COACHING WITH PURPOSE:
LEARNING ENCOUNTERS FOR EDUCATIONAL CHANGE

BY RACHEL LOFTHOUSE,
TRISTA HOLLWECK
AND JASEN BOOTON

Together we unlock every learner's unique potential

At Hachette Learning (formerly Hodder Education), there's one thing we're certain about. No two students learn the same way. That's why our approach to teaching begins by recognising the needs of individuals first.

Our mission is to allow every learner to fulfil their unique potential by empowering those who teach them. From our expert teaching and learning resources to our digital educational tools that make learning easier and more accessible for all, we provide solutions designed to maximise the impact of learning for every teacher, parent and student.

Aligned to our parent company, Hachette Livre, founded in 1826, we pride ourselves on being a learning solutions provider with a global footprint.

www.hachettelearning.com

Although every effort has been made to ensure that website addresses are correct at time of going to press, Hachette Learning cannot be held responsible for the content of any website mentioned in this book. It is sometimes possible to find a relocated web page by typing in the address of the home page for a website in the URL window of your browser.

Hachette UK's policy is to use papers that are natural, renewable and recyclable products and made from wood grown in well-managed forests and other controlled sources. The logging and manufacturing processes are expected to conform to the environmental regulations of the country of origin.

To order, please visit www.HachetteLearning.com or contact Customer Service at education@hachette.co.uk / +44 (0)1235 827827.

ISBN: 978 1 0360 1396 7

© Rachel Lofthouse, Trista Hollweck and Jasen Booton 2025

First published in 2025 by
Hachette Learning (a trading division of Hodder & Stoughton Limited),
An Hachette UK Company
Carmelite House
50 Victoria Embankment
London EC4Y 0DZ
www.HachetteLearning.com

The authorised representative in the EEA is Hachette Ireland, 8 Castlecourt Centre, Dublin 15, D15 XTP3, Ireland (email: info@hbgi.ie)

Impression number   10 9 8 7 6 5 4 3 2 1
Year   2029 2028 2027 2026 2025

All rights reserved. Apart from any use permitted under UK copyright law, no part of this publication may be reproduced or transmitted in any form or by any means, electronic or mechanical, including photocopying and recording, or held within any information storage and retrieval system, without permission in writing from the publisher or under licence from the Copyright Licensing Agency Limited. Further details of such licences (for reprographic reproduction) may be obtained from the Copyright Licensing Agency Limited, www.cla.co.uk

Cover photo: Shutterstock/Shirstok
Typeset in the UK.
Printed in the UK.
A catalogue record for this title is available from the British Library.

About the authors

Jasen Booton's career spans 30 years in the field of primary phase education. He has worked globally in roles such as advanced skills teacher, instructional coach, senior leader and university teacher educator. He served as the founding director of learning and teaching for a multi-academy trust and teaching school. Jasen completed his master's in learning and teaching at the University of Oxford and continues to be an active member of the Oxford Education Deanery. As an accredited European Mentoring and Coaching Council (EMCC) coach, he passionately supports changemakers in Africa to drive social change. Jasen currently serves as a consultant in the Kingdom of Tonga, using a coaching approach to co-construct the primary phase curriculum and support the growth and development of teachers and Ministry of Education personnel.

Trista Hollweck is a pracademic who integrates the worlds of research, policy and practice. She is a former secondary teacher, vice-principal and school district consultant at the Western Quebec School Board in Quebec, Canada, and leads educational research and practice networks at local, provincial, national and international levels. Trista is a CollectivED senior fellow and adjunct professor at the University of Ottawa where she researches collaborative-based professional learning and teaches graduate courses on mentoring and coaching in professional contexts. Trista is a proud mom of three and is committed to supporting schools and systems to improve education for all students within and across educational systems globally.

Rachel Lofthouse is former professor of teacher education at Leeds Beckett University, England. She founded CollectivED, a research and practice centre with a focus on coaching, mentoring and professional learning. Rachel has been engaged in coaching in education for almost three decades, as a practitioner, researcher and professional development facilitator. Her work has allowed her to engage with and lead local, national and international professional and academic networks. Before joining Leeds Beckett University Rachel worked as a secondary teacher and middle leader in schools in the North East of England and as a teacher educator, researcher and course director at Newcastle University. Rachel retired after 34 years as an educator to pursue a new career drawing on her skills of dialogue, support and advocacy. Her commitment to coaching, done well, remains.

Contents

Synopsis ix

Acknowledgements x

Foreword – Jim Knight xii

Introduction xv

Part 1: Coaching in education

Chapter 1 Learning encounters 5
    Encountering coaching with purpose 5
    Learning encounters as authors, contributors and readers 6
    Encountering each other as learners 9
    Beyond encounters to change 11
    CollectivED as space for learning encounters 12
    Encountering emergent expertise within a rhizomatic community ... 13

Chapter 2 Encountering coaching in education 17
    Defining coaching 17
    Role of contracting in coaching 19
    Understanding differences in coaching approaches 21
    Differentiating coaching from other collaborative professional learning .. 23
    Coaching processes, frameworks and models 26

Chapter 3 Encounters with coaching origins and theory 31
    Origins and influences 32
    A tentative and emerging evidence base 33
    Theoretical encounters 33

Chapter 4 Sensemaking: from core skills to guiding principles of coaching 43
    Underlying coaching principles 44
    Coaching way of being 46
    Core skills and techniques 47
    Accompaniment 48

Chapter 5 Exploring the concept of purpose 51
    Making sense of what really matters to you..51
    How might values shape our sense of purpose?.....................................52
    Moving forward *with* a sense of purpose 54
    Sensemaking analogies 55
    A scholarly sense of purpose...56
    Coaching *with* a sense of purpose versus coaching *for* a purpose 57
    The purposeful progress model...60
    Coaching *with* a sense of purpose is 'life-worthy' learning 61

Part 2: Encounters with coaching through our practice and research

Chapter 6 Unique learning opportunities: encountering coaching through practice and policy 67
    Emergent encounters with coaching 68
    Developing coaching insights through contextual awareness 70

Chapter 7 Coaching kaleidoscope: perspectives on coaching from a career in research and practice...73
    First encounters with coaching..73
    Intentional encounters with coaching...77
    Encountering tensions in coaching 82
    New encounters through CollectivED: coaching as an evolving and maturing practice 84
    Encounters beyond silos..88

Chapter 8 A patchwork quilt: stitching the pieces together 91
    Encounters with past experiences 91
    First encounters with coaching and mentoring......................................96
    Extended encounters with coaching..100

Part 3: Contemporary coaching: encounters from the CollectivED community

Chapter 9 Coaching as a way of enhancing teaching and learning 109
    Encounter: coaching with a shared focus on teaching and learning principles...111
    Encounter: enhancing teacher coaching using video 115
    Encounter: an instructional coach perspective.....................................118
    Encounter: developing and deploying an instructional coaching team ...120
    Encounter: student peer coaching in a primary school........................122

Encounter: developing opportunities for engagement in coaching 124
Encounter: student coaching for wellbeing 126
Encounter: learning to lead pedagogical coaching 128

Chapter 10 Coaching as a way of enabling and empowering others 135
Encounter: developing and leading inclusive coaching 136
Encounter: coaching for attunement and advocacy 139
Encounter: executive and leadership coaching 141
Encounter: a coaching approach to leadership 143
Encounter: creating a safe space through coaching 144
Encounter: coaching to promote agency, meaning and purpose 147

Chapter 11 Coaching as a way of shaping culture 151
Encounter: passing it on, from being coached to embedding coaching ... 152
Encounter: coaching for student and staff wellbeing 158
Encounter: challenging the status quo through embedding coaching as a national qualifications provider 161
Encounter: achieving a coaching approach across a multi-academy trust 164
Encounter: developing a whole-school coaching way of being through guided conversations 166
Encounter: coaching for personal growth and development across the school community 167

Chapter 12 Coaching as a way of sustaining change 175
Encounter: reflections from the CollectivED Award lead coach 176
Encounter: thriving and flourishing through a culture of coaching 179
Encounter: creating momentum for change through conversation 185
Encounter: instructional coaching and beyond 188
Encounter: developing a whole-school coaching ethos 191
Encounter: embedding and sustaining coaching 192
Encounter: growing our own through enhanced professional development 194
Encounter: professional learning – coaching, autonomy and community 197

Chapter 13 Coaching as a way of developing purposeful conversational spaces 207
Encounter: dilemma-based coaching 208
Encounter: co-coaching for reimagining a positive direction for education 220

    Encounter: attuned authentic coaching for teachers (AACT)..................223
    Encounter: Flourish programme 230
    Encounter: holding the space for story exchange as collaborative
    curriculum innovation...235

*Chapter 14 Coaching as a way of enacting social justice, equity
and decoloniality* **241**
    Encounter: empowerment and equity through executive and
    systemic coaching..243
    Encounter: coaching in Indigenous communities............................. 244
    Encounter: coaching within the BAMEed Network...........................247
    Encounter: coaching for climate change and active hope 249
    Encounter: wayfinding as a way of conceptualising coaching..........251

Part 4:   Coaching, context and change

Chapter 15 Contextual coaching, collaboration and wellbeing......................**263**
    Contextual coaching and coaching terroir 264
    Collaborative professional learning..265
    Contextual coaching as collaborative professionalism and contribution
    to school improvement..270
    Coaching and educator wellbeing 274

Chapter 16 Coaching efficacy: knowing what works **279**
    Problematising the concept of efficacy..279
    Starting with a theory of change for coaching.................................283
    Understanding how coaching functions as an activity system 289
    Cycles of growth enabled by coaching 295
    Using the approaches to explore what and how coaching works
    in context 299

Chapter 17 Coaching, change and the 5As **303**
    Individual change..304
    Organisational and systemic change... 311
    The 5As model: five dynamic phases of educational change 316

*Chapter 18 Coaching connections: sensemaking through the
CollectivED community* **323**
    Making sense of coaching in interacting contexts 323
    It takes two: unique individuals and micro-contexts of coaching.........325
    Flexible, situated and informed coaching 327

Learning through coaching: creating individual and
organisational potential 329
Unseen, unbidden and unique coaching outcomes 331
Changing culture to cultures of change..333
Finding and sustaining purpose: coaching values and goals....................336
Coaching way of being: agency and transformation 338

Epilogue A call to action and advocacy 343
References 349
Additional resources 377

Synopsis

A book for anyone working in education with an interest in understanding and developing coaching with purpose. Explore how coaching creates supportive relationships between colleagues, provides educators with opportunities and space to be valued, seen and heard, and personalise professional learning and development. With over 30 international case studies of coaching, in combination with unique perspectives drawn from research and practice, this book will enable you to experiment with and evaluate coaching in your own context. The expertise and insights offered will ensure that coaching supports professionals to make autonomous, situated decisions, find their niche and utilise their talents, and enhance wellbeing and feelings of hopefulness in education communities.

Acknowledgements

We could not have written this book without members of the CollectivED community and the wider professional community beyond CollectivED. We thank them for their past, present and continuing work to engage in, improve, research, facilitate, lead, understand and share coaching in education in all its guises. We appreciate the huge strides that they have made and helped us to make. Their work has created a diverse landscape of coaching which has changed the opportunities, confidence and capacity of many others to shape learning and wellbeing for others.

We are immensely grateful to the contributors to this book (named with their consent). Between them they have written and contributed to case studies, attended focus groups, read draft sections and responded as critical friends. Original case studies were gathered through research which was ethically approved by Leeds Beckett University. We have enjoyed our encounters with them as authors and know that they are all agents of change.

Laura Anthony, Paula Ayliffe, Sheila Ball, Mhairi Beaton, Mark Bennett, Rose Blackman-Hegan, Ann Booton, Ceri Boyle, Debbi Briggs, Natasha Carman, Victoria Carr, Melanie Chambers, Anne Clements, Sarah Cornelius, Mark Dowley, Tracy Edwards, Hazel Farrer, Dan Ford, Cathy Gunning, Pinky Jain, Joanne Kane, Jim Knight, Adam Kohlbeck, Casey Kosiore, Asif Lorgat, Jess Mahdavi-Gladwell, Catriona Mangham, Brendan Marshall, Vicky Martin, Andrew Mears, Jasmine Miller, Neil Mullen, Chris Munro, Amanda Nuthall, Lizana Oberholzer, Nicola O'Keefe, Stacey Postle, Rebecca Prescott-Mail, Jean Ramsey, Emily Ray, Rebecca Raybould, Ana Sanches de Arede, Tom Shaw, Laura Smith, Mark Steacy, Mary Stephen, Lisa Stephenson, Catherine St. Ville, Jim Thompson, Stephanie Thomson, Rachel Tomlinson, Lucy Vincent, Emma Vlaeminck, Sue Webb, Olivia White, Victoria Whiting, Hannah Wilson, Antony Winch, Lucy Wood.

In addition we personally thank past and present colleagues, research supervisors and partners at Newcastle University, Leeds Beckett University, University of Ottawa, University of Toronto, Aberdeen University and Leeds Trinity University. We also draw on work enabled by the following schools, local authorities (LA), regional school boards, teaching school alliances and multi-academy trusts, governments, non-governmental organisations and companies: Northumberland LA, Worcestershire LA and Derby LA, Western Quebec School Board, ClarityTec, Swaledale Alliance, Symmes/D'Arcy McGee School, Carr Manor Community School, Leeds Learning Alliance, Integrity, Tongan Ministry of Education and Curriculum Development Unit, Leadership Committee of English Education in Quebec, Growth Coaching International, the Curriculum Foundation, Tribes Learning Communities and Instructional Coaching Group. CollectivED has been privileged to be partners in several European Erasmus+ projects, with the PROMISE and RAPIDE projects being key in developing coaching practices. Some aspects of our coaching work has been funded and in this book we refer to projects funded by Newcastle University, the Department for Education in England, Teacher Development Agency, CfBT, National College of School Leadership, the World Bank, the National Education Union, Erasmus+ at the European Union, Paul Hamlyn Teacher Development Fund, and the Social Sciences and Humanities Research Council (SSHRC) in Canada.

We are also immensely grateful for the support, patience and encouragement throughout the writing years from members of our families.

Foreword

Most of us dedicate a lot of time to trying to get better. We may be trying to cook the perfect omelet, or improve our parenting, or play Beethoven's Hammerklavier Sonata, or lose a few pounds, but right now, most of us, I suspect, are trying to get better at something. In fact, the act of getting better, learning how to do something new, to notice aspects of life we've never seen before, or how to improve at the things we do every day, that act is so common to humanity that I suspect it is a universal longing in people. No matter where we are, or who we are, most of us want to be better parents, spouses, teachers, people. And when we get better, when we are able to see or do more, it can feel joyful.

My experience, at least, reveals that learning is life-giving and something we want to share with others. I remember when I first learned how to use an internet browser (it was Netscape) to get on the internet. It was such a joy to be able to find so much information at my fingertips. I was teaching a course on contemporary authors, and each week I used to spend an evening at the Toronto Library doing research on the author we were going to study. After the internet, I could learn in a few minutes what it used to take me an entire evening to discover.

Part of the fun of learning how to use Netscape was sharing it with my friends because when they saw how the internet could help them do what they wanted to do, they, too, felt the joy of learning. They would enthusiastically thank me for sharing this new amazing tool just as I had thanked my mentor who helped me get access to the internet. My Netscape experience reveals a lot about how learning and getting better work. It is joyful and life-giving to get better, and it is also joyful and life-giving to share that learning with others.

Since getting better is such a huge part of our lives, we naturally seek out ways to get better at getting better. One of those ways, and perhaps the most popular one, is to work with a coach. In the past decade, interest in coaching has exploded. Most people recognize, as Atul Gawande wrote in 2011, 'Coaching done well may be the most effective intervention designed for human performance' (Gawande, 2011). Today, we can get coaches to help us with just about anything. There are nutrition coaches, sleep coaches, wilderness survival coaches, and lucid-dreaming coaches. In fact, coaching is so ubiquitous that there probably should be coaches that help us choose our coaches.

Many coaches work in professional fields, such as education. In fact, coaching is one of the most popular forms of professional learning in education globally today.

Some approaches to coaching are grounded in the research, traditions, and writing on forms of conversations that help people get better. Other approaches, unfortunately, appear to be hastily constructed to cash in on a popular trend. Educators can find it difficult to know how to distinguish between snake oil and a powerful force for change. That's why I'm so grateful for this wonderful book, *Coaching with Purpose,* by Rachel Lofthouse, Trista Hollweck, and Jasen Booton.

In *Coaching with Purpose,* the authors don't propose one simple approach to coaching. They provide us with a wealth of resources so that we can make our own sense of coaching. This shouldn't be a surprise because sensemaking is one of the authors' foundational concepts. The book contains four sections so that we can understand the traditions, research, and lived experience of coaching in four different ways:

Part 1. Foundational Concepts revealing coaching as a mutually humanizing relational and reflective practice fostering agency, trust, and professional growth;

Part 2. Lived Experiences and Insights where the authors discuss their own successes and challenges designing and implementing coaching;

Part 3. Case Studies from over 30 educational settings showing the power and diversity of coaching, and;

Part 4. Context, Efficacy, and Change describing the potential for coaching in educational settings.

Lofthouse, Hollweck, and Booton describe and draw upon many different models and traditions of coaching, but there are some key ideas that recur throughout the book. For the authors, coaching is a human-centered, dialogical way of interacting that helps people achieve purposeful goals so they can make lasting improvements in teaching, learning, and organizational culture. The authors also describe a variety of pathways to those goals, describing several different coaching models. Finally, the book demonstrates the power of learning communities as many of the ideas in the book come from the CollectivED network of educators.

At its heart, *Coaching with Purpose* is about what truly makes coaching effective—relationships, reflection, and meaningful conversations that lead to real growth. Lofthouse, Hollweck, and Booton don't offer a one-size-fits-all solution. Instead, they provide a rich, research-based exploration of coaching that honors the complexity of learning and change.

This book reminds us that coaching, when done well, is a profoundly human endeavor. It's not about imposing solutions but about partnering with others to make sense of challenges, build trust, and create lasting improvement. Whether you're a coach, a teacher, or a leader, *Coaching with Purpose* offers insights that will deepen your practice and expand your understanding of how coaching can transform education. If you're serious about coaching, this book deserves a place on your shelf—but more importantly, it deserves to be put into practice.

Jim Knight

February 2025

Gawande, A. 'Personal best'. *The New Yorker*. (3 October 2011) https://www.newyorker.com/magazine/2011/10/03/personal-best

Introduction

Choosing to read a book about coaching has the potential to change you, change others and change organisations. It is not the act of reading that matters; it is the agency you have as a reader to determine what you are curious about and how open you are to provocation, support and challenge. Indeed agency underpins coaching, too, influencing what learning we bring to it and take from it, in either role. We invite you to bring agency to your encounters with this book.

You will find that this book is not a quick read, and actually it might warrant slow reading. It has certainly come about slowly: it has taken over three years to write and is based on many more years of work. We open the book by setting the scene on coaching in education and the significance of purpose. We provide insights into how our individual roles in coaching, teaching and leading and in supporting teachers' development and learning have been influenced by encountering coaching and how this has been influential in forming our understanding and evidence base. As co-authors we have invited fellow members of the coaching community, many of them part of the CollectivED network, to share examples of coaching, and they make a unique contribution to this book, and we feel really privileged to have explored, discussed and reflected upon these contributions. The book concludes with a focus on coaching context, coaching efficacy and purposeful change.

As you encounter this book it is worth recognising its origins. As co-authors based on both sides of the Atlantic we have shared the writing process and see this book as a way of sensemaking from our own knowledge and experience related to coaching in education. Our knowledge originates from four key sources, all of which have been drawn on in our writing:

1. our engagement with the coaching literature, both peer-reviewed and professional sources
2. our own systematic research in the field of coaching in education, as doctoral students, as academics and pracademics, as individuals, in collaboration with each other and in wider project teams
3. our engagement with practitioners and researchers currently working in the field, primarily through CollectivED, of which we are all members, but also through our work with organisations such as Growth Coaching International (based in Australia) and Instructional Coaching Group (based in the USA), Erasmus+ research and development projects with European partners and the ICSEI community (International Congress on School Effectiveness and Improvement)
4. our own direct practice as coaches, teachers, school leaders and teacher educators, in education advisory roles, as programme leaders of professional development and master's and PhD level courses in coaching, and as supervisors and examiners of postgraduate scholarship and research related to coaching.

In addition to our pre-existing knowledge and experience, writing this book has itself been a research process. We have gathered new accounts of coaching in education, we have undertaken thematic analysis and we have been in conversation with current coaches and leaders. This has been undertaken in line with ethical approval gained from Leeds Beckett University.

Navigating the book

The book is written in four parts. Each part is introduced with key elements to look out for and a summary of the chapter contents. Many of the chapters include 'encounters'. Each encounter is an example of coaching in an educational setting. There are a small number of coaching encounters that are returned to several times across the parts of the book. This is because we use them to illustrate key developments or ideas which reflect the progress of our work on coaching.

In part 1 we explain the use of our term 'learning encounters' and introduce the ways that we have experienced, researched and built community through our encounters with coaching in education. We provide definitions, a brief history and theoretical underpinnings of coaching in education and acknowledge a range of coaching approaches, skills and stances. We also focus on purpose and use this as a way to explore the roles that coaching can play.

In part 2 we draw on our own lived experiences and how we have encountered coaching as researchers and practitioners. In each chapter in this section we reveal more detail about coaching approaches, the intended purposes of coaching, the design and difficulties of implementation and the tensions and affordances that emerge.

In part 3 we extend the evidence base by sharing a wide range of case studies of coaching gathered through the extended CollectivED community from diverse education contexts. These examples are presented as individual encounters and organised under themes that emerged through our analysis of them.

In part 4 we focus on context, coaching efficacy and change. These 3Cs are significant if the potential of coaching to support positive and purposeful improvement is to be realised. We need to situate and adapt coaching in more sensitive ways, not just add it as another burden, we need to make sense of its actual impacts, not just account for it in simple metrics, and we need to understand the educational ecosystems that coaching intersects with and can shape over time. Finally, we draw together key themes and insights from the four CollectivED focus groups that were held to discuss the chapters on context, coaching efficacy and change to make connections between their coaching and purpose.

As you read the book you will find that the chapters have different styles. This is partly because of our shared writing process, but also because they have different origins and evidence bases, and serve different functions. Some chapters provide historical context, exploring how coaching in education emerged over time, and include our own narratives of engagement with coaching. Some chapters are heavily rooted in research, giving insights into how coaching has been studied and developed using research methodologies and analysis, and drawing on a wide literature base. These chapters therefore also provide windows into the expanse of further possible reading. Others create opportunities to learn from the curated case studies of an international and cross-phase coaching community, with the integrity and authenticity of their individual voices maintained. Some chapters articulate our sensemaking or synthesis in relation to contemporary issues of coaching in education.

Considering we describe our own encounters with coaching through research and practice in part 2 of the book using the metaphors of 'kaleidoscope', 'patchwork quilt' and 'wayfinding,' it makes sense that the varied chapter styles and foci reflect a complex and dynamic collage of ideas and encounters. We provide 'endnotes' at the end of each chapter. The endnotes are a reflective space. We add final thoughts as co-authors, and in some endnotes include reflections from members of the CollectivED community. We have added possible talking points for you to use in conversation with others and ideas for action. References are provided at the end of the book. Writing from different geographical contexts, we have encountered some differences when it comes to some wording and spelling. For any shared writing in this book we defer to using standard British English spelling and phrasing, but you are likely to notice that we also include the original spelling used by the authors in our quotations. We have done our best at the start of each section of the book and in the chapter endnotes to offer you, our readers, a golden thread that we hope helps to stitch this coaching story together.

Our book is a call to action and advocacy for coaching. Even a well-researched and hopefully well-read book is just a text. The difference it can make is in the hands, minds, hearts and actions of its readers.

Part 1
Coaching in education

What to look out for in part 1

In this section you will encounter:
- an exploration of CollectivED as a space of reflection, gathering, inspiration and learning
- a discussion on how coaching is defined in CollectivED and the broader literature base, along with some of the approaches, frameworks and models used in education
- a description of the roots, history and theoretical underpinnings of coaching
- an outline of core coaching elements, skills and principles, and an introduction to conceptual tools to support sensemaking
- an examination of purpose and what this means for coaching in education.

We open this book by sharing some of the ways that we have encountered coaching as educators in our multiple roles and contexts. These have been formative learning encounters. Our engagement in coaching spans decades, and while the current use of coaching across education settings fascinates us, we acknowledge the significance of the history of coaching and the theories that have underpinned its development or explain its impact. Coaching is often advocated to support educational change, but it is not always defined with clarity. This may be because a short definition cannot summarise what is a complex activity, or perhaps because as coaching has become branded it is used as a means of commerce and for organisational and policy influence. We illustrate a range of coaching approaches in part 1, seeking out similarities and underlying principles that might help create a coherent sense of what coaching is (and what it is not). We are not interested in coaching in education sustaining and perpetuating hierarchy or silos.

As educators there are motives and values which give meaning and purpose to our work. To accept the status quo is to believe that what we have created and sustained so far is enough for the future. It would be an anomaly for educators to not want to see new communities empowered by learning, the talents of individuals nurtured and scaffolded to create promising futures, and to lead and contribute to organisations which have a positive impact on society. We have deliberately considered the title 'Coaching with purpose' and dedicate a whole chapter in part 1 to what we mean by 'purpose'. This matters because if we invest in coaching, we invest in people, and people have the power to bring about purposeful change. But not all change has equal merit. Coaching may be a popular addition to education, but we do need to be conscious of the opportunities that it affords and the impacts of the changes that result.

Coaching is an activity that allows for the individual. It gives them a protected space, a chance to think and focus, a source of inspiration for future decisions and actions. While it should be person-centred, coaching is not individualistic and it is not an indulgence. Coaching might be experienced as a privilege, but one that is not unique to a few. Coaching can create a growth zone, personally and professionally. Despite its potential, the adoption of coaching in education should not herald another round of non-negotiables, add further burdens or lessen the choices that individuals have. Engagement in coaching should be possible but not obligatory. Coaching can also create growth zones in organisations, through developing shared understanding, shared ambition and shared purpose. We see growth as a desirable outcome of coaching and we value the opportunities for divergence rather than the safety of convergence as it continues to develop.

In part 1 we set our foundations for the book in five relatively short chapters. The chapters can each be read separately or combined to get the full understanding of what we mean by our book title 'Coaching with purpose: Learning encounters for educational change'. Whereas chapter 1 explores the idea of 'learning encounters', chapters 2–4 focus on coaching in education, and chapter 5 examines 'purpose'. We hope that together they create an opportunity for you to revisit and build on your existing knowledge and experience of coaching in education.

Chapter 1
Learning encounters

Teachers are not performers in the traditional sense of the word in that our work is not meant to be a spectacle. Yet it is meant to serve as a catalyst that calls everyone to become more and more engaged, to become active participants in learning.

bell hooks (1994, p. 11)

Encountering coaching with purpose

We know that in most education settings the overwhelming sense is one of expectation. As educators we are expected to generate opportunities, to create conditions in which others can achieve, to corral available resources for greatest impact, to demonstrate we are both evidence-informed and responsive to the here and now. So, when there is so much to do, and so much to prove, is it legitimate to ask 'why coaching'?

We extend bell hooks' proposition about teachers acting as catalysts not performers to our beliefs about ways that coaches can work with purpose in education. As such we invite you to read this book as a way to explore the ways that coaching can create educational change across a wide range of settings. We believe that coaching can bring ideas and talents into focus, can disentangle dilemmas, can weave together research and practice, and can create positive momentum for change. We invite you to engage with the evidence base, the professional development practices and the impacts of coaching as you read.

We would like this book to help you to start and continue conversations: as coaches, as teachers, as leaders, as decision-makers and as researchers.

Like the most engaging conversations we encounter, we hope that this book offers an experience of connection, provides new insights and provocations, allows a sharing of perspectives, creates opportunities for affirmation and helps to refine focus or generate ideas that have impact.

We do offer a starting point. Through our work individually and through CollectivED we promote coaching because we advocate for teachers and leaders as learners. We believe that coaching offers a unique opportunity for educators to have powerful conversations about their own work. Coaching can help educators to create supportive professional relationships based on trust and curiosity. Coaching can reconnect educators with each other, with a sense of purpose and perspective and with their potential. Coaching can create a time and space to focus the mind, which is essential in the busy lives of educators.

As such, coaching can play a significant role in helping educators make sense of how to create the conditions which enable children and young people to flourish. In doing so, coaches help educators remain in learning mode. Teachers and leaders can become:

- more open to new ideas
- more able to connect knowledge and experience
- more confident to face challenges
- more curious about others.

Coaching is an emerging field in education which has gathered momentum in recent years. The implications of this are that many models have developed, some of which are linked to programmes or initiatives while others are stand-alone. Some of the common educational coaching models, frameworks and approaches are discussed in more detail in chapter 2.

Learning encounters as authors, contributors and readers

This book acts as an invitation to engage thoughtfully and creatively with the phenomenon of coaching in education. Without doubt, coaching has become more common. In different education contexts it has become connected with leadership development, been deployed alongside mentoring as induction and support for early career teachers, become associated with enhancing and embedding specific teaching and learning routines, enabled individuals in underrepresented groups to gain promoted posts and been developed as a way to support children and young people and their families. We write with all of these in mind, but of course we also write with limitations. We cannot cover all bases, all research, all coaching models. We do intend to write with purpose. In that way, our writing mirrors our belief that coaching can create opportunities to find, refine, heighten and to achieve our purposes as educators.

There are three authors of this book and many contributors. Collectively we have many years of experience during which we have researched, designed and undertaken coaching in multiple contexts. We recognise that in education coaching has plural meanings and we also appreciate that it can become conflated with other activities including mentoring, consulting, training and counselling. In order to make this book make sense to others we have to first make sense of coaching for ourselves. We are doing so by deliberately building on the work of the CollectivED community, drawing on the legacy of our engagement in and with research and practice, and making sense of the current opportunities that coaching can create in education.

This book will be appreciative. We will acknowledge that coaching can make a positive difference, that coaches can bring value to educational communities and settings, and that one of the joys of coaching is that it is still an evolving practice. We do not anticipate that this book will answer all the questions that you may have as readers about coaching, but we hope that you read this book as a 'learning encounter' itself.

As authors we will bring authenticity and honesty to writing this book. We are ourselves educators and we are still learning. We offer insights rather than presume expertise. As authors we have taken time in conversation with each other long before writing. We have worked tentatively towards greater clarity. We have expected to learn from each other, to challenge each other's thinking and to share the writing load with a sense of solidarity. The shape of this book has evolved significantly since it was first conceived, and that is as a result of these ongoing encounters.

As authors we engage in formal and informal learning contexts; we teach coaching in professional postgraduate courses; we meet with the CollectivED communities and hear their coaching insights and dilemmas; we create new opportunities to support educators who want to make a positive difference through coaching. We also coach, and have coached, students, teachers and leaders. Our networks, coachees and partners are local, national and international and we value the diversity and breadth of knowledge we draw on. As researchers we have created opportunities to learn with and from others. We come to writing this book with a background in undertaking research, including on coaching, but with a determination to keep an enquiring mindset. This book gathers together case studies of coaching, many of which have not previously been published. We have also conducted focus groups to explore the themes of the book and incorporate the multiple perspectives gained from these within the book.

As readers we invite you to encounter coaching with us. You may have read many books on coaching, or indeed none. You may have been coached, been a coach or even dismissed coaching in the past. You may compare and contrast what we offer here with what you have encountered elsewhere. You may find yourself using what you learn to add to your advocacy of coaching or you may find yourself responding 'yes, but…' to some of what we write.

As readers we ask that you encounter this book with learning in mind. We are not offering neat coaching packages for consumption, we are not pitching for business and we are not picking over what is offered as coaching through other platforms or organisations. We hope that you will read with curiosity and compassion. Our case-study contributors are working with curiosity and compassion in their own contexts. They share their experiences with a generosity of spirit and as learners. They are not handing over a coaching formula but instead opening a window into their work.

Above all, we encourage you to read with a sense of purpose. When reading, view this book as a sensemaking tool, just as we have in writing it. Take ideas that challenge you and dwell on them for a while, explore them in conversation with others and use them to develop your own reasoning and practice. Find ideas that resonate with you and reflect on why they do and how they might enrich your work. Explore coaching as an organising concept to augment your understanding, rather than as a blunt tool to win an argument. Use the book to encounter coaching in education and judge how you might use it to create purposeful learning encounters with others.

Encountering each other as learners

Perhaps the unexpected element of our book title is 'learning encounters'. It surprised us as authors when it emerged through our conversations. We were drawn to it as an expression which unlocks a world of possibilities and hope. We describe coaching as a relational space in which we can encounter a sense of purpose, opportunity, hope and achievement. Our experience, research and encounters with others working in this field show us that as educators experience positive, fulfilling and impactful change in their own work, they can feel more optimistic about their own capacities and the value that they bring to the lives of their learners. This is why coaching matters.

Engaging in coaching often provides a chance to focus, to create motivation for action and to reorientate decisions to purpose, thus coaching can feel re-affirming. However, coaching is not an end in itself. Within education settings and in support of education capacity building, coaching is deeply concerned with learning. Coaching should enhance the opportunities for, experiences of and outcomes from learning. We consider the learning of adults and young people in education settings to be reciprocal and equally significant, and that coaching offers growth opportunities for both.

In very simple terms there are probably two key ways in which we as authors conceptualise learning: learning can be convergent and divergent. These determine how we design learning environments, through curriculum, pedagogy, resource allocation and policy. They also determine how learning is assessed and how achievement is acknowledged.

Convergent learning is typically learning in which we anticipate, seek out and reward convergence. In professional learning terms this might include an expectation that colleagues are exposed to the same knowledge, acquire the same skills and implement them with fidelity to an overarching schema or pre-determined set of behaviours. In contrast to this, more divergent learning welcomes and plans for a wider range of possible desirable outcomes. In professional learning terms this might create conditions in which engagement with breadth of knowledge is privileged and a repertoire of skills are recognised as valid in context, so that greater autonomous decision-making and self-determination are encouraged.

In terms of teacher learning the difference might also be framed as a desire for 'adherence' – learning to do the right thing – or as the promotion of 'enquiry' – learning to make sense of teaching (Lofthouse et al., 2020). In reality, of course the contexts in which educators work are probably aided by both a degree of adherence and an openness to enquiry. An interesting question is how coaching objectives align with adherence or enquiry conceptualisation of professional learning and as such whether they encompass, encourage or constrain convergent or divergent learning outcomes.

In connecting the ideas behind our book we start with the ambition that in education we can use coaching to create and sustain learning encounters through which we find and support the knowledge, skills and humanity in ourselves and others. As such, coaching is a practice which can help create, develop and sustain human activities, conducted by individuals and groups as a response to evolving contexts and situations. This is because practices (noun) are influenced by individual values and beliefs, decisions, experience and expertise. They are dynamic actions which embody language, relationships and physicality. Practices can stagnate, but they can also be altered through practising (verb), allowing them to be understood and refined with intent (Lofthouse, 2019a). Coaching can create the opportunity for this refinement.

We see this in reality in the work undertaken and illustrated in our case studies. They represent coaching as collaborative, relational, iterative and developmental and as such they demonstrate how coaching can create conditions for individuals to use their talents to flourish, for organisations to experience sustainable growth, for heightened professionalism and for community building in education.

Chapter 1 Learning encounters

Beyond encounters to change

Our reflections on learning encounters may not easily align with your experiences of coaching in busy educational workplaces. You may reflect on them as desirable, but not achievable. You may wonder how they fit with tight teacher training schedules, non-negotiable teaching routines, high-demand leadership roles, accountability and a constant call to lever up ever-increasing educational performance. You may even dispute our premise. If that is so, we encourage you to pause and reflect a little.

The risks are that coaching could just become the next additional burden in educational workload; that the outcome of its implementation is increasing or reducing the perceived status of colleagues; or that it is introduced as a package without offering the school community a sense of ownership and an opportunity to attune it to their setting.

To avoid these issues we hope that this book gives you a chance to think about how coaching can help educators to articulate their values, gain confidence in their work and shape the purpose of education and to feel valued and sustained by others. By conceptualising coaching as learning encounters, our purpose is to emphasise the relational dimension of coaching. We see coaching as a way that educators can work and learn together, unleash their potential and build a legacy of compassion, expertise and hope.

Perhaps the most original part of this book is the development and evidencing of a new dynamic model of educational change. This is articulated in part 4 (chapter 17) and is based on five phases of change, which go from 'awareness' to 'advocacy'. In our synthesis of existing research and an analysis of the examples of coaching gathered for this book we have been able to conceptualise this framework. We explore it through two lenses. As coaching itself evolves as a professional learning and support practice in education settings, the five phases of change can be detected in how coaching develops and becomes integrated into the setting, aligned with purpose and changing the ways that the education community work with and for each other. In addition we recognise coaching as one of the underlying mechanisms which foster the five phases of change to support the broad alignment of purpose, practice and culture in settings.

Thus, while this book stresses the importance of encounters, we do not limit these to fleeting moments or occasional conversations or temporary working relationships. We see encounters as the foundation for the evolution of educational practice and the flourishing of individuals in sustainable flourishing settings and systems.

CollectivED as space for learning encounters

This book arises out of CollectivED, building on research and practice development undertaken both individually and collaboratively by the authors and the wider CollectivED community. CollectivED is a research and practice centre based at Leeds Beckett University in the UK. Since 2017 we have built an international community of educators with a shared interest in coaching, mentoring, supervision and professional learning and development in education. Part 3 of this book contains a curated collection of coaching case studies from the CollectivED community.

The CollectivED community forms a network or 'collective' which aims to expand the available knowledge base on coaching, mentoring and collaborative professional learning and to work and meet together to develop new approaches, to share experiences, insights, ideas, research and practice. CollectivED members are invited to gather, learn with and from one another and to contribute to a variety of knowledge mobilisation activities, such as virtual and in-person meetings, professional development opportunities, working papers, podcasts and research presentations. Contributors to CollectivED outputs, including working papers and engagement events, are invited to become CollectivED Fellows and we also host the CollectivED Award, which is the thematic focus of the case studies curated in chapter 12. We refer to the CollectivED community as 'rhizomatic'. It is a non-hierarchical, non-linear, complex and dynamic network with its members creating new and often unexpected opportunities and collaborations with and for one another.

The values and purpose of the CollectivED community include increasing the opportunities for positive educational change through enhanced professional agency and wellbeing. As such, coaching is a common thread running through much of our collective work. CollectivED has evolved over time rather than through strategic or operational planning. Its story to date is based on conversations between educators. These conversations can take place in a single moment, span projects over time and segue into a range of contexts and opportunities for engagement.

Through CollectivED, research, enquiry and development are activated, and several local, national, online and international projects and partnerships have focused on coaching. In particular we have undertaken:

- collaborative action research and co-creation projects focusing on developing coaching approaches and partnerships to enhance pedagogy and decision-making
- publication of open-access working papers, think pieces and blog posts contributed by over 100 educators, creating a significant archive based on research and practice in coaching, mentoring, collaborative professional learning and supervision in education
- research and analysis of coaching in education with a focus on coaching characteristics, efficacy and context.

The work of CollectivED and its community forms an integral part of this book and it is situated in a wider review of coaching and educational purpose.

Encountering emergent expertise within a rhizomatic community

When we first planned this book, we thought of asking the perceived coaching experts and thought leaders to add their reflections. In the time it took to write this book we continued to meet informally with coaches, leaders and mentors through the CollectivED community who frequently shared powerful thinking from their use and development of coaching in multiple contexts, and in reality they are our experts. Expertise is not a commodity, it is not bounded and it is not static. Expertise in coaching cannot be traded, codified and canonised. Coaching insights, coaching confidence and coaching impact are contextual and develop over time, through participation, engagement with a range of sources and emergence within coaching communities. This depends on the opportunities for such encounters and the capacity to remain curious and develop critical and creative thinking in relation to coaching. That is the premise of this book.

The CollectivED community has become a critical mass allowing practice, research and innovation to be shared and co-constructed through an organic, reciprocal and emergent professional learning community. Unlike many professional development programmes educators have discretion about participation in CollectivED opportunities and make deliberate decisions that they recognise as having value for them. This has helped to build momentum and motivation for individual practice-based developments away from the network. Through its rhizomatic character the community has become curriculum (Cormier, 2008); it is neither linear nor simply objective-led. It is in this space, and others like it, that so much interesting work on coaching has evolved and change has happened.

Chapter 1 endnotes

Final thoughts

We opened this chapter with a quote from bell hooks, an American educator and theorist. Thirty years ago she urged teachers to see themselves as catalysts not performers, enabling 'everyone to become more and more engaged, to become active participants in learning'. It is hard to envision teachers' capacity for engagement of others without themselves being active participants in their own ongoing learning. While there are many forms of professional development, active participation is a personal stance and cannot be assumed. In a recent think piece Rachel suggested that as educators:

> *[...] we create our own golden threads [...] features of our working worlds which sustain our commitment; help us create meaning and allow us to navigate some of the inherent tensions and complexities in our education contexts and roles.*

She went on to propose that:

> *[...] teachers' internal golden threads create their own lived curriculum through which they experience unique professional development. [...] coaching has the potential to contribute to this*

golden thread, [as] meaning-making, intentional conversations, through which the values that educators hold about their work, their students, wider community and future society can form part of the personal and professional sense-making.

Lofthouse (2024, pp. 108–109)

The lived curriculum experienced by teachers is thus based on learning encounters, including those enabled by coaching, and within both organisational structures and rhizomatic communities, in collaboration with others and as individuals. We hope that our encounters with coaching and coaching communities in education, which have formed our lived curriculum and are the basis of this book, now contribute to yours.

Talking point

We use the term 'rhizomatic' to describe the engagement, learning and impacts of the CollectivED community. You might like to explore together the idea of rhizomatic learning experiences. How have you encountered them in your personal and professional lives? How do they contribute to your insights, skills and sense of self as an educator? What might limit your own or your colleagues' engagement in rhizomatic learning communities, and would you want this to change in the future?

Ideas for action

Why not try to make sense of your own 'golden thread' or help a coachee to do the same? To do this you might select a specific area of your work and trace back the ways that it has evolved over time. What role (if any) did coaching play?

Chapter 2
Encountering coaching in education

If coaching is the answer, what is the question? (Christian van Nieuwerburgh)
Rachel Lofthouse and Christian van Nieuwerburgh (2019, p. 68)

'So, what is coaching, exactly?' is a question you may have asked or been asked. In this chapter we define coaching, describe how coaching differs from mentoring and other collaborative professional learning activities, and acknowledge some of the different coaching in education processes, frameworks and models you may have come across. Although you may read this chapter independently from the others included in part 1, we do build upon this foundation in the following two chapters.

Defining coaching

Coaching is a co-created, collaborative and respectful learning relationship. This growth-oriented partnership of ongoing support and challenge evolves over time through structured conversations and ultimately (when done well) leads to positive change. Coaching is 'inherently multifaceted and ambiguous' (Gallucci et al., 2010, p. 922). Perhaps this ambiguity is not surprising as coaching can be found in a multitude of disciplines with varying conceptualisations and definitions, including business, leadership, medicine, human resources, philosophy, psychology, organisational development, sport and education.

As introduced in chapter 1, we describe coaching in education as a relational, positive and appreciative space in which educators can encounter a sense of purpose, opportunity, humanity, hope and achievement. It is a human-centred process of sustained and focused professional dialogue in which the coached educator (coachee) is given an opportunity to develop their pedagogical practice by gaining greater insights and/or developing specific skills to enhance their professional repertoire. In a nutshell, coaching is 'personalised professional support to teachers through discussion about their practice' (Lofthouse et al., 2010a, p. 7). As an inside-out process, coaching is led by the coachee and scaffolded by the coach. As a growth-oriented and reciprocal learning process, both the coach and coachee are provided with opportunities for reflection and responsive decision-making. Importantly, coaching is not a 'done to' process; it can lead to educators gaining enhanced self-awareness and a better understanding of the teaching and learning context.

Descriptions and definitions of coaching which resonate with us include:

- partnering with clients in a thought-provoking and creative process that inspires them to maximise their personal and professional potential. The process of coaching often unlocks previously untapped sources of imagination, productivity and leadership (International Coaching Federation, 2024)
- a collaborative solution-focused, results-orientated and systematic process in which the coach facilitates the enhancement of performance, life experience, self-directed learning and personal growth of individuals and organisations (Grant, 2006)
- the process of equipping people with the tools, knowledge and opportunities they need to develop themselves and become more effective (Peterson and Hicks, 1996, p. 14)
- a human development process that involves structured, focused interaction and the use of appropriate strategies, tools and techniques to promote desirable and sustainable change for the benefit of the coachee and potentially for other stakeholders (Cox et al., 2010, p. 1)
- a form of helping relationship, where one person builds a relationship with another (or a team or group) with a view to

- supporting them to make positive changes in their life and situation (Adams, 2016, p. 5)
- calling someone forward to learn, improve and grow, rather than to just get something sorted out (Bungay Stanier, 2016)
- the art of facilitating the performance, learning and development of another (Downey, 2003, p. 21)
- unlocking people's potential to maximise their own performance. It is helping them to learn rather than teaching them (Whitmore, 2009, p. 11)
- a method of work-related learning that relies primarily on one-to-one conversations (de Haan, 2008, p. 19)
- a collaborative process of facilitating a client's ability to self-direct learning and growth, as evidenced by sustained changes in self-understanding, self-concept and behaviour (Stober and Parry, 2005, p. 14)
- a managed conversation that takes place between two people that aims to support sustainable change to behaviours or ways of thinking; focused on learning and development (van Nieuwerburgh, 2014, p. 5).

Many of these coaching developers and authors have also influenced the wider CollectivED community and you can read more about how and why in part 3.

Role of contracting in coaching

Contracting within coaching is fundamental, although not always as explicit in education settings as in other contexts. Central to this is the fact that coaching is not a 'done to' process. Participating in coaching should always be with informed consent rather than by obligation. In the teaching profession the workforce is typically managed, hierarchies of leadership responsibility exist, and there are expectations of engagement in continuing professional development (CPD). This can lead to an assumption that practices such as coaching can just be applied without consideration of the ethical issues associated with contracting. Writing about executive coaching, in which a balance is sought between the individual coachee and the organisation, Lee (2013) acknowledges that while contracting is central, it remains poorly defined. This same balance is common in education. Lee suggests that 'executive coaching rests on a foundation of assumptions that give purpose and shape to the contracts' (p. 41) and given that this book deliberately links coaching and purpose we consider an awareness of the characteristics of contracting as worthy of consideration. For Lee (2013), there are four underlying issues: formality, balance, clarity and trust.

- **Formality** indicates that coaching in its truest sense is distinct from the 'myriad of casual conversations people have with each other' (Lee, 2013, p. 41) as well as from other practices such as mentoring, consulting or being supervised.
- **Balancing** the sometimes complex relationship between individual and organisational goals and the advantages gained by coaching, and issues of funding and access to coaching are pertinent.
- **Clarity** is dependent on all parties understanding the roles and responsibilities, expectations and purpose of coaching. Clarity can be confused with being deliberate about outcomes from the outset and this is not always helpful when coaching often allows for issues to emerge along the way. Having said this, there are essential components that need clarification if informed consent is to be truly given, such as issues related to confidentiality, and if a coachee is going to be able to actively participate.
- Contracting should create a platform for **trust**, which a safe psychological environment in coaching depends on. Despite this, contracting can also be perceived as a barrier to trust, especially if the start of the coaching is dominated by the formality of a coaching agreement rather than the establishment of a trusting relationship over time.

Writing about developing coaching contracts, van Nieuwerburgh (2014) suggests nine topics to consider in a coaching contract, although the level of recommendation for each one is dependent on the nature and context of the coaching. His suggestions are operational issues (number of sessions, location, etc.), shared understanding of coaching, financial arrangements, agreement and withdrawal, ethical conduct, confidentiality, competence, permissions and personal style. In their school guide to coaching teachers Lofthouse et al. (2010a) acknowledged that every school in their research (based on secondary schools in several regions of England) had a unique version of coaching teachers, but that these were commonly based on cycles. Rather than always focusing on contracts specifically, schools had paid attention to establishing the 'coaching partnership' and 'climate', which often addressed the relevant 'contracting' issues proposed by both Lee and van Nieuwerburgh above. These included enabling a sense of ownership by the coachee (rather than overt direction from the school), having a degree of choice regarding coaching pairings, being provided with assurance of adequate time to conduct coaching, with an agreed schedule being developed for coaching cycles, the confidentiality of coaching conversations, and with agreed mechanisms for sharing outcomes of coaching.

Understanding differences in coaching approaches

Within the field of coaching, there are many different and effective ways that coaches work with colleagues. One way to describe the differences between the different coaching in education processes is to examine the extent to which the coach's expertise and ideas are brought into the learning conversation, which can be categorised as facilitative, directive, dialogical or transformational.

- A **facilitative** coach is often referred to as the 'sounding board'. Coachees are seen as capable individuals with strengths and resources and the ability to develop their own insights. The coach uses a range of skills to facilitate reflection, analysis, observation and experimentation and supports the coachee to learn new ways of thinking and being (Aguilar, 2013, p. 23). As much as possible, coaches refrain from sharing their own expertise or suggestions and encourage reflective practices, personal responsibility and self-directed learning through questioning, active listening and appropriate challenge in a supportive and encouraging climate (Campbell and van Nieuwerburgh, 2018). Cognitive (Costa and Garmston, 1994, 2016), ontological (Sieler, 2010), solutions-focused (Jackson and McKergow, 2007), evocative (Tschannen-Moran and Tschannen-Moran, 2010, 2018) and GROWTH (Campbell and van Nieuwerburgh, 2018) coaching are often described as facilitative processes.

- **Directive or instructive** coaching is also known as the 'master and apprentice' model. In many ways, directive coaching is the opposite of facilitative coaching: the directive coach has specialised knowledge and shares their expertise. The relationship between coach and coachee is respectful, but not equal. Directive coaching works from the assumption that the coachee may not know how to use best practices and generally focuses on changing a coachee's behaviour. This type of advocacy coaching is often used to support the implementation of new initiatives or programmes and is sometimes referred to as, or overlaps with, mentoring. Responsive coaching (Goodrich, 2024) falls into this category.
- **Dialogical** coaching involves 'thinking partners'. The coaching relationship is equal and neither coach nor coachee withholds their expertise, strategies or ideas. At times, the coach may model or teach specific evidence-based practices, but they aim to balance advocacy with enquiry. Dialogical coaches use coaching conversations or 'dialogue' to challenge and support the coachee in describing precisely what they want to achieve, setting goals and examining how to get there. Instructional coaching falls into this category and is described by Jim Knight (2018) as 'coaches partner with teachers to analyse current reality, set goals, identify and explain teaching strategies to hit the goals, and provide support until the goals are met' (p. 3).
- **Transformational** coaching works to surface the connections and leverage change between the individual, the institutions and systems in which they work and the broader educational and social systems (Aguilar, 2024). Drawing on the coaching work of Hargrove, this type of coaching is grounded in systems thinking (Senge, 2006), which looks for how interrelationships and patterns of change across different levels in a system and context can have an impact on an individual's way of being. Elena Aguilar outlines transformational coaching in her new book *Arise* (2024), and systemic coaching (Hawkins and Turner, 2020; discussed further in chapters 14 and 17) would also fall under this category.

Although the purveyors of different coaching models emphasise how their model differs from others, coaching is best seen as a 'big tent' (Woulfin et al., 2023) aligned with multiple theories and shared features.

We find it helpful to think about the different types of coaching as part of a 'continuum'. At one end of the continuum, coaching conversations are described as 'less directive' (i.e. facilitative) and, at the other, 'more directive' (i.e. instructive). Munro and Campbell (2022, p. 29) offer the following diagram that helps to conceptualise a continuum of learning conversations (see Figure 2.1).

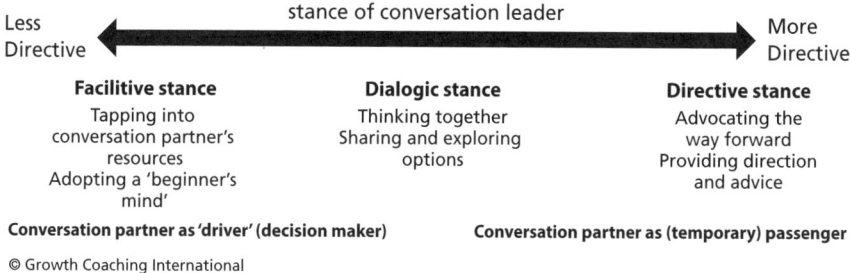

Figure 2.1 A continuum of learning conversations

Depending on the context, relationship, coaching process and needs of the coachee, the coach might move along the continuum and adopt a different 'stance' (Booton et al., 2023). Stance is described as 'a combination of how the conversation leader consciously "shows-up" – their way of *being*; and what they *do* in the conversation – how they use coaching' (Munro and Campbell, 2022, p. 30). Stance is dynamic, agile and responsive. The coach is confident and capable of offering a discerning ear, hand or thought according to the needs, wants, resources and energy of the coachee. A coaching way of being is described in more detail in chapter 4 and referenced frequently throughout the book.

Differentiating coaching from other collaborative professional learning

In the process of defining coaching, it is also important to highlight how it is similar to and yet different from other collaborative professional learning activities such as mentoring, supervising, training and consulting. In CollectivED, we believe that each of these collaborative relationships can play a role in teachers' continuous professional learning and development and improve school effectiveness. What becomes important, however, is to understand when, how and with whom to use the different activities. Using the same continuum presented above, supervising, training and consulting would obviously fall on the more 'directive' end of the continuum due to their hierarchical nature and core activities of instructing, leading, teaching and evaluating. When it comes to situating mentoring on this continuum, things get a little trickier. In CollectivED, we categorise mentoring as a directive and formalised process whereby a more experienced and knowledgeable educator (mentor) provides guidance and support to a less experienced colleague (mentee). One helpful way to think about the difference between these different collaborative-based relationships is the role of advice-giving. For Michael Bungay Stanier (2020) 'building a coaching habit is about staying curious a little longer and rushing to advice-giving a little more slowly' (p. 3). This is in obvious contrast to supervising, training and consulting where the expectation is that advice will be given. Similarly, advice-giving is a welcome part of the mentoring process since, as Rachel notes in her personal narrative in chapter 7, it is mentors' understanding of the training or working context and of the expectations that this places on the mentee that forms the basis of their mentoring work.

In the educational research and practice literature, the terms 'mentoring' and 'coaching' have conflicting interpretations and usage and can be used interchangeably. The terms can even be understood differently by people working within the same context and programme. Although there are clear similarities between the two collaborative professional learning processes, we see them as distinct but interrelated and complementary. As discussed in chapter 7, in her doctoral research, Trista (Hollweck, 2017, 2019a) used a Möbius strip to represent the multi-faceted and fluid nature of mentoring and coaching within a teacher induction context (see Figure 2.2).

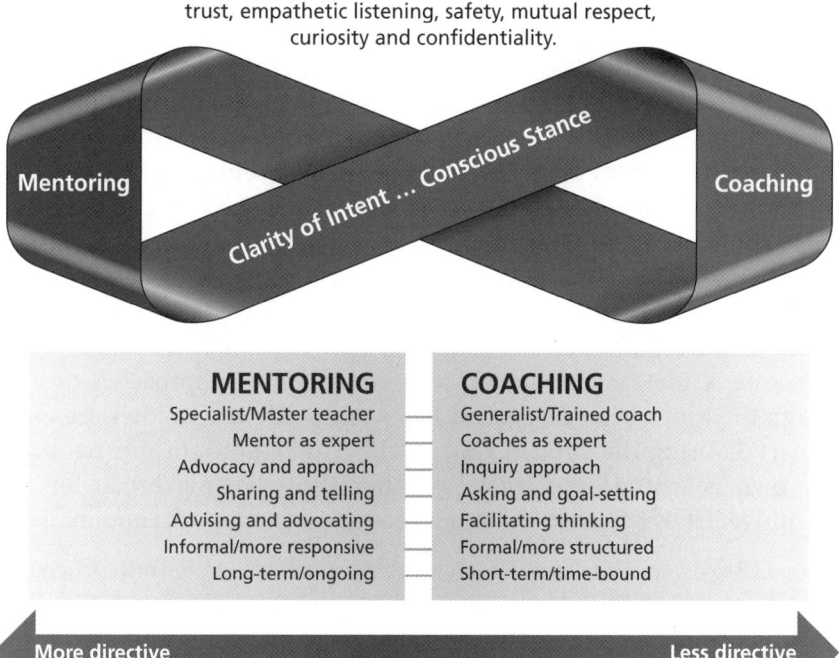

Figure 2.2 Mentoring and coaching in teacher induction. © Trista Hollweck, 2017

Rather than present mentoring and coaching statically on a continuum, the Möbius strip 'reflects the human quest for continuity and infinity within the bounds of space and time' (Tschannen-Moran and Tschannen-Moran, 2018, p. 42). Although we are aiming for definitional clarity in this book, we believe what is most important is that those responsible for and participating in collaborative professional learning and development activities such as mentoring, coaching, consulting, training and supervising have a shared understanding of what the different terms mean and how they differ. One way that helps us navigate this complexity is the concept of *accompaniment* which we discuss in more depth in chapters 4 and 8.

Coaching processes, frameworks and models

There are many different coaching processes, frameworks and models that are used in education. These structures can be best understood as an overarching framework that helps structure and signpost a coaching conversation and help move a coachee towards their goals or achieve change (van Nieuwerburgh and Love, 2019). As coaching tools, they provide shape, direction and guidance and often are presented in a step-by-step manner. Our research and coaching experiences have shown that it takes time and practice to get comfortable with a coaching model. It can feel very mechanical and awkward at the start, but as the coach gains confidence and competence, a model can be a powerful coaching tool. Different coaching frameworks speak to different coaches and we encourage coaches to learn about and try different models. Much depends on the resources and training provided, but it is possible for coaches from the same school or jurisdiction to prefer different approaches or even design their own bespoke process like some of the case studies presented in part 3. Using the curated CollectivED case studies in this book and our own coaching experience, we offer the following broad but not definitive list of common coaching processes, frameworks and models:

- **GROW model**: one of the most common coaching processes. Co-created by Alan Fine, Alexander Graham and Sir John Whitmore, the GROW model was popularised in the 1980s in Whitmore's *Coaching for Performance* (2009). The GROW acronym stands for goal, reality, options and will (or Way forward). As a model, it helps the coachee to think about their situation and instil a sense of personal responsibility and forward momentum. Additional letters have been added to the model in different coaching provisions, such as I (issues) in I-GROW (Wilson, 2011), T (topics) in T-GROW (Downey, 2003) or T (tactics) and H (habits) in GROWTH used by Growth Coaching International (Campbell and van Nieuwerburgh, 2018).
- **STRIDE model**: developed by Will Thomas (Thomas and Smith, 2009), it stands for strengths, target, reality, ideas, decision and evaluation. Anchored in an appreciative stance, the framework starts with and celebrates the coachee's strengths and aims for the process to be a positive experience.

- **Impact cycle**: integral to instructional coaching (Knight, 2007), the impact cycle is described as a dialogical process for helping teachers set and hit powerful PEERS (powerful, easy, emotionally compelling, reachable and student-focused) goals. The three parts of the impact cycle are identify (identifying a clear picture of reality, goal, strategy), learn (research, explain, model strategies) and improve (confirm direction, review progress with data, make adjustments, plan next steps).

- **Thinking environment**: based on the work of Nancy Kline (2009) the thinking environment is a philosophy of communication that forms the basis of a teaching pedagogy and coaching approach. Its ten components or principles are attention, appreciation, ease, encouragement, diversity, information, feelings, equality, place and incisive questions. As described on the 'Time to Think' website, 'The quality of everything we do depends on the quality of the thinking we do first. The quality of our thinking depends on the way we treat each other while we are thinking.' Chapter 13 provides a more in-depth discussion of Kline's thinking environment.

- **5Ps model**: also referred to as the 'see it, name it, do it' coaching model (Bambrick-Santoyo, 2016), this is a directive coaching process that includes classroom observations and feedback. The 5Ps are 'Provide precise *p*raise, *p*robe, identify *p*roblem and concrete action steps, *p*ractise, *p*lan ahead and set a timeline.' This model informs incremental coaching or BASIC coaching (Buck, 2020).

- **LEAD model**: part of evocative coaching (Tschannen-Moran and Tschannen-Moran, 2010, 2018), LEAD stands for listen, empathise, appreciate and design. This facilitative process uses David Cooperrider and Diana Whitney's (2005) appreciative inquiry SOAR (*s*trengths, exploring *o*pportunities, framing *a*spirations and identifying *r*esults) process and 4D model of discover, dream, design and destiny from design thinking.

- **OSKAR model**: this solution-focused process (Jackson and McKergow, 2007) is an acronym of *o*utcome, *s*ituation, *k*now-how, *a*ffirm and action, and *r*eview. It focuses on solutions and finding what works rather than analysing an issue or problem. This model has also been referred to as OSCAR (Gilbert and Whittleworth, 2009) with the C representing *c*hoices rather than know-how.

- **Dialogic orientation quadrant (DOQ)**: developed by Haesun Moon (2022), this solution-focused brief coaching model is a quadrant with the x-axis focused on timeline (past–future) and the y-axis on the content of the coaching conversation (negative–positive) described as positive/preferred future (Q1), positive/resourceful past (Q2), negative/troubled past (Q3), and negative/dreaded future (Q4). The DOQ is featured in the purposeful progress model we present in chapter 5 and referenced again in chapter 14.
- **Cognitive coaching conversation map**: cognitive coaching (Costa and Garmston, 1994) is a three-step process of a planning conversation, an observation and a reflection conversation that helps teachers explore their assumptions or 'invisible thinking' behind their practice. Conversation maps are used in each step to: clarify goals; specify success indicators and a plan for collecting evidence; anticipate approaches, strategies, decisions and how to monitor them; establish personal learning focus and processes for self-assessment; reflect on the coaching process and explore refinements.
- **Four phases of transformational coaching**: the transformational coaching (Aguilar, 2024) process has four phases: surface (current reality), recognise (impact), explore (emotions) and create (new practices). A transformational coaching conversation takes, alternately, both facilitative and directive stances and is anchored in five principles of compassion, curiosity, connection, courage and purpose.
- **SPACE model**: the SPACE model (Weiss et al., 2017) stands for *s*ocial context, *p*hysiology, *a*ction, *c*ognition and *e*motion and is used for assessment and intervention in cognitive behavioural coaching and therapy. Each of the components in the model is equal and explores the interconnected areas of behaviour, mind, mood and body, and their relation to environment.

As authors and in CollectivED, we strongly believe that there is no one 'right' coaching process, framework or model. Rather, research has shown that it is the coach's belief in their selected process that can lead to a successful coaching partnership (de Haan, 2008). Our suggestion is for coaches to explore a variety of approaches, play with them in your coaching conversations and adapt the one(s) that works best for you, your coachee and your context.

Chapter 2 endnotes

Final thoughts

This chapter outlines a breadth of coaching approaches which have contributed to coaching in education. Given this diversity, a critical component of success is how well linked the coaching approaches adopted are to the purposes intended for coaching. Establishing relevant and reliable coaching partnerships, which may include contracting, with appropriate attention paid to suitable arrangements and clarity of shared expectations, is essential for purposeful activity. Ensuring coaching is undertaken with informed consent promotes forms of agentic, active participation. Contracting can seem like a business-like approach, and the term is not always used in education coaching. Indeed few of the encounters with coaching in this book, including those from the CollectivED community, explicitly refer to contracting. This does not imply a lack of care for the clarity and shared understanding that successful coaching requires, as our case studies illustrate. Such care and consideration form the basis of the ethical dimensions that should underpin coaching and we invite you to engage with this book with this component in mind.

Talking point

We opened this chapter with a quote from van Nieuwerburgh which he commonly asks during conferences and workshops, 'If coaching is the answer, what is the question?' Considering that this book focuses on coaching with purpose (a concept further explored in chapter 5), you might find it helpful to post this question in conversations with others. As you enquire into their perceptions of what coaching might be 'the answer' to, you may expand your own thinking about the potential of coaching in education.

Ideas for action

If you work in a setting that uses coaching already or you are a coach, you may like to review the definitions and key features applied to the work and consider how they align with those identified in this chapter. You might start with the definitions of facilitative, directive or instructional, dialogical and transformational coaching. In doing so you should also take the opportunity to check that the terms that you use are appropriate or whether concepts and practices of coaching have drifted over time.

Chapter 3
Encounters with coaching origins and theory

There is increasing awareness among coaches of the need to ground their practice in a solid theoretical understanding and empirically tested models, rather than the standardised implementation of 'one size fits all' proprietary coaching systems.
Anthony M. Grant and Michael Cavanagh (2004, p. 1)

In this chapter we look beyond the definitions introduced in chapter 2 to explore the historical, theoretical and disciplinary roots of coaching in education. We adopt a more systematic style to summarise important background knowledge from a large and diverse body of practice and research literature to explain how and why coaching is conceptualised and practised in the ways that you may encounter it in your environment, in other literature or in the case studies captured in this book. We hope this will ground coaching in education in a wider context and spark a more in-depth exploration of what can seem like a hot new educational phenomenon.

The roots of coaching stretch back into antiquity and across continents and cultures. In the *Sourcebook of Coaching History*, Vikki Brock (2014) traces coaching's numerous and far-reaching origins and points out that Eastern philosophers were among the first coaching practitioners. She also highlights some of the challenges facing the field:

> *A child of many parents – among them psychotherapy, management consulting, self-help, motivation, continuing education, and of course, athletics – the early practice and theory*

> *of coaching was characterized by a confusing number of models and standards, all borrowed from coaching's root disciplines and frequently applied without a comprehensive understanding of the origins and purposes of those models and standards.*
>
> Brock (2014, p. 1)

In our own research and practice work with Canadian Indigenous communities and in international settings like Tonga, it has been important – and humbling at times – to recognise that most of the coaching literature is anchored in a Western perspective and that coaching's guiding principles and practice of accompanying someone as they learn has been around since time immemorial.

Origins and influences

The term 'coach' itself originated in the northern Hungarian town of Kocs (also pronounced Kochi), which was known for building a particular kind of horse-drawn carriage, known in English as a 'coach' in the 1500s. Since these 'coaches' took people from point A to point B, the term was used to describe private tutors at Oxford University in the 1840s who would help students pass their examinations – taking them from where they were (point A) to where they wanted to be (point B) (Evered and Selman, 1989). The term was then most often associated with traditional sports coaching until it was revisited by Harvard educationalist and tennis expert Timothy Gallwey in his 1974 book *The Inner Game of Tennis* (Gallwey, 2024). Gallwey de-emphasised the importance of skill instruction in coaching in favour of supporting players to manage and reduce internal states that might be interfering with their performance (e.g. fear, doubt, inattention, distraction) (Adams, 2016). Gallwey later parlayed this conceptualisation of coaching into the business world where it was introduced to Sir John Whitmore. Whitmore, often referred to as the father of modern-day coaching, was trained by Gallwey and is best known for his book *Coaching for Performance* (2009), where he introduced key coaching elements like powerful questioning, goal-setting and the GROW framework.

A tentative and emerging evidence base

While there were some practice-based texts and fewer than ten coach-specific peer-reviewed papers in the early 1990s, the popularity of coaching research and practice has significantly increased since that time (Grant and O'Connor, 2019). However, the bulk of this work has been described as 'atheoretical' (Stober and Parry, 2005) and critics argue that coaching remains 'largely undertheorised, and an awareness of which theories have been applied in the field is lacking' (Elek et al., 2024, p. 16). Theory in this instance refers to 'a set of concepts and the proposed relationship between them' (Maxwell, 2005, p. 42) that are presented as conceptual models or frameworks designed to help explain how the world 'works'.

For Anthony Grant (2014), the difference between professional coaching that draws on solid theory and research is stark when compared to overhyped coaching adapted from personal development and motivational programs: 'Without critical thinking, without proper evaluation, without informed reflective practice, the field of coaching has the very real potential to be lost and submersed in a sea of hyperbole, mumbo-jumbo and plain wishful thinking' (p. xiii). Like Grant, CollectivED supports more evidence-informed practice and calls for greater attention be paid to the theoretical, philosophical and disciplinary roots that underpin effective coaching.

Theoretical encounters

There are a number of influential theories which inform the coaching practices found in the CollectivED community. These include but are not limited to adult learning theories, positive psychology, self-determination theory, self-efficacy and person-centred theory. Since coaching theories draw from a variety of disciplines, the following is best viewed as a short primer focused mainly on some psychological theories and approaches related to the self, behaviour and learning. In part 4 we also explore theories related to human and systemic change as well as social and professional learning.

Adult learning theory

In most cases, coaching is a learning process for adults. Two key adult learning theories that underpin coaching are Malcolm Knowles's *andragogy* and Jack Mezirow's *transformative learning*.

Andragogy

Developed in the 1970s, andragogy was described by Malcolm Knowles as the 'art and science of helping adults learn' (Knowles, 1984). He posited that adults will be most successful when they are active participants in the learning process, accompanied, challenged and supported, and attention is paid to their surrounding context. Knowles developed a set of five assumptions for andragogy:

1. Adults are self-directed, seek choice and autonomy in the learning process and accept responsibility for the outcomes.
2. Adults come to the learning process with a depth of experience, knowledge and capacity and value real and relevant experiences that build on these resources.
3. Adults learn when they have reason to do so and focus on what is most useful to them in their daily work and personal lives.
4. Adults value topics that are problem-oriented, active learning strategies and consistent and relevant feedback.
5. Adults are intrinsically motivated and goal-oriented, seeking goals that are realistic, important and aligned with their personal and/or professional needs.

Transformative learning

Critical reflection is pivotal to transformative learning, which is understood as an adult form of metacognitive reasoning. Defined by Mezirow (2003), 'Transformative learning is learning that transforms problematic frames of reference – sets of fixed assumptions and expectations (habits of mind, meaning perspectives, mindsets) – to make them more inclusive, discriminating, open, reflective, and emotionally able to change.' Transformative learning involves critical reflection of assumptions held and can be supported by interactions with another. The four principles of transformative learning are:

1. Adults exhibit two kinds of learning: instrumental (e.g. cause/effect) and communicative (e.g. feelings).
2. Learning involves change to meaning structures (perspectives and schemes).
3. Change to meaning structures occurs through reflection about content, process or premises.
4. Learning can involve refining/elaborating meaning schemes, learning new schemes, transforming schemes, or transforming perspectives.

In her new book *Arise: The Art of Transformational Coaching*, Elena Aguilar (2024) sums up adult learning with seven principles:

1. Adults must feel safe to learn.
2. Adults come to learning experiences with histories.
3. Adults need to know why we have to learn something.
4. Adults want agency in learning.
5. Adults need practice to internalise learning.
6. Adults have a problem-centred approach to learning.
7. Adults want to learn (p. 417).

Positive psychology

Positive psychology (PP) is described in the Sage *Handbook of Coaching* (Boniwell et al., 2010) as 'a scientifically rooted approach to helping clients increase wellbeing, enhance and apply strengths, improve performance, and achieve valued goals' (p. 158). An umbrella term, PP grew from the humanistic movement that became popular in the 1960s. Rather than focusing on malady, deficit and dysfunction, applied positive psychology focuses on the importance of positive emotion, understanding and developing positive traits, and introducing strategies that build on the strengths within individuals and organisations to optimise functioning. Some of the popular PP interventions include strengths-spotting using the values in action (VIA) survey of character strengths, which lists a person's top strengths with a short description, gratitude writing and positive reflection activities like 'three good things'.

Wellbeing theory

Wellbeing is at the heart of positive psychology. In his book *Flourish*, Martin Seligman (2011) defined wellbeing as a multidimensional construct that bridges the hedonic aspect of feeling good (positive emotion) with the eudaimonic aspects of living well (relationships, purpose, mastery, growth and autonomy). Five elements combine to contribute to human flourishing and form the evidence-based PERMA framework: *p*ositive emotion (the subjective measure of happiness and life satisfaction), *e*ngagement (the subjective measure of being absorbed in a task), (positive) *r*elationships (with others), *m*eaning (the subjective experience of belonging to, or serving something which you believe is bigger than yourself) and *a*ccomplishment (experiencing achievement or success). Each element has three properties (Seligman, 2011, p. 16):

1. It contributes to wellbeing.
2. Many people pursue it for its own sake, not merely to get any of the other elements.
3. It is defined and measured independently of the other elements (exclusivity).

Emotional intelligence

An integral part of positive psychology, the concept of emotional intelligence (EI) (or emotional quotient, EQ) was coined by John Mayer and Peter Salovey (Mayer et al., 1999), who defined it as the ability to perceive, understand, manage and use emotions to facilitate thinking. Reuven Bar-On (2010) described it as 'an array of interrelated emotional and social competencies and skills that determine how effectively individuals understand and express themselves, understand others and relate with them, and cope with daily demands, challenges and pressures' (p. 54). The most familiar model of EI is the one popularised by Daniel Goleman (1998), who presented it as a framework to understand the role of emotions in human behaviour, decision-making and relationships. The Goleman model is made up of four main components: self-awareness, social awareness, self-management and social skills.

Appreciative inquiry

Appreciative inquiry (AI) is a collaborative, strengths-based approach to supporting change in organisations and other human systems. Developed by David L. Cooperrider and colleagues at Case Western University in the 1980s, AI 'involves in a central way, the art and practice of asking questions that strengthen a system's capacity to apprehend, anticipate, and heighten positive potential' (Cooperrider and Whitney, 2005, p. 3). AI is anchored in eight assumptions:

1. In every society, organisation or group, something works.
2. What we focus on becomes our reality.
3. Reality is created in the moment and there are multiple realities.
4. The act of asking questions of an organisation or group influences the group in some way.
5. People have more confidence and comfort to journey to the future (the unknown) when they carry forward parts of the past (the known).
6. If we carry parts of the past forward, they should be what is best about the past.
7. It is important to value differences.
8. The language we use creates our reality.

Using a strengths-based or affirmative approach (Hammond, 2013), AI assumes that each human system has a positive core of strengths. Its methodology and activities focus on centring the values, beliefs and capabilities of organisations when they are 'at their best' and on building upon these collective understandings of these assets (Cooperrider and Whitney, 2005). AI is most commonly associated with design thinking's 4D model of discover, dream, design and destiny and the SOAR process of discovering strengths, exploring opportunities, framing aspirations and identifying results.

Hope theory

Hope is defined as 'goal-directed thinking in which the person utilizes pathway thinking (the perceived capacity to find routes to desired goals) and agency thinking (the requisite motivations to use these routes)'

(Snyder and Lopez, 2007, p. 189). Developed by Charles Richard Snyder (2002), hope theory is based on three core assumptions:

1. **Goals**: human behaviour is generally goal-directed.
2. **Pathways**: hopeful thinkers imagine multiple workable ways to achieve goals.
3. **Agency**: hopeful thinkers instigate change and persevere to achieve their goals.

Hope researchers have shown that higher hope corresponds with improved academic and athletic performance, physical and psychological wellbeing, interpersonal relationships and work performance.

Self-determination theory

According to Richard Ryan and Edward Deci (2000), 'Human beings can be proactive and engaged or, alternatively, passive and alienated, largely as a function of the social conditions in which they develop and function' (p. 68). Self-determination theory (SDT) is described as a psychological framework that explores human motivation and personal development. Ryan and Deci introduced SDT to behavioural science in the 1970s and argued that all humans have three innate psychological needs that contribute to intrinsic motivation:

1. **Autonomy**: the desire to feel in control of one's decisions.
2. **Competence**: the desire to feel capable of mastery and accomplishment.
3. **Relatedness** (or **belonging**): the desire to feel a sense of connection to one's peers.

Intrinsic motivation challenged the traditional belief that the way to 'improve performance, increase productivity, and encourage excellence is to reward the good and punish the bad' (Pink, 2011, p. 19). In his book *Drive*, Pink (2011) also includes 'purpose' as a key element contributing to intrinsic motivation, which he describes as the desire to do what we do in the service of something larger than ourselves. In SDT, goal-setting plays an important role, but Pink includes a caution: 'Goals that people set for themselves and that are devoted to attaining mastery are usually healthy. But goals imposed by others – sales targets, quarterly returns, standardised test scores, and so on – can sometimes have dangerous side effects' (p. 50).

Person-centred theory

Person-centred theory is attributed to psychotherapist Carl Rogers (1961), who argued that people are self-actualising, capable of growth and are ultimately their own best experts. Rogers builds on Abraham Maslow's (1943) work in humanistic psychology, which stated that human motivation is based on people seeking fulfilment and change through personal growth. Self-actualisation denotes people who are fulfilled and doing all they are capable of. When in a social environment where a person feels safe, understood, valued and accepted, their potential will be realised. For Rogers (1961), empathy (i.e. understanding), congruence (i.e. genuineness and authenticity) and unconditional positive regard (non-judgement) were the three 'necessary and sufficient conditions' for a successful and humane relationship. 'If I can provide a certain type of relationship, the other person will discover within himself the capacity to use that relationship for growth, and change and personal development will occur' (quoted in Adams, 2016, p. 39).

Motivational interviewing

Motivational interviewing (MI), developed by William Miller and Stephen Rollnick (2013), is a collaborative person-centred strategy that is often linked to coaching. The four steps used in MI are engaging, focusing, evoking, and planning, but the effectiveness of MI depends on the interviewer's 'way of being' (see chapter 4) and the interpersonal relationship within which MI is used. Miller and Rollnick (2002) explain this as 'the way in which one communicates can make it more or less likely that the person will change' (p. 8).

Solution-focused brief therapy

As indicated by its name, solution-focused brief therapy (SFBT) focuses on helping individuals to develop new behaviours to resolve problems. The solution-focused model developed by Steve de Shazer and Insoo Kim Berg (2021) is based on the premises that the future is 'created' and that small changes in the present can lead to big differences in the future. The principles that guide this approach are:

- Focus on solutions not problems.
- Start with the premise that people are competent.
- Expect success and progress.
- Make the least change to attain the greatest result.
- Keep on doing what works.
- Stop doing things that don't work.

The SIMPLE coaching model (Jackson and McKergow, 2007) builds on these propositions: *s*olutions not problems, *i*n between (the action is in the interaction), *m*ake use of what's there, *p*ossibilities (past, present and future), *l*anguage (simply said) and *e*very case is different.

A popular SFBT intervention used in coaching is the *scaling technique*, which asks the coachee to use a scale from 1 to 10 to describe the problem and consider the next small step using their available resources to move towards their 'preferred future' (Moon, 2024) or what they picture as their 'perfect' ten. For Moon, the emphasis is on positively 'moving forward' and progressing up the scale rather than the number, which aligns with the goals of positive psychology.

Self-efficacy/social cognitive theory

In self-efficacy theory psychologist Albert Bandura (1977) states that the extent to which people are motivated to pursue their goals and desired results is related to their confidence and belief in their own capacity and capability: 'Efficacy expectations determine how much effort people will expend and how long they will persist in the face of obstacles and aversive experiences. The stronger the perceived self-efficacy, the more active the efforts' (p. 194). The two guiding principles for self-efficacy are:

1. whether an individual believes they are capable of adequately performing the behaviour needed to reach the outcome (efficacy expectations)
2. whether an individual believes that if they perform the behaviour adequately, it will get them the outcome they are hoping for (outcome expectations).

Collective efficacy, which we discuss in chapter 15, builds on Bandura's theory and is described as the shared belief that through working together, or collective action, people can reach a common goal and make a difference. In education, Jenni Donohoo's (2017) research on collective teacher efficacy has shown that educators who work together to build a shared sense of efficacy can influence student outcomes and increase achievement for all students. Collective efficacy is more than just professional collaboration; it requires trust, a shared sense of purpose, structures and supports for authentic collaborative-based learning opportunities, access to evidence-informed practices and ongoing feedback and reflection (Elliott et al., 2022).

Chapter 3 endnotes

Final thoughts

We opened this chapter with a quote first published two decades ago, but which we think is now very pertinent in education. Grant and Cavanagh (2004) were wary of 'standardised implementation of "one size fits all" proprietary coaching' and argued for a strong theoretical grounding for coaching. The summaries offered in this chapter create an initial route through relevant theory. They help to remind us that as adults our learning needs to be considered in ways that are appropriate and allow for self-determination and self-efficacy. A challenge in education settings where children and young people are the principal learners is to remember not to rely on assumptions of learning based on experiences of working with the curriculum, assessment and behaviours more typical for that age group. The theoretical grounding for coaching is also useful when distinguishing between teaching, training and coaching, whatever the age range.

Talking point

Andragogy is introduced in this chapter as being central to adult learning theory. The short account of andragogy given might be a really powerful stimulus for discussion. This may produce interesting reflections from colleagues about their own learning as adults, both within and beyond the profession.

Ideas for action

The scaling technique introduced in this chapter is an intervention drawn from SFBT, which is commonly used in coaching. If you do not already use this as a coach, you might like to try it out if a problem is central to the coaching conversation. Invite the coachee to use a scale from 1 to 10 to describe the problem and consider the next small step using their available resources to move further up the scale. What might it take to reach '10'?

Chapter 4
Sensemaking: from core skills to guiding principles of coaching

Sensemaking is not an event, but is ongoing, focused on extracted cues, driven by plausibility, and tied to identity construction. Individuals pay attention when something in their surroundings does not fit with their usual routines, and use their experience to find patterns that help to explain new situations.

Karen Seashore Louis (2010, p. 18)

We hope that when you read the coaching case studies found in part 3 of this book, it will be evident that members of our CollectivED community have experience, training and alignment with diverse coaching approaches, models and frameworks. Within this community we continue to draw on a growing understanding of the history, theoretical and disciplinary roots and shared guiding principles to inform our evidence-informed research, practice and discussions around coaching. We do this to address the fact that while there is no shortage of coaching books promoting and advocating for certain core coaching skills, strategies and processes, the field still 'lacks understanding of what the key components of coaching are, how and why they "work" and, as such, which aspects to emphasise when taking coaching to scale' (Elek et al., 2024, p. 1).

We have included 'sensemaking' in the chapter title because this ongoing process is fundamental in our evolving understanding of coaching in education. There are core elements of coaching we have come to know in theory, observe in others and be able to do in our own educational realities. There are ways of approaching educational spaces and relationships that we have witnessed as a coaching way of being and stance. There are unfamiliar ideas that we have become attuned to over time, and that shine a light on coaching principles and purpose. We recognise in ourselves and in others the ways that sensemaking becomes enacted and embodied by coaches.

This chapter first draws out the underlying principles of coaching that lead to the focus on the 'how-to' of coaching. As coaching scholar Anthony Grant (2013) stated, 'while "coaching" might imply a "monolithic" activity, the term refers to a diversity of practices aimed at generating individual or organisational change' (p. 16). Yet there is a difference between 'doing' coaching and 'being' a coach. Christian van Nieuwerburgh (2014) argued that effective coaching requires three key elements: a 'way of being', a set of skills and techniques, and a clear process (p. 12). We outlined examples of processes, frameworks and models in chapter 2 and noted that members of the CollectivED community have experience with and use a variety of different educational coaching frameworks and models. As such, we do not promote a particular type of coaching process in this book, nor do we introduce a new product into an already congested space. Similarly, in this chapter we do not go into depth around the other key coaching elements of the 'way of being' and core coaching skills and techniques. Rather, they are offered as a learning encounter and an invitation to explore the literature that focuses on these elements. We conclude this chapter with the less well-known concepts of 'accompaniment' and 'wayfinding' that we have found to be useful sensemaking tools for the CollectivED community. Both are rooted in specific cultural and linguistic traditions and help extend our future focused thinking about coaching with purpose and what that means for education.

Underlying coaching principles

Coaching is often identified as one of the most effective methodologies to support individual and group professional learning and development (CUREE, 2005; Kraft et al., 2018; Kraft and Blazar, 2018). These assertions

Chapter 4 Sensemaking: from core skills to guiding principles of coaching

have led to an ever-increasing influx of coaching programmes available to educators that are called instructional, incremental, GROWTH, cognitive, transformational, solutions-focused, ontological, evocative, dilemma-based, blended, BASIC, responsive, systemic and so on (see chapter 2). With so many different options and offerings, it is no wonder that educators can feel a sense of confusion and even overwhelm when they first begin to explore what coaching is and how it might fit into their practice or context. In some ways it is easier to reflect on what coaching might 'do' or what purposes it serves rather than start with the variations in how coaching works or looks like in the educational landscape.

Coaching is grounded in shared principles and we can relate these to the purpose of coaching: the role we want it to play in educational communities. These principles also have an ethical foundation, related to the establishment of a shared understanding of the purpose of coaching and the value of that purpose, clarity in relation to the coaching approach and informed consent. The key principles are represented in Table 4.1.

Table 4.1 Linking the principles and purposes of coaching

Key principle of coaching	Coaching purpose
Coaching is a managed conversation.	The bulk of the coaching work is facilitated through dialogue, where the nature and focus of the talk are on learning and development that aim to catalyse changes in the coachee's behaviour, thinking and/or beliefs (van Nieuwerburgh, 2014).
Coaching is purposeful.	Coaching is action-oriented. The coaching partnership is working towards an established goal that is meaningful for and owned by the coachee (Moon, 2022).
Coaching is reflective.	The coach and coachee work together to critically examine the past, learn from mistakes and challenges and build on strengths and previous successes (Grant, 2013).
Coaching is human-centred.	Effective coaches work from a lens of unconditional positive regard for their coachee and believe people are competent and their own best experts: 'We must think of people in terms of their potential, not their performance. Human potential is realized by optimizing individuality and uniqueness, never by moulding someone to another's opinion of what constitutes best practice' (Whitmore, 2009).

45

Key principle of coaching	Coaching purpose
Coaching is relational.	At the heart of effective coaching is a trusting and collaborative relationship that forms between the coach and coachee. Partnership principles (Knight, 2016, 2022) such as equality, choice, voice, dialogue, reflection, praxis and reciprocity lead to better conversations and create a space in which teachers and others in the education system can feel heard and valued.
Coaching is collaborative.	The coach and coachee use a structured (but not rigid) process to learn with and from one another, whereby their shared knowledge and skills are brought to the fore to be worked with and extended through co-construction (Lofthouse, 2019b).
Coaching creates purposeful and positive change.	The coach and coachee are both invested in working together to reach a personal and/or professional improvement goal that will lead to a change in behaviour, belief or being (Grant, 2013).
Coaching is contextual and dynamic.	Coaching has interactive properties: it is influenced by context and it also influences context. Effective coaching is attuned to its setting and it adapts and changes based on the input and needs of its context (Hollweck and Lofthouse, 2021).
Coaching is a way of being.	'Coaching is not merely a technique to be wheeled out and rigidly applied in certain prescribed circumstances. It is a way of managing, a way of treating people, a way of thinking, a way of being' (Whitmore, 2009).

Coaching way of being

A coaching 'way of being' relates to how we show up in the world and how we experience and express our emotions. Linked to Rogers' (1961) person-centred theory (see chapter 3), it consists of various character traits like integrity, authenticity, empathy, reliability and trustworthiness. A coaching 'way of being' is the key factor in an effective coaching relationship and requires high emotional intelligence, the ability to form trusting relationships and a commitment to seeing the potential in others (Aguilar, 2024; de Haan, 2008; van Nieuwerburgh, 2014). Whereas coaching skills, techniques and processes can be taught and learned quite easily, a way of being is more complex and develops over time. It is about 'noticing', which van Nieuwerburgh and Love (2019) describe as being present and attuned to the coachee and their needs. Ultimately, a coaching way of being is the element that makes coaching a craft rather than a set of techniques to follow. It doesn't matter how confident and skilled the coach, if the coachee doesn't trust or respect them, the interpersonal relationship will not be as strong and coaching is unlikely to be successful. We have found the work of Jim Knight (2016, 2022) on 'partnership principles' to be an excellent resource to better understand a coaching 'way of being'.

Core skills and techniques

At its core, coaching is a 'conversational process and a set of easily learned skills' (van Nieuwerburgh, 2017, p. 5). As noted earlier there is no shortage of resources on key coaching 'moves' or practices and many are linked to the psychological theories and approaches we introduced in chapter 3. These skills can include:

- building trust in the coaching relationship
- asking powerful questions to provoke and invite reflection, enquiry and action
- empathic, intentional and focused listening (paying attention and showing that we are paying attention)
- clarifying and elaborating to expand on an idea or check for understanding
- summarising, rephrasing and paraphrasing key ideas shared by the coachee
- setting goals that are impactful and owned by the coachee
- strength spotting
- inviting multiple perspectives
- giving and receiving feedback
- making suggestions (not too quickly, too often or too directive).

There are numerous resources and tools available to help coaches develop the skills and techniques listed above. We encourage you to explore each of these practices in more depth and to use the references and additional resources we provide as a springboard to future learning encounters.

As authors, we have direct experience that learning to coach is part of an individual change process (see chapter 17) and we each draw on different learning encounters with coaching. It takes time, experience and support to learn the core skills of coaching, practise techniques, build performance and gain proficiency and expertise (van Nieuwerburgh and Love, 2019). In her doctoral research examining the impact of learning to be a coach from the experienced educator perspective, Trista's participants reported that it took them around three years to fully gain confidence and capacity as an effective coach (Hollweck, 2019a).

Accompaniment

Working in the dual-language context of Canada and refining her sensemaking related to the relationships between coaching and mentoring have led Trista to consider the concept of 'accompaniment'. A further encounter with accompaniment can be found in chapter 7, in which Trista articulates key experiences of her research and practice in coaching. As co-authors we have been exploring through a variety of CollectivED events the use of accompaniment as a sensemaking tool to help expand our own and others' understanding of mentoring and coaching as stances and as a way of being (Booton et al., 2023).

The term 'accompaniment' has the same root as the Spanish verb '*acompañar*' and the French noun '*accompagnement*', with the literal meaning of 'accompanying' in English. Described by American researcher Brené Brown (2021), accompaniment is practising the courage to walk alongside someone to help them to get better at doing what they do: 'a commitment to be with people – not pushing them from behind or leading from the front, but walking with them in solidarity' (p. 262). Rooted in social liberation theology in Latin America, accompaniment is 'an intentional practice of presence' (Wilkinson and D'Angelo, 2019) and best described by American medical anthropologist and physician, Paul Farmer (2011) as an 'elastic' term:

> It has a basic, everyday meaning. To accompany someone is to go somewhere with him or her, to break bread together, to be present on a journey with a beginning and an end. There's an element of mystery, of openness, of trust, in accompaniment.

Chapter 4 Sensemaking: from core skills to guiding principles of coaching

The companion, the accompagnateur, says, 'I'll go with you and support you on your journey wherever it leads.'

Farmer (2011, p. 190)

Accompaniment has been a part of the educational context in the Canadian province of Quebec since 2000. There, accompaniment designates an approach to collective mobilisation and is used as an umbrella term that encompasses a wide variety of collaborative-based professional learning and development approaches (Hollweck and Baradaran, 2022). As a process of change and transformation, accompaniment represents a reciprocal learning journey where educators from different backgrounds and experiences work together respectfully as equals to improve their practice day by day and become more confident and competent in their professional life (see Booton et al., 2023; Chestnutt et al., 2024). In CollectivED, we believe that the term accompaniment makes space for and recognises the different ways that educators work with and support one another to meet the needs of their students, improve their practice and, ultimately, flourish.

Chapter 4 endnotes

Final thoughts

In the opening quote, Louis links sensemaking to identity construction. We argue that sensemaking is an intentional outcome of coaching. Therefore, we make the link between coaching in education and identity formation of teachers, leaders and students who engage in coaching. This can also be asserted if we recognise coaching as an opportunity for teacher learning, which Beijaard (2019) suggests is influenced by the teacher's aspirations, learning history, beliefs about education and biography. As such, coaching does not start with a clean slate coachee, it is not a clinical exercise and it cannot be expected to be experienced, appreciated and learned from in the same way by all. The capacity of the coach is based on the skills that they bring, the techniques that they can draw upon and their coaching way of being. These enable the coach to work individually with coachees, drawing on a set of key principles which we have outlined in this chapter. These principles create the opportunities for sensemaking and the space for continued identity formation. We have extended these with the two additional concepts of accompaniment and wayfinding. We find these of value when we consider the way that coaches support coachees in activities which have personal and professional purpose.

Talking point

In this chapter we quote Brené Brown, who describes accompaniment as 'a commitment to be with people – not pushing them from behind or leading from the front, but walking with them in solidarity'. This concept of solidarity is also explored in chapter 16 when cycles of growth (CoG) enabled by coaching are considered. You may find it interesting to reflect as a coach and with other coaches about accompaniment and solidarity. Do these concepts resonate with you and, if so, how would that be recognised in your practices of coaching?

Ideas for action

If you are a coach, you might seek permission from a coachee to record a coaching session. You could then watch this back with them and notice the skills that you bring to the session. The list of skills offered in this chapter might be a good place to start. Be considerate in relation to potential power imbalances when inviting a coachee to help you and when you are undertaking this. This activity would be a good task as part of coaching development, perhaps working with other coaches to record coaching sessions with them for review.

Chapter 5
Exploring the concept of purpose

Purpose is the aim around which we structure our lives, a source of direction and energy. Through the lens of purpose, we are able to see ourselves – and our future – more clearly.

Richard J. Leider (2015, p. vii)

Making sense of what really matters to you

You might associate the word 'purpose' with the philosophical question: 'What's your purpose in life?' It's a really big question and probably one that you need time to think deeply about. It may be helpful to consider how your own values shape your sense of purpose. If you are clear about what matters to you, then your values may guide your purposeful journey in life. The title of this book draws attention to 'coaching with purpose' in the field of education. We believe the concept of purpose needs, and deserves, to be explored more broadly, before applying a lens to the contexts of coaching and education. In saying that, we expect educators interested in the practice of coaching will see familiar language and imagery that resonates.

In the context of coaching frameworks, the concept of purpose is not typically emphasised or used as a foundational element. While purpose can certainly be a significant underlying motivation for individuals seeking coaching, traditional coaching approaches often focus more on goals, actions and strategies, rather than delving deeply into existential or philosophical questions of purpose. With this in mind, this chapter on purpose in coaching does not draw extensively on schools of thought from other areas of practice, but rather serves as a statement of belief regarding the potential value and impact of purpose within the coaching process.

In simple terms, the concept of 'purpose' may refer to the motivation and reason behind someone's actions and behaviours. As alluded to earlier, a purposeful existence often provides meaning to our actions and helps us understand our role in the world. Having a sense of purpose can provide individuals with a direction of travel, drive and fulfilment. It is important to recognise that human beings are unique individuals; finding and defining one's purpose is both personal and subjective.

As co-authors, we recognise that we spend a great deal of time pondering over the meaning of words – we feel it is important to clarify the meaning of three concepts that are strongly entwined. We view a deep connection between the concepts of purpose, values and goals. If we're not careful though, these words may become clichés – overused, shallow and ultimately ignored. An issue with communication arises when teachers consider such words meaningless jargon or 'edubabble' (Woolman, 2018)! As co-authors, we fundamentally believe language helps us to make sense of the world. In order to engage in meaningful dialogue, it is helpful to have a common, shared understanding of key conceptual language. From experience, due to time pressures, this doesn't happen automatically in schools, and when it does the conversations are often at a surface level.

This leads us to unravel two of these elegantly woven conceptual threads. We admit the metaphor of weaving is often used to discuss complexity in education, but some clichés just make sense. We will unpick the meaning of values and purpose and how they influence each other.

How might values shape our sense of purpose?

We begin by explaining what we mean by a 'sense of purpose' from a broader, conceptual perspective. On the front cover of Michael Bungay Stanier's (2022) *How to Begin* is a powerful provocation: 'Open the book and start doing something that matters.' In his book, Bungay Stanier refers to the word 'worthy', with respect to setting a 'worthy goal' (p. 19). He acknowledges that the word 'worthy' might be thought of as 'perhaps a little high and mighty', but states that the word is 'less about an abstract moral rating' and more about the 'worthiness' of making a commitment. As co-authors, we feel that Bungay Stanier's description of 'worthiness' aligns closely with our use of the phrase 'sense of purpose'. For us, exploring a person's sense of purpose is a worthwhile coaching conversation. If we use the metaphor of 'learning journeys' and conceive that values shape our sense of purpose, then the coaching intention would be for a coachee to set off with a strong feeling and belief that there is 'value' in the journey ahead. We examine how values influence and shape our sense of purpose through the following:

1. **Clarity**: knowing what values are important to you can help you gain clarity of thinking by providing a framework for decision-making and guiding your actions. When you are clear about your values, you have a better understanding of what matters most to you and what you stand for. This clarity can help you prioritise your goals and choices, filter out distractions and stay focused on what aligns with your values. It can also help you make decisions that are in line with your beliefs and principles, leading to a more coherent and consistent thought process. Ultimately, understanding your values can provide a sense of purpose and direction, which can contribute to clearer, more focused thinking. Significantly for us, we see values shining light on our sense of purpose. Putting it simply: values provide clear guidance and help shape our sense of purpose.

2. **Alignment**: when a person is clear about their values, they can align their actions and choices with what truly matters to them. Values act as a moral compass for decision-making and behaviour. Values help us check that our actions and choices are aligned with our sense of purpose.

3. **Fulfilment**: when we consciously align our actions with our values and sense of purpose, we are more likely to create conditions for a 'well-lived life' (Knight, 2022). In his book *The Definitive Guide to Instructional Coaching*, Knight (2022) states 'coaching invites teachers to move closer to a life where what they believe on the inside aligns with what they do on the outside' (p. 195). While this

quote speaks to 'alignment', it also highlights how aligning one's beliefs with actions can lead to fulfilment in both personal and professional life.

4. **Motivation**: in his book *The Power of Purpose*, Richard J. Leider (2015) poses a crucial question that chimes loudly with us: 'What gets you up in the morning?' Intrinsic motivation, driven by our values, makes it easier to stay committed to moving forward with a sense of purpose.

5. **Ethics**: values can serve as ethical prompts, nudges and reminders in fulfilling one's purpose. When we clearly understand how values inform purpose, there is a synergy between our actions and belief system.

In summary, values shape our sense of purpose. The alignment of values and purpose contributes to greater clarity, fulfilment, motivation and ethical decision-making: we have an authentic reason to get up in the morning and experience a 'well-lived life' (Knight, 2022).

Having considered the importance of starting with a sense of purpose, we will now discuss the relationship between the three conceptual threads: purpose, values and goals.

Moving forward *with* a sense of purpose

As previously discussed, values help shape our sense of purpose. The ability to define our purpose allows us to take aim and move toward our purposeful, 'preferred future' (Moon, 2022) or 'vision' using typical leadership language. In simple terms: be 'future looking'.

Goals are specific, measurable targets that we set in order to make progress towards our preferred, visionary future. Purpose provides direction and clarity; for us purpose also provides the energy and momentum to move forward. Goals act as milestones and indicators along the path towards the future we desire. Goals are more concrete and provide actionable steps and measurable outcomes. Arguably, a goal is a means to making 'purposeful' progress. Without a clear sense of purpose, the goals may feel imposed by others and not owned. The goals may be met, but there is no joy in the journey! Sadly, we have worked with high-achieving schools where the culture is toxic. Outstanding pupil outcomes lead to goals ticked off, but every teacher hated the process. As co-authors, this is why we feel so passionately about values aligning with goals.

We strongly believe values play a crucial role in goal-setting, referenced often in the foundational coaching theories outlined in chapter 3 and described as one of the core coaching skills introduced in chapter 4. Values help us prioritise our goals and ensure that they align with core beliefs and principles. When goals align with one's values, the pursuit of those goals becomes more purposeful. Values also act as a guide for decision-making when faced with choices that impact the pursuit of goals. For us, importantly in a collaborative school culture (Gruenert and Whitaker, 2015), there is a unity of purpose and sense of solidarity. When meeting goals along the way to the preferred future, values help us to discuss if the journey so far was positive and purposeful. If not, then acknowledging this deviation from our agreed collegial purpose allows teachers to return to the purposeful route. In all honesty, we recognise in ourselves that we gave little attention to values as early career teachers. But now, with a greater depth of understanding, informed by lived experiences, we advocate the importance of clearly understood and embodied values. We feel strongly that this aligns with the concept of teacher agency: teacher voice, choice and ownership.

In summary, purpose, values and goals are inextricably linked. These woven threads help form and influence an individual's and a group's journey towards personal and professional growth. We appreciate that negotiating a united sense of purpose within educational organisations is essential to navigating the tension between individual values and collective goals. As co-authors, we are firm believers that setting goals supports teachers to take actionable steps. However, we would suggest that the key, initial question might focus on 'What's your purpose?' instead of 'What's your goal?'

Sensemaking analogies

Above we introduced the following three concepts:

1. **A sense of purpose** gets us out of bed in the morning (Leider, 2015) – it provides us with energy and overarching intention.

2. **Values** are moral compasses – they act as guiding principles and health checks that continue along our purposeful journey of growth.
3. **Goals** importantly serve as the milestones towards fulfilling our purpose. In essence, goals exist to facilitate purposeful progress. Goals serve our purpose.

We've never met an educator or coach who doesn't appreciate a good analogy. So, to help us with sensemaking, we offer the often used imagery of a ship's journey to explore the relationship between purpose, values and goals:

1. **A sense of purpose** helps us make sense of the journey and navigate toward new territories. If we have reason to care about the destination, we are more likely to sail in uncharted waters.
2. **Values** are like the compass that guides the ship. A moral compass provides guidance and ensures that the ship navigates the course.
3. **Goals** are like specific waypoints along the voyage. Goals help with charting the course, breaking the journey into smaller, achievable steps.

In this analogy, the ship's purpose provides the intention, influencing its entire journey – importantly it's the wind in our sails. The compass (values) guides the ship to stay on the right course. The goals represent the visible and tangible checkpoints that help us to assess how well we are progressing towards the ultimate destination and desired future.

A scholarly sense of purpose

As researchers, we believe that it is important to acknowledge the scholarly shoulders we stand upon. The following academics have written about the concept of purpose from various fields of study. Their studies and thinking are broad in nature, but the commonality is the focus on a human way of being.

- **Viktor Frankl**: the Austrian psychiatrist and Holocaust survivor Viktor Frankl (2006) examined the concept of purpose in his book *Man's Search for Meaning*. Frankl highlighted the importance of

finding meaning and purpose in life, especially in troublesome and adverse conditions.
- **Richard Ryan and Edward Deci**: in the field of education, these psychologists are viewed as 'motivation' heroes. As discussed in chapter 3, they coined self-determination theory, which explores the influence of purpose on human motivation and wellbeing. Their studies emphasise how the concepts of autonomy and competence interconnect with a sense of purpose.
- **Carol Dweck**: Dweck's (2006) influential research explores the power of purpose in fostering a growth mindset. She suggests that having a growth-oriented purpose can lead to greater resilience, learning and achievement – in coaching we might align this to human flourishing and growth.
- **William Damon**: the developmental psychologist William Damon (2008) highlights the importance of purpose in adolescent and adult development. His research particularly resonates in these post-Covid times, arguing that a sense of purpose may impact positively on personal growth and wellbeing.

As co-authors, we find it both reassuring and exciting that many scholars are currently exploring the concept of purpose through different lenses and disciplines, including psychology, sociology and philosophy. This leads us to discuss how we view the significance of the concept of purpose within the field of coaching. We will examine the distinction between coaching *with* a sense of purpose and coaching *for* a purpose and offer our interpretation about why the choice of language matters to us.

Coaching *with* a sense of purpose versus coaching *for* a purpose

At the early stages of planning this book, we realised that the language of purpose is often cited as having different meanings in processes of change. In fact, we debated whether the title of our book should be coaching *with* purpose or coaching *for* purpose. Perhaps you feel that we are overthinking this and that the phrases are interchangeable. Influenced by our reading, discussions and findings, we believe there is a useful distinction to be made between coaching *with* a sense of purpose and coaching *for* a purpose. We will give some focus now to elaborate for clarity.

Coaching *for* a purpose

Our search of literature showed many instances when the word 'purpose' was used synonymously with vision, mission and sometimes goal. For us, this implies the concept of purpose aligns with a future outcome – something you want to achieve. 'What's your purpose?' is perhaps used to mean 'What's your end result?' We can see real relevance here in a coaching conversation: 'What's your purpose?' is asking a coachee to imagine their preferred future or destination. The purpose may be seen as a vision of what you are aiming for and working toward. Using the metaphor of 'learning journeys', the coaching intention is to help the coachee envision a reason *for* their journey and see clearly that the journey is *for* a purpose. In 'solutions-focused coaching' (Jackson and McKergow, 2007; Moon, 2022), one might find it helpful to align the desired future with the expression 'forward- or future-focused purpose'. We view coaching *for* a purpose as aligning with coaching conversations that centre on picturing and achieving desired results. The expression 'If you can see it, you can be it' seems to chime with the concept of coaching *for* a purpose as we view it.

Coaching *with* a sense of purpose

As alluded to earlier in this chapter, the word 'purpose' is also often used with reference to personal motivation. When we ask 'What's your purpose in life?', we are asking 'What gets you up in the morning?' or 'What do you really care about?' In Tonga, Jasen poses the question: 'What shines light in your life?' which has great resonance for the nation that is first to see the dawn of a new day. These questions prompt you to reflect upon your 'sense of purpose', focusing on exploring self-determination and agency. When we are clear about what we value in life, then our sense of purpose gives us energy and drive to fulfil our commitments. However, we must emphasise that coaching *with* a sense of purpose is not exclusive to the start of the process. Once a coachee has an initial understanding of what they really care about, then all the coaching conversations that follow will speak to that driving sense of purpose. When actions are taken to achieve goals along the journey of change, the discussion will examine and shine a light on any 'purposeful' progress. In this book, we view coaching *with* a sense of purpose as the initial and ensuing coaching conversations that provide momentum and sustained energy for purposeful progress. A united sense of purpose between a coach and coachee provides the will for the coaching and affords the way to move forward together.

Shining a light on both coaching *with* a sense of purpose and coaching *for* a purpose

If, like us, you find it helpful to make a distinction between coaching *with* a sense of purpose and *for* a purpose, then it is useful to offer a conceptual image and metaphor (see Figure 5.1).

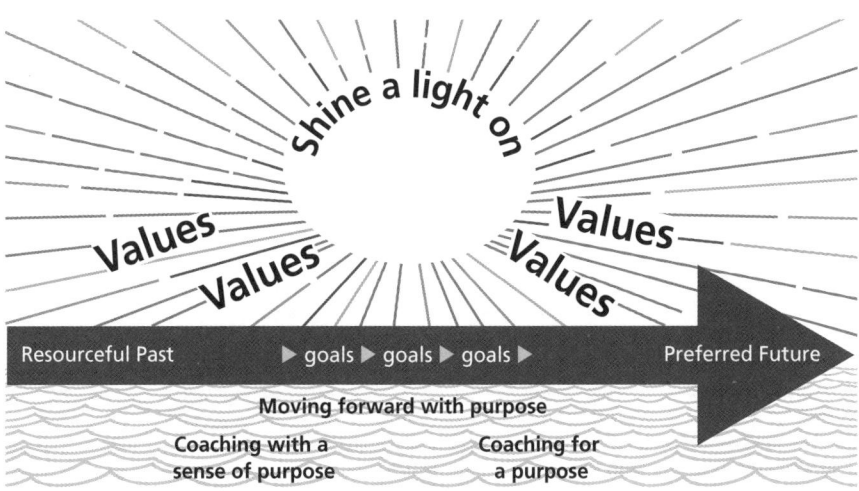

Figure 5.1 Purposeful progress model. Source: © Jasen Booten

For us, *clarity* of purpose is the unifying concept, where coaching conversations support a clarity of thinking throughout the journey of positive change. Shining a light is our metaphor for clarity. We emphasise the word 'positive' as we strongly believe that a coaching approach explores positive pathways and may indeed enhance wellbeing (Campbell and Nieuwerburgh, 2018). Not everyone views it this way, but we are very much aligned to principles espoused in the growing field of positive psychology introduced in chapter 3. As Haesun Moon (2022) puts it: 'I hold on to the assumption that people want to see positive differences in their life' (p. 6).

The purposeful progress model

The purposeful progress model builds upon Haesun Moon's (2022) dialogic orientation quadrant (DOQ) (see Figure 5.2) previously mentioned in chapter 2.

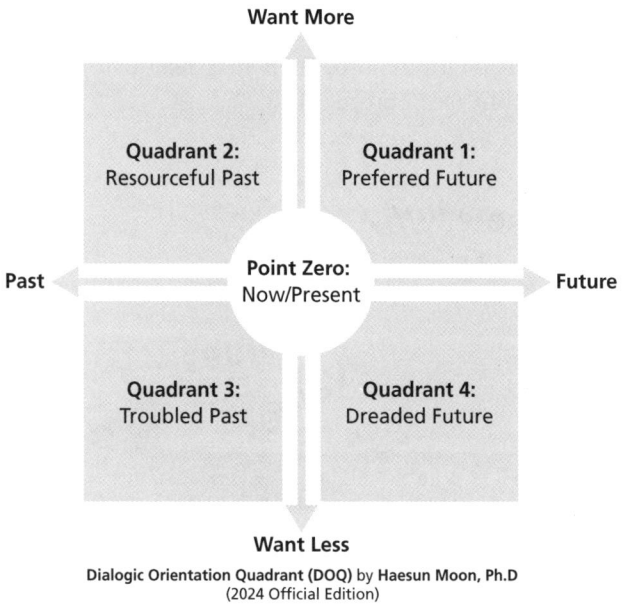

Figure 5.2 Dialogic orientation quadrant

Moon poses the question: 'Where do you most frequently dwell in your stories?' The DOQ supports coaches to listen attentively and shape the coaching conversation to highlight 'what's wanted and what's already working in that direction'.

We view coaching conversations as the means to shine a light on both aspects of coaching purpose. In fact, we would argue that strong rays of light need to be shone simultaneously on the initial, motivational sense of purpose and the future-focused purpose. And, of course, throughout the journey, we need to illuminate the actions taken to achieve the goals. Not only does the light provide clarity, but also energy. For us, the energising effect of coaching conversations is one of the most fulfilling and positive benefits of coaching; we become 'fit for *the* purpose'. Importantly, shining light involves being clear on how our values shape and influence our sense of purpose. As alluded to earlier in the chapter, when our goals align with our values, the light continues to shine a route ahead.

Coaching *with* a sense of purpose is 'life-worthy' learning

David Perkins is an American educator and researcher. Notably he is a professor at the Harvard Graduate School of Education and a founding member of Harvard Project Zero. His research focuses on the development of thinking and understanding in individuals and organisations.

Perkins (2014) coined the phrase 'life-worthy learning', which refers to a vision of education that goes beyond simply acquiring knowledge and skills for academic success. You may align his phrase with the concept of 'life-long learning', but for us 'life-worthy learning' implies a life of learning *with* a sense of purpose. Perkins argues that life-worthy learning develops students' knowledge, skills and dispositions necessary to tackle the challenges of living in an uncertain world. You may have heard of the acronym VUCA (Volatility, Uncertainty, Complexity, Ambiguity) to describe a challenging and unpredictable environment. For us, VUCA situations feel extremely relevant as we write this book, living in a post-Covid era, with countries at war in Europe and the Middle East. Perkins claims that if students are to engage in meaningful and authentic learning experiences, they need to be able to think critically, solve problems, make decisions, collaborate and apply their learning in real-life situations, especially in a VUCA world.

We view both coaching *with* a sense of purpose and *for* a purpose to be closely related to the idea of life-worthy learning. In an educational context, purpose may refer to the idea that learning should have a meaningful and relevant intention, direction and outcome. For us, purposeful progress rings true with the idea that life-worthy goals may lead to life-worthy achievement. Arguably, when education is driven by purpose, students are more engaged and motivated because they can see the value and relevance of what they are learning. Here is a definite nod to Ryan and Deci's SDT mentioned earlier in chapter 3. Ideally, knowledge and skills acquired can be applied to critically examine issues, generate solutions and make a positive impact on the world. In the context of life-worthy learning, purpose is fundamental in the educational process; education needs to move beyond the transmission of content and instead focus on helping students discover and develop their own sense of purpose. We would describe these coaching conversations as 'valuable'. As a linguist, Jasen is fascinated by word derivation. The prefix 'val' typically means 'worth' or 'strength'. So it makes sense that the word 'values' is derived from the ideas of 'importance' and 'power'. In the word 'validate', the prefix 'val' conveys the meaning of 'making something valid or confirming its worthiness'. To validate something means to confirm or approve its validity or correctness. In the expression 'I feel validated', the word 'validated' is used to indicate that one's feelings, beliefs or actions have been confirmed or approved by others, thereby giving them a sense of worth, acceptance or legitimacy. It suggests that the person's feelings or actions have been recognised or supported by others, enhancing their self-esteem or sense of value. Our values serve as a foundation for shaping our sense of purpose, as they represent what we consider valuable and worthy in our lives. By identifying and embracing these values, we are able to assess and prioritise what is truly important to us.

We view purpose as a vital aspect of life-worthy learning, providing learners with a sense of agency and direction, perhaps also a feeling of self-belief and belonging. This strikes us as raising the timeless philosophical question: 'What is the purpose of education?' This in turn leads us to the important enquiry question steering this book: 'What is the purpose of coaching in education?' For us, we believe that all learning in life needs to be worthy and purposeful. Drawing upon Kemmis et al. (2014), we hold that education serves a dual purpose: 'to prepare people to live well in a world worth living in' (p. 27). On one hand, education equips individuals with the knowledge, skills and capabilities needed to flourish and thrive in life and, on the other hand, education helps shape the kind of world we live in. This dual purpose of education highlights its importance not only for personal growth and development, but also for the collective wellbeing of communities and the world at large. It strikes us that the field of social psychology will become increasingly important in showing how the individual shapes the group and how the group shapes the individual.

Chapter 5 endnotes

Final thoughts

In this chapter, we aimed to explore the concept of purpose as an affirmation of the potential value of coaching *with* a sense of purpose and *for* a purpose, and believe that purpose, values and goals are inextricably linked. We recognise the benefit of setting goals to support coachees to take actionable steps and argue that this can be well placed within coaching conversations which are valuable and energising because they prompt coachees to reflect upon their 'sense of purpose'. Additionally, we offer the provocation that sustaining change in organisations is more likely when stakeholders share an authentic 'united sense of purpose' which is often arrived at through meaningful and purposeful dialogue.

The new coaching case studies that we encounter in part 3 of this book, sourced through enquiry with the CollectivED community, clearly show how the concept of purpose resonates with CollectivED coaching practitioners. As educators they are dedicated to fostering a coaching practice and culture that recognises the transformative power of purpose. Through their commitment to empowering individuals, instilling trust, promoting social justice and equipping students with essential life skills, members of CollectivED exemplify the profound impact that a sense of purpose can have on personal growth and organisational success. By embracing the belief that purpose underpins all endeavours, they strive to create lasting positive change within both individuals and the broader learning community. Purpose creates a powerful framework that not only supports thinking around meaning and goals but also leads to long-term benefits like job satisfaction and staff retention. In our case studies we encounter many defined purposes of coaching, including engaging students to take action in relation to climate change, advocating social justice and promoting a sense of empowerment in new and aspiring leaders, ensuring that teaching and the curriculum equip young learners with essential life skills.

Talking point

How would stakeholders in your setting view the importance of establishing a united sense of purpose? How feasible is this across the community? Who do you consider to be members of that community? Is 'purpose' more concrete than 'vision'? Some organisations create 'purpose statements' instead of 'vision statements' – how might this influence or affect the culture within your organisation?

Ideas for action

You might like to undertake a SWOT (strengths, weaknesses, opportunities, threats) analysis related to 'purpose', either as an individual educator or within your team. Identify a 'future-focused' purpose and consider what strengths and weaknesses exist within your locus of control or immediate environment in relation to it. Also recognise what threats and opportunities you perceive from the current policy or practice situation that you are in. Keep these reflections tight, focused on the specific purpose you have identified. You might then note how coaching might help you, or others, further explore the strengths, weaknesses, opportunities and threats. Perhaps coaching is a valid approach to allow for curiosity, address tensions, choose 'active hope' and consider the ways ahead.

Part 2
Encounters with coaching through our practice and research

What to look out for in part 2

In this section you will encounter:
- examples that illustrate how coaching has shaped education practices and settings over several decades
- insights into how coaching has been used as a developmental tool to address local and national priorities
- reflections on research related to coaching and key themes emerging over time

- personal narratives through which the role of coaching and wider professional experiences became woven to create sensemaking opportunities.

Over the course of our careers we have encountered coaching in a wide range of ways. In part 2 we explore how some of these encounters have informed and influenced us. Each author takes one chapter and in each a selection of encounters with coaching are outlined. Given that we have different professional backgrounds, have worked in different education settings and locations and have had different professional roles, the three chapters help to illustrate the diversity of coaching in education. They also show our connections with coaching and how engagement with it has shaped and been shaped by research and development opportunities over time. These chapters provide insights regarding where our understanding of, and advocacy for, coaching stem from.

As co-authors we share a belief that to be powerful coaching needs to be better understood. We took several more years to write this book than we first planned, in part because of our other commitments, but largely because we kept learning along the way. We also wanted to draw substantially on the insights of many others whose work has led them to, or been sustained by, coaching, and who share our commitment to coaching with and for purpose. In order to engage authentically, meaningfully and ethically with others we needed to be sure of our own foundations and principles. These three chapters help elucidate the nature of these and what they are framed by.

We invite you to learn from our direct encounters with coaching. This is a book which we hope helps join the dots between coaching practice, research and theory. In order to do that in our writing we had to also undertake our own sensemaking. It is also a book which expresses tensions and explores opportunities, often influenced by education context or policy. In writing from our own experiences we hope these elements start to be revealed. Each of us has been working in education for several decades and we would claim to have developed phronesis, or knowledge we use wisely in context, in relation to coaching. Our phronesis has been heightened through our engagement with the CollectivED community over time.

Chapter 6
Unique learning opportunities: encountering coaching through practice and policy

The person who is self-focused understands how their self relates to the needs of others [...] Your awareness of your self has a critical impact on your confidence as well as your competence.

Tim O'Brien (2015, p. 53)

In this chapter Jasen explores his first encounters with coaching and ends by introducing his most recent professional experiences in Tonga. He gives emphasis to experiences which highlight the significance of starting out and remaining open to opportunities for professional learning. He reflects on how our personal sensemaking is unique to our experiences, but also valid in creating our potential to support others. Jasen's experience of teaching and leading development in education spans decades, but as the years pass he realises that there is so much more that he needs to learn. His experiences show that context really matters and that we really cannot achieve sustainable change on our own. His account also illustrates the relationships between practice and policy, including how he as an individual has used his practitioner expertise to support policy-making.

Emergent encounters with coaching

I have worked in primary education for over 25 years, as a teacher, advanced skills teacher (AST), senior leader, local authority school improvement adviser, governor and founding director of a multi-academy trust. I consider myself lucky to have had several career paths and professional lives. Before teaching I was fortunate to experience coaching in the corporate world of global business and enterprise. In recent years I have studied, gained a coaching accreditation and practised coaching, and I am now able to look back and see when I used a 'coaching approach' in my teaching career without actually realising it. Van Nieuwerburgh (2014) explains that a person can 'do' coaching without 'being' a coach' (p. 13). I appreciate that I was 'doing' aspects of coaching, more by accident than design. My experience of coaching was emergent rather than intentional. For many years, my understanding of the coaching elements was patchy and very much at a surface level; I would describe myself as having once been an 'accidental coach'.

Encounter: accidental coaching as an advanced skills teacher

My first exposure to coaching in education was as an AST in primary schools in England. AST roles were policy-driven and funded in England and Wales from 1998 to 2013. I always found the title problematic, alienating perhaps, seemingly placing me on a platform as the 'excellent teacher' who knew best – certainly not an image of working in partnership. Placing these feelings aside, my role was one that I took seriously. As an AST I supported vulnerable teachers, often working in schools that had failed a government (Ofsted) inspection; the teachers were under intense pressure to improve, with some facing competency procedures. Having taught in two schools in 'special measures', I understood the feelings of inadequacy – the fear of failing and the possibility of losing your job and sense of identity. As an AST my main motivation was to support teachers to believe in themselves. In formal terms the coaching conversations generated goals linked to school improvement focused on raising standards of achievement; when a school is failing in England this is a given. However, it was apparent that the personal goal for most teachers and leaders working in special measures schools is to survive the process.

Chapter 6 Unique learning opportunities

My job description as an AST clearly pointed to school improvement; ASTs were expected to develop teachers and leaders, often so that schools moved out of a failing category. My AST status was awarded in light of my expertise in learning and teaching; I would frequently question my ability to coach effectively, as no formal training was provided for coaching. In truth, I lacked many coaching skills and did not routinely follow a conversational framework. As such I was often the 'accidental coach', but I realise in hindsight that I was on the way to 'becoming' a coach. I strongly valued the concept of partnership; people mattered in the process of developing practice. My coaching 'way of being' was hugely important to me, even if I did not realise it at the time. There were many aspects of my AST role which I now recognise align with components of teacher development approaches of instructional coaching.

Encounter: an unexpected coaching conversation

One of my proudest achievements as a teacher was joining the leadership team of a primary school in special measures and leaving the school six years later with the category of outstanding. A key reason for recounting this milestone event is that during the latter inspection the lead inspector asked me two key coaching questions: 'So Jasen, what are your future goals for the school, and how will you take people with you?' Up until this point I had felt that conversations with those holding me to account were interrogatory and directive. This inspection conversation was different – the goals were not given; I was being asked to generate my own, in the best interest of the school community. It took six years to be genuinely asked a powerful coaching question – and it felt good to be trusted to steer the school forward to a sustainable future.

Encounter: being coached in a new role

Having gained a reputation for working successfully in special measures schools, the local authority offered me a fresh opportunity to develop learning and teaching across the county. It was in this post that I began to focus more on coaching and significantly developed my coaching way of being. My new line-manager was a true coach. I always felt 'well-held' by him (Drago-Severson and Blum-DeStefano, 2019). My induction was a steep and sometimes scary learning curve, but rather than 'tell' me what to do (even when I wanted answers) my manager 'offered' suggestions, but only when he could sense real frustration. I now understand that he expertly modelled a 'coaching stance' (Booton et al., 2023), a concept we discuss in chapter 2. He believed in me; and as a highly respected leader and educator, his trust in me was powerful.

I worked alongside a colleague who was developing the concept of 'learning conversations' for primary phase pupils in the local authority. I enjoyed learning alongside him. He had a gift to inspire change in others with a sense of warmth and good humour, coupled with intelligence. He brought out the very best in people – he was much more than a guide on the side; he helped me think more clearly and more deeply. The learning conversations resembled coaching conversations. The conversations were between teachers and pupils, and also pupil and pupil. They focused on goal-setting, identifying support and recognising signs of progress.

Developing coaching insights through contextual awareness

Encounter: the advisor–coach dynamic

My personal understanding of coaching has been enhanced through engaging in professional coaching qualifications, acting as a coach supporting leaders working towards a school mental health award and being a regular participant and contributor in the CollectivED community. Perhaps the most influential coaching juncture of my career in education, where my learning about coaching practice increased dramatically, was the result of addressing a professional dissonance.

For six years I worked for the local authority as a 'learning and teaching adviser'. It is the word 'adviser' which I have reflected on and am now informed on by Bungay Stanier's 2020 book *The Advice Trap*. Crucially, the nagging, nightmare question raised for me was: 'How can you really be a coach, when your title includes "adviser"?' In fairness, at one point the word 'adviser' was questioned; I distinctly remember the LA leadership team toying with a new title incorporating 'coach'. However, it seemed too radical, so the image of an 'advice monster' has clawed me ever since. So, did I coach or did I advise? In truth, I did both, but I was distinctly aware of when I was advising, and, let's not pretend, vulnerable teachers and leaders under the microscope ask for your advice. But I'd like to highlight that I have supported many 'excellent' teachers and leaders working in schools in special measures. These practitioners definitely benefited from coaching; they knew the goals they wanted to achieve, and they did achieve them over time. My title may have been 'adviser', but I certainly coached those who had a clear vision for themselves. We also discuss the role of advice-giving in relation to different collaborative-based relationships like coaching, mentoring, supervising and training in chapter 2.

Encounter: wayfinding and coaching

Alongside continuing to work in England in a range of education roles, in recent years I have been fortunate to be appointed to work in a partnership project supporting the co-design of the new Tongan primary phase curriculum. I am working as a consultant for a non-governmental organisation. My role includes providing training and development to all the primary school practitioners from the 36 inhabited islands. It's an incredible opportunity for personal growth, but I also feel a huge weight of responsibility to best serve the young learners of Tonga. Through this project I have encountered wayfinding (discussed in more detail in chapter 14) and this has been influential in my current sensemaking about coaching. Fa'avae (2021) defines wayfinding as 'a process of orientation whereby people navigate the physical as well as the social and spiritual spaces' (p. 71). As I reflect on my own experiences of coaching, it makes sense that I relate it to orientation and navigation through the duration of my career. In addition, my engagement with wayfinding is supporting an awareness of the significance of decolonising coaching, a theme we return to in chapter 14, where a fuller encounter with wayfinding is provided. This has genuine resonance in the globalised world of education and education policy.

Chapter 6 endnotes

Final thoughts

Jasen has selected a number of intersections between his work as an educator and coaching. Practice is always influenced by policy and, as such, practitioners enact policy through their everyday work. However, practice is always emergent, nuanced and situated, not simply a clinical enactment of what is written in a framework.

Talking point

In this chapter there is evidence of the 'advice trap' in real life. Jasen is not suggesting that advice is unhelpful, but he is illustrating the dynamic that exists in the position of advice in coaching. You may find this an interesting subject for discussion. Is being an adviser implicit in your job roles or others' expectations of you? When do you consciously step aside from this? How do you feel about advice given to you as a professional and what circumstances affect this?

Ideas for action

Jasen appreciated how a former colleague helped him 'think more clearly and more deeply'. In your work as a coach or leader, this might be a useful indicator of success. You could ask a closing question: 'Is your thinking about what we have been discussing clearer or deeper as a result of our conversation?'

Chapter 7
Coaching kaleidoscope: perspectives on coaching from a career in research and practice

> *The most innovative learning spaces are open, reciprocal and participatory – learning doesn't really work as a spectator sport.*
>
> David Price (2013, p. 81)

In this chapter Rachel frames direct research encounters by situating them in her own professional journey and in relation to relevant aspects of the contemporary educational contexts. Each encounter exemplifies a situated and purposeful use of coaching to enhance educational outcomes, professional learning and/or wellbeing. Some also illustrate the purposeful research-based development of coaching practices in education as a means of better understanding how coaching functions and how it might be enhanced.

First encounters with coaching

Recently, during an online network meeting of experienced educators now working as coaches, I hosted a conversation in which we talked about school staffrooms. The coaches reflected on a general loss of staffroom culture, teachers having less time to spend there, fewer colleagues meeting up for coffee and a chat and the transition of staffrooms from social spaces to workstations in which teachers are rarely offline or off duty. The final remark of this conversation was that 'before coaching we had staffrooms'. This provoked me to reflect. When I was a secondary school teacher in the 1990s, working in schools in the North East of England, we had staffrooms which hummed with conversation, where wisdom and wisecracks were passed on, where corners were occupied by the sceptics, where tea and toast were consumed and in which pigeon holes, noticeboards and a single telephone created lines of communication. When I visited student teachers in the 2000s, I was often first welcomed by their mentors with a mug of coffee in their staffroom. More recently my school visits suggest that teachers rarely have sufficient time to sit and chat, but it is common for me to talk to teachers in settings where a busy schedule of coaching has been emailed to all staff. In this context I have found it interesting to reflect on my own encounters with coaching as a practitioner and researcher over that 30-year time span.

Although this is a retrospective chapter, providing a narrative of coaching research over several decades, in some parts the present tense is used. This typically indicates that research findings still have validity in current education settings. In much of this chapter, I refer to 'we' rather than 'I'. This is appropriate because I have been fortunate to work with colleagues at two universities and with teachers, leaders and other researchers from across the education sector. Rather than naming each individual in the encounters I cite them in the references to the publications that resulted and I have focused on those encounters which can be explored further in a range of literature.

Encounter: coaching with a focus on teaching thinking skills

I first encountered coaching in the 1990s. Throughout this time, I was fortunate to be part of local networks in which teachers worked collaboratively and over a sustained period to develop pedagogic approaches for teaching thinking skills within the curriculum. We met regularly, designed, shared, taught and observed lessons, and crucially talked a lot about teaching, learning, cognition and metacognition. We developed a shared understanding and common language and we scaffolded each other's understanding and development (Lofthouse, 2018).

Over time our work in teaching thinking skills in networks matured and there was an ambition to create more capacity for teaching thinking skills in the schools where seeds had been sown. To do this we needed to expand the number of teachers and subjects engaged in the pedagogic and curriculum development work. This ambition led to funding for a school-based research consortium. It was as part of this project that I first became a coach, with the opportunity to coach colleagues to support them to integrate teaching thinking skills into their subjects in the school in which I worked. This work was based on the cognitive coaching approaches which were being developed by Costa and Garmston (1994), with the project creating an opportunity to apply and adapt their thinking to our context.

As coaches in this project we used a cyclical approach to coaching. The structure included pre-lesson coaching conversations in which the teacher and coach discussed plans for teaching in the context of the students, the curriculum and the teacher's concerns and interests related to teaching thinking. This discussion foregrounded and informed my observation of the lesson as the coach. In addition, parameters of the observation were negotiated with the teacher being coached. The observation was sometimes augmented by video-recording the lesson to allow both myself and the teacher to review aspects together. Following the observation the coaching conversation wove together elements of the pre-lesson conversation, the observation and allowed consideration of next steps. Across the project, coaching occurred in sequences of coaching cycles, usually between three and five per teacher, perhaps over a term. This helped build a sustained opportunity for learning and development, and crucially also helped the coaches and coachees become more confident in this new mode of working together (Leat et al., 2006).

The teachers who participated in this project to develop thinking skills lessons supported by coaches kept diaries of their experiences. The contents of the diaries were coded and analysed by researchers. The diaries showed patterns that can be described in six phases.

1. **Initiation**: teachers were initially motivated as teaching thinking skills aligned with their interests. They enjoyed the CPD but showed some anxiety and hesitation about developing practice. They valued working with trusted partners in the project.

2. **Novice**: teachers became more involved and began to experiment with teaching thinking skills. They experienced ups and downs but also sought out informal feedback and support from the project coordinators and school-based coaches.
3. **Concerns**: it took effort to sustain changes in teaching. Teachers' expectations of teaching thinking skills rose but were not always met and some were frustrated with the work and/or had concerns about personal efficacy.
4. **Consolidation**: as coaching and networking continued, teachers' confidence grew. They recognised their progress and shared experiences and learning with others, thus developing common language. A sense of momentum emerged in the group.
5. **Expansion**: teachers linked new practice and wider educational objectives. They sought out new knowledge and accommodated new ideas and skills into their repertoire.
6. **Commitment**: teachers reported shifts in professional identity as they sought new opportunities to support professional learning of others. They became advocates for new pedagogic approaches and gained a stronger sense of agency.

While this initial experience is now over 25 years old, being a coach in this project was one of those 'sticky' professional moments for me. It might have been that the focused, productive, collegial conversations in the thinking skills networks created the foundation for my understanding of the nature of coaching talk. I was able to consciously aim to recreate these types of conversations as a coach, creating the opportunity for exploratory talk, deep reflection, co-construction and professional decision-making. It also felt significant that as a coach I too was experiencing expansion and commitment phases, both in relation to my further advocacy for teaching thinking skills (which I retain even now) and also my professional identity. Developing and then reflecting on the six phases outlined above formed the seeds of understanding the importance of how change happens for individuals and professional communities.

Encounter: potential and pitfalls in sustaining coaching

Towards the end of the school-based research I was appointed as a university teacher educator and researcher. Given my own experience as a teacher coach, and also as a mentor for student teachers, it was probably inevitable that my first research interest as a new academic was related to teachers coaching teachers. This interest persists and continues to intersect with my broader role in teacher education and in developing an informed, expert and sustainable teaching profession. In my first decade as a lecturer in education I worked alongside colleagues to weave together emergent research into teacher coaching and the development of master's modules on mentoring and coaching. Themes that continue to resonate in my academic life started to emerge. As teachers shared their views about coaching in research interviews and informally in professional development sessions, there was a strong sense that coaching 'felt good'. However, it was more complicated than that: coach training and finding time to coach was not enough.

Interviews with teachers for this emergent research indicated that coaching gave them a chance to improve their teaching. They also talked about their enjoyment of coaching. The process of coaching seemed to unpack accumulated layers of meaning and led teachers in unexpected directions. When they used video, it enabled them to see the lesson and their teaching from 'alternative perspectives'. As such, coaching helped to create a climate in which teachers continued learning through collaboration, reflection, analysis and dialogue. However, the teachers also talked of difficulties encountered. It was evident that real commitment was required from the institution to provide time for lesson observations and coaching sessions. For coaching to work well, strenuous efforts had to be made to get rid of power and establish a relationship based on trust (Lofthouse and Leat, 2006).

Intentional encounters with coaching

Despite the tensions that the early research above revealed, I have always been persuaded by the potential for coaching between teachers to create a space for reflection, collaborative and situated learning, and support for developing practice. This form of coaching allows a focus on curriculum, pedagogy, behaviour, relationships and formative assessment. It shines a light on the day-to-day work of teachers and opens up opportunities for workplace learning. These opportunities exist in everyday teacher conversations but can be heightened through coaching. As my career as an academic continued, further research opportunities to explore coaching ensued.

Encounter: coaching dialogue dimensions and co-construction

Van Nieuwerburgh (2014) describes coaching as a managed conversation and this begs the question about the characteristics of coaching dialogue. A common description of coaching dialogue is that it is based on the coach asking powerful questions to promote reflection. Hence active listening and effective questioning are seen as core coaching skills. However, from my own experience as a teacher coach, I was already aware that this was not sufficient. I knew that my role had been more than just to ask questions. An opportunity to explore this further arose when the research centre that I was part of was funded to conduct a two-year research project related to teacher coaching. Through this we gained and shared an evidence base of a wider range of coaching dialogue dimensions (Lofthouse et al., 2010b). By analysing transcripts of teacher coaching conversations a series of coaching 'dimensions' which were characteristics of the dialogue were identified. It was then possible to track their occurrence and significance in coaching conversations and use this to help coaches become more conscious of their role in scaffolding the discussion and coachee's thinking.

The coaching dimensions included:

- the focus for the discussion
- how stimulus was used to invite participation and reflection (e.g. shared viewing of a lesson recording or pupils' work)
- the tone of each aspect of the conversation (neutral, positive or negative)
- reference to past, current or future timescales
- the scale of attention (e.g. a critical incident, a planned episode, a lesson as a unit, a curriculum plan, a broad theme, principle or professional routine, whole school or social aspects)
- range of interaction functions, such as question, explanation, evaluation, challenge and suggestion, which might come from either the coach or coachee
- co-construction.

The interaction functions are significant because they indicate the purposes, processes and outcomes of interaction. The final but significant coaching dimension was co-construction. Co-construction indicates cognitive development occurring with the conversation. It is the point at which reflection and learning through coaching are greatest.

Using the coaching dimensions proactively with coaches allowed levels of development in teacher coaching to be defined. These enabled coaches to consider how they were currently practising and how and why they might aim to further refine their coaching. This is an appreciative conceptualisation of coaching dialogue and its development, rather than one which starts in deficit. All the levels of coaching described were valuable. This conceptualisation also illustrates the fact that coaching is always a two-way conversation and relationship and, as such, coachees have a role in understanding and contributing to the quality of the practice. We used the research evidence to identify progression in the quality and impact of coaching dialogue to a level we named *co-constructive collaborative coaching*, which was described as:

> *The coach and coachee collaboratively develop ideas, building on the successive contributions of their partner. There is significant focus on enhancing learning opportunities. The questions that they ask each other allow them to successfully explore their own understandings. Through reflecting on, and responding to, each other's contributions they identify alternative pedagogic approaches. This leads to exploratory talk related to opportunities for professional learning and development and the ways in which they might analyse the impact of this on pupils' progress. As such this is a knowledge-creating process.*
>
> Lofthouse et al. (2010a, p. 31)

It was clear from our research that being aware of these coaching dimensions helped coaches and coachees engage more intentionally to enable the coach to scaffold the coachees' thinking. As researchers and practitioners we were able to use the coding of the coaching dimensions to design new professional learning for coaches. By combining dimensions to create the levels of coaching development we were able to make sense of how coaching might become more productive. Tools can thus help make coaching or mentoring more purposeful and can be used judiciously and flexibly to aid navigation of this coaching–mentoring dynamic.

Encounter: developing an enquiry model of lesson observation

As I continued to work as a teacher educator and researcher, I also retained a keen interest in mentoring. A common factor of skilled mentoring and coaching is the ability to select and use tools which support reflection, professional learning, development and self-actualisation appropriate to the context. Alongside the work on coaching dimensions I was also researching other tools such as how using video to capture classroom practice aided discussion between the mentors and student teachers, and the reconceptualisation lesson observation approaches. Working within an initial teacher education context allowed the development and testing of a new tool (designed as an enquiry-based proforma) for lesson observation and feedback. Questionnaires, focus groups and interviews allowed the perspectives of mentors and students teachers to be analysed. By structuring lesson observation around focused questions generated by the student teacher, the mentor adapted their typical approaches and entered into discussions which created opportunities for framing and reframing professional experience and learning. This supported divergent learning outcomes. The student teachers gained greater education insights and developed more nuanced and contextualised teaching (Lofthouse and Wright, 2012). The enquiry-based approach to lesson observation has crossed into coaching practice in some settings, being a transferable tool that can be used with careful intention.

Encounter: applying the coaching dimensions

During this initial period of my own research and practice development I tended to use the broad definitions offered by the Centre for the Use of Research Evidence in Education (CUREE) in their *National Framework for Mentoring and Coaching* (CUREE, 2005). Working across both practices in the context of initial and continuing teacher education gave me a chance to think about how tools could be usefully deployed to enhance the development of practice. Beyond the initial research I found new opportunities to test the validity of the coaching dimensions in supporting teacher coaching practice and its development across a range of research and practice partnerships (including school-based support and supervision of dissertations).

Teachers working in three different contexts on their own coaching and mentoring practices focused on the coaching dimensions to understand, describe, analyse and improve the quality of their specific coaching and mentoring conversations. Using the dimensions allowed the relationships between the intent and characteristics of their practice to be explored and thus helped the teachers to plan for, and be more responsive within, their coaching and mentoring meetings. It emphasised the nuanced quality of dialogue in context. The resulting self-knowledge enabled the teacher-coaches to experience productive practice development, helped to clarify the roles of different types of professional dialogues in schools and illustrated how better conversations are part of building trust between coaching participants (Lofthouse and Hall, 2014).

As a former mentor and coach I found this aspect of my work as a teacher educator highly engaging. I was working with practitioners to develop a research-based pedagogy of coaching and mentoring by marrying up the purpose for professional learning with the approaches being used. Tools can help make coaching or mentoring more purposeful and can be used judiciously and flexibly to aid navigation of this coaching–mentoring dynamic. Specifically the research was revealing how coaching dialogue is not just a skill to be acquired but is indicative of, and formative in, the characteristics of the relationship between the coach and coachee, and of how the professional context influences this. For example, in non-hierarchical relationships exploratory talk between coach and coachee and sharing of curiosity and vulnerabilities are more likely than in line-management or performance-monitoring relationships. The conceptualisation of tools for coaching and mentoring was valuable. Such tools have the ability to 'make a particular activity different: faster, slower, richer, more focused, more efficient, more sustained' and as such can be conceptualised as catalytic tools (Baumfield et al., 2009). Developing their knowledge base allowed coaches and mentors to make appropriate coaching decisions at the 'plan, do and review' stages of their own work.

Encountering tensions in coaching

While developing more CPD and postgraduate study for coaches it was important that we understood coaching better, not only from the research literature but from our intelligence on the ground – the teachers and school leaders working in the field. The more we talked to practitioners and reviewed emerging evidence, the more the tension between the perceived promise of coaching and the realities of making space for it to work in schools became palpable and, indeed, on occasion, emotive. We were thus exploring the dynamic of teacher coaching in schools impacted by the performance-driven policy and practice pressures and affordances.

Encounter: coaching as a culture clash

We undertook conceptual research using sociocultural theory to explore why coaching does not transplant readily to schools, particularly in England, where the object of coaching activity may be in contradiction to the object of dominant activity in schools – meeting examination targets. In this context, coaching often struggles to meet expectations. The research indicates that the results agenda, or performativity culture, in many schools is so strong that either coaching is introduced as part of the dominant discourse, which meets resistance from staff, or, where it develops in a more organic, 'bottom-up' approach, it may clash with managerial cultures that demand accountability and surveillance, and this does not sit well with trust-based coaching partnerships. It is thus necessary for coaches to manage the boundary between trust-based coaching and performativity agendas (Lofthouse and Leat, 2013).

As we continued to work closely with teachers who were developing or had been assigned coaching roles, this culture clash became ever clearer. In addition to the performative system drivers impacting on schools as contexts for coaching, the fact that many of the emerging coaches were more familiar with mentoring seemed significant. Mentoring can be distorted away from the personal learning needs of the new teacher due to the links between qualification, induction into the norms of a school organisation and compliance with professional standards (Hobson and Malderez, 2013; Wilson, 2014; Lofthouse and Thomas, 2014). The outcome can be that mentoring conversations are sometimes didactic or instructional, driven by target setting and checking, and do not always engage the mentee as a proactive participant in professional dialogue. Teachers also told us that their experiences of performance management observation and feedback can be similar. These experiences of mentoring and performance management can be formative – creating conversational and behavioural habits that are sustained in coaching. Other teachers reported that even when coaching starts as a confidential and personalised learning opportunity, it gets swept up by the performance management system of the school or ascribed a role linked to the school's (rather than their own) CPD priorities. Schools are busy places and coaching uses up the most precious resource, that of teachers' time. Managing this and the expectations that are generated is problematic.

It was understanding these conundrums and seeking to respond to them which was continuing to hold my attention. It has not always been easy to tease out the specific differences between coaching and mentoring, particularly as they have gained currency, leading to some interchangeability in their application in education settings. We explored some differences in chapter 2. The key difference is probably in the overall stance adopted by the coach or mentor to create the relationship with the coachee or mentee. One of the constant debates I have found myself having with reference to coaching in schools is the extent to which a coach should or should not offer feedback or advice. This question sits at the heart of the mentoring and coaching dynamic, particularly where mentoring is strongly aligned with specific training or career phases.

Traditionally it has been considered that mentors are expected to offer advice as the more experienced partner in the mentoring relationship. It is mentors' understanding of the training or working context and of the expectations that this places on the mentee that forms the basis of their mentoring work. Mentors are also often part of an assessment system to judge competency, compliance or progress. This was certainly the role of the mentors I worked with in our teacher education partnership.

In contrast, coaching is often positioned as non-advisory and non-judgemental. It is argued that coaches allow the existing, but perhaps overlooked, knowledge, expertise and motivations of the coachee to be brought to the fore through an opportunity to be reflective and to rehearse emergent ideas. Coaching and mentoring practices can be consciously merged, for example, a coach being open to offering their insights if elicited by the coachee in the coaching conversation, or a mentor stepping into a more nuanced coaching role at an appropriate stage in a mentee's development. Going beyond the traditional role definitions through more exploratory research seemed helpful and more recently I have found 'stance' useful, as introduced in chapter 2 (Munro and Campbell, 2022; Booton et al., 2023), and Trista's work on accompaniment in this area compelling, as introduced in chapter 4 and elaborated in chapter 8.

Encounter: understanding teacher collaboration for developing teaching

Teachers are often encouraged to work in partnerships to support their professional development. We undertook a small-scale piece of research related to three such partnerships: mentoring, coaching and an adapted lesson study. They had common practices of one-to-one meetings, planned activity and shared reflection and had the intended function of developing teaching practices. The participants' perspectives on these practices were investigated through a multiple case study using semi-structured interviews. The degree to which their experiences could be considered to be collaborative was established based on an analysis of the extent to which there was evidence of working 'together', not just working 'with', and of working towards a common goal, pooling knowledge and problem-solving. Collaboration for the development of their own teaching practices allowed teachers to engage in more informed decision-making and to construct a shared understanding of the nature of the desired learning outcomes and how they might be achieved in their own contexts. The teachers indicated that this experience often ran counter to their experience of the school cultures driven by performativity (Lofthouse and Thomas, 2017).

New encounters through CollectivED: coaching as an evolving and maturing practice

In 2017, as a newly appointed professor, I launched CollectivED as a research and practice centre, now known as CollectivED The Centre for Coaching, Mentoring, and Professional Learning. This further refined my professional and academic focus and also provided a welcome opportunity to connect with others committed to understanding and unleashing the potential of coaching in education. In addition to supporting coaches developing their own coaching repertoire, I was gaining a growing interest in how the repertoire of coaching continues to be extended in education. It has been fascinating to see the range of ways that coaching has evolved, the different purposes that it can have and the ways that people engage with it. Three early research projects conducted within CollectivED are outlined here.

Encounter: coaching in formation

Our first CollectivED event was based on a conversational encounter between six coaches. I undertook a thematic analysis of these conversations that was formative in understanding the contemporary coaching landscape in education (Lofthouse, 2019b). Coaching has been evolving as a form of professional development for teachers and school leaders for several decades and now exists in many forms. This study focused on the work of six coaches in England, using an adapted focus group approach to discover how they explained and conceptualised the value of their practices. As the coaches' conversations with each other emerged, details of the nature of their work, and their reflections on it, were elicited which were analysed thematically while also paying due attention to individual narratives. Although coaching is not easily defined, this study demonstrated the significance of relationships and dialogue in coaching and the structures and protocols that support that. It suggested that coaching is suited to helping individuals dealing with authentic challenges, professional interests and dilemmas experienced in complex educational settings, while also acting as a counterweight to some of the consequences of performativity. The study also suggested that coaching may be a valuable means to deploy the expertise of experienced professionals to support an education system exposed to problems of retention of both teachers and school leaders (Lofthouse, 2019b).

Encounter: interprofessional video-based coaching for communication-rich pedagogies

A coaching project which proved innovative and sparked my curiosity was an interprofessional model of coaching which brought primary and early years teachers into a coaching relationship with children's speech and language therapists. This created a unique opportunity for collaborative action research as I was able to work alongside the speech and language therapists to co-construct a coaching approach and also work with the school staff to understand their ambitions for their own pedagogies and their experiences of coaching (Lofthouse et al., 2016). In several nursery and primary schools in a multicultural area of economic deprivation in an inner city in England, speech and language therapists developed a new video-based coaching approach for teachers and teaching assistants. They shared the joint aim of creating communication-rich pedagogies in classrooms with high numbers of children who were learning English as an additional language (EAL). The approach was informed by models of teacher coaching (Lofthouse et al., 2010a) and video interaction guidance (Kennedy et al., 2015) and was rooted in professional learning which makes deliberate and explicit work processes, learning activities and learning processes (Eraut, 2007). The aim of the coaching was thus to ensure that research and practice evidence related to children's speech and language development became a vehicle for the teachers' and teaching assistants' professional development.

A theory of change approach was used to evaluate the impact, allowing a conclusion that specialist video-based coaching can play a significant part in enabling bespoke professional learning. In particular it was evident that the coaching approach created a neutral, non-judgemental space in which teachers' own interactional practices could be exposed and made open to co-construction based on the relationship between their pedagogic knowledge and skills and the speech and language therapists' knowledge and skills related to speech, language and communication (Lofthouse et al., 2016). Further consideration of this example of intra-professional coaching is provided in chapter 15, which explores how we can judge coaching efficacy.

Encounter: leadership coaching

In broad terms it was the hope that coaching headteachers would create this combination of confidence, competence and wellbeing support that resonated with me when I was invited to evaluate a year-long headteacher coaching programme. It was my first foray into researching leadership coaching, and I was curious. Over the last decade the coaching of educational leaders has grown alongside coaching teachers. Indeed, in England at least, it is the basis of what seems to be a flourishing entrepreneurial education support sector as well as a much-needed peer-support coaching community working in voluntary capacities. Working with the teachers' union which had commissioned both the coaching provision and the evaluation was an important lesson in considering resource implications, sustainability and the transfer of lessons learned from coaching into continually evolving practice in the resource-limited education sector. What we learned was not just about coaching, but also about the lived experiences of headteachers, their personal and professional dilemmas, how they felt challenged and supported in existing systems and what hopes they had for their own capacities and leaders and for the profession (Lofthouse and Whiteside, 2020).

The coaching had a positive impact on headteachers' self-belief and confidence, and coaching helped them to place greater priority on their physical health. Coaching also helped them to address their common feelings of isolation in role. These gains had a reciprocal benefit in managing the demands of the job and reducing the 'erosion of resilience'. Coaching supported headteachers to develop and maintain effective management approaches, giving them time to prioritise the issues that need resolving, developing their competence in decision-making and working positively with and empowering colleagues. It also supported their strategic leadership, giving them a chance to develop a 'clear road map' and 'clarity in direction'. The coaching conversations were productive. They provided space and time and allowed focused, supportive and supported reflection. This was dependent on the skill of the coach and also the acknowledgement of the importance of 'identity work' which explored personal values as well as professional challenges. This programme was successful because of the quality and independence of the coaching provision. Coaches brought depth of experience and strong understanding of how to enable headteachers to engage in productive thinking which then enabled them to develop new approaches in their professional and personal lives. The coaches also supported them to explore their values and seek opportunities to align these with their leadership roles (Lofthouse and Whiteside, 2020).

A clear implication from this research was that coaching of headteachers has the potential to help maintain a sustainable school workforce.

Learning from the headteachers and the coaches about their experiences of coaching led to the core theme of the research conclusions, which was summarised by the report title 'Sustaining a Vital Profession'. This concept of sustainability across the teaching profession has become a critical one for me in my current work. It has taken me back to my original discipline of environmental science, to ecological and systems thinking and to applying these ways of exploring and analysing education systems and practice in my work.

Encounters beyond silos

A way of working which extends from my initial to my recent years in teacher education and support has been to create teacher professional learning cohorts or research partners who formed a medley of practitioners. Emerging partnerships and programmes were always a little unpredictable and required us to think beyond the traditional silos and hierarchies that characterise much of the education landscape.

Working beyond silos generates genuine sensemaking moments for me as well as the professionals who came together to learn and develop. There is something very reassuring and refreshing about having a space in which to be credited with expertise because no one else in the room has ever welcomed a toddler to their first days in nursery, while also calming an anxious parent and working in a free-flow open-plan setting. Similarly, it is affirming to hear teachers from numerous schools across a city express their desire to work collaboratively to meet the diverse needs of the city's students, regardless of whether they will ever meet them in person.

I relish working outside of silos, seeing the boundary crossing that I undertake and enable in others as means to create learning opportunities. When artists and teachers work together, a strange magic happens in classrooms. When speech and language therapists and primary teachers share their specific expertise, they can co-create new communication-rich opportunities for learners. When project partners from multiple European countries work together over several years, the outcome goes well beyond the project website.

Working beyond silos is something that led me to found CollectivED, the research and practice centre, in which we focus on coaching, mentoring and professional learning. CollectivED became my true maker-space, a community of educators with a wide range of roles working in diverse settings who share a commitment to supporting the professional learning of others. It is a community naturally suited to sensemaking.

Forming CollectivED has afforded the opportunity to add a new space to the educational landscape in which coaching can be understood and experiences of coaching can be shared. This has evolved through formal research, through European partnership projects, through more organic enquiry, through written pieces collated as working papers and blogposts, and often through conversation. As a community we have a collective interest in the role that coaching can play to sustain and enhance education communities, and the quality and impact of their work. While this chapter closes with the formation of CollectivED and draws on three research projects that resulted, many more of the coaching encounters extend the story. Part 3 is dedicated to coaching case studies curated from the CollectivED community. Part 4 includes research and analysis undertaken through the maker-space that is CollectivED.

Chapter 7 endnotes

Final thoughts

In this chapter Rachel has drawn on a long and diverse professional and academic engagement with coaching. In a recent think piece Rachel wrote that coaching can 'connect teachers' professional experiences, allowing them to become the warp and weft of their own lived curriculum' (Lofthouse, 2024, p. 110). The kaleidoscope of coaching experiences shared here have certainly formed a warp and weft of the decades that Rachel has been an educator. They also illustrate the essential relationship between practice and research in enabling coaching in education to become meaningful and worthy of further development and scholarship.

The research included in this chapter offers insights into how coaching can help teachers to refine their core practices and we are thus watching the rise of models of instructional coaching in England with interest. It is clear that not only do many teachers value the opportunity to focus on their classroom practices, to gain insights and develop new skills, but they also find coaching to offer a 'feel-good' effect, especially when compared with other forms of professional development. Some of this can be associated with the growth of their competence and confidence in their teaching role, but it is also afforded by their sense of being given time by another professional to do so, and to develop and sustain new professional relationships and have someone who they could rely on to work with them over time. For some teachers at least, coaching creates a workplace wellbeing boost.

Talking point

This chapter opened with a quote from David Price's book *Open: How We'll Work, Live and Learn in the Future* (2013), in which he suggests that innovative learning spaces are open, reciprocal and participatory. This proposition resonates with the coaching research and CollectivED community that Rachel has led and participated in, as does the connection he makes between working, living and learning. Price goes on to suggest that being a spectator does not work in learning. Does the coaching that you have experience of feel open, reciprocal and participatory? Do coaching encounters create, reinforce or break down silos?

Ideas for action

This chapter has 'kaleidoscope' in the title and presents multiple examples of coaching in education, emerging over time and in relation to context. If you have coaching provision in your setting, you might like to undertake a kaleidoscopic review of it. How has it evolved, in what ways is it creating new patterns of activity and opportunity, and how are relationships being altered? Following the review, consider who the findings are most relevant to, how to share them and what would be helpful as next steps.

Chapter 8
A patchwork quilt: stitching the pieces together

This is a drawing together of threads,
A piecing together of the past and the future,
A time to stop and consider where you've been,
Where you're heading

Cassandra Ellis (2012, p. 6)

In this chapter Trista explores the many twists and turns in her encounters with coaching. The presented encounters follow Trista's ongoing learning as a researcher, practitioner and pracademic and explore the many ways coaching can be used in our personal and professional lives.

Encounters with past experiences

When I am asked about how I first encountered coaching and mentoring in education, it has never been a simple answer, and this chapter reminds me of how all the seemingly disparate parts of my professional career can be stitched together to help me tell this story. I titled this chapter to draw on the metaphor of the patchwork quilt that I used in my doctoral thesis. It helped me make sense of the emerging pattern between teachers' professional learning and development, coaching and mentoring, and teacher evaluation. Once again, I find the quilt a useful way to connect a series of eclectic elements and tell the story of my past, present and future in this personal narrative.

Encounter: quiltmaking and pracademic positionality

A practical item to keep oneself warm, the patchwork quilt tells a story about its quilter: 'An encounter with a quilt is incomplete if it does not include some understanding of the people who made it' (Pellman and Pellman, 1984, p. 6). From the fabric blocks chosen to the overall quilt design, the quilt is a powerful *text*-ile. In this chapter, each encounter, or fabric block, that I present can be viewed as a story on its own but also forms an intricate element of the larger quilt pattern that I'm stitching. I did not journey alone and am grateful to all those who have accompanied me along the way.

When I started my PhD in 2013, I had an established career as a teacher, vice-principal and district consultant. Despite professional experience and gaining a master's in education (MEd), I was intrigued by how much I did not know but was still responsible for as a leader. I came to my doctoral studies from a stance of a 'pracademic' (Hollweck et al., 2021; Hollweck, 2020; Campbell et al., 2023), a term more frequently used outside of education (Hollweck et al., 2022) and which refers to someone who 'spans the ethereal world of academia as a scholar and the pragmatic world of practice' (Walker, 2010, p. 1). As such, I work at the nexus of practice and research and try to balance practical relevance without compromising methodological rigour and theoretical depth (Nesbit et al., 2011).

I now borrow from both concepts described above and often describe myself as a 'pracademic quilter' as I endeavour to stitch together different encounters from research, practice and the space between – my fabric blocks – to tell my story. In this chapter I explore some of the critical incidents from my past and present that have informed my experience with coaching and what has brought me to co-writing this book.

Encounter: early career teaching

My teaching career started in 1996 in rural Japan. This two-year experience was my first time as an 'outsider' to a culture and it imprinted on me the importance of mentorship and support for individuals new to a culture, community, district or school. After Japan, I completed my postgraduate certificate in education (PGCE) in Scotland. My contrasting school placements across Edinburgh (rural, urban and private) gave me insight into the ways school cultures differ even in the same region. There is no 'one-size-fits-all' approach in education – everything is always contextual. That said, I was also struck by how similar secondary students are whether they live in Japan, Scotland or Canada, which reinforced my belief in the importance of relationships and relational pedagogies when it comes to working with and supporting teenagers through their secondary studies.

Encounter: accompaniment and systemic change

After Scotland, I got my first 'real' job as a Grade 8 English teacher in an English-language school in the Western Quebec School Board (WQSB) in the province of Quebec. In Canada, education is a territorial and provincial responsibility, so teaching and learning can look very different depending on where you live or work. The school board where I worked serves anglophone students in 25 schools (kindergarten to Grade 11) across a diverse geographic catchment roughly the size of Ireland. The district's large geography and diversity (yet small population) make professional development and teacher collaboration challenging. Historically, it has also struggled to attract and retain teachers, especially in rural sites and in specialised subjects such as French, mathematics, science and special education.

This job coincided with the launch of a new large-scale provincial reform called the Quebec Education Program (QEP), which had significant implications for all elements of schooling, including ways teachers understood and engaged with curriculum, evaluated students and worked together. To support teachers with the major systemic change, the province introduced the Accompaniment Research Training project in 2002 (Lafortune et al., 2009). Accompaniment is described as 'support that individuals receive in learning situations so that they may progress in their construction of their knowledge' (Lafortune and Deaudelin, 2001, p. 1). Accompaniment activities were described as meetings where the changes in the professional lives of participants were discussed and studied and interactions with peers to 'activate prior experiences, give rise to socio-cognitive conflict, make the most of any such conflict that arises in discussions, co-construct in action, track down erroneous conceptions, and profit from self-awareness arising from certain constructions' (p. 10).

It strikes me now how much these activities sound like coaching. As a new teacher, my involvement in the Accompaniment project fostered relationships with educators and researchers across the province and gave me insight into the implementation of large-scale reform from a system perspective. It also sparked my interest in the concept of accompaniment that we describe in chapter 4 of this book. I wanted to know more about how educators can work alongside one another and accompany each other through individual and systemic change. This interest brought me to lead an Accompaniment Practice and Research project in 2019–22 to 'examine and capture innovative mentoring, induction and professional learning and development support structures available to teachers and leaders across the province and to build a network that fosters the sharing of these promising practices' (Hollweck and Baradaran, 2022, p. 8). Coaching also featured prominently in this research.

Encounter: exploring and leading teachers' professional learning and development

Part of my role in the Accompaniment project was to bring back what I was learning and to accompany colleagues in my school. Luckily, this project dovetailed with another influential professional learning experience: participation in a five-year project in instructional intelligence (II). II is best described as the integration of content knowledge, assessment, knowledge of how we learn, instructional repertoires, personal/professional change and systemic change. I met with other participants six times a year to learn about and practise instructional concepts, tactics, skills, strategies and graphic organisers. We also explored classroom management and how to create a safe and caring learning environment for students.

As a newly qualified teacher, this initiative offered me a chance to build strong collaborative relationships with new and experienced teachers from different schools around the district. After three years, I took on a teacher leader role at the school board and became an II trainer while also teaching secondary English. I focused my master's research on the ways in which II influenced WQSB teachers' experience of large-scale systemic change. My research supported my own experience that the II initiative was well implemented, impacted the way teachers taught and was instrumental in helping them through the organisational change process. Disappointingly, however, a change in top leadership led to its cancellation. This experience taught me critical lessons about systemic change, the importance of shared understanding, and the need for buy-in from all stakeholders in an educational system. 'Bottom-up' initiatives also need support (resources, financing and advocacy) from the 'top'.

Encounter: relational pedagogies and circling

During my time with the WQSB, I was fortunate to experience training that promoted intentional relational pedagogies and was introduced to the social technology of circling, in which spaces are created for sharing individual and collective ideas and needs. Seeing the power of circling for my own students, I wanted to learn more about how circles could be used beyond the classroom. I encountered the growing social movement restorative justice (RJ) and learned more 'about learning to live in a better relationship with oneself and others' (Boyes-Watson, 2008, p. 8). A process long evident in Indigenous communities, especially prior to colonisation, RJ requires a paradigm shift to ensure relationships are just, caring and honouring. This idea is also explored by Jasen in chapter 14 as he encountered the Indigenous Pacific concept of *talanoa*, described as respectful and collective discourse. Although RJ is often misunderstood in schools as a programme focused on correcting individual behaviour (Reimer, 2018), a more comprehensive view of it in education is that it builds, strengthens and restores relationships. It is focused on 'learning communities that nurture the capacity of people to engage with one another and their environment in a manner that supports and respects the inherent dignity and worth of all' (Evans and Vaandering, 2016, p. 8).

These encounters with relational pedagogies and facilitating learning experiences that honour and empower others have been foundational to my work in teaching, leading and coaching. Interested in the impact of RJ and relational pedagogies on the engagement of teacher candidates and influence on their own classroom practice, I conducted a research study with teachers one year after they were part of my 'Building healthy, safe and supportive learning environments' course (Hollweck et al., 2019). Although findings were positive, I was struck by the challenges many of the participants faced when implementing this way of working in their new schools: 'Teachers' professional learning, especially for new teachers, is shaped by the school context in which they operate, a context that itself is strongly influenced by its surrounding community and society' (p. 18). This is when I began to get really interested in building and maintaining flourishing school cultures.

First encounters with coaching and mentoring

Although Quebec's Education Act 2020 stipulates that teachers must 'collaborate in the training of future teachers and in the mentoring of newly qualified teachers' (Ministère de l'Éducation, 2020, Section 22, para 6.1), what this looks like in practice varies across the province. In fact, individual school boards and schools are responsible for their own teacher recruitment, induction and CPD. Against this backdrop, my first formal experience with coaching and mentoring was in 2006 when I became vice-principal at a large secondary school in a newly blended junior high and high school with a shared leadership team. It was my role to build relationships across the two teams of staff – no easy feat as neither school community supported the merger. With a large number of new teachers across both schools, I focused on building a supportive learning community and introduced mentoring by experienced staff. The impact of both support structures was noticeable in the feedback from participants and in the retention of staff the following year.

Encounter: designing, leading and researching a mentoring and coaching programme

Based upon the success of our school's informal mentoring programme, I was inspired to see what was possible with a more formal process of induction and mentoring across the school district and proposed an induction initiative to the school board directors (Hollweck, 2017). This became the Teacher Induction Program (TIP), which was piloted in 2008 and fully implemented in 2009. TIP still has three clear aims:

1. to retain effective teachers new to the district
2. to provide leadership and professional growth opportunities for veteran staff
3. to improve teaching and learning across the school district.

At the start of the TIP we used a pre-packaged mentoring kit bought from the USA to train our 'mentors' but quickly realised that we needed to design a more bespoke and contextual professional learning provision. As the part-time district consultant responsible for TIP, it was at this time that I realised that I needed a better understanding of mentoring and coaching. Although the 'kit' referenced coaching as a component of mentoring, I was beginning to get the sense there was much more to coaching and it would be an important approach for teachers' professional learning and development.

With a paucity of coaching literature and conversation situated in the Canadian context, I started my doctoral research to examine mentoring and coaching within teacher induction. I continued to work part-time leading the TIP so was able to play around with new ideas that I was learning about mentoring and coaching and also use my research to hone in on some of the problems of practice with which we were wrestling. One of the first activities we did as a TIP community was to define what mentoring and coaching meant in our context. As presented in chapter 2, mentoring and coaching were described as distinct but interconnected approaches that share guiding principles. We used the Möbius strip to present our co-constructed conceptualisation and outline how mentoring activities were more directive than coaching. In the TIP we now use the term 'mentor–coach' (MC) to represent the different stances experienced educators may use (Booton et al., 2023). We also use the notion of a fellowship to represent the reciprocal, supportive and honouring partnership between experienced teachers and teachers new to the district called 'teaching fellows' (Hollweck, 2019a). Since its launch in 2008, the TIP pattern continues to evolve and change in response to participant and key stakeholder feedback. Since I stepped away from my TIP role in 2016, it has changed, improved and flourished under the leadership and direction of the new consultants.

Encounter: professional learning networks in coaching

One of the most significant findings of my doctoral research was the importance of professional learning networks (PLNs) for MCs (Hollweck, 2020). We know that effective coaching depends on the quality of the relationship, the nature of the setting it occurs in and the skill of the coach. However, as we noted in chapter 4, it takes time and practice to become a confident and competent coach. Whereas participants in my research found themselves natural mentors, it took them around three years to become effective coaches. In chapter 17 we go into more depth about the individual change process that can happen when teachers learn to coach. At the WQSB, a PLN was established to bring together MCs from around the district to learn with and from one another, share experiences and engage in CPD focused on coaching. In PLN sessions, educators would begin in a circle to gather as a coaching community to connect and share experiences and then, based on their interest and needs, would be introduced to different coaching processes and techniques like the 'I-GROW' model, Michael Bungay Stanier's 'seven essential questions' and Jennifer Abrams' 'having hard conversations' framework (see chapter 4). Beyond providing support, resources and professional learning for MCs, the PLN also enabled the district to gather critical feedback on the TIP, as well as build shared understanding and consistency in coaching objectives and processes. The PLN was also an opportunity for interested members to take on a leadership role and facilitate gatherings and mentorship for any new MCs.

My interest in collaborative-based professional learning and social structures continues to drive my research activity. Most recently, I have been examining how to map distributed leadership using social network analysis (Chestnutt et al., 2024). I am particularly interested in the role coaches play as middle leaders in their schools, their influence on school culture and how they broker knowledge and beliefs.

Encounter: coaching and wellbeing

Another area of interest for me is the relationship between coaching and educator wellbeing. Subscribing to the view that students thrive when teachers thrive (Hollweck, 2019b), in my doctoral research I examined the ways in which the MC role influenced experienced teachers' wellbeing. I used Seligman's PERMA (positive emotion, engagement, relationships, meaning and accomplishment) framework (see chapter 3) as a theoretical basis to analyse participant interviews. I discuss this research in more detail in chapter 15. Despite many participants describing the MC role as positively contributing to their sense of professional (and personal) wellbeing, I was struck that 'for others, negative mentoring and coaching relationships were reported to be emotional and added to their workload and stress level. Thus, although the MC role was found to offer powerful benefits to experienced teachers, it is not a panacea for teacher wellbeing' (Hollweck, 2019b, p. 327). Teaching fellows in my research also shared similar responses. While the majority of respondents to my questionnaire were 'very positive' about their experience working with an MC, others struggled: 'My mentor–coach made my first year in the WQSB much more difficult' (Hollweck, 2019b, p. 205). This tension raises two questions for me that I still wrestle with: Can anyone (learn to) be an effective coach? Can everyone be coached?

Encounter: coaching and performance management

The experiences described in this chapter demonstrate how important support, resources and advocacy from those in leadership positions (those at the 'top') are in systemic change. In the TIP, mentoring and coaching was a relatively organic and grassroots initiative, but we also had unwavering support from our board's director, who secured ongoing funding for MC professional learning and advocated for the process to the leadership team. However, TIP was not the only board-wide initiative that the board was engaged in (Hollweck, 2019a). Influenced by external partners from England, a high-stakes (job vs no job) teacher evaluation system for new teachers to the district was adopted. Thus, the challenge for me became how to balance the board's focus on 'quality assurance' with 'professional growth': 'Rather than view these goals as incompatible and competing, they are viewed as essential, mutually supportive, and inextricably intertwined elements that support continuous improvement in the total evaluation process' (p. 64). However, that understanding was not always shared across different schools. One area that was especially contentious was the use of formal classroom observations within the evaluation. In the words of one teaching fellow: 'It feels as though your whole teaching career depends on a 20-minute observation when we are supposed to be lifelong learners. Does this observation truly reflect a supportive and encouraging system or does it encourage an elimination program?' (p. 70). Despite the positive and supportive experience of working alongside an MC, the performance-management process created tensions within the TIP, although more recent changes that have ended the formal classroom observation by the TIP team have resolved some of these.

Extended encounters with coaching

In 2019 I designed and taught my first online asynchronous graduate course described as an 'exploration of mentoring and coaching through the lens of professional learning and leadership with focus on students' professional contexts'. Students engage with defining coaching and mentoring, historical and theoretical underpinnings and the three key coaching elements: way of being, skills and techniques, and coaching process (see part 1). We also explore change and systemic change in relation to coaching and leading coaching cultures (see part 4). Students come from diverse disciplines including health professions, business, education, leadership and sport. The course includes academic and practice activities and assessments and has grown from one section to three across three different modalities: lecture, online asynchronous and online asynchronous.

This academic and interprofessional role complements my engagement with CollectivED, alongside a growing concern with mentoring and coaching as a culturally responsive practice. Recent opportunities to extend my thinking to the necessary challenges related to decolonising coaching form a key component of my current work. Some of the related encounters are introduced in chapter 14.

I'm grateful for this new opportunity and, as I look to the future, I hope to continue to gather new fabric blocks for my ever-growing and evolving patchwork quilt.

> *Quilts have the transformative potential to stitch seemingly disjointed fragments together to make a beautiful whole.*
>
> Hollweck (2019a, p. 50)

Chapter 8 endnotes

Final thoughts

As Trista's personal narrative shows, coaching can feature in professional lives at each stage, from new teacher to leader, and can align with a range of opportunities, roles and projects. This illustrates the value of ensuring that coaching is not understood unilaterally or pigeon-holed into narrow purposes or with inflexible approaches.

Talking point

This chapter explores the many encounters or fabric blocks that contribute to Trista's professional patchwork quilt. What has brought you to coaching? Who do you read and learn from when you engage with coaching in education? What influences do our own encounters play in stitching our coaching quilt? What new encounters will help you think critically and deeply about coaching in your context? What connections can you make to your past and present to guide your purposeful future?

Ideas for action

If you are a coaching leader or advocate, you might like to select a 'go-to' resource that you think will challenge others to extend and enhance their understanding of coaching.

Part 3
Contemporary coaching: encounters from the CollectivED community

What to look out for in part 3

In this section you will encounter:
- a unique collection of coaching case studies written by educators from several countries, working in diverse education settings and with a range of purposes and impacts

> - invaluable insights from the CollectivED community about how coaching has evolved in their settings over time, including the challenges and successes
> - descriptions of how coaching draws on models and tools, but is frequently adapted and contextualised to ensure suitability and build impact
> - consideration of coaching as ways of enhancing teaching and learning, enabling and empowering others, shaping culture, sustaining change and developing purposeful conversational spaces.

When coaching is introduced in education, it is often used because there is a sense that change is needed or that external policies and newly adopted norms of practice cause anxiety and educators in a setting have to catch up, comply or prove themselves. However, sustaining any new activity requires resources and these are often constrained in education settings. In our work with CollectivED we have found it interesting to explore with others their experience of coaching, their settings' perceived priorities for change, and the relationships between change and purpose, and between purpose and values. We are also interested in how coaching supports the orientation of effort and challenges participants to explore their values and often to adjust their practices in light of this.

Despite the relationship between coaching and change we are wary of coaching in schools which is lauded as a 'game-changer' or which is rolled out at speed and at scale without a sense of context or consideration of ongoing resources required and with relatively limited opportunities to elicit voice or encourage agency in its development. We are also wary of coaching offered as a 'one-size-fits-all' approach. We acknowledge the surge of individuals and organisations who have adopted the mantle or identity of coaches in education and we welcome an expansion of the development and potential of coaching. However, we are concerned about the risks of monetising coaching as an endeavour because it needs more than entrepreneurial spirit for it to be sustainable and impactful. In broad terms there is a risk that coaching itself becomes performative.

In contrast we advocate for the concept of coaching as a 'way of being' as well as a 'way of doing' and a 'way of knowing'. When all three are combined, we see interpersonal, intrapersonal, practical and cognitive domains of collective professionalism through coaching coming together. We acknowledge that in many non-Western, less neo-liberal education systems, the foundations and principles of education practice and of coaching are often intertwined, to the extent that there is no significant need for naming coaching as a distinct activity within education. We are also interested in the concepts of 'wayfinding' and 'accompaniment', which were introduced in chapter 4. Coaching is not a 'done to' process; it is an intentional, growth-oriented and courageous practice where individuals accompany others in solidarity and equal partnership to help them get better at what they do. Rather than seeing coaching as the means to reach a given solution or specific destination or to tailor practice or thinking to boundaries set by others, we propose coaching as an experience of 'wayfinding' through encouraging exploration, close observation, adaptability, heightened awareness, problem-solving and connection. This 'wayfinding' aligns with a strong sense of purpose; we believe that finding and sustaining a sense of meaningful purpose is at the heart of coaching.

In this part of the book we explore contemporary approaches to, uses of and challenges related to coaching in a wide range of education settings. To understand the breadth and depth of coaching practices which are in current use, we draw on case studies from the CollectivED community and beyond and present these new encounters to add to those already presented in the book. In supporting, developing and curating coaching approaches we dispute the singularity of '*the* way' to coach, because we appreciate and acknowledge nuance, contextualisation and evolution of coaching over time, a stance which was highlighted in the research report 'Improving Coaching: Evolution not Revolution' (Lofthouse et al., 2010b). In reading these case studies, you will encounter different coaching processes, models and frameworks. In CollectivED it is less about the specific coaching tools you use and more about how you use them. These new case studies of coaching provide evidence of the realities of coaching, the roles it plays, the potential it offers and the challenges which are grappled with.

Gathering and curating the case studies of contemporary coaching

In these chapters are contributions from educators leading and innovating in coaching in their schools and other settings, as well as individuals working as freelance coaches, researching coaching and others who have developed coaching within networks. We hand over the authorship of these case studies to the coaches and school leaders who have shared them, and each voice is different. As authors we have added our reflections. These are made as a means of demonstrating how we encounter these coaching accounts and how they inform our own thinking or stimulate questions related to each focus area.

These contemporary encounters with coaching were collected between 2022 and 2024, and most describe coaching that has been evolving for many years, including before, during and following the period of pandemic lockdown. These new encounters are not intended to be fully representative of the diverse range of uses, contexts and approaches of coaching in education; neither are they proposed as universal best practice examples. What they do provide are interesting encounters with how and why coaching has been adopted and developed, what difference it is felt to be making, and the sorts of decisions that are made along the journey. Some case studies represent coaching in particular school or college settings, some represent the way that individuals work with coachees from many settings and others make direct links to programmes, networks and organisations within the education sector. As time elapses, some of the case studies are encountered in the past tense, while others give us a chance to discover coaching which is ongoing and emerging.

As you read the encounters presented in part 3, it will become clear that they are written in different styles, lengths and voices. Some of these encounters include references to coaching approaches or specific authors who have influenced the coaching developed in the settings. The encounters are curated authentically, so that you can read them as a direct and deliberate sharing of ideas and practice. Unless the contributor does so in their own writing, we have opted not to break up the voice of our contributors by using in-text citations, but the relevant references and resources are included at the end of the book.

The encounters are grouped in six chapters:

- Chapter 9: Coaching as a way of supporting teaching and learning
- Chapter 10: Coaching as a way of enabling and empowering others
- Chapter 11: Coaching as a way of shaping culture
- Chapter 12: Coaching as a way of sustaining change
- Chapter 13: Coaching as a way of developing purposeful conversational spaces
- Chapter 14: Coaching as a way of enacting social justice, equity and decoloniality

Chapter 9
Coaching as a way of enhancing teaching and learning

Transformative professionalism involves not only individual attributes but also collective strategy on the part of those engaged in any educational enterprise. It means that new forms of work organization are established between teachers, in particular that the hoary chestnut of teacher privatism, isolation and individualism is dispensed with.

Judyth Sachs (2003, p. 26)

Coaching teachers with a focus on their classroom routines has become big business in parts of the education world. Teacher coaching has deep roots in different models of instructional coaching, including the work of Jim Knight (2018, 2022) and Paul Bambrick-Santoyo (2016) and much-cited evidence bases (e.g. Kraft et al., 2018), and has also been developed as an 'in-house' approach to CPD, with teachers working with peers as coaches (including work by Lofthouse et al., 2010a; Hollweck, 2019a). The growth in teacher coaching provision sits alongside CPD programmes (e.g. the Early Career Framework in England), a surge in the influence of cognitive science in teacher training and the development of digital platforms, artificial intelligence and video, and is supported by intensely marketed publications, conferences and qualifications. Given this, it could be argued that the sector is awash with teacher coaching solutions and that school leaders wanting to adopt coaching for this purpose just need to select the model that best suits their school's needs and budget.

In the CollectivED community there remains a strong stance towards adopting a creative, critical and collaborative approach to development of teacher coaching, as well as to the practice of teaching itself. Coaching ideas are often blended, contextualised and allowed to evolve over time. We advocate for a move towards transformative professionalism and acknowledge that this goes beyond classroom repertoire to teaching stance, which includes reflection, humility and integrity with a goal of empowerment and agency for learners. Coaching could be seen as a response to the call made by Sachs (2003) for transformative professionalism, but we approach that with caution. While Sachs states that transformative professionalism is 'concerned with mutual engagement around a joint enterprise […] improving student learning outcomes', she also indicates that it 'questions and criticises taken-for-granted practices and structures' (Sachs, p. 16). Coaching to a formula or for the development of a predetermined teaching technique needs to itself be questioned and critiqued. In this vein we discuss the concepts of context, efficacy and change in relation to coaching in more detail in part 4.

This chapter invites you to encounter a number of examples of teacher coaching from primary, secondary and further education settings. Interesting as discrete case study examples, they are even more powerful as a collective in showing the different ways coaching is understood and enacted in practice. We hope you keep them in mind and even return to this section as you continue your reading. Each case study is followed by reflections made by us as co-authors that share how we have encountered them and where possible draw connections to some of the ideas presented elsewhere in this book.

Although less common in the field, there is a growing interest in coaching students to support them in their journeys through education, to help them develop self-awareness and the ability to gain focus and a sense of purpose and perspective as learners. Alongside adults coaching young people there is also the opportunity for the students themselves to become peer coaches. We have included case studies of student coaching happening in the CollectivED community as additional encounters in this chapter and wholeheartedly support growing this movement in schools.

Encounter: coaching with a shared focus on teaching and learning principles

Lucy Vincent leads a coaching team of ten people at Harrogate Grammar School (part of the Red Kite Multi-Academy Trust), a large non-selective state secondary school in Yorkshire in the UK. Lucy writes:

How and why coaching is used

At Harrogate Grammar School (HGS) coaching takes place to support teachers becoming better teachers, through self-reflection, clear and honest discussion, with a clear focus on seven principles of teaching and learning that we use across the school. Coaching sits within the performance review work of the school, which is aligned with that of the multi-academy trust (MAT) made up of 13 schools. The MAT has three pillars of performance: self-awareness, growth and collaboration, which are centred around the colleague and designed for our people to thrive. Each teacher has a minimum of two coaching cycles every academic year.

Coaches undertake 10–15-minute lesson visits, then ask the coachee to choose a time that suits them to have a coaching conversation, usually within the following few days. The conversation lasts between 30 minutes and an hour – maybe longer if necessary – with actions agreed. This may result in another lesson visit or a joint learning walk. It may result in more intensive coaching. There are two cycles in each academic year. These conversations now take place in the coaching room – a dedicated space where staff are able to speak freely and openly, without the worry of being seen or heard by other colleagues or students.

For those colleagues who are not following national designated coaching and mentoring approaches created for early career teachers we follow a clear pattern in our coaching conversation: What was seen? How can the learning climate be improved? What options do we have? What are the next steps? Our approach is influenced by research into Leadership Matters' 360 Tool, the Centre for Creative Leadership's situation–behaviour–impact (SBI) model, Jim Knight's impact cycle, Andy Buck's BASIC model and Kim Scott's radical candour, alongside professional experience gained through current national leadership and coaching training.

How coaching emerged and evolved

Harrogate Grammar School has undertaken lesson observations, with feedback meetings and gradings given, for many years. It felt like a process that was undervalued, and was certainly a process that teachers felt was being done 'to them' – and not 'with them' or even 'for them'. We wanted to reshape this. By focusing on collaborative thinking and looking at the notion that all educators want to improve, we moved from lesson observations to lesson visits; lesson gradings disappeared. We wanted to use the lesson visits as a springboard for a conversation regarding teachers' classroom practice. Over time, the school's learning team (colleagues from each faculty) helped develop the HGS seven principles of teaching and learning. This fits with our school's values and pillars of excellence; all are focused on improving the learning climate in every classroom. Coaching conversations are now based on 'The seven principles'. Colleagues now know them, understand them, plan lessons using them and in the coaching conversation we use the language of them. It is these principles we want to improve upon, and this is what we base our coaching on at the moment.

In terms of coaching questions, these have also developed over time as the coaching team have become more familiar with the wording and responding to the temperature of the coachee. We started with a script, with various options of wording available. As the coaches have grown in confidence – in themselves and in the process – this has relaxed and as a result the conversation is now a conversation and not a question-and-answer session.

Changes and improvements have been possible due to the staged rollout of coaching and regular feedback to enhance and develop the process. Previously we had to use classrooms or senior leaders' offices for coaching conversations, which we recognised as less than ideal due to the hierarchical inference. We now have a coaching room, as described above. The information that is recorded during coaching conversations has also been streamlined. To aid the coachee to concentrate on their thinking the coach records the notes. Initially the coach sent a lengthy and detailed email to the coachee reflecting the conversation and outlining the agreed actions. This was time-consuming and the coachee didn't really know what to do with it. Using the 'What was seen? How can the learning climate be improved? What options do we have? What are the next steps?' model, we now have a simple grid. The coach fills it in during the conversation, using the first three sections to verbally reflect or 'play back' the conversation, before agreeing the next steps. This document is seen by the coach and the coachee throughout the conversation. It is then scanned and immediately sent to the coachee. If they wish to upload this and use it as part of their appraisal evidence, they can, but it is their document, reflecting their process, enabling their actions to move their teaching forwards.

When we began coaching, time was limited so coaches coached whoever they could, where it fitted with the timetable. Now coaches are assigned to faculty areas. Each coach meets with the faculty leader in the first instance. They discuss the culture and the teaching and learning focus of the faculty area and look at the faculty development plan together. From here the designated coach coaches each teaching member of that faculty, aligning the teacher development with the faculty development. Listening to Andy Buck recently, coaches are then able to see if the culture and vision is 'lived or laminated'. This process is also proving useful in gathering practice to share in learning walks, where appropriate. Going forward, I have proposed that each faculty leader also has a coach to support their leadership. The school has three pillars: culture, curriculum, and teaching and learning. Each faculty leader currently has a senior leadership team link, focusing on curriculum and data, but dovetailing a coach in would support the culture and teaching and learning pillars.

Impacts of coaching

Early reflections from colleagues on their coaching experience were overwhelmingly positive, with some of the comments being:

> *I really like the fact that this approach is a lot more based on our own view of our lessons, targets and classes. The guided questions that allow us to reflect on what worked, our strengths, what we would like to focus on, etc., with guidance and ideas from the coach, which was really valuable. This is better than before as observations are only a snapshot of a lesson rather than*

> discussing the bigger picture, which the coaching conversations allow.
>
> The fact the conversation doesn't just focus on the 20 minutes of the lesson that was seen. Observers can miss really important/more exciting activities when they only drop in for part of a lesson. This conversation gave me the opportunity to talk about the types of activities that work well in my lessons, etc. and I left with ideas about how to improve my own practice.
>
> It was an opportunity to think about my practice in a different way than I had been used to; I was able to clearly reflect on how to move forwards, in line with the school principles, compared to the old 'what went well, what could have been better' style reflection.
>
> It helped me be reflective; prompted me to really think about my teaching. There was more time for me to reflect and less time with the observer just making judgement/suggestions.
>
> The fact it didn't feel like a judgement, just a chance to discuss my classes, where I am at with my teaching and the next steps I want to take.
>
> Previous observations have left me feeling very demotivated, this wasn't the case this time. Emphasis on what could be developed was empowering.

By the next coaching cycle some colleagues who needed greater support were very open to this. Open and honest conversations took place so coachees knew they would be offered regular lesson visits, with the coach and coachee working together to improve specific practices. Trust was built, practice was better, outcomes were improved. Coaching is now firmly embedded within the school culture. Learning walks take place with regularity, to share good practice with colleagues. Colleagues are open to lesson visits and the open-door culture of the school continues to be valued.

Continuing challenges

As part of a MAT we are grappling with the cultural change of moving away from system-led processes to the opposite experience for performance reviews. Developing a coaching culture for all staff – teaching and non-teaching – will take time and rely on skills development and buy-in by all stakeholders. We accept that this may take years, however, we are already changing and with each quality conversation, we will get nearer to our goal of a truly safe and effective learning environment. At school level, the initial challenge was quite simply to gain staff buy-in. Changing perspective and opening colleagues' minds took place intensively over the space of one term; it was received really well, as outlined in the results of the staff survey. Colleagues are open to the process, so now we look to see how we drive this forward, continuing to improve teaching, and to see the outcomes in students' results.

Reflections

As we encounter the description of teacher coaching from Harrogate Grammar School, we are struck by the ways that coaching has been developed to both consolidate and enhance the desired characteristics of teaching and learning. In her leadership role Lucy treads a fine balance, ensuring that coaching is engaged in by all teachers, while wanting their experiences to feel personal and meaningful. As a leader she also needs to be able to understand and evidence its impact, so that its continuation is appropriate, secured and valued.

Encounter: enhancing teacher coaching using video

Jim Thompson is an experienced school leader and coach based in New York State. He works with school districts and schools providing a video instructional coaching programme for teachers, working closely with Casey Kosiorek, a district superintendent who sets the conditions for coaching. Casey's interest in coaching came from playing American football and watching film and wanting to apply this to improving teaching. Casey continues to support this work, stating that 'we started with 10s of teachers and now have 100s volunteering' and that he sees 'more effective teacher reflection and better instruction for students' as a result. Jim writes:

How we use coaching

Our coaching work is undertaken at public K–12 (kindergarten to Year 12) schools in western New York State. At Hilton Central School, for example, we are in the eighth year of video coaching. We use a differentiated coaching model creating cohorts of teachers across a range of video-based coaching programmes. Each consists of a series of online meetings and video projects which I mentor. Our various programmes are underpinned by Jim Knight's books *The Definitive Guide to Instructional Coaching* and *Better Conversations* as well as Harvard's Best Foot Forward research. Teachers are supported to read and unpack key chapters then engage in a video project with coaching practices at the heart. For example, we encourage peer coaching between members of different programme cohorts based on Jim Knight's *Impact Cycle*. The programmes are voluntary and positive 'word of mouth' sustains our work. Coaching happens with me and with peers where they share a video project.

How this coaching approach developed

I was an elementary principal for 20 years. During the last ten years of my career I was fortunate enough to hire assistant principals. My last two assistant principals were Dr Dan Murray and Dr Casey Kosiorek. Our discussions always focused on what's best for kids. We all came to the conclusion that the system where principals conducted formal evaluations and teachers 'endured' professional development after professional development without any coaching really wasn't impacting student learning. We started looking especially at the work of Jim Knight. Knight said the 'teachers don't know what it looks like when they do what they do'. About ten years ago Dan and Casey became district superintendents and asked me to work with some of their teachers, inviting them to video some of their practice, meet with me in a confidential and non-evaluative way and see what might happen.

Jim Knight's work has always been key with the *Impact Cycle* being foundational to our coaching approach, along with Harvard's Best Foot Forward research. Teachers take a 'selfie' video of their practice, identify a goal important to them to work on which would advance student learning and then partner with their coach to dialogue on where they are and what it would look like if the goal was reached. The key value that we wish to nurture and grow is Knight's 'partnership approach'; inferring 'power with…not power over' and always remembering that 'one size doesn't fit all…one size fits one'. Partnership principles such as equality, choice, voice, dialogue, reflection, praxis, and reciprocity are the DNA of our work. Our work is also affirmed with Michael Bungay Stanier's *The Coaching Habit* and *The Advice Trap* and Megan and Bob Tschannen-

Moran's *Evocative Coaching*. We wrote our own book *A Quick Guide to Video Coaching* (Amazon) by Casey Kosiorek and Jim Thompson. In the realm of helping coaches develop a repertoire of instructional strategies, the work of Doug Lemov (*Teach Like a Champion 3.0*) and the inspiration of Tom Sherrington and his book *Rosenshine's Principles in Action* and others impact our work. We are also inspired to be CollectivED Fellows and enriched by the work of Professor Rachel Lofthouse, who founded CollectivED.

Each year more and more teachers asked to be part of this programme. I then trained additional teachers as full-time instructional coaches and I was asked to be director of instructional coaching. Over the years teachers have kept requesting video coaching across multiple districts and even through the pandemic we sustained cohorts in our entirely voluntary programmes. During the pandemic we switched from in-person meetings to using Zoom for workshops and adapted to an approach that works online. On a personal level this was not easy, I have experienced 'imposter syndrome', especially trying to be earnest with extending empathy and grace to teachers who were enduring the most challenging times in modern educational history.

Impact of video coaching

Because the program is entirely voluntary, one impact we see is that teachers see great value with video reflection and true partnership coaching. We have significant sign-ups each year because of very positive 'word of mouth'. Teacher after teacher tells us it was one of the most transformational professional learnings they've ever undertaken. They have shared stories about how video has been so powerful in giving them clarity. Jim Knight says that 'Video is rocket fuel for learning.' Teachers tell us about both small and large victories emerging from video reflection and partnership coaching, real impacts with student learning and a much greater sense of that 'collective teacher efficacy' that Hattie writes of. The mere fact that the work continues to be funded is testimony to what they feel about its importance.

Reflections

Sometimes coaching is described as a way to hold a mirror up for a coachee to promote reflection so they can get a picture of their reality and solve their own problems. Using video is a powerful means to do that. The video-recording will always be partial, but what is made visible and audible is accurate, and thus provides an excellent stimulus for consideration, analysis and discussion with a coach.

The idea of video-recording may feel daunting for some educators, especially if they are teaching in high-stakes, high-accountability institutions. Capturing and amplifying strengths is appreciative rather than reductive and is a good basis for coaching.

Encounter: an instructional coach perspective

Chris (a pseudonym) was employed as an instructional coach for five years at a large K–12 school in Sydney, Australia, with a particular specialisation in primary grades kindergarten to Year 4. Chris reflects on that work and how his understanding has evolved.

Recognising objectives and tensions in coaching

The central purpose of coaching in this context was to lead teachers to transform practice and improve student learning. As a coach it was my role to model effective high-yield strategies which enable and support each student's engagement with literacy, numeracy and the national assessment framework related to general capabilities. This was achieved through both a commitment and dedication of the co-planning, co-teaching, co-debriefing and co-reflecting with teachers as individuals and in both small and large groups. As a coach I was assigned to a group of teachers. They were not so much invited but expected to be coached either individually or in teaching teams, and there was no opt-out/in.

The coaching model used was a hybrid model that had been developed prior to my arrival. It was reflective of the following models:

- AITSL (Australian Institute for Teaching and School Leadership) approach of planning, contracting, coaching, reflecting
- Lyn Sharratt and Michael Fullan's co-planning, co-teaching, co-reflecting, co-debriefing model
- Jim Knight's impact cycle approach.

When I was a novice instructional coach, Jim Knight's impact cycle was the most useful as it helped develop an internal structure or schema for my role. In my context, we espoused his 'partnership principles', but they were not enacted and this became a primary tension in how I worked.

Developing more nuanced insight

My coaching approach evolved and became more reflective of a more nuanced understanding of coaching, not merely instructional coaching. Following the work of CollectivED, I became aware that instructional coaching is but one thread in the tapestry of professional learning within a school and accordingly I developed an approach that acknowledged the teacher as already being 'creative, resourceful and whole'. Whereas before I would be 'deployed' to 'fix' instructional practices in teachers (particularly beginning teachers), I now push back against partnering with someone based on the demands of a leader and operate from a stance of relationship, dialogue, context and unconditional positive regard.

Typically the outcomes of coaching are 'measured' by traditional student/class/school improvement metrics. I am interested in student improvement, but I also appreciate that not all improvement can be noticed in data spreadsheets, particularly as they can be weaponised and used to justify policy and pedagogical direction, as well as negatively influence teacher judgement or assessment. While I am interested in student improvement at individual, class and school level, I am now also drawing on Nora Bateson's concept of 'warm data' and 'data storytelling' in providing nuance and detail to what is essentially a complex and agile system.

Reflections

Through Chris's honest account we encounter the inherent complexities of coaching in organisations which are often hierarchical and performative in culture, but which also espouse and aim to live out values of support and partnership. Adopting coaching can shine a light on tensions. It can also provide a focus and means to both imagine, advocate for and enact change. Chris's use of emotive language such as 'weaponised' reveals the reality of certain coaching approaches that are not really 'in service' of the coachee's thinking and purpose. When a coachee feels well held (Drago-Severson, 2004; Drago-Severson and Blum-DeStefano, 2016) conversations can be challenging – but never harmful!

Encounter: developing and deploying an instructional coaching team

New College is a sixth form college of over 1400 students in Doncaster, England. It is part of a trust which has two further colleges that use the same coaching programme. Ceri Boyle leads the coaching programme in the college as assistant principal with responsibility for teaching for learning and lead for professional development. There is a team of three instructional coaches: Debbie Briggs, Rebecca Prescott-Mail and Nicola O'Keeffe, with similar teams in each partner college. Ceri writes:

How and why coaching is used

All teaching staff and progress tutors at college set a professional learning priority as part of their appraisal and professional development cycle each year. One of our core Trust values is commitment to continuous improvement and the coaching programme supports this. Coaching is designed to meet our aim to further personalise CPD for staff. All teaching staff and progress tutors are invited to be coached and can nominate themselves for one of four cycles throughout the year. They can re-enter the programme if there is space available. In addition, all early career teachers are supported by the coaching team, as are new staff to support their induction.

There is a dedicated CPD slot within the timetabled day each week and this is often protected for time to work on personal professional priorities. Coaches are also given time to ensure that they have capacity and flexibility to work with coachees. Flexible approaches are offered to ensure part-time staff are not adversely affected by loss of non-contact time; for example, offering fortnightly sessions over two cycles. We also have a policy whereby staff can set work for classes to allow them to visit peers to observe strategies in action.

Our coaching approach is largely based on Jim Knight's *Impact Cycle*, using the identify questions to support teachers in reflecting on their performance. The PEERS (powerful, easy, emotionally compelling, reasonable) target-setting approach has been very useful in supporting all teachers in setting specific, student-focused targets. The ADAPT (attempt, develop, adapt, practise, test) approach used in the *Walkthru* programme has also been a useful scaffold to build granular approaches and useful reflection.

It is sometimes difficult to ensure time is built in to reflect and busier times of year can be a barrier to the success of the programme due to increased workload. Being mindful of this at a strategic level has minimised the issues with flexible scheduling, varied or extended coaching cycles or postponed coaching cycles.

How coaching emerged and evolved

The 'teaching for learning leads' carried out research into different coaching models, which led to choosing Jim Knight's *Impact Cycle* as a supporting programme for our Trust approach. Having decided on some key principles and structural decisions, a proposal was submitted to the CEO and executive team to approve. The next stage was to appoint excellent coaches and we agreed a consistent set of questions and tasks which would identify coaches who could demonstrate the ability to work with colleagues who might be highly skilled and experienced. Once appointed, the Trust coaching team were all involved in a two-day residential with training sessions from all of the teaching for learning leads and opportunities to support the building of the programme around a set of consistent starting principles. Following the residential, each coaching team put the programme into practice with time to plan, collaborate, reflect and adapt before each cycle of coaching. The Trust coaching team have an online community to share good practice regularly and also meet annually to reflect and evaluate the programme in order to agree improvements and priorities before the next academic year. The Trust teaching for learning team, led by Stuart Nash, meet each half term and ensure that the coaching programme is being evaluated and that we also provide opportunities for the coaches to continue their professional development.

Impacts of coaching

We issue an evaluation after each coaching cycle and these have been overwhelmingly positive with staff sharing 'soundbites' to promote the programme to colleagues. There has been a sharing of experience through end-of-year teachmeets and the coaching team have contributed to CPD workshops to broaden the reach of their work as well as developing them professionally, too. Staff surveys have highlighted positivity around the personalised nature of CPD and this seems to be reflected in strong retention. Developmental learning walks have shown evidence of positive improvements with coached staff speaking openly about the strategies they have developed and the impact on students. At institution level, this is supporting an appreciation of personalised approach and fostering confidence in teachers to seek support with their professional development.

Reflections

The coaching programme developed at New College is so well grounded that it already feels quite mature. Ceri and the coaching staff have worked strategically and pragmatically to create the provision and then engaged in their own professional learning and a process of co-construction to build the quality of what they do. Coaching has been embedded as part of the staff's CPD provision and they are invited to nominate themselves if they feel it supports their personal professional learning goal. Dedicated time to coach, support for coaches' ongoing learning and development and feedback after each coaching cycle are considered, as is attention to coaching for new staff members. Thinking systemically in this way leads to an attuned and responsive coaching provision and greater staff buy-in and retention.

Encounter: student peer coaching in a primary school

Vicki Martin and Anne Clements are both qualified coaches and passionate about using the coaching 'way of being' and key coaching skills within their school. They have established and modified a leadership training programme of students coaching students within Royal Oak School in Auckland, their large multicultural primary school in New Zealand. Vicki and Anne write:

How and why we have developed student peer coaching

Our school values are Care, Respect and Empower. Coaching and the coaching process allow our children to focus significantly on the empower aspect.

All students in Year 5 are invited to a coaching conference where they receive some knowledge and understanding of what coaching looks like in our school. Following on from the conference, they can put forward an application to become a coach if they are interested. From this point the application process begins and students put themselves forward to be interviewed for this leadership role as coaches.

Once selected we then spend a term training the student coaches using the GROWTH framework (goals, reality, options, will, tactics, habits) from Growth Coaching International (GCI), where the student coaches are given plenty of opportunity to learn about, refine and develop key coaching skills. Student coaches then coach other students within our school for 20 weeks a year. These coaches are coaching weekly in different classrooms from Year 3 to 6 on their learning goals, so that each child in our school has two coaching sessions each term.

With our school values at the heart of the coaching process we follow the GROWTH coaching framework as a means for empowering both our student coaches and the children they coach (coachees). We extensively discuss trust, noticing, active listening, empathy, strengths, asking good questions and ISMART goal-setting (inspiring, specific, measurable, achievable, results driven and time-bound), also from GCI. We have found this to be a logical and thorough process for children to follow and understand.

What has motivated us in coaching?

Initially we qualified to become coaches and instantly recognised how this aligned with our school values and wanted to bring coaching into school somehow. We worked with senior leaders to help them gain an understanding of the coaching process and appreciate the value of coaching within our school context. We have coached teachers to support their professional goal-setting. This grew and evolved over time to encompass our students. Naturally as 'empower' is a key value, we realised that this perfectly aligns with the essence of coaching. Our students coaching students leadership programme was established in 2020 and is now incorporated into our school's 'way of being' as a key set of skills that we offer to our students to take into their future. Both the coaches and coachees have a role and, although different, it relates back to our school value of being empowered.

Impacts on students

There are two main objectives: first, for the coaches to be empowered facilitators, comfortable in supporting others to discuss and action goals; second, for the coachees (Years 3–6) to be empowered to self-select goals they wish to develop and work through an action plan with a coach.

We see this working. Children are identifying and valuing things that are important to them and are being accountable to make steps towards achieving their goals. Coaching and all that it encompasses has become a 'way of being' within our school. The expectation is that all our learners are empowered to make improvements and strive to achieve goals. Coaching assists in the development of a growth mindset because students are thinking about goals, making steps to achieve them and understanding the process from start to finish with more clarity. This helps them to calmly face challenges and understand the thinking behind goal-setting.

Reflections

This is our first encounter illustrating how coaching can be directly experienced by children and young people. Multiple strands intertwine here. We are excited by the opportunities created for the students themselves to be coached and also to become a coach. We also value the learner-centred approach to change which allows for unique encounters and impacts bound by a structured programme and support. There is also a sense of the power of the school community with a coaching way of being proactively created by those within it. It is clear to see that authentic pupil agency is a strong cultural pillar at Royal Oak School. There is a powerful sense that young learners are nurtured to develop holistic learning dispositions. The coaching approach in this school fosters a culture of kind, caring critical thinkers.

Encounter: developing opportunities for engagement in coaching

Stacey Postle is headteacher of Beaumont Primary School, a single-form primary school in Bolton, England. The community is relatively affluent but there are pockets of economic deprivation. Over 85% of the pupils are from minority-ethnic families and there are an average number of pupils with special educational needs and disabilities (SEND). Stacey writes:

How and why coaching has been developed

When I entered the profession, I was on a fast-track teaching programme with National College and I first learned the benefits of coaching then. I have since tried to bring this to each school I worked at, but with no success. It was only when I became a headteacher that I could use coaching to its full advantage. In our school, coaching is used as a vehicle for CPD for both teachers and teaching assistants. Most of our CPD relates to developing pedagogical approaches to support individual teaching repertoires. As the headteacher I was initially the coaching leader who introduced coaching and have since handed this over to a member of the senior leadership team (SLT) with Nicola as my coaching champion. We have a model in which everyone is a coach and a coachee. All staff are trained and all staff are involved three times per half term. It is a part of everyone's performance management targets.

We use the STRIDE model to support coaching (strengths, target, real situation, ideas, decision, evaluation). Our CPD is led in-house and is focused on the needs of the school based on our instructional round information. For example, I lead 'pace and routine' as an inset training session and then this is the coaching topic that staff are to use during their coaching time. We use Padlet to record updates and findings.

When we first introduced coaching the first term, it was very interesting. I led a training day and introduced all staff to coaching and the benefits. At the start I asked staff to just enjoy coaching – no hidden CPD or meanings. It was just about enjoying coaching and building rapport. One teacher used the fact she couldn't afford to buy a house and was coached through this problem and ended up buying an apartment instead. To maintain momentum in coaching I have provided time within the school day to make sure this works. I expected too much initially and reduced it from weekly coaching to three times per half term. When staff are absent, some people miss out, so we need to make sure groups or pairs are fluid when needed. We always talk about 'the answer always lies within'. Now it is a systematic approach that has developed into a process that people enjoy and see merit in and it helps drive school improvement.

Impacts of coaching

Coaching has brought a lot of positives to my school. For individuals, the quality of their teaching repertoires has been enhanced, relationships between staff have developed professionally and they have professional discussions with ease. As a school, the quality of teaching and learning is exceptional. Recent external inspection results, parental happiness, staff morale are at an all-time high!

Reflections

This encounter shows a deep commitment to developing a culture of coaching in a school, underpinned by a united sense of purpose. We appreciate Stacey's honesty around the challenges she faced bringing coaching to some of her schools and managing her expectations against the realities of a school day and availability of staff. The power and potential of an engaged and advocating leader who is involved in developing and adapting the coaching programme are clear. How coaching is introduced and implemented in a school or jurisdiction matters for its sustainability and staff buy-in.

Encounter: student coaching for wellbeing

Jean Ramsey is a former teacher and developed coaching for students prior to her retirement. She now coaches students in a sixth form in a secondary school in Oxfordshire. Jean writes:

How and why coaching is used

I use coaching to help post-16 students cope with anxiety and overwhelm, with a special focus on supporting neurodiverse students, including those with hitherto undiagnosed ADHD. The young people are referred to me by the student support staff who work as part of the pastoral team in the sixth form. They liaise with the young people and their families to see if they would like to participate in coaching. If the invitation is accepted, the support staff give me a heads-up on what the young person is struggling with and I coach them for 30 minutes once a week, initially for six weeks, but often the support is extended. We work out a time that suits them and their studies; sometimes we meet online but usually in the sixth form in a confidential space. To support the students in the coaching sessions I tend to use Will Thomas's STRIDE model, but I have also been using Michael Bungay Stanier's '7 questions'. However, I have been coaching for so long now I kind of go with the flow.

Development and impacts of the coaching approach

Before I retired as a teacher, I designed my own student coaching approach in school. I started with a pilot group of boys who were at risk of underachieving at GCSE. I coached them for 30 minutes for six weeks with the coaching time built into my timetable. I treated them as clients and took the sessions very seriously. I was scrupulous about confidentiality within the school's safeguarding policy. I realise now I was meeting their unmet needs for empowerment, fun and belonging. The number of exclusions fell; they got their GCSEs and classroom behaviour improved as they were engaged. That made coaching an easy sell to my colleagues. The coaching developed and I became the in-school expert and more coaching was built into my timetable. I shared top coaching tips in our school newsletter. I became interested in coaching staff, too, especially around behaviour management. Coaching became recognised throughout the school as another helpful strand in student wellbeing support. The school brought me back in once I retired to continue the model which works so well.

Over time I have become involved in 'positive intelligence coaching' with Shirzad Chamine. I ask my young clients to do a brief online test to see what their main 'saboteurs' are (limiting beliefs), then we look at simple mindfulness techniques to get them out of their heads and into their bodies. I teach them how to tap into their 'sage' powers – the opposite of the saboteurs. The young people seem to respond well as they see the simple exercises helping them to build up their mental stamina and resilience.

The outcomes of coaching are happier, more resilient young people, families, staff and whole school community. People seek me out. Their eyes light up when we meet!

Reflections

The focus here on facilitating coaching conversations that overcome limiting beliefs shows the synergies between coaching, talking therapy and positive psychology. Jean's account also illustrates a dynamic change process when learning to coach, something we discuss in more detail in chapter 17. Some people are resistant to innovations such as coaching and need to see it working to believe it, an idea that is worth holding onto if you are responsible for implementing coaching or want to see it develop in your context.

Encounter: learning to lead pedagogical coaching

The British School of Brussels (BSB), Belgium, is an all-through international school with 1350 students from 70 nationalities aged from one to 18 years. The curriculum offers a bespoke, skills-based, inquiry-driven approach adapted from the UK national curriculum to meet the needs of the diverse student population. Emma Vlaeminck is a professional learning partner at the school and started inquiring into coaching in 2019 alongside two members of operational staff. This has led to the development and implementation of pedagogical coaching, and she is now the whole school lead coach. Emma writes:

Inquiring into coaching

The professional learning inquiry that my colleagues and I started in 2019 explored the case for coaching at BSB. Coaching seemed to be a way forward to support and sustain high-quality teaching and learning. Coaching also resonated with the ways of working in the professional learning community (PLC) through which we nurture collaboration, trust, careful listening and meaningful questioning. Our PLC at BSB is a staff- and student-led whole school model. It values the inquiry and collaboration of all our community members. We share expertise and learning within and beyond the school to build collective capacity and ultimately make a difference to learning outcomes for learners. There is another encounter with this structure and vision at BSB in chapter 12.

An important backdrop to our work in developing coaching was the separation of the two functions of professional development and performance management. The latter only helps manage performance; the former supports individual professional growth. Having recognised this dichotomy, the school decided in 2016 to move away from a performance-management approach to a much more autonomous and personalised way of learning that builds on the strengths and interests of everyone. After having tried out different models of reflective practice, the school has developed its own framework for pedagogical coaching not as an evaluation tool, but to allow professional individual growth. Finally, pedagogical coaching supports our school's vision of working towards high-quality teaching and learning in an atmosphere of staff learning together in a non-judgemental way and modelling learning by being learners themselves. Pedagogical coaching in particular, when two teachers connect to undertake a process of change, is a powerful example of this.

Creating the pedagogical coaching model

When I became a professional learning partner, I wanted to address a concern that I had that teachers (too) often work in isolation and this can sometimes affect motivation or inhibit innovation. Coaching seemed to me a powerful way to remind people what they are good at. What particularly resonates with me about coaching is that it is about playing to your strengths, enhancing student and staff agency, stimulating insights and awareness to make a difference. The professional learning community offered me a platform where I could explore, sense-test, articulate what coaching at BSB could look like. Rapidly, I came across the GROWTH model (from Growth Coaching International) and Jim Knight's 'instructional coaching' and started to play with it in various situations. Additionally, I attended training sessions, listened to podcasts, read articles and books and practised coaching conversations to upskill myself. I am now the whole school lead coach at BSB.

As we developed our pedagogical coaching model we diverged from Jim Knight's approach because we saw the benefit for the coach and coachee changing roles so that participants have experience of both. This seemed more consistent with professional learning (PL) practice at BSB because of its emphasis on the fundamental reciprocity of teaching and learning. Another aspect that is unique at BSB is that we can coach in several languages (English, French and Dutch). When you're being coached, you are vulnerable and speaking another language adds to the challenge. Speaking one's mother tongue can facilitate the coaching conversation. We put strong emphasis on choosing the coaching partner. It is crucial that both partners have trust in each other to allow a structured, respectful and confidential coaching conversation.

There are three steps in our pedagogical coaching process:
1. the **inquiry time** – 30 minutes. Through a series of questions, the coach helps the coachee define their goal. It is important that the coachee articulates a goal as precisely as possible. One, for the coach to focus on what is wanted and, two, for the coachee to ultimately measure the impact of a new strategy.
2. the **visit** – 15 minutes for a focused observation by the coach.
3. the **conversation time** – 30–45 minutes. Again, through careful questioning, the coach is here to raise awareness, to stimulate insights and not to come up with solutions. The coach needs to listen carefully and hold back as much as possible. The outcome of the conversation time for the coachee should be to have gained more clarity about the next steps, meaning how to implement a new strategy to come closer to their goal.

Once this cycle is completed, a second cycle starts with the same focus but a different strategy. After the first two cycles, the roles are reversed. A resources toolkit is being developed to gather data and evidence about the coaching partnerships that have taken place.

Pedagogical coaching is now available for all teaching staff across primary and secondary. It is offered not only to newly qualified teachers but also to experienced teachers. Coaching works in an invitational way – it is not imposed and is entirely staff-led. Teachers are encouraged to find a coaching partner they trust inside or outside of their faculty or section of school. If they do not have a partner, I offer to connect like-minded colleagues.

Embedding pedagogical coaching

Coaching sessions, in many forms, have always been on the agenda for our PL days, which remain a powerful way to encourage staff to try it out. Presentations during primary and secondary meetings have also been the opportunity to promote coaching across the school. We supported a group of 12 teachers who implemented pedagogical coaching initiatives as part of their autonomous professional learning (APL). This coaching group led a session during the PL days where we modelled a coaching conversation, which proved an effective way of sharing ideas and practical suggestions. More recently ten teachers from primary and secondary volunteered to take part in a pedagogical coaching group. They had chosen their coaching partner with whom they stayed for the whole year and in addition we met four times during the year as a group. These meetings were about learning what our pedagogical coaching model is, practising key coaching skills, such as questioning and active listening, as well as sharing our experiences implementing the cycle. Those who have gone through this process will receive a certificate to acknowledge their commitment to and their skills in pedagogical coaching. Alongside this group, the English and media faculty started pedagogical coaching initiatives to allow space and time to reflect, and also to forge strong relationships through better conversations.

Prospects and challenges for pedagogical coaching

As I look towards the next school year, it is evident that levels of interest in participating in pedagogical coaching are high and I believe that people are now becoming more reflective about their practice and thus are more intentional. There is a space to discuss ideas and to be heard. Good conversations happen in the corridors. In some meetings, I feel that we know we won't be interrupted, which helps deeper reflection, which is one of the key elements of coaching. Recent feedback from participants includes:

> *I think that actually inviting someone in to observe you can be empowering for both.*
>
> *Coaching helped me realise the true impact of my teaching on the learning of students in the class, not just what I had assumed the impact was.*
>
> *My three key takeaways: Sharpen my listening skills. Eagerness to talk needs to be reduced. Don't judge anyone.*
>
> *The whole process felt valuing – personally and professionally – a really positive experience.*

Even though foundations for growing coaching are in place thanks to the PL community, some challenges remain: principally how to develop coaching across our school in an invitational way. Coaching cannot be imposed upon someone, but it needs enough traction to flourish further. How can we build trust further to encourage people to take risks and try out new things? And how do we make time for things that matter?

One possible answer is to dedicate time for training sessions and make cover available for those who wish to enter a coaching relationship to remove practical barriers and build a sense of resourcefulness. Starting with early followers and champions in the hope of creating a ripple effect seems also to be effective. Now it is growing, how can I scale this up without losing the integrity of the model?

Reflections

The role of strong values-led leadership with clarity of purpose in developing a systemic, integrated coaching approach throughout the organisation is clear in this encounter. This ensures that the design and implementation of the school's own pedagogical coaching framework are attuned to their setting, staff and school vision. At the start Emma noted the challenge that many coaching programmes face: how to navigate coaching in relation to evaluation and performance management. The school leaders have held fast to their purpose for coaching to not be an evaluation tool but rather allow for professional individual growth with a basis in choice rather than compulsion.

Chapter 9 endnotes

Final thoughts

Researching and writing about teacher professionalism led Judyth Sachs to consider the significance of working collectively. In the opening quote for this chapter she calls for individualism and isolation to be dispensed with by teachers (Sachs, 2003, p. 26). She does not explore coaching in this context, but the encounters revealed in this chapter create a strong case for enhancing teaching and learning through a variety of collaborative in-school coaching approaches. Most teaching occurs (either in reality or in essence) within four walls and behind a classroom door, with many teachers experiencing only occasional observation from colleagues, often as a form of monitoring or scrutiny. These case studies indicate the value of deliberately knocking down some of those metaphorical walls, increasing the opportunities to share, discuss and co-construct our core work in education. This becomes particularly important when resolving tensions and building shared understandings related to the purpose of education. Coaching with the learners and learning in mind makes for purposeful and productive conversations about teaching.

Talking points

Each of the encounters in this and the following chapters are written by educators who have become informed advocates for coaching in education. We discuss the significance of advocacy in chapter 17. Who are the advocates for coaching for teaching and learning in your setting or wider network? Are they coaches, coachees or leaders? What opportunities do they have for sharing their work and insights? What would you like to learn from them?

Ideas for action

You might find it helpful to look through the encounters in this chapter and to draw comparisons between them and your work as a coach, and/or the arrangements and intentions for coaching in your setting. From this review you could identify aspects that could help you to develop or expand your coaching approach. Perhaps take just one insight into action, first reflecting on 'what' you might do, 'why' it might be appropriate, 'who' would be open to trying it out, 'when' and 'how' that might be adopted. Don't aim for an overhaul, but notice what could evolve through small steps, and don't forget to consider how you would make sense of the impacts.

Chapter 10
Coaching as a way of enabling and empowering others

As coaches I see our role as helping clients to get in touch with their own humanity, which inevitably means engaging with broader themes affecting all lives today.

Geraldine Gallacher (2022, p. 110)

Outside of education and sport probably the greatest uses of coaching are executive, leadership and life coaching. The underlying principle of both executive and leadership coaching is that organisations rely on the capacity of high-performing people in critical senior roles to make good decisions, to remain focused and to maintain their wellbeing to avoid burnout. In education, too, it is common to coach leaders and aspiring leaders and sometimes this is part of a wider coaching culture, but when resources are tight, or leadership turnover is rapid, it may be seen as a priority. In the education sector, ensuring leadership roles are open to, aspired to and undertaken by experienced teachers who are representative of the profession and the diverse communities we serve remains a challenge, and coaching has also been introduced as one way to address this. Coaching is also used by some as a leadership approach. Some headteachers, for example, make a conscious decision to work with their colleagues based on a coaching stance, building opportunities for coaching conversations and seeking to promote agency in the profession.

Coaching is thus associated with empowerment, in terms of supporting individuals to develop confidence and skills to move into new roles, as well as in developing teams who share responsibility and take risks towards a common purpose. Coaching can also be offered with the purpose to empower people to gain agency and act according to their values, perhaps helping them to feel they have more power or capacity when faced with challenges. In this respect coaching should not aim to paper over cracks, but to encourage individuals to acknowledge and address systemic characteristics of society and organisations, such as inequality and anxiety about change. In this chapter we encounter case studies that illustrate coaching to lead and empower, and once again we offer reflections on each one.

Encounter: developing and leading inclusive coaching

After working in a range of international schools Olivia White was employed in an international school in Romania. One of her leadership roles was leading a team of instructional coaches from Early Childhood (EC) to Grade 12, as well as working with leaders to develop a coaching culture. Back in the UK now, Olivia reflects on the coaching work in the school. Olivia writes:

How and why coaching was used

We aimed to use coaching to support teachers to make decisions about their classroom practices and most importantly have positive effects on student learning. We also aimed to use coaching as a vehicle to build a culture of trust and respect. But getting started was hard. For a long while people didn't know what I was talking about. They used the word 'coaching' to mean any conversation. The team and I pushed back hard on hearing 'I will coach them into doing that!' and 'I am sending in the coach to fix that!' Some misconceptions remained in some areas of the school.

However, we developed three coaching objectives:

1. to change the culture of 'doing' into one of reflective practice for the leadership team and wider faculty in the school
2. to build an instructional coaching programme to support teachers in their classroom through the use of goal-setting, learning and practice, focusing on student learning
3. to build a culture of personal growth for all in the school, moving from a teaching environment to a learning one.

These objectives aligned with my own coaching journey. I am an instructional coach (by trade and tradition) and first became an instructional literacy coach in Singapore eight years ago. I have been researching coaching since. I was trained there in 'cognitive' coaching and saw how this changed the way people in work interacted with one another and how trusting the relationships could be. In Romania, I was leading coaching more broadly across the school. I coordinated and advocated on behalf of the instructional coaching team.

How coaching continued to evolve

Once coaching was introduced, we found time for both teachers and leaders to have a coaching experience. If they requested coaching the coaches were on standby to jump into action at any point. Teachers could ask for coaching simply by booking us on our digital calendars. We tried to find release time if possible, but often the time was made by the teams as they began to value it highly. Training for coaching was carved out of meeting times and we started each meeting engaging in an element of coaching such as the 'partnership principles' or unpicking 'trust'.

We also used Growth Coaching International's model as a whole school approach including their GROWTH model. This was useful in giving people a simple framework – we acknowledged at all times that other people had other models – as long as the model placed the coachee in the driving seat, we were happy that people were having conversations. Instructional coaches used Jim Knight's *Impact Cycle* to support their work in classrooms, coupled with the GROWTH model. We worked hard to provide research beyond what is easily found in the field and the usual 'first stop' for coaching. Some of our coaches went on to postgraduate study in coaching and brought their learning back to the school.

Impacts of coaching

Coaching had a positive impact on the people who were willing to engage and, as time went on, more and more staff were having professional and thoughtful conversations. People saw a shift in the culture of the school, particularly within the middle leadership group. For a sustained period I was focused on early childhood where teachers felt their work was often perceived as less than their high school counterparts. Coaching and the coaching mindset gave us the opportunity to talk about their pedagogy, implement best practices and position them as drivers in their own learning and development. As momentum picked up, teachers began asking for coaching and they became more comfortable turning on the video camera and recording their lessons, and they told me it is the best professional learning they have had. I know the impact because they showed me, as they began running workshops, presenting their expertise internationally, leading learning and sharing their experiences via testimonials.

The change in culture was slow but promising. As coaching took hold, we felt more comfortable to try new things, we voiced our opinions and we innovated with our programme, all the time ensuring we were aligned with research. When I left the school, I left as a teacher who had benefited from our approach and a sense of positivity. I left a legacy of two years of instructional coaching and a three-year plan for growth of both the instructional and facilitative coaching programmes. I left a team of coaches and middle leaders who knew what coaching is… And most importantly what it isn't and who had the tools to push forward in their careers and their research for what they know is impactful in education.

How I changed as a coach

My coaching approach began with a focus on growth and student impact. Over time I realised that working with teachers meant that I needed to trust that teachers know their students very well and therefore I have to know the teachers really well. So my focus became adult education. I started to enjoy adult conversation more and more and began to really see the impact that teacher growth and confidence had on their students. I found myself to be a reluctant (at first) mentor and quickly gained a reputation for being well researched, practical and thoughtful, so the focus of my conversations became broader rather than single subject/strategy based. Over time, I moved from being an instructional coach to being a pedagogical leader and I took my beliefs about leadership and coaching into this new role. I led from a place of compassion and was focused on ensuring that every person – secretaries, admin assistants, teaching assistants, teachers and principal – enjoyed their year of growth. I listened intently, offered support and grappled with what it meant to lead and want to coach all at the same time. I now see myself as a coach and mentor who can leverage coaching expertise to help build the capacity of middle leadership and have a passion for leading change and growth in systems using the principles of coaching!

Reflections

Developing and sustaining a coaching culture has been integral in Olivia's leadership roles. It is clear to see how the values of trust and collaboration have been pivotal in facilitating teachers' professional growth. Olivia recognises that it is not easy to build a shared understanding of what coaching is and what it isn't and this is often useful to address misunderstandings about how coaching fits with performance management. Engaging with those willing to participate is a good starting point to begin to change a culture and recognise that the process will be slow. It was interesting to read how Olivia is focused on her own professional growth by exploring adult learning theory and what it means to be both a mentor and a coach in different roles.

Encounter: coaching for attunement and advocacy

Cathy Gunning has been interested in coaching since she was a headteacher and using insights from training she implemented a distributed leadership and coaching approach. She is now a freelance education adviser, teacher, coach–mentor, with specialisms in early years and foundation stage (EYFS) and looked after and adopted children. Cathy writes:

Leadership and coaching

As a leader I was struck by the words of Margaret Wheatley's *Leadership in an Age of Complexity: From Hero to Host*. I realised we can't lead alone and together we can build each other up for greatness. My core purpose as a coach is to enable leaders and teachers to feel encouraged, more confident and empowered in their roles overseeing and delivering the EYFS. Particularly in these turbulent tough times, teachers of young vulnerable children have to be great advocates and well-attuned individuals with professional and personal confidence. I think it is important that we build teachers and leaders up, to raise up the next generation. Because every child does matter.

Developing as a coach

I undertook the postgraduate certification (PGCert) in coaching and mentoring for education practitioners at Leeds Beckett University.

This lifted me onto a new path of a 'coaching way of being' following redundancy after lockdown. I now use my coaching and mentoring as a teacher specialising in early years and birth to seven. I interweave my lived experience as a therapeutic parent with my professional experiences and primarily work to support, enable and inspire an attuned coaching way of being.

As a freelancer I coach-mentor anyone who invites me through various commissioned and partnership roles. Currently I am coaching teachers and leaders in the EYFS and in primary and nursery schools and settings across a diverse sector. As a coach–mentor I focus on building trust and relationships. I draw on Kline's thinking environment components and an attuned way of being which focuses on the coachee/mentee co-constructing their journey or co-creating their possibilities (chapters 2 and 13). Coaching gives them space, time to talk and a guarantee of being listened to. There are times when I advise, make suggestions and model, and these help to deepen pedagogical thinking.

Impacts and challenges of coaching in the EYFS sector

The key observable impacts of my coaching work, corroborated by feedback and evaluation, include the growth in confidence experienced by coachees. It also enables them to develop better EYFS pedagogy and more attuned practice. Attuned practice means that practitioners include and accept (and love) every child as uniquely themselves. Coaching also supports teachers and leaders in having a voice and being an advocate for children and young people for regulatory bodies and external agencies.

However, the contexts within which I coach are challenging. The leaders and teachers I work with show such grit, resilience and brilliance despite their circumstances. I am grateful to know them and partner with them. There are weekly pressures of teaching and leading, and added realities related to staff absence and shortages, stress, redundancy, budget cuts and EYFS reforms. These negatively impact on consistency and on relationships and the capacity for team building and growth. As a responsive and attuned coach–mentor I have to work with these challenges: coachees' aims and circumstances change, which means that coaching is always emergent and ever-evolving. Sometimes it's just as simple as surviving, turning up and knowing all children are safe.

Other times there are breakthroughs in powerful thinking spaces where transformation is evident.

Reflections

Cathy's coaching work centres children and her purpose is to empower teachers and leaders to do their best work for the children in their care. As an early years practitioner and advocate, we recognise Cathy's passion for holistic pedagogical approaches and how she utilises coaching to nurture and enhance learning opportunities. We also appreciate that Cathy doesn't shy away from pointing out the challenges and pressures that educators face, such as staff absence and shortages, stress, budget cuts, redundancy and reforms. Effective coaching is intertwined with the realities of the coachee and must be 'emergent and ever-evolving'.

Encounter: executive and leadership coaching

Catriona Mangham works as a coach for Multi-Academy Trusts (MAT) in England, coaching executive leaders across primary, special and secondary schools. She also coaches individual clients in other industries or regarding personal coaching needs. Catriona holds an Institute ILM L7 Executive Leadership coaching qualification. Catriona writes:

My role as a coach

I am an executive leadership coach in education, supporting leaders to be more strategic, and I also provide professional support through both personal and careers coaching. My coaching work began as part of my role as a school principal before moving to being director of strategy for a MAT, where I developed a coaching strategy. I also run my own coaching company which supports education leaders and creative leaders as well as individuals on personal coaching.

How I have developed coaching to support MAT leaders

In my MAT, leaders at all levels have access to coaching on request. All leaders who work at principal level and above have coaching as a right. Two of the schools in the MAT are developing coaching at all levels. I also work with another MAT coaching their leaders who request it. All coachees complete a pre-coaching questionnaire to explore their readiness for coaching and a post-coaching questionnaire to reflect on its impact.

I am a 'transformational' coach and I use SPACE (social context, physiology, actions, cognitions, emotions) and adapt this according to the circumstances. I use visualisation and storytelling within my work. I particularly work with the work of Professor Paul Brown around neuropsychology and coaching. I have matured as a coach over time. My approach was formulaic at the start, keeping to models and key questions. Over time I have allowed the coaching conversations to flow and the client to lead me. I listen very well and will go back to early comments and aspects of their conversation. The more experience I have, the more I allow the session to evolve rather than try to shape it.

Challenges and impacts of this type of coaching

Occasionally coachees think that they are being coached because they are failing (there then needs to be some coaching around self-perception!). I have to be clear with institutions that as their leaders are in a coaching client relationship with me all conversations are confidential. The biggest challenge is managing the boundary between coaching and therapy. Many clients will have barriers to moving forward due to behaviours that come from past trauma. I am trauma informed so have to be careful not to step into therapy. The lines are sometimes blurred for a coach.

It is difficult to isolate coaching in terms of impact as there are so many variables at play but individual feedback from the leaders I coach is very strong in terms of their own confidence in leadership. This relates to institutional impact as leaders feel empowered and able to think strategically and to challenge themselves and others.

Reflections

In this case study, Catriona's credibility as a school principal before becoming a director of strategy is worth noting, as is her reflection that her reliance on coaching tools lessened over time. It is evident that Catriona benefits from experience and training in other spaces, such as trauma-informed therapy, and how this is relevant as she navigates her coaching stance.

Chapter 10 Coaching as a way of enabling and empowering others

Encounter: a coaching approach to leadership

Victoria Carr is the headteacher of a primary school in Cheshire, England, and is also a reservist in the British Army. This is a unique combination and has allowed her to develop valuable insights. Victoria writes:

How I have developed as a coach and how it was developed and received in school

In both the army and school contexts my coaching role is the same and involves developing junior members of staff and supporting a learning environment. As a coach and validated leader with specific roles I lead by example through creating a culture of coaching and developmental conversation.

I now know that coaching has always been my approach but, as a result of being asked to lead on a master's module on school leadership, I realised that what I was doing was classed as coaching. I chose to learn about the range of coaching styles, including the GROW (goal, reality, options, will) model, many elements of which I was naturally using before implementing a number of them more deliberately to find the one that suited me best. Now I operate a more holistic, intuitive and mature approach that transcends any model. Over the years I have become more confident and competent and no longer need the handrail of a model, rather I implement a coaching style across many domains in my role to best effect.

Time is always a barrier as there is never enough of it! When I arrived at my current school, the staff were in crisis and had been for a prolonged period during which they had not enjoyed consistent leadership. This presented issues as there was a lack of trust initially about my style of doing things. In time, and with the consistency required, I was able to demonstrate my commitment to coaching and its positive outcomes and this was hugely beneficial to the overall wellbeing of staff as well as their professional growth. The school culture means that we have a range of coaching methodologies from ad hoc sessions where we explore decision-making (both before and after an event takes place) to explore learning at point of need for all staff, to more formalised coaching sessions which are built around a specific point (such as leadership or curriculum delivery).

Impacts of coaching

Individuals feel empowered to both make and take decisions and learn from their outcomes (both negative and positive ones). This gives staff members the agency and licence to be thoughtfully creative and fearless in their decision-making and execution of plans and this means we have a dynamic and forward-leaning school. As an organisation the benefits are that we are not complacent, we are all constantly learning in a safe and supportive environment, nobody feels limited to one 'right' answer and we are emboldened to build on the ideas of others to best effect for all stakeholders.

Reflections

There is a genuine feeling of calm, measured confidence in Victoria's account. She describes coaching as always having been her approach so she is able to build on this way of being to develop further competency and confidence in her coaching skills and process. Like many experienced coaches, Victoria started by using coaching models but now works more intuitively as her coaching has matured. Her sense of purpose instils trust from teaching staff, and it feels likely that this transmits to the wider learning community. It strikes us that Victoria's diverse experiences provide her with a purposeful way of being and purposeful way of leading.

Encounter: creating a safe space through coaching

Jasmine Miller has a coaching role across multiple settings. She is a qualified and accredited coach with Chester University and the International Coaching Federation (ICF) and has recently certified as a coaching supervisor. Jasmine writes:

Why I coach

My interest in coaching was first stimulated when I was principal in a 5–19 special day and residential school. I was interested in further professional development and a former colleague had shared a coaching qualification course that they had been through which sounded interesting and a good opportunity to further understand myself as a leader. As a coach the central purpose is to create a safe space where people feel listened to, without interruption, and can explore ideas/areas/concepts that they wish to think about and find a way forward with.

Developing as a coach

When I qualified as a coach, I went through the Practical Barefoot Programme alongside the Chester University qualification for personal and business coaching. The course brought together individuals from a wide variety of backgrounds and industry, which I found really refreshing and insightful. The course was very practical and, as we learned about different models, approaches and research, we used triads for practice and I had volunteer clients back in my school. I was also keen to try things I had learned to support school culture. Meetings were a starting point and I utilised Nancy Kline's meeting structure to support the change. Everyone in the meeting was reassured that they would all be given time to speak and people were not to be interrupted when they were speaking. Agendas were prepared with questions to think about ahead of meetings, and each meeting would finish by each person sharing one thing they were grateful for about the colleague sitting beside them. It took a few weeks for the reminders about interruptions to stop and a noticeable change in the way our meetings produced outcomes and resolutions as opposed to additional lists of things to do!

My coaching approach has developed over time as I have become fully comfortable with being in the moment and staying with the 'not knowing' and remaining curious. As a teacher, this was probably my biggest learning curve as a coach. Realising that I didn't need to have or provide all the answers.

My current coaching

My current coaching maps onto my past and present professional roles and relationships. I use different frameworks and models in my coaching, including Nancy Kline's principles related to 'thinking environments' (chapters 2 and 13), Growth Coaching International's GROWTH framework (chapter 2) and Jim Knight's guidance on 'Better conversations'. I have used different hot-seating frameworks for team and group coaching. In coaching supervision I have found the 'seven-eyed' model of supervision useful. There can be different challenges depending on the context. One such challenge is when other leaders within a setting prioritise a performative culture over a coaching culture. This has a direct impact on levels of trust and relationships within an organisation and, in my belief, the success of coaching.

I coach the director of a centre for children with special needs in China who is also studying an online inclusive education course. Our coaching relationship started over 10 years ago, when I first connected with the centre in China when I was the principal of a school in Scotland, and continued when I moved from a principal to founder and director of my own coaching business. The outcomes of this coaching relate to clarity and application of my coachee's study into practice. The coaching conversations support the inclusive outcomes for the nursery students and the development of staff (individual and institutional level).

I now have a leadership role in a college in the UAE and provide coaching to the staff that request it. They use coaching to work through a particular dilemma that they are facing or to focus on an area related to teaching and learning. The coaching approach is as part of my leadership style and I engage in lots of different conversations internally and externally. Remaining curious and non-judgemental is key within the conversations so that I can understand the different cultural context that I am in here and how to best benefit our students from this community. The coaching outcomes relate to staff professional development. Staff have regular 1:1 meetings where there is an opportunity to hear back about progress made in particular areas individuals have focused on. At present coaching is not used across the whole leadership team so it is difficult to get an understanding of impact at institutional level.

I am also an associate for a socially driven coaching and training provider and work with individuals within the Scottish Government who can seek out 1:1 coaching for their own wellbeing and am a research supervisor for the MSc in applied positive psychology and coaching psychology (MAPPCP) course at the University of East London.

Reflections

Jasmine approaches coaching from a position of curiosity using a blend of coaching approaches to best serve her learners. We see that values such as respect, trust and humility shape the purposeful coaching approach that Jasmine adopts in her leadership roles. It also strikes us that Jasmine views the evolving field of positive psychology as an important influence in the future developments of coaching philosophy and practice.

Encounter: coaching to promote agency, meaning and purpose

Adam Kohlbeck is a deputy headteacher of Birkbeck Primary School, in England, and co-founder of EduPulse. In his leadership role Adam has been working to develop approaches which help to enable and empower others as coaches and teachers. Adam writes:

How and why coaching was developed

In recent years I have worked to create a model of coaching that encourages coaches to use their coaching sessions to promote agency in their coachees. I am motivated to do this because I am aware that in England we have one of the youngest teaching workforces in the developed world (OECD, 2023). It is not just the profile of class teachers which is becoming less experienced. Those with responsibility for developing others are also becoming less experienced as the continual exodus of experienced teachers from the profession takes hold.

I believe that there is value in considering this problem from two viewpoints. First, the questions of why teachers keep leaving and how we can keep them in the profession. Second, the concern about how we can support those responsible for developing others with a framework for using coaching to support thinking. Happily, I believe there is a close relationship between the two and so they could be simultaneously addressed. As a leader I adhere to the proposition that job satisfaction and retention are supported by working with meaning and purpose, and agency is one key factor in establishing agency and purpose.

My current coaching

The work I do to support other coaches sits within my remit as professional development (PD) lead in school. Coaching is based on a framework for considering teaching purpose in any given moment of a lesson or teaching sequence. Coaches and teachers meet first to discuss the area the teacher would like to work on and then refine this down to a proposed goal. This follows a conversation that the teacher has already had with me, as the PD lead, during which I support their reflection on their teaching and some initial thinking about where they would like to work. This means that they go into that first session with their coach in control of the conversation.

After the coach and teacher meet, a form of evidence about the teacher's practice is collected. This can be through observation or shared or staggered watching of video (the teacher chooses). The coach's questions focus on the desired purpose of a particular moment within the teaching. The idea is to help the teacher consider their purpose first so that they are then able to identify the different options, or strategies, open to them to enact that purpose. The coach's role is to encourage the teacher to believe in their choice by facilitating continual conversational interaction between purpose and strategy. The coaching has five non-sequential components: secure attention, utilise memory, communicate meaning, ensure thinking and enable practice.

Emerging evidence of the impact of this approach is positive. It seems that coaches feel they have a framework to support their coaching while teachers feel that the framework positions them firmly as decision-makers. While scaffolding and agency are often presented as paradoxical in the field of coaching, I believe that this paradox can be reconciled and I remain fascinated by the long-term impact of our initiative.

Reflections

It is powerful to read about Adam's process in developing a coaching framework that is anchored in teaching purpose and fosters agency in the coachees who work in a system with significant retention and recruitment challenges. As he rightly notes, it is not only class teachers who are less experienced but also those in leadership and professional learning roles. For Adam, coaching offers an important framework to support thinking around meaning and purpose which hopefully will lead to long-term benefits like job satisfaction and even staff retention.

Chapter 10 endnotes

Final thoughts

An interesting common feature of these encounters, which explore how coaching has been used to enable and empower others, are the connections made between the choices underpinning, and engagement in, coaching and the wider contexts. As the opening quote suggests, this allows coaches and coachees to engage 'with broader themes affecting all lives today' (Gallacher, 2022, p. 110). This implies that the purpose of coaching is not simply unilateral. In these encounters coaching is not seen solely as a means to provide a crutch or a route map for the individual to support their journey, but instead as an opportunity to engage reflectively, knowingly and with purpose with the complex landscapes within which the journey takes place, helping to reshape not just the coachee but their context as well. This is equally important for adults and young people as they learn to become agentic in their professional or personal communities.

Talking point

What do the words 'enable' and 'empower' mean to you? Outside of coaching, what or who has made the most difference in empowering or enabling you? What might you learn from this reflection that could influence the coaching you offer or support in the future?

Ideas for action

As you coach, consider making anonymised notes of the themes that emerge which act as barriers or create concerns for your coachees. Which of these are systemic or institutional rather than particular to the coachee? As you recognise themes try to be proactive in deepening your own understanding of the issues, by identifying opportunities to learn from reading, the media or networks. In doing so you may become more confident to ask nuanced questions and to contribute to discussions and decisions where you have influence outside of the coaching role.

Chapter 11
Coaching as a way of shaping culture

The nature of the non-linear dynamics of an open living system fits with emergent practice rather than best or good practice. [...] Emergent practice is all about adaptation and experimentation. [...] Emergent practice allows for the ongoing search for the best 'fit' to a problem so the 'form' is always assessed based on its ability to serve the higher purpose of the organization.

Kathleen E. Allen (2019, p. 72)

As coaching evolves over time in education settings it can become woven into the context and become a significant component of the culture. This can occur through strategic planning and actions, where advocates for coaching seek multiple opportunities for it to impact positively in the setting. There are roles for both leaders and participants in sustaining these efforts to promote, develop and evaluate coaching with, and for, purpose.

Coaching can also shape culture less deliberately and more organically. For example, there may be a range of formal and informal coaching occurring, but not under the umbrella of a specific priority or overseen by a particular leader. Some of the coaching may be being accessed independently from the school. However, with time such coaching activity may have a positive legacy and perhaps become more visible to decision-makers in the setting who start to join dots or to appreciate and aim not to disturb the emerging culture.

In this chapter we encounter education settings in which coaching is shaping culture. These include small-scale approaches adopted across a whole context making a tangible difference to the ways the school community functions. We also encounter case studies of multi-layered coaching activity, usually representative of engagement with, and the evolution of, coaching over sustained periods. In several of these case studies the role of coaching in supporting wellbeing is also evident. There is a sense of schools as communities in which both adults and young people work and learn, where achievement is underpinned by relational support, where students are seen as contributors and where the skills and potential of teachers, leaders and non-teaching staff are recognised as equally vital in the life of the organisations. These encounters illustrate how coaching shapes these cultures.

Following each encounter we offer our reflections.

Encounter: passing it on, from being coached to embedding coaching

Dan Ford works at an independent day school in Glasgow, UK, as a teacher of geography. He is a former head of department and head of house who is an accredited coach with the European Mentoring and Coaching Council (EMCC), having completed a training course with Growth Coaching International (GCI). He also has professional recognition for coaching in Scotland with the General Teaching Council for Scotland. Dan has led the development of coaching at the school in conjunction with the school leadership team (SLT). Dan writes:

How and why I have developed coaching

I was working as a head of house when I started my coaching journey. I wanted to support my students and colleagues more effectively but also develop my own leadership and communication skills. I originally started to learn about coaching as I was looking for another way to support my students. Having been coached I understood the benefits of coaching and its potential in schools. As I learned more, I wanted to improve the quality of the communication across the school – the way staff work with each other, pupils and parents. I realised coaching could be the way to do this. Over time I have become more interested in staff development and how colleagues can develop their classroom teaching and leadership skills. Coaching has developed in my context over six years and I have been fortunate to be well supported by the school's rector (principal), who is also enthusiastic about the benefits coaching can bring to education. The rector and his leadership team have helped create a forward-thinking and progressive school where staff are allowed to implement new ideas and have the freedom to do it.

The training I have had with GCI has allowed me to work with and meet inspirational people like Professor Christian van Nieuwerburgh. As a result I introduced the GROWTH model to the school (Campbell, 2016b). This is an easy-to-remember and flexible model with a 'solutions-focused' approach to coaching conversations. This means coaching (in the right hands) is generally a positive experience for all involved. The GCI training teaches the coach to focus on the future and 'what is working' rather than 'what is not' and aims to utilise people's strengths while all the while keeping the coachee at the centre of the conversation. For me, coaching people is a real privilege as I can help people to develop their ideas and interests and gain clarity about how they can move forward.

Coaching for colleagues

I work in conjunction with SLT to develop coaching within the school. Throughout we have exchanged ideas, but I have always been given the freedom to get on with things without being micromanaged. An example of change is that our professional review and development (PRD) system now uses a coaching approach rather than an appraisal-based system. As part of the PRD all teaching staff are coached if they feel comfortable to do so. Middle leaders and SLT have received training in a coaching approach for the purpose of managing these conversations. Staff choose who they want to be their designated coach for the forthcoming academic year and who they want to discuss their personal professional development. The coach then meets with the coachee formally twice in the year (at the start and end of the year) and informally whenever they wish. As a result, staff have greater autonomy, agency and more support. It has enabled a great deal of innovation and development as well as giving SLT the knowledge of where to target resources. Staff can choose one target or more to work on as long as one of those is related to the school development plan in some way. This change has been well received by staff and a more thorough evaluation is planned, but as one deputy head has commented:

> *With staff, it has led to conversations with more understanding about what role each party plays and what they are hoping to achieve; it also develops capacity in staff to think deeply about the issues they face at work or areas that they wish to develop and has led to a surge in new developments, initiatives or highly specific personal targets. Ultimately it has changed the way people think, and the way the model has been adopted across a range of school areas means that this type of thinking is highly likely to be sustained and to become the norm over time.*

Working alongside the school's teaching and learning group, I also run projects using coaching to develop teaching. This enables staff to be self-reflective, share thoughts and ideas, and engage in professional learning with each other. We drew on the 'unseen observation' programme (O'Leary, 2022) and have been supported by Joanne Miles to facilitate this change. Feedback from those who participated in the pilot was encouraging, with colleagues describing the experience as 'essential', 'motivating', 'thought-provoking' and 'creative'. From there I set up the 'unseen leadership' programme, which has been adopted by SLT due to its self-reflective nature and the dedicated time it gives them to enhance their own leadership while working on an important school-related target of their own.

I also provide individual coaching sessions to colleagues if there is no conflict of interest. I have coached teachers at all levels on several topics, including new members of staff taking on positions of responsibility, applying for new posts within school, career coaching and leading new projects/initiatives within school, among other things.

Student peer coaching

I run a peer-coaching programme which involves sixth form (S6) students supporting their younger peers. Here the aim is to support those students who are struggling academically with a focus on those in exam years. Pupils cannot take part without parental approval and the peer coaches are trained in coaching skills, the GROWTH model and relevant child protection information. Each pupil supported meets weekly with their S6 peer coach and fortnightly with a member of teaching staff who also employ a coaching approach to help the students. Staff volunteer to give up their time in this way and it is another invaluable layer of safeguarding as well as academic support. The idea for using peer coaching came from reading a series of research articles including, Passmore and Brown (2009), Browne et al. (2012) and van Nieuwerburgh and Tong (2013).

Peer coaching has proved to be a successful intervention to support younger pupils in exam years, which can be hard to navigate. In the first year of the programme, 2018–19, there were 13 candidates being coached by members of S6 and out of 52 exam entries 48 of those were at grades A–C. Since then the peer-coaching programme has grown and not all students take to it, with some withdrawing from the programme altogether, but they are the minority, and the key is trying to make sure it is the right intervention for them. Positively, both coaches and coachees have reported seeing benefits from the experience. One head of department wrote about the programme:

I witnessed one of our S6 peer coaches coach their young charge to a small, yet no doubt, important goal. The beginnings to access self-actualisation at this stage can only be empowering not only to themselves but importantly to those they come into contact with. After all, is this not the point of teaching and learning?

Feedback from some pupils who have been coached includes:

I now understand how to effectively tackle revision.

I feel [learning] isn't as hard as I used to think it was.

I was more positive about my learning and ability.

He allowed me to set small goals every week, that made a big impact, as it is easier to achieve these.

Some comments from the peer coaches include:

[Coaching] allowed me to understand how different people approach the same thing in different ways and made me more open to trying different approaches.

I have developed my patience and ability to work with others from younger year groups and those with a different mindset and varying levels of motivation.

What motivates me?

I believe the training I have had in coaching has changed the way I teach in the classroom: I listen more effectively, I ask better questions to facilitate discussions with the pupils and I notice more about the students and how they are. I think my experience of coaching has helped me to develop better relationships with students and consequently there is a greater chance of learning being successful and this is empowering for me and hopefully the students.

The more I coach, the more I realise that the benefits of a coaching approach allow people to reflect and think about how they can resolve their own challenges and develop ideas in a non-judgemental space. I have enjoyed working with people in this context and I am always impressed with how people can find solutions to things they are seemingly unclear about at first. Over time I decided that I wanted to become a qualified coach and set up a coaching service for staff as a positive way to support them. Education can be a challenging and fast-paced environment, so coaching my colleagues allows me to help people to take a step back, gain clarity, reflect on things and as a result they are often more focused, clearer and motivated to continue with their work. I believe coaching is valuable to teachers at all levels as they need time to think and explore their ideas in a safe space without external pressures distracting them. Personally, I find it interesting, rewarding and a real privilege to be able to listen to people working in so many different parts of the school, with different aims, but for the primary objective of making school a better place for our learners.

Throughout, I have tried to establish coaching within the school in a way that has been research led, so it is more credible, informed, tried and tested. Learning more and having the freedom to use coaching to try to improve education for staff and pupils have been extremely rewarding and I hope to take things further by developing a coaching culture at the school, so coaching is the vehicle for the way we do things.

Acknowledging the challenges of change

It is always a challenge to manage my normal teaching commitments with my coaching work and home life. As is the case in education there is always a lot to do! Things don't always go to plan and don't always work as schools are complex, busy places with a lot of moving parts to them.

I've also learned to recognise that coaching is my passion, but it is not always a priority for everyone else and the challenge of keeping it relevant, current, without it becoming 'too much' has been something I have had to keep in mind. I have tried to make sure coaching is used because it is the right tool for the job, planned, researched and strategically implemented, otherwise it risks becoming another 'white elephant' in education. Similarly, because of my other commitments some believe progress with coaching has been slow, but that has benefits, too, as I would rather let things develop in a planned way rather than rush and get it wrong. The peer-coaching programme has supported more pupils this year than ever before, but in such a busy environment and with more demands on staff and pupils it can be hard to find enough people who can give up time effectively.

Importantly, I need to be mindful when coaching colleagues that I have a dual role in the school. I need to be clear about this distinction to maintain the trust of my colleagues and, as discussed earlier, I make sure there are no conflicts of interest and what I do is ethically correct. As a result I am very clear about what I will and will not coach people on, and as an accredited coach with the European Mentoring and Coaching Council (EMCC) I regularly undertake supervision and continual professional development, which is extremely useful at helping me develop and stay on top of things. I can confidently say that coaching has changed the way I teach, and work with colleagues, and one day I would like to use coaching more to serve those in education. I hope to work with SLT so that coaching develops in such a way that it is embedded in the fabric of the school. There is a lot to do, but it is an exciting start!

Reflections

Dan notes the challenge of managing his own enthusiasm and capacity to commit to creating change through coaching with the realities of wider school life and priorities. His advocacy is powerful and his recognition that urgency is less important than creating sustainable change is essential. Dan advocates for coaching to be research led, to ensure its credibility. The coaching is invitational and develops in spaces where it is most useful and needed. As a classroom teacher, Dan highlights how coaching has improved his classroom practice and relationship with colleagues, but he also notes some of the tensions that exist in this 'dual role' and credits the value of being an accredited coach in guiding his ethical practice.

Encounter: coaching for student and staff wellbeing

Laura Anthony is learning manager: coaching, counselling and mentoring at a girls' secondary school (11–16-year-olds) which, combined with a co-educational sixth form (16–18-year-olds) and a primary school forms Herts and Essex Multi-Academy Trust. Coaching is used to provide early intervention to improve and consolidate individual wellbeing within the school, with an initial focus on student wellbeing and an extension into becoming a core strand of the staff wellbeing offer. Laura writes:

Developing a coaching approach

We have been a coaching school now for a decade and, prior to this, our student support was very much around mentoring. The need for an alternative came about when I had been working with a bright Year 11 student (final year of secondary school) with incredibly difficult home circumstances, who I mentored and seemed to spoon-feed throughout that year. We were thrilled when her results were good enough to get her into our sixth form, but without the close support she had received lower down the school, she crashed out of full-time education within three weeks, unable to cope with the transition. It was a watershed moment for me as I realised that I had failed to provide her with the tools and understanding to become resilient and be able to independently navigate any difficulties in her life. So I looked around to see what else was available and by chance I found a local school that was coaching. They allowed me to train as their first external trainee and then I came back to our school suggesting that this was the only way forward if we were to offer our students a worthwhile intervention. A number of us trained as coaches and pre-Covid, we regularly ran coach training courses for staff here and from other local schools.

Once we became immersed in coaching, there were so many aspects that I hadn't anticipated, such as the 'unseen' value of staff-to-staff coaching. Having a non-teaching member of staff coach a teacher or senior leader (or the other way around) forged much deeper and more meaningful relationships that, once the coaching was over, remained rooted. This manifested as a real appreciation of each other and thereby encouraged a much more unified staff body – we were spending time with, and getting to know well, colleagues who we normally probably wouldn't even come across in the school day. I was equally taken by the flexibility of coaching: that a passing conversation could often be enough to stimulate new thinking and move individuals forward and that anyone with a basic understanding could have the power to facilitate change.

Influences on our coaching approach

Our original coaching training framework was the GROW model (goal, reality, options, will) and this served as the basis of the coaching work we undertook and trained others in. Our coaching work was also underpinned by research undertaken for a master's degree. This enabled us to complement the work we were doing on the ground with research-based learning that supported how we were developing our practice. The final year was an action case study that focused on our 'inside-out' coaching work and its outcomes. In essence this is an understanding of how we work as human beings, that individual thought creates our experience of the world.

Recognising the impacts of coaching

Creating coaching capacity does have challenges, particularly in creating the time needed when the school day is already very full, and in securing the finances to create staff capacity and enable training. Despite this we are confident of its value and the cumulative effect over many years.

When we developed the 'inside-out' coaching, we invited all our Year 11 students to a session where we served tea and biscuits and they could learn more about it. We ended up with a core group of 15 or so students and spent the following weeks and months talking to them and just pointing towards how our thinking makes our experience of life. What was fascinating is that the more challenging students got it really quickly and, for some, it became transformative beyond school, supporting them in their relationships with family and peers. As we looked back at the end of that academic year, very unusually we had not had to make specific arrangements for any students for their exams (for example, being in a smaller room or sitting by the door). The whole year group appeared calmer as we approached the summer exams, a fact that other colleagues commented on, and target grades in our little group were met and sometimes exceeded. It felt very much like the ripples in a pond when a stone is thrown in. The individual changes had happened organically and we could only conclude that as the feeling in the year group was so different to previous years, our students had shared with their friends what they had seen themselves about this understanding and this had helped to lighten the stress and anxiety more generally. The 'inside-out' coaching understanding continues to develop and is now being utilised in our local National Health Service (NHS) young people's social prescription service.

Now students and staff are able to self-refer for coaching and students can be also advised of the offer by staff they are in contact with, as appropriate. In essence, coaching has helped us survive what were becoming very real issues around wellbeing and mental health, which Covid then exacerbated further. Pre-Covid we were already experiencing high levels of stress and anxiety, while at the same time external support was diminishing. Having an effective early intervention that our coaching culture and ethos in school have provided has become key in effectively building and maintaining wellbeing and reducing the number of students needing referrals to be made. That is not to say that they are not being made; we are in a changed landscape post-Covid with very high levels of complexity, stress and anxiety, but coaching enables us in many instances to step in early and help students get back on track before the issues get too big. We know that this is a positive contribution to individual wellbeing from their ability to access their education/life thereafter and the door remains open to them to re-engage whenever it is needed. On an institutional level, coaching is scaffolding the wider need for support through, for example, the use of coaching conversations to support the way we interact and work together across the board, with all our stakeholders within our school.

Reflections

Laura demonstrates that coaching conversations can have significant social and emotional benefits for students in this highly supportive setting. Having the time to be heard seems so valuable for learners and the positive 'ripple' effect is far-reaching. A culture of purposeful coaching is equipping students with a repertoire of life skills to draw upon. Student wellbeing along with academic achievement is at the heart of coaching in the setting and it was interesting to read about the expected benefits Laura noted that extended into deeper connections and relationships among staff. Laura describes a watershed moment that brought her to coaching, illustrating that critical incidents that don't go as we expected in the moment can lead to growth. It is heartening to see how the school's bespoke 'inside-out' coaching continues to develop beyond the school and into the local NHS.

Encounter: challenging the status quo through embedding coaching as a national qualifications provider

Until recently, Catherine St. Ville was the director of improvement at LLSE, which is a designated provider of the Department for Education National Professional Qualifications (NPQ), with the strapline 'Leadership Learning Securing Excellence'. Her role was to research and determine the coaching approach, set expectations and develop strategy for the way the company works to support school leaders. She is also an executive coach and a former middle and senior leader in schools. LLSE leads the work of delivery partners across over 90 local authorities in England and abroad, with international participants from over 30 countries and a main hub in Dubai. As growth since 2021 has been rapid, LLSE has adopted an intentionally scalable coaching approach to continuous improvement. Catherine explores how a holistic coaching approach supports large-scale partnerships as well as the programme participants. Catherine writes:

How and why LLSE use a coaching approach

The aim of our coaching approach is to nurture agency and self-determination and provide high levels of bespoke support and challenge so that those we work with can be the best they can be. We also want our partners to have confidence to collaborate with LLSE in the true sense of the word to provide the best for the schools, organisations, stakeholders and students they serve. We do this to build capacity, championing a self-sustaining system. Our NPQ partner leads are being coached and the NPQ participants are being coached. By using a coaching approach to facilitating professional development, the NPQ participants are put at the centre of their learning experience and empowered to be deep thinkers, through reflexive reflection, making their learning relevant and portable to their own contexts. The curriculum structure encourages and supports this, the facilitators know how to create the climate and maintain an open, challenging and enabling environment, and the coaches know how to listen, ask probing and insightful questions, helping the participants to form new habits that lead to sustainable change. The coaching approach used in our partnership working means that every partner believes they have a voice and is able to excel within their own contexts.

Leaders at LLSE believe in consistency of opportunity and outcome, rather than uniformity. Partners are consistently encouraged to become proactive and self-determined, within the expectations of their contracts. The coaching approach to continuous improvement is transforming our partners' experience and understanding of approaches to quality review and improvement. The well-defined and articulated expectations provide the foundations on which the partners can build. These are beyond compliance and grounded in recent and corroborated research into the many topics related to adult professional development. Partners have easy access to a plethora of real-time information and data, the acknowledgment that they are the absolute experts in their own contexts, and an expectation that they are best placed to evaluate their provision and execute improvements to the quality of professional development and their leadership thereof.

Influences on the coaching approach

The coaching approach is based on the premise that a coach's role is to listen actively and attentively for meaning, be emotionally intelligent and read body language, ask probing and insightful questions, and to be a thinking partner. Although we share the GROW model with the programme coaches, we base our professional learning model around the Boyatzis' process of self-directed learning, which connects coaches to all aspects of the model from visioning and supporting accurate self-evaluation to honing the learning agenda and encouraging reflexivity throughout the reflection processes. We do not believe that there is a need to dictate a single rigid approach for the coaching of particular groups of either participants or delivery partner team stakeholders. We believe and expect ourselves and those who work with us to be deep thinkers and to use their expertise and our expectations to inform their thinking. The NPQ coaches are provided with a briefing session and additional professional learning opportunities, as well as regular communities of practice discussions and newsletters.

Challenges and impacts of coaching

It is not easy to hold true to the principles of coaching as a newly and rapidly expanding organisation. We have high expectations of partners that exceed compliance and use a wide research base to inform the approach to continuous improvement which might be viewed as overly ambitious. However, the coaching approach bolsters sustainability across the partnerships, meaning that although support may be intense at the start, the scaffolding can gradually be removed as time progresses.

The outcomes have been numerous and varied. Every delivery partner has a robust and accurate self-evaluation of their NPQ provision, which considers the seven questions for continuous improvement. These relate to the impact of the active professional development ingredients and the leadership of the NPQs. The questions ask the extent to which these elements improve the leadership development for the participants, rather than merely asking if a series of processes are occurring. Participant feedback provides the first reference point, where hypotheses are created for further investigation. Participants' work, summative assessment outcomes, synchronous session evaluations, conversations with participants, facilitators, coaches and school leaders, and retention rates all add to the wide evidence base. As a result of the coaching-style quality review meetings that I hold following the receipt of the self-evaluation, delivery partners are empowered to share effective practice and identify areas for improvement, often enacting and having evidence of the impact of these improvements before we meet. The whole system is very agile and changes can be made at speed. Every delivery partner is able to bring the impact of their distinctiveness to various forums to share them with other delivery partners and more widely. They often say that this feels like a genuine partnership and they feel valued, listened to, and can take charge of the quality of professional development in their contexts.

Reflections

From Catherine's contribution we can see the complexity in building a self-sustaining system with coaching at its core. We appreciate the challenges faced by a provider facilitating national professional qualifications. There is no impression of compliance and fidelity limiting the organisation's agile coaching approach. It strikes us that 'reflection' and 'reflexivity' are pivotal to developing future leaders of learning in an uncertain environment. A key element in this work is well-defined and articulated expectations that aim to transform the delivery partner's experience and understanding of approaches to quality review and improvement. There are many links that can be made to performance management in schools.

Encounter: achieving a coaching approach across a multi-academy trust

Victoria Whiting is a qualified coach who has worked with colleagues at Achievement Through Collaboration Trust, a multi-academy trust (MAT) based in the North West of England, to develop coaching approaches. The coaching takes place in various guises across all four primary and secondary schools within the MAT. Three of the schools within the trust are in challenging contexts located in Blackburn and Blackpool with significant levels of economic deprivation and the associated challenges. Victoria writes:

Why I became a coach

I believe in the importance of empowerment and wanted to break out of the oppressive nature of hierarchy within the education sector. This is what prompted me to begin my coaching journey. I am one of a number of qualified coaches within the MAT and I provide training for staff in the organisation who wish to adopt a more 'coaching approach' to their leadership. I am also an instructional coach and support other coaches to design coaching cycles and deliberate practice sets.

How and why coaching has developed in the MAT

We use coaching for a number of key purposes and our focus areas have expanded over time. Everyone in the MAT is being coached in one form or another and schools are actively trying to adopt a coaching culture for both staff and students. Some of the MAT schools have specific timetables to accommodate coaching, while others are more ad hoc and responsive.

We started coaching at the executive leadership level of the trust, adopting executive coaching models. This was then extended to performance coaching across all leadership roles. We then focused on teachers' practice and pedagogy using deliberate practice and instructional coaching as regular features of our continuing professional learning and appraisal, including for early career teachers. We now also focus on student coaching to increase student confidence and resilience, using mental toughness coaching. To underpin our coaching we use Arbinger mindset models from the Arbinger Institute, such as 'meet to learn' and their '3A+ approach' alongside the GROW model as a basic premise for engagement in a coaching conversation. To succeed we have had to acknowledge and solve problems related to staff perception and reluctance and address the time and cost implications.

Having stuck with it over several years we now see greater collaboration between colleagues, an increase in wellbeing and efficacy, stronger relationships and increases in risk-taking and innovation. We have also experienced an increase in resilience from our students and an openness to engage in dialogue about performance and goal-setting. The growing interconnectedness and increasing consensus discourse around coaching are helping to build a place where staff and students feel safely challenged and consistently supported.

Reflections

Victoria is candid in her description of her purpose for engaging in coaching to dismantle oppressive hierarchies in education. Recognising the aim to develop a coaching culture across the trust, it is helpful to read that like other systems Victoria faced issues of staff perception and reluctance in relation to time and cost. It is heartening to hear that 'sticking with it' in the face of these challenges has led to tangible benefits that are being recognised.

Encounter: developing a whole-school coaching way of being through guided conversations

Rachel Tomlinson is the headteacher of Barrowford Primary School in Lancashire, England. While she does not describe herself as a coach, she thinks carefully about the types of conversations that she and her colleagues are having in school. Rachel writes:

Coaching conversations

I use and promote coaching-type conversations in school to ensure high-quality education for all in our setting. I love having 'problem-solving'-style conversations that explore themes deeply and I encourage everyone in our school context to do the same.

To do this we have developed what we call a LEARN framework and use it relatively informally but frequently.

LEARN stands for:

- Listen
- Explore
- Alternatives
- Reflect
- Next steps.

As we used LEARN to frame our professional conversations with each other, parents and partners, we also created a Scribblepad to capture these informal 'moments' of LEARNing. This means we ensure LEARN conversations are noted and valued. Colleagues are encouraged to keep their Scribblepad LEARN record, knowing that it may have value later to recall and refer to.

The LEARN framework supports professional development and focuses our minds on better teaching and learning outcomes. We also see it providing psychological safety for staff, parents and children to enable them to grow.

Reflections

The LEARN framework is used in Rachel's school for 'problem-solving'-style professional conversations. It is interesting to read how these conversations extend beyond educators and include all members of the school community. We were intrigued by the school's use of Scribblepad to ensure the conversations are not only noted and valued but contribute to future growth opportunities.

Encounter: coaching for personal growth and development across the school community

Laura Smith is the coaching lead and assistant headteacher at Merchant Taylors' School, an independent day school for boys aged 11–18, in London, UK. She has undertaken a range of coaching qualifications, having first been introduced to coaching at a national education event, and has worked with the headteacher to support the development of a coaching strategy for the school. Working closely with her colleague, Sally Hale, she is now responsible for running coaching courses for all new staff members, advanced courses for existing staff, introductory courses for parents, and organising coaching triads among staff as well as coaching staff. Laura states that the core purpose of coaching at the school is supporting the school community (whether pupils, teachers or parents) in personal growth and development. Developing coaching within the school has been a sustained and multi-layered process, and one which has faced challenges along the way. Laura writes:

Establishment of coaching in the school

I was introduced to coaching through Graydin's simple Heart-Head-Step model. This is the model that our coaching is largely based on, although I have incorporated elements from other coaching programmes over time. Our school's journey into coaching began in 2017, when a group of staff attended the Graydin coaching course and staff coaching trios were set up, with about 30 regular participants. The following year more staff volunteered to attend the course and some colleagues were trained by Graydin to run the courses 'in-house'. Over the first three years, over 100 members of staff attended the two-day foundational course. Initially, heads of house and other key stakeholders such as our head of careers, the SEND team, school counsellor and prep school leads were asked to attend the course. Next, heads of department were signed up. Subsequently the number of staff in coaching trios grew.

Alongside the training and trios, a new professional development review (PDR) system was developed by the pastoral deputy head, which was based around a series of coaching conversations with a final goal agreed by staff member and overseeing mentor. Coaching inset and more training for staff on how they might use coaching to improve their teaching skills was first introduced in 2018. At the same time we began to adopt coaching approaches with pupils. They were asked to use coaching tools such as a fulfilment wheel to reflect on their academic learning, and there was a series of off-timetable coaching workshops with pupils. In 2019 and 2020 this work was further embedded. We began to run an advanced coaching course for staff in-house and a pupil self-review and coaching booklet was introduced for use in tutor time.

After the pandemic, in 2022, staff were introduced to instructional coaching using WALKTHRUS. As part of our teaching and learning programme, all staff were paired up and asked to complete instructional coaching cycles to enhance their own teaching practice. We have just completed our third year of instructional coaching partnerships and this has been well received by staff.

In order to develop our vision of the whole school community benefiting from coaching, we also ran the first coaching course for parents back in 2021. We advertised to parents what we have been doing with coaching skills in school and invited them to come along to a three-week evening course, running for two hours per week, to learn more. We have now tailored the course to offer specific coaching strategies for building better communication with their children and this has been very well received.

Now all new teachers to the school attend a mandatory one-day coaching course and existing staff are invited to attend an advanced course. All staff are invited to form a triad with colleagues and are given protected coaching time on their timetables when they will not be called to meetings or required for cover lessons. Parents are invited to attend a three-session programme. Staff PDR meetings are conducted following a coaching model and staff (with few exceptions) set their own targets. Coaching booklets are used during tutor time with all pupils in the school and tutors are trained to have coaching conversations with tutees in timetabled self-reflection and coaching time each half term. Pupils can be referred for a programme of 1:1 coaching sessions once tutors and heads of house feel that they have run out of support strategies. Our Year 11 pupils are trained in coaching skills as part of their 'middle school leaders' programme and we have embedded three hours of coaching lessons into the Personal Social Health curriculum for Years 7 and 8. Next, from summer 2024, we are working on training Year 12 pupils to become peer coaches.

Addressing the challenges and misconceptions

By requiring staff to attend the course there were of course some who were resistant – the 'captives' as Graydin calls them. Quiet grumbles of 'Spare me another fad' and 'Where's the actual data that this is in any way effective?' could be heard in corners of the staff room. It doesn't take much for the cynics to unite when an initiative is imposed upon them and this was absolutely our experience. In fact, after the first year, there was quite a toxic undercurrent of dissent from some quarters. This was not helped by a strangely quasi-religious narrative that emerged separating the 'believers' and 'non-believers' and those who might be 'converted'. Fortunately, some of the central figures in this circle of cynicism were leaving the school that summer. Paired with the decision that all new staff to join the school would need to complete the course as part of their induction, the voices of dissent began to quieten. We decided to publicly dismiss the 'cultish' talk and clarify the key aims and direction of our coaching plans to create a more positive tone. Making it clear that coaching was here to stay was important; it allowed those who didn't enjoy the ride to either put up or… disembark.

One of the most challenging and enduring issues we have faced is staff misunderstanding – particularly at the outset. In the first couple of years comments such as:

> *I can't teach by asking pupils what they think the answers are. I need to tell them, so coaching doesn't work.*
>
> *This is dangerous. We are not counsellors, we are teachers. We are not qualified for this.*
>
> *I don't have time to have coaching conversations in tutor period – there is too much else to do.*
>
> *I don't need coaching myself – I don't have any issues.*
>
> *There is no proof that coaching works.*

Many of these comments reveal significant misunderstanding about what coaching is and how it can be helpful in a school context. It became clear that the foundation course was not enough to give staff sufficient grounding. In response, we adapted our in-house training to spend more time exploring the spectrum of help, including the differences between mentoring, counselling, direct instruction and coaching. We have emphasised more carefully the fact that coaching is a tool which teachers can pick up and put down as required when the context is appropriate. Being clear that coaching is quite often not the appropriate form of help has dispelled some of those misunderstandings and given staff more confidence to decide when a coach-like approach to conversations with pupils, parents or colleagues would be beneficial.

Publicising the positive impact that coaching had had for many staff was a turning point in staff seeing the benefits and variety of ways in which staff were using coaching effectively in their day-to-day roles. Inviting, rather than instructing, staff to attend the advanced training course (which was initially two days but has now been trimmed down to one) has done two things: first, it has provided staff with more practice, tools and confidence to be coach-like. It has created a desirable difficulty and a status which has been beneficial for staff seeking pastoral advancement. Second, it has subtly reinforced our unwavering stance: we believe that coaching is infinitely beneficial to our school community and is here to stay.

Impacts of coaching

Institutionally we believe in creating autonomy, independence and empowerment. Coaching has done a lot at institutional level to demonstrate this belief. The PDR system, dedicated staff training staff, the pupil coaching booklets and protected time for tutor–pupil coaching and the parental coaching skills courses all demonstrate the values we believe in. Staff responses in evaluations indicate its impact and these include:

> *In my regular coaching trio, we have been looking at how we want to improve as teachers. Taking time to step back and talk through the fine details of how effective my feedback has actually been or ways I can use questioning more skilfully, for example,*

has made me a more effective and efficient teacher. No doubt about it.

The connection I've made with other staff through two days of coaching has been more effective than ten years' worth of organised school events.

Today, a boy came to see me who looked absolutely shattered. Consequently, we had a mini-coaching chat which totally changed the direction of what I had planned. In our meeting next week, he's going to tell me what he's done to try and increase the amount of sleep he gets.

Coaching has given me practical tools to practise compassion (our core value at MTP) more effectively in my work as a senior leader and a teacher: it's made me a better listener and helped me to understand what's motivating the person I'm with.

Reflections

Laura's account demonstrates some of the challenges of implementing and sustaining coaching across a school community. The complaints she shares from colleagues, based on misunderstandings about what coaching is and isn't, are familiar. The leadership team's approach to look at ways to better support teachers with coaching adheres to their purposeful and firm stance that coaching has an important place in the school. Gathering evidence and feedback is essential to supporting the change process and it was interesting to read about how they have built upon different coaching processes and training to develop their own bespoke approach to professional learning.

Chapter 11 endnotes

Final thoughts

Schools and other education providers are complex organisations, with limited resources and a natural momentum that builds as cohorts of learners enter and progress. Maintaining shared purpose across these communities can be challenging, even among employees. Organisational culture impacts on the experiences of everyone in the setting. The culture is also created by everyone in the setting and coaching can become influential in ways of working, ways of relating, ways of leading and ways of learning. Coaching can create spaces for growth, allow voices to be heard, help to refine practice, and build a sense of solidarity and shared purpose. However, coaching can also reinforce cultures that cause anxiety or strengthen hierarchies of influence, leading to lack of agency for some members of the community. Being alert to how coaching is shaping culture is essential.

This chapter opened with the proposition that coaching can shape cultures in education settings, through both deliberate and more organic means. The six encounters probably blur this distinction. In each case coaching is planned for as a purposeful approach to influence the setting and the ways that education is framed and provided. Some also demonstrate how coaching is explicitly used to help leaders sustain a focus on wellbeing in the setting. They all illustrate what Allen refers to in the opening quote as 'non-linear dynamics' with coaching being an 'emergent practice' where 'adaptation and experimentation' are ongoing (Allen, 2019, p. 72). Cultures in education settings are the manifestations of collective behaviours and knowledge. Coaching can become integral to these manifestations, keeping cultures alive and ensuring that learning also creates opportunities for enhancing rather than entrenching educational cultures.

Talking point

If culture can be described as the attitudes, behaviours and habits that exist in a community, what do the coaching practices adopted in your setting tell you about the coaching culture? To what extent is the coaching culture an extension of the wider culture in the setting and are there any examples of how coaching itself is changing the attitudes, behaviours and habits of the professionals, learners and other participants in the community?

Ideas for action

Educational settings often adopt acronyms and slogans, which can become orientated towards performative purposes (such as posters or routinised behaviours) and risk being clichés rather than culturally resonant. In her encounter, Rachel Tomlinson described the LEARN framework that is used to support a culture of deep conversations in her primary school. You may find it helpful to run a reality check with regards to similar frameworks, acronyms and slogans in your setting or to describe your own work within and possibly beyond coaching. Are these helpful? Do they genuinely have shared meaning? Are they authentic or cloned from elsewhere? Do the coaching practices draw on or create new frameworks? Do these escape into the wider culture in ways that make a positive difference? On reflection you may like to either edit some of the terminology or make more concerted use of it to strengthen the relationships between coaching and culture.

Chapter 12
Coaching as a way of sustaining change

The future doesn't take form irrationally, even though it feels that way. The future comes from where we are now. It materialises from the actions, values, and beliefs we are practising now. [...] If we want a different future, we have to take responsibility for what we are doing in the present.

Margaret Wheatley (2009, p. 68)

The CollectivED Award

The CollectivED award enables educational providers to make coaching, mentoring and professional learning a guided strategic priority for school development. The award focuses on the creation of an implementation plan which guides the whole school community through a process of building the skills and knowledge needed to bring about whole-school improvements in coaching, mentoring and professional learning.

The award provides a framework through which CPD leaders collate evidence of initiatives that work towards demonstrating a commitment towards excellent practice by making coaching, mentoring and professional learning a part of a school's core business. Award applicants work with a CollectivED coach to create a personalised action plan for their school community or organisation.

Over time the portfolio of evidence is reviewed against the competencies of the framework, allowing it to be verified against bronze, silver or gold levels.

In this chapter we encounter the coaching journeys of schools that have each been successful in the CollectivED Award described above. Despite this common characteristic they are each unique and include primary, secondary and cross-phase schools in England, Europe and Australia. The encounters with these schools illustrate mature coaching engagement, creating opportunities for sustained culture building, new forms of leadership and enhancement of the support offered to colleagues across a range of roles. Several of these are extended case studies, evidencing many years of work in this area, often involving building and rebuilding programmes and teams, the realities of grappling with dilemmas and tensions that occur as coaching is developed and the strategic decisions made along the way. By grouping these together we acknowledge the time and effort taken to work towards the CollectivED Award, but we do not propose to elevate the quality or impact of their work above that of the encounters in the previous chapters.

The first encounter in this chapter is shared by the lead coach for the award itself, who explains how she uses her educational and coaching experience to facilitate conversations with leaders in schools who are undertaking the award. Each of the other encounters is written by the members of staff who led the work towards the CollectivED Award in their school.

Encounter: reflections from the CollectivED Award lead coach

Rose Blackman-Hegan is the lead coach for the award and in this role helps to build coaching cultures and uses coaching-type approaches as a way of supporting schools to reflect and plan their year-long journey through the award. Rose writes:

My background as a coach in education

I work as a freelance coach and facilitator across all education settings. As an educational coach I have supported teachers and school leaders in a range of settings. I also facilitate coaching training workshops. My interest in coaching developed through my own experiences of being coached while a senior leader. Through the coaching process I was able to find space to challenge my thinking, explore alternative approaches and develop confidence and agency to make change. I was initially introduced to the GROW model through my own coaching training. As a new coach it can be helpful to have a model or framework to inform your practice. Over time I have learnt to be more flexible during coaching conversations and work outside of one single framework.

In one of my roles I work as the Lead Coach for the CollectivED Coaching, Mentoring and Professional Learning in Education Award. An aspect of this role involves providing coaching support for schools who complete the award. I bring experience as a senior leader in the secondary sector as well as a chair of governors for a sixth form in the UK. I am also able to draw on experience from working with a national educational charity, providing leadership training across all stages of educational provision.

Coaching within the CollectivED Award

The CollectivED award competencies are structured to assist the lead in reviewing all aspects of the school's provision. As the coach, using the school's self-assessed diagnostic, I will initially focus on areas that they have selected as areas for development alongside celebrating any areas of strength. The GROW model I find most useful in this context. This approach enables a quick determination of what the school's goal is, where the current reality is, where the lead has the influence to make changes and how they will make these changes as well as what they hope the impact to be.

Each school elects who will be the lead on the award. My role as coach is to work with the lead in developing their action plan that they will implement over the 12 months of the award process. There is no set approach or model of coaching used: this is determined by the needs of the lead and the school. At times there will be more than one person involved in the coaching process, for example, the lead on the award and a colleague who may be responsible for professional development or for initial teacher training.

The key to coaching on the award is to first determine what level of expertise exists within the school. If a school embarks on the award with very little understanding of what coaching is, there will be a need for some preliminary groundwork, this can involve some coaching training where appropriate. I undertake conversations with a coaching approach, with questions posed from anywhere within the range of non-directive to directive. In some instances, I may adopt a coaching-mentoring approach.

If a school and award lead already have an in-depth understanding of coaching, it is possible to approach the coaching relationship differently. For example, I may approach conversations with a more nuanced model of coaching. In all instances, my role is to support the school in building a coaching culture through reflection on what they currently do and how to plan for changes where these are needed. I do not offer suggestions or alternatives; I may direct leads to other schools that could be helpful to them, but my role is purely to help them find the best solutions in their own specific context.

My central purpose as award coach is to coach and support schools in developing and successfully delivering a personalised action plan. Schools generally undertake the CollectivED award as a way to review and refine their provision. Some schools have very little experience of coaching and use the award to learn how to introduce coaching to their setting. This may be through a single lens, such as using coaching to develop pedagogical approaches, or from a wider perspective, for example, to develop a whole-school coaching culture. A few schools start the award with a great deal of coaching experience, where coaching approaches permeate almost all layers of the school. The majority of schools have experience of mentoring, primarily through initial teacher training provision. Similarly, all schools are familiar with the requirements of professional learning for staff. In each area the award provides a structure from which schools are able to reflect and improve. One school stated that 'the award framework provided a helpful structure, ensuring that each strand of the work undertaken was tied together across the school community'.

Gaining clarity and acknowledging tensions through the CollectivED Award

A significant tension is the range of influence the award lead may have in developing and building a coaching culture within their school. For example, if the lead is in a position of seniority in the school hierarchy, they are likely to be able to introduce changes that can develop the school's coaching culture. If, however, the lead has little influence on school decision-making then the possibility of developing a coaching culture is often more challenging.

In my role the main aim is to support schools in achieving the award. Beyond this I hope to develop the lead's confidence and agency in their coaching role in their setting. The impact of my coaching work at an institutional level is clear as the schools progress through and ultimately achieve the award. At an individual level this is less easy to determine other than through direct feedback from the award leads, both during the award process and after the award has been granted. However different school leads engage with the award, all will take time to reflect and plan on where they currently are and what changes they wish to make. The period of reflection is key and in my role as coach I will spend some time with the lead on exploring what the outcomes of their reflection process have been. Through the clarity developed following this time of reflection a clear plan can be developed.

Reflection

Rose's contribution sets the stage for the rest of the case studies in this chapter. It is clear that the purpose of the award is focused on professional growth and support. There is a feeling of openness to this award, with agency existing for the award coaches as well as for school leaders engaging with it. Tensions can exist in building a coaching culture and it is useful to consider this in relation to our discussion on systemic change in chapter 17.

Encounter: thriving and flourishing through a culture of coaching

Mark Steacy is assistant principal with responsibilities for whole school systems as well as professional learning and development in an all-through school in Malaysia which caters for students aged 3–19. There are over 800 students, with a growth of around 60% in the past two years. The school vision is to develop students who are the 'complete person', not just as learners, but as people in the school community regardless of their age. Part of his role is to help provide pathways for all teachers to grow individually as well as develop the capacities to contribute to the growth of the teams and of the entire school as a learning organisation. There are strong relationships between school purpose, pedagogical principles and coaching. Mark writes:

Purpose of coaching

The central purpose of coaching in our school is to provide the conditions for all staff to thrive and flourish in a learning environment based on people improving and growing both professionally and personally over time. The Japanese concept of 'kaizen' is central to this belief. Schools need to be places where adult learning is a way of life (not just merely a single 'initiative') as the conditions adults experience become the conditions that are recreated for students in the classroom. An important part of coaching is, therefore, to help our educators become better aware of their own purposes and values as whole people as well as how they can realise their 'hidden potential'.

This means that, as a school, we have a responsibility to provide professional learning pathways which put the holistic, long-term growth of our educators (not just as individuals, but also as being able to make a positive contribution to teams and communities) over the course of their entire careers at the centre. These pathways need to build the capacities of educators to help build a strong set of core values and to be able to respond to situations in creative and compassionate ways. Underlying our coaching system, as well as other professional learning and development pathways, are the values of respect (we value and build on the strengths of others), compassion (we act on feelings of empathy and listen with the intent to understand), curiosity (we have the courage to imagine and act on new possibilities), humility (we enter learning opportunities open to learning) and integrity (we live, not laminate, our values).

Developing our pedagogical framework

As our educators teach different age levels and subjects and come from a wide range of educational and cultural backgrounds they bring varied prior learning experiences and expectations. They hold many different, sometimes competing, conceptions of effective teaching and learning. To develop a deeper shared understanding we brought together people from different sections of our school to share what they felt was essential to effective teaching and learning, to identify the common ground rather than to focus on differences or what works only for a specific group of students or subject area. This led to a framework based on pedagogical principles which has allowed the development of a shared language across our school community and a coherent understanding of what our collective purpose as a school community is, as well as what our responsibilities are to each other and our student body. In contrast to focusing on the 'delivery' of information related to a specific teaching practice and then moving quickly on to something else, we adopt principles of communities of practice and explore each pedagogical principle for around three to four months. This gives us time, space and opportunities for teachers to develop a deeper understanding of effective teaching and learning.

Our coaching practices and influences

All teachers in our school have a coach or a mentor to have growth-focused coaching conversations with. Teachers who are looking to join our school are made aware of what we offer in terms of professional growth and development and that there is an expectation that we want to see a commitment to professional growth over time. When new teachers start at our school, they are assigned a 'mentor' to support them during their 'settling-in' period. Staff who have been at our school for longer than six months are assigned a coach who can support a sense of ownership of the next steps required for their development (although this does not mean that this person does not switch back to the role of being a 'mentor' where the situation requires). When we launched our coaching and mentoring system, we used Elena Aguilar's Behaviours, Beliefs and Beings framework initially to help people to understand that when we merely change our surface-level behaviour without updating our underlying beliefs and ways of being, we do not necessarily change for the better, and hence we do not grow or develop in the longer term as educators or people. Lately another framework based on three Bs (Being, Becoming and Belonging) has been more widely used. Integral to coaching is our own teaching and learning framework of pedagogical principles.

All professional conversations, including coaching, mentoring and communities of practice, are based on Partnership Principles (synthesised by Jim Knight). These are equality, choice, voice, dialogue, reflection, praxis and reciprocity. These partnership principles form the basis for how people are invited and encouraged to think about their own growth as well as what we can do together to make more of an impact on student learning. They also allow the richer dialogue to take place to tap into what they bring with them to our school community as well as how they can develop the unique gifts that everyone brings to a school community. We also draw on the GROWTH framework from Christian van Nieuwerburgh and John Campbell. Additionally, a spectrum from a more directive mentoring approach to a non-directive coaching approach has also been used to highlight the fact that sometimes the stance of the person facilitating the conversation needs to change as a conversation unfolds. Frameworks and metaphors related to the natural world around us are also used in coaching, including learning from rainforests, planting seeds, shamrocks and growing mango trees.

Part of my interest in coaching has been stimulated from the world of long-distance running as running is a key part of my own daily routine. I had previously worked with a running coach for a couple of years before becoming self-coached as a runner. While coaching in distance running is a different context from the work that takes place in schools, there are lots of shared underlying principles. This includes putting the long-term growth and transformation of the 'practitioner' at the centre of the process, assuming positive intent in all situations, building positive relationships based on respect and reciprocity, using non-judgemental dialogue, developing mental models and giving people the skills and capacities they need to take on more responsibility for their own growth.

Developing coaching and professional learning over time

Our approach to professional learning and development has been developed over a number of years. The first foundations were set during a change of school ownership as well as a transition to a new campus. This saw the school move away from formal graded lesson observations and a quantitative appraisal system and enabled non-contact time every Friday afternoon for staff to learn and grow together. During the extended pandemic school closures we focused on professional development to enable learning online as well as support student wellbeing from a distance. Pathways to support the development of our early career teachers as well as our middle leaders were additionally established in 2021 due to the significant number of staff who were new to teaching or new to middle leadership. When we were able to return to learning in the physical school campus at the start of 2022, this allowed us an opportunity to reset (again). During this time, we launched our coaching and mentoring approach to professional growth and created and implemented our teaching and learning framework. We explored our first two pedagogical principles of our teaching and learning framework, one at a time (these two principles focus on purpose and language) in 2022 and our next three pedagogical principles in 2023 (these three pedagogical principles focus on the learning environment, checking for understanding as well as deep learning). During 2024, we are focusing on our sixth and seventh pedagogical principles (these focus on learning strategies and metacognition). We are also starting to focus on curriculum development as a whole school community to support the developments being made with pedagogy this year. Next year, we will explore our final pedagogical principle of embedding learning over time before circling back to our first pedagogical principle (as with everything else, we start and end with purpose). In the years following this, our other pedagogical principles will be revisited. The duration and intensity of exploring two or three pedagogical principles, one at a time, over the course of an academic year will stay the same.

Recognising and addressing challenges

Challenges in developing this work are associated with any organisational development initiative. This can be summarised by a version of Peter Senge's laws of systems thinking: 'Yesterday's "solutions" become today's "problems".' If something 'worked' in the past, there may be times when people do not want to move forward from this particular way of being (or doing). A specific manifestation of this in our context has been due to the recent increase in student numbers, which means that a more personalised approach with smaller student numbers no longer works. This is where effective coaching can play a key role as it potentially can allow others, in a safe, non-judgemental space, to consider situations from different perspectives and return to what the bigger picture is as well as what the current 'reality' asks for. Another issue associated with embedding a culture of coaching is ensuring there are enough quality coaches and mentors for all teachers. At the beginning of the approach, there were fewer people able to be effective coaches and it mainly fell on senior leaders to fill this role. Over time, through a pathway which focused on the development of middle and senior leaders, the number and quality of coaches and mentors has increased.

Another common challenge is that sometimes people want others to be able to provide them with the 'solution' to their 'problem' or 'fix' it for them rather than being willing to invest in the necessary development of thinking skills and self-commitment that is required for longer-term development over time. Some of this is potentially caused by previous compliant-based appraisal systems which unintentionally create 'learned helplessness'. There is also a limiting assumption that a 'leader' is a person who 'tells others what to do'. Like any challenge, there is no 'quick fix'. With a consistent focus on key messages over time (e.g. leadership is a 'choice' that is available to anyone and the role of (formal) leaders is to coordinate systems based on shared purposes, teach others and steward the future of the organisation). This can be done through the sharing of conceptual frameworks through which there is scope to reduce the impact of these related issues over time. Another key part of the process is helping people to imagine new possibilities and co-create the necessary steps to be taken to move forwards for the benefit of all concerned (where no blame is required). Like most longer-term plans, patience, compassion and commitment are key.

Understanding impact

Indicators of impact include a significant number of educators who have been internally promoted to another role, including six of our current teachers who started out as teaching assistants, eight middle leaders who joined us as teachers and six (of eight) of our current senior leaders who have been internal appointments. Staff are increasingly seeing students outside of their school sections and are starting to embrace a shared purpose and common journey. This is evidenced by the fact that teachers are not just showing interest in the development of students in their own section but recognising that we all have a responsibility to all students regardless of what their current 'year level' is. New staff to our school community have also shared their observations that our school is 'different' from others, especially in terms of students' ways of being as well as being clearly focused on the development of all people (staff and students alike). How people respond when 'things go wrong' can also be a useful indicator of where people are at in terms of their thinking. During some challenging circumstances in the past few months, there has been a willingness on the part of staff to recognise that there is a bigger picture hidden 'beneath the surface' and that requires additional people to help out and do something extra to help alleviate the issue. In the past, negative judgements and blame would have been more prevalent.

Reflection

Values clearly shape the sense of purpose at this school and as a result standards of achievement are not only high but also sustained. From Mark's contribution we can see how the purpose statement is folded into all its professional learning activities and that the school is focused on the wellbeing and development of all its members (both staff and students). It is also clear that thoughtful consideration has been made to the short- and long-term goals of the school as they work together to embody a coaching culture.

Encounter: creating momentum for change through conversation

Hollybank School (a pseudonym) is a two-form entry primary school in the East of England. There are a high number of pupils with SEND and EAL. Some families in the school community are experiencing increased deprivation, while a significant number are more affluent families who might have traditionally chosen the private sector. The school's headteacher writes:

Creating a coaching culture

We have used coaching to give greater autonomy to staff, so they feel empowered to lead their own career paths. I wouldn't describe myself formally as a coach, but I use coaching techniques all the time when having discussions with staff, parents and children. I have put systems in place in school where coaching conversations can take place both privately within a positive appraisal context and more openly where staff can come together collaboratively to talk about all sorts of learning related themes and issues. Staff now routinely expect me to ask them how they are doing, not just in terms of their wellbeing but how they are developing professionally and how as a school we can help their development further. I know this from the master's research that I have carried out recently, which, although is primarily about our headship model, has allowed me to hear first-hand the impact of having a coaching culture in school.

We use 'spirals of inquiry' as a model for nearly everything in school. This is not a coaching model, but it does provide a framework (spiral) that allows us all to ask questions and then check out those questions or hunches that we have. What we are aiming to do is to encourage people to ask questions, whether that be about their own practice, about the children they are teaching or about the curriculum they are covering. We want people to be inquisitive and active rather than passive about their professional learning.

I have worked hard over the last eight years to create this culture, because it was very much lacking when I started out in this profession. I am only in the position I currently hold because of certain individuals over the years who asked me the right questions at the right time. These questions directed my thinking and encouraged me to join networks that would allow me to think more deeply and bravely – which I believe are traits that I demonstrate still today.

Development over time

It started over eight years ago, when I could hear people naturally talking in the staffroom about how they were either developing professionally or how they wanted to develop in the future. So I took advantage of this really positive aspect and set up 'tea and chat' sessions where staff came together to talk about education and learning more widely. Each week had a different theme which might have been linked to a particular article or topic, and staff from all areas of school, including support and admin staff, came together over a cup of tea. This led to having 'lesson chats', which I wrote about for the CollectivED working papers, where two people would come together to plan a series of lessons, often one of the pair would be the subject lead, and where together they would plan and then evaluate the lessons that had taken place. In time this led to more informal sessions where a member of staff would ask a few colleagues about a particular lesson, e.g. whole-class guided reading. One of the teachers would model a lesson with a class during assembly with others watching, followed by very supportive follow-up chats over the next few weeks as they developed their own expertise and offered their own advice and encouragement to others.

Now all staff members are exposed to some coaching, it is their choice whether they wish to take opportunities further. They are all exposed to elements of coaching because of the culture in school. Everybody's appraisal conversations begin with a set of questions where we start by asking 'Can you name two people in school that believe in you as a professional?' This is quickly followed up with:

- How has this knowledge influenced your practice?
- What have you learnt recently about your practice?
- What are some of the areas where you would like to grow further?
- Ideally, what would your next steps be both in the short term and long term?
- How can we help you achieve these goals?
- What do you envisage as potential problems this year? What can you/we do to avoid these?
- Try to summarise the impact you have in one sentence.

These questions are asked three times a year. Depending on the answers given and the willingness of the participants further coaching scenarios may then follow.

Finding a network of support

I have stopped talking about this approach with my local school cluster; they seem to have a very different approach to how schools should be run. I think they manage what others might be telling them to do – either because they are part of a large multi-academy trust or because they think they don't have the time to have this type of approach. This sounds harsh, but that is how it feels. This is why I have, over the years, chosen my networks carefully and why CollectivED is so important.

Reflection

The invitational approach is foundational to the success of the staff development at this school. The coaching way of being is evident in how they approach staff development and their use of a variety of frameworks and coaching techniques. Building on and strengthening established frameworks like the 'spirals of inquiry' support coherence across the school and it was interesting to read about how what started as an invitation to a 'tea and chat' developed organically into formal and empowering collaborative activities. Although local networks of support are lacking, the external network of CollectivED offers the author a community to accompany their work.

Encounter: instructional coaching and beyond

Frankfurt International School (FIS) is one of the oldest international schools in Europe and was founded in 1961. It caters for approximately 1800 students from over 60 nations across two age-based campuses. FIS is a family-oriented and internationally minded not-for-profit school. Antony Winch is one of two instructional coaches at the school. Antony writes:

How and why coaching is used

In my opinion, the central purpose of coaching in my context, and in any context, is to help teachers grow in order that their professional development better supports the young people they teach.

In our school, coaching is voluntary. Everyone is regularly invited to take part and colleagues (mainly teachers) can choose if they wish to form a coach/coachee relationship or not. The length of the time colleagues commit to coaching is entirely up to them. They can be coached every eight-day cycle or have just a one-off meeting or class visit. Colleagues have complete control over their participation. Some colleagues who have been at the school for five years and undergone a performance review cycle may be encouraged to work with a coach on certain pedagogical aspects, but this is voluntary. We mainly coach teachers, but our role is not exclusive to teachers. We have coached senior school leaders, learning support coaches, an instructional coach, tech integrators and building management colleagues.

We have drawn mainly on the instructional coaching work of Jim Knight (2007, 2020, 2022), Boughton and Beere (2013), and Andy Vass (Hook et al., 2006; Vass, 2016), and the coaching work of Sir John Whitmore (2017). Consequently, we use a GROW (Whitmore, 2017) or iSTRIDE (Beere and Broughton, 2013) framework depending on the coaching context.

I read widely and this shapes my coaching. For example:

- From *First Break All the Rules* (Buckingham and Coffman, 2005) and Mark Buckingham's work with Ashley Goodall on *The Feedback Fallacy* (2019), I have adopted three principles: I would care for the people I work with, help them to develop and build on their strengths. This means that I tell my coachees when I see something going well, I am more careful with my language of feedback and I use what the coachee knows to lead them to their preferred future.

- From *Helping* by Edgar H. Schein (2009), I took the art of humble inquiry, and I remember to address inequalities in a coaching relationship and balance these out between coach and coachee. I never have all the answers and am comfortable to admit when I am unsure how to proceed, e.g. 'I don't know what to do next to be helpful.'
- From *NLP at Work* by Sue Knight (2009), I try to use similar language to that of the coachee and draw on the concept of CLEAN questions (questions that are simple to understand and follow) and I use anchoring to move from one state to another.

Other influential writers for me have been Daniel H. Pink (2011) on motivation being based on autonomy, mastery and purpose; Heidi Grant Halvorson (2012), particularly related to goal-setting and realistic optimism, and Boyatzis, Smith and van Oosten (2019), who remind me of the importance of being in a positive state to change and using vision of change as an anchor for positive states.

I also use tools to support coaching, with my favourite physical tool being my 0 to 10 ladder – 10 being where the coachee wants to be, and 0 being when they are nowhere near it. It is a simple but effective way to help someone see their reality – how close or far they are from their preferred future or goal. The other physical tool I use is coaching picture cards ('52 deep pictures for coaching, training and therapy' made by metaFox), which I use intermittently to transition teachers positively from a classroom state of mind to a creative ideas coaching state of mind. Normally in the middle of the year, I survey my coachees about our coaching meetings. This survey has been a useful tool and so has an evaluating coaching document we created based on Jim Knight's work (2022).

How coaching emerged and evolved

In my last school, where I was assistant head of school, we had a rigorous evaluation cycle three times a year when teachers were observed and assessed. This stressed teachers who only focused on their grade and it was only used as a key performance indicator for the company who owned the school. There was no learning for teachers, and it did not help them grow into better teachers. My head of school and I decided to try something new and, unbeknown to the company, we brought in Andy Vass and changed the observation cycle to a coaching cycle. We trained up everyone in the school who could speak English to be a coach. We then made heads of department and other leaders in school responsible for coaching other colleagues. This was a mistake. Some heads of departments made very good coaches but others did not. I realised that coaching is not something everybody has the necessary skills to do.

In my coaching sessions, I saw the potential in individualised professional development for people and holding them accountable to their goals and dreams in a non-threatening manner. After three years, I quit my job to be a dad to my son and to write fiction. During this gift of time, I was able to reflect on my achievements and failures. Coaching was something I was proud of and I continued to read books/articles on the subject. After four years, I wanted to get back into education and at the same time my current school was advertising for an instructional coach. The timing was unbelievably perfect. I am now six years into my current position. Over time and influenced by my reading, my coaching has developed in ways that I feel benefits my coachees. This includes the art of helping, neurolinguistic programming, how the brain works, motivation and self-determination theory, dealing with stress and using positive psychology. Since the pandemic, I have wondered, and written about, whether 'instructional coach' is a misnomer and that 'coach' is a more accurate description now (Winch, 2022). Or maybe, like the coachees I work with, my instructional coach role simply continues to grow.

Reflection

Throughout this extended encounter there is a sense of momentum and growth. This is not the same as a relentless urge for change but represents a responsive and iterative process in which people, practices and place are in an evolving relationship with each other. Antony also reflects on the importance of pausing, allowing him to take stock, take time and gain new perspectives. This reminds us that we should not see change as a race but as a journey, underpinned by a desire for professional learning.

Chapter 12 Coaching as a way of sustaining change

Encounter: developing a whole-school coaching ethos

Natasha Carman is the principal at Moor End Academy, a secondary school in West Yorkshire in the UK, located in an area of significant deprivation. Although students arrive at the school with attainment scores below national average, the nationally applied progress scores indicate that when the students leave the school they have made well above the expected level of progress. The school is part of a multi-academy trust (MAT). Natasha writes:

How and why coaching is used

Anyone and everyone can be coached! Some of our office staff and our business manager have been coached, and our head of school is currently being coached…and everyone in between! Staff are actively encouraged to use coaching as a high-quality and bespoke form of professional development that has sustainable impact.

Coaching is a kind of 'ethos' that permeates through much of what we do. For example, feedback from learning walks or observations is structured in a coaching conversation. Over recent years, all staff have been trained as coaches and many (teaching and non-teaching) have accessed coaching as part of their professional development offer. We have also used 'dilemma-based coaching' (see chapter 13) as a format for senior leaders across the MAT. Coaching in our organisation is very much about professionals identifying something they would value some support with, and we then pair people up according to areas of specialism and experience.

The majority of our coaches are internal, although sometimes experts from the MAT support with this – usually around middle leadership development. People who have opted into being coaches have 'profiles' that others can look at to select a coach or they can ask for coaching in a certain area and be allocated somebody with this specific area of expertise. The head of school and a middle leader oversee coaching as part of wider professional responsibilities.

How coaching developed

Our focus on coaching started a few years ago when we identified that there was a gap from the intensive mentoring of early career teachers to the wider teaching staff whose appraisal model involved them in two meetings per year. We also reviewed induction processes so that all new starters have the support of another member of staff as they familiarise themselves with the school. Initially, some staff had negative perceptions about coaching being something that happened to people who were 'failing'! We have worked hard to refute this. We use GROWTH coaching as our model in school, although we use a lot of research by Clutterbuck and are starting to develop something more specific to education as a unique sector. Some of our coaches have completed the *'Olevi: Power of Coaching'* qualification so they access materials there. Completing the CollectivED Award provided us with a clear 'golden thread' and sense of direction for this work.

We will keep going because staff feedback indicates colleagues reporting better wellbeing and feeling more able to manage challenging work situations more effectively.

Reflection

Natasha's enthusiasm for inclusive coaching is contagious. It is helpful to understand that the majority of coaches are internal and that there is system support through involvement by the head of school and a middle leader. Like many of the case-study schools, it is interesting to see how coaching grew from an established mentoring programme and was first perceived from a deficit perspective. Developing a bespoke coaching model is beneficial in this context.

Encounter: embedding and sustaining coaching

Mark Dowley is the associate head (staff development and consulting) at Brighton Grammar School, a boys' independent school in Melbourne, Australia. It has 1500 students from early years to secondary age and 248 staff (130 full-time equivalent teaching staff). The school is based in a high socio-economic area of Melbourne and has a supportive community with a growing academic culture and focus on positive masculinity and wellbeing. The school also hosts the Crowther Centre for Applied Educational Research. Mark is author of the Classroom Management Handbook *and is a certified instructional coach with the Instructional Coaching Group. Mark writes:*

Why and how coaching is used

Our staff development is based on four motivational principles: purpose, connectedness, mastery and autonomy (from self-determination theory, see chapter 3). The purpose statement for our coaching team is 'We are a support service to teachers. Coaches are thinking partners who help develop teachers' instructional practice and wellbeing.' The main coaching that occurs is 'instructional coaching'. We also have a leadership coaching program and teachers coaching students through our house/tutor/form group program. There are multiple student/student coaching programs as well. Coaching is supported by a system of professional reading, workshops and management.

Our coaches are all internal. The roles are positions of responsibility, similar to a head of faculty/department. Roles need to be applied for and applicants go through an interview process and work samples test. I oversee the coaching program as an associate head leading staff development and as director of instructional coaching.

All coaching is optional. Coachees are invited to join the program after workshops and presentations. Colleagues at all levels of experience are being coached. The form of coaching varies. We take a more directive approach to coaching for new teachers and leaders and a more facilitative process is used for experienced colleagues.

How coaching developed and is sustained

We started with peer coaching using a GROWTH model and moved to instructional coaching using Jim Knight's *Impact Cycle*, initially with just one coach. As the impact data was positive, we were able to justify time and resources for more coaches. After three years we identified a need for leadership coaches. Over time we have built our own models of both instructional and leadership coaching, based on our early experiences. Our leadership coaching uses a mix of growth, cognitive and ontological coaching frameworks (see chapter 2). After eight years, we have 16 coaches with time allocation for coaching (equivalent to four full-time coaches) and 90% of staff volunteering to be coached. Our staff development program now makes us a school of choice for teachers who wish to improve their practice and develop their leadership skills.

Our coaching team supports other schools to develop coaching programs. We facilitate a staff development network here in Australia, host 'Coaching in Action days' where teachers from other schools come to learn how to coach, visit real classes and practise coaching with experienced coaches.

There are challenges, including upholding the principle of choice and creating a performance management system that sits outside coaching. Fortunately, we have strong leadership support that provides us with the resources required to maintain an effective program.

We are continually developing and training new coaches and inducting new staff into our culture of coaching. We continue this work because the feedback we gather is so positive: at an individual level we have feedback data from all coaches (coaching feedback survey) and we also track engagement at the individual and school level. This has been improving year on year, coinciding with our best-ever results in six of the last seven years and record enrolments.

Reflection

It is clear from Mark's contribution that this is a mature coaching culture and they consider coaching at all levels. Even for a school that has experienced significant success there remains the perennial tension with how coaching sits alongside performance management. It was interesting to read about how the school perceives coaching as a leadership role and has developed a process to become a coach, how coaching is supported and ways they introduce the coaching to new staff through induction.

Encounter: growing our own through enhanced professional development

St Teresa's Roman Catholic Primary School is in Irlam in Salford, UK. It is a one-form entry school with 239 pupils on roll, 11% of whom speak English as an additional language and 7% of whom receive free school meals. Joanne Kane is assistant headteacher who led the school through the CollectivED Award. Joanne writes:

Putting coaching into context

As a whole school we have embraced a school improvement motto of 'Better never stops', taken from Team GB. We have established a sustainable culture of coaching, conversations and learning at the heart of what we do. Staff are encouraged to drive their own continuing professional development and to share this with others in school and beyond our setting. Staff within the school are empowered to pursue profession-wide learning and opportunities. We work in partnership with various professional bodies to share good practice, deliver initial teacher training, act as primary support providers, train mentors regionally and embrace professional mentor roles. We believe in 'growing our own'.

How coaching is used

All teachers and teaching assistants engage in coaching. We have worked with an external coach who was an educator and a sports coach for Team GB. Internally the senior leadership team members have created peer-to-peer partnerships based on professional conversations and dialogue. GROW lesson feedback was introduced and all staff have embraced this. As staff have engaged in sharing their practice, including outreach work and supporting others, their coaching roles have developed. As assistant headteacher I work alongside the headteacher to lead the coaching within our school in collaboration with other leaders. We ensure staff have appropriate resources and training to fulfil their role confidently and have opportunities for ongoing professional development. We encourage staff to look for their own courses, research and accreditation opportunities.

Coaching is based on what we need as a school and as individuals and relates to personalised career planning. Coaching is thus linked to whole-school projects, curriculum leadership and teachers working collaboratively to research, trial and then change our policy and practice. It is also embedded through engagement with professional qualifications, for example, teaching assistants completing an apprenticeship, early career teacher induction and support, and future leaders gaining accreditation through National Professional Qualifications.

How coaching emerged and continues to develop

Honest and open dialogue has been the starting point for establishing coaching. Based around our school mission of 'We grow together' we put wellbeing, professional collaboration and trust at the heart of our coaching approach. Our journey began with senior leaders working with an expert coach to create a leadership development programme. Staff training sessions centred on coaching and we developed professional dialogue, opportunities to collaborate with peers, coaching conversations, training and support. All staff were part of this process and our coaching has evolved over seven years. We are now more open to asking questions about our practice and the 'So what?'

The wellbeing of staff and children is also very much part of the coaching. We engage with peer-to-peer coaching and collaborate as a staff team to identify common goals but also as individuals to pursue learning opportunities and support professional growth. We look at the 'intent, implementation and impact' but also the 'why'. We allow the time and space for coaching conversations to happen and the opportunity to trial new things within classroom practice. Colleagues are encouraged to attend national coaching conferences and events, to use social media for professional development, to read up-to-date research and share their learning with each other.

It is not always easy to sustain this work. Time and funds provide a challenge when trying to cover staff for time out of class to pursue CPD and research projects. We need to ensure the balance of embracing new learning and research while maintaining the role of full-time class teacher or curriculum leader. Keeping staff wellbeing at the heart of any improvements has been essential. Undertaking the CollectivED Award ensured that coaching remains high on our agenda and encouraged us to 'dig deeper' into all the aspects of coaching, including staff wellbeing, collaboration, honest dialogue and opportunities for professional enquiry and an openness to be agents of change.

Impacts of coaching as part of planned development

When looking at the impact of coaching many things are not quantifiable. However, developing the curriculum and the role of curriculum leader has been a major focus of our school development plan and of our coaching work. This has provided the staff with the opportunity to create a broad, balanced, bespoke curriculum for their subject area, making sure pupils' outcomes are achievable and enjoyable. The impact can be seen in staff subject knowledge, confidence and leadership. This has then had a positive impact on teaching and learning with improved outcomes for all learners. Working with 'experts' and outside agencies to provide greater opportunities for staff and pupils has shown a very positive impact on stakeholders throughout the school. One example was staff having the freedom to engage in discussion, time to read, research and take a greater look at the different ways to approach marking and feedback, including the opinions of the pupils across school. The outcome was evidence-based practice that live marking was most effective, meaning fewer books going home to be marked in the evening or weekend, and pupils benefiting from teacher input in the moment.

Reflection

It was fascinating to read how coaching at the school is intertwined with sport and Team GB, evidenced in its school improvement motto. Leadership is a critical component of this school's coaching culture and ensures that coaching does not become another burden but is integrated into the wider work of the school. Although coaching impact is not always 'quantifiable', as Joanne notes, after seven years the impact is being found in the involvement of staff, quality of teaching and learning and the meaningful changes that have been made as a result of coaching.

Encounter: professional learning – coaching, autonomy and community

The British School of Brussels (BSB) is a not-for-profit, all-through International School with 1350 students from 70 nationalities aged from 1 to 18 years. The school is made up of 350 staff from diverse backgrounds. Melanie Chambers is whole school deputy (professional learning), and Melanie Warner is the former principal. They write:

Coaching within a culture of professional learning

Our vision is to be a community of learners and to achieve this, we aim to have: the highest quality of teaching, learning and support; a healthy, vibrant and progressive culture where children and adults successfully learn together.

At BSB we believe that the most valuable resource we have is each other and we can learn from one another irrespective of our positions in the school. We believe that within BSB we have the knowledge, skills and understanding to create the best practice; the optimism, positivity and trust to participate, share and collaborate; the curiosity to ask questions and be open to future learning.

BSB has a strong and established professional learning community that is staff and student led. Its nature is one of collaboration and joint work which holds dialogue at its core. Coaching is an essential tool to enable us to engage in our professional learning conversations. We intentionally create time and space for this to take place both formally and informally. Dialogue is a necessary part of our professional learning and a way to create innovative approaches and next practice; it allows divergent thinking to come together and new ideas to emerge, and we recognise that the key to making this happen is to equip staff with the skills to hold these learning conversations, essentially to be able to expertly bring coaching into their discussions.

There is a high degree of trust at BSB and increasingly leaders at all levels encourage and establish conditions in their departments for trusting dialogue. This is clearly established through our ways of working that we have built upon since 2016. The principles of the professional learning community (PLC) at BSB being:

- collaboration
- careful listening and meaningful questioning
- critical feedback
- professional learning sustained over time for self, others and the organisation.

Professional learning (PL) at BSB is based on a model of choice, trust, PL sustained over time and reflective practice. Coaching supports this learning. Our PLC has been strengthened by both formal and informal processes. Examples of more formalised roles and processes that have supported its growth are the creation of professional learning partner (PLP) roles and our BSB autonomous professional learning (APL). Coaching is an essential component of their success.

As a PLC we are committed to developing the conditions for its success by creating a climate of trust, commitment and collective responsibility where, as colleagues, we feel confident to identify areas for learning, set challenging objectives and take risks, and see setbacks as an opportunity to learn rather than be blamed. In addition, we are encouraging colleagues to help one another. Working in a peer-to-peer way, we provide the support and training to help support staff to fulfil these assumptions – and coaching is a powerful tool in this process.

Autonomy and accountability

Our aim through APL is to ensure all staff are supported to be reflective practitioners, active participants in our own PL and accountable for developing our professional capabilities. At BSB all staff are supported in their APL. This can take a variety of forms but giving staff opportunities to work in other areas of the school or outside of their normal role is a key part in developing staff and building their career around their natural competencies. Our school principal supports noticing, identifying and nurturing strengths of all of our staff, including where these lie outside our original formal roles. Coaching is a vital tool to uncover these strengths within and allow staff to go deeper in their development. All staff consider their APL on a biennial basis and are supported by their line manager or PL leads to explore the best path for their career and learning throughout the two years. We make priorities in our PL budget that not only cover staff to follow courses, work with coaches or complete a formal qualification, but also free staff up to work collaboratively, visit different settings and form sustainable connections beyond the school.

It has been significant that our colleagues have shaped the PL space, leading their own initiatives with the support of school leadership who believe that self-accountability or peer accountability carry more importance than any hierarchical accountability. All of our staff, both teaching and learning and operational, sit as equal partners in our community and as staff we have collaboratively shaped our PLC together. We have witnessed that PLC growth needs collaboration and interaction – there is very much a social aspect to it and it takes time for genuine professional collaboration where we are not just working together, but really engaging with each other for the common goal of improving outcomes for all the learners in our community. We firmly believe that taking time to create this culture pays off.

Our professional learning ecosystem involves trusted external friends whose roles include formal and informal coaching. We also give all staff the opportunity to connect with our trained staff confidants who work alongside our PLPs to deepen and strengthen our staff wellbeing.

Development over time

Since our PLP roles took shape in 2017, we have witnessed our staff-led professional learning projects develop through specific transitionary stages. They often start out as foraging and enquiry, which lead to experimentation in practice, a series of reflection, review and reform cycles, before then sharing the findings and recommendations at a leadership level to enable the project to go deeper, be shared more widely, given some structure and then, importantly, sustained.

Since 2019, three PLPs have worked collaboratively to develop our whole-school vision for coaching in line with our whole-school development priorities for reflective practice, following the enquiry–experiment–review–formalise stages of this BSB PL model. Their initial enquiry was broad, but we engaged in a lot of reading, including books and papers on coaching and thinking (authors including Jim Knight, Nancy Kline, Christian van Nieuwerburgh, Chris Munro, Margaret Barr, Rachel Lofthouse and Trista Hollweck), and more widely on professional learning, self-determination and motivation. During the initial enquiry and experimentation phases, the PLPs witnessed how several established structures could add a frame to support and guide the growth of coaching within the school. We drew on work from Growth Coaching International including the GROWTH model and the Global Framework for Coaching in Education (Campbell and van Nieuwerburgh, 2018). The use of this model has allowed the PLPs to naturally divide into specialised areas of enquiry: APL coaching and pedagogical coaching to support professional practice; student coaching to support success and wellbeing; and leadership coaching.

Additionally, one of our PLPs has been developing a new hybrid or nuanced form of coaching to support operational staff in their specialised areas of work. Seeing it this way allows a recognition of the complexity of its development and the significance of the creation of links across the school. It has grown organically from staff need in a bespoke setting, drawing similarities with the concept of 'contextual coaching' (Hollweck and Lofthouse, 2021; see also chapter 15). All of our PL focus areas grow at naturally occurring rates, which will inevitably see some projects reach the more formalised stages quicker than others.

One of our PLPs who has been inquiring into pedagogical coaching has become a GCI-trained coach. Her study into pedagogical coaching has moved through the enquiry, experiment, review phases into the more formalised stage. Building on the 'instructional coaching' model of Jim Knight, we now have a form of pedagogical coaching at BSB that all staff can choose to follow as an APL option within the reflective practice pathway. In chapter 9 Emma Vlaeminck writes about establishing pedagogical coaching through this structure.

CollectivED has been part of our development journey. The CollectivED Award brought energy, motivation and learning as it pushed our thinking, research and models beyond our own context. The wider connections through CollectivED professionally challenge our thinking and encourage depth and breadth to our enquiries by working alongside knowledgeable and experienced professionals. In the CollectivED community we are connected to other like-minded practitioners and it gives the strength to speak openly about our work in a trusted and experienced community.

Sometimes we ponder on what comes first, a coaching culture or coaching practice. Based on the experiences in our setting, it has not been a binary choice of culture versus coaching – both have been intertwined in a nuanced way and our view is that they work best when they are interconnected, rather than as separate entities, as by building those interrelated aspects at the same time it appears to create a more sustainable system; essentially, a component can't be seen as an add-on if it's too intertwined to pull apart from the rest.

Impact of coaching

We have a self-accountable model and consider wide forms of evidence that we can use to evaluate our learning. For us, this has included seeing a marked improvement in more formalised data, such as examination results, but the impacts on wellbeing, agency and mindset seen in staff feedback have been particularly significant. Coaching has been an important tool to support the professional practice of all of us as colleagues, in both teaching and operational roles. In doing so we have amplified to wider aspects to our roles and consequently have made more connections with others across the whole school community.

Staff feedback indicates that coaching has helped to connect colleagues around areas of practice; replace judgement with curiosity; provide a space for colleagues to think; develop models of practice to share with self, others and organisation; facilitate the exchange of knowledge between practitioners; strengthen creativity and imagination and allow for effective self-accountability. PLPs have witnessed how coaching has energised and empowered staff; brought a sense of feeling valued and respected; provided a space for practitioners to recharge and has given our learners a voice. The learning outcomes that our PLPs have witnessed show how coaching has built capacity; equipped us with skills to give better feedback; fostered curiosity; built leadership capacity; underpinned a way of being through better conversations; supported our autonomous professional learning; enabled PL to be sustained over time and developed meta-cognition and self-awareness.

In terms of student coaching, speaking with staff coaching our older students, we have seen how it has supported them to manage their workload and post-18 study and life choices. Listening to leaders who have been coached, we have seen how it has re-energised, developed skills, built an ability to engage with others in a process and create a sense of achievement. We have found that a bespoke (or tailored) approach in terms of the support we offer each leader has worked best, drawing on a range of approaches. One of our leaders recently reflected saying 'I appreciated being able to share my concerns and anxieties with a trusted coach. Moving forward I would like more staff to be able to have the opportunity to work with a colleague who can take time to listen and reflect with them.' Other leaders noted 'Coaching helps leaders to feel supported so that they can do their very best work [...] Coaching provided an opportunity to rehearse ideas and gain clarity [...] and become a more "human and humane" leader.'

Staff who have been working on pedagogical coaching noted that the changes they made to their teaching spanned out across all of the lessons they taught, not just the changes they made for the class they were observed with. Their joint pedagogical coaching has focused on developing specific areas of practice, such as better modelling of subject-specific skills, like source inference, or helping students get more out of feedback. In turn, this spotlight on practice has led to better learning outcomes for further students in other classes, too. Furthermore, they have reflected on how pedagogical coaching felt like 'someone saying I really care about what you're doing and want to help you to improve. And I want to give you my time to do that and [...] feels a bit indulgent. It feels like a bit of me time.' Their dialogue has signposted us to clear examples of what we see when coaching has impact. For all of our coaches and mentors, we have witnessed how they themselves have become learners from others through their practice as they commit to themselves as a learner. The impact that such collegial learning has ultimately makes a difference to the learning experiences of our students, which is the main goal as a learning organisation. One of our mentors reflected: 'Mentoring makes you have a spotlight on your own practice and your mentoring skills. The development and learning in terms of team teaching and planning was powerful. It changed the whole culture of the department, built trust, fuelled discussions, improved communication, sharing of ideas and developed our learning environment.'

Reflections

BSB's deliberate and attuned approach to coaching has woven it into the fabric of the school and its continued development is in response to the setting and led by the staff. Coaching is not an add-on: it is a way of being and a way of working in the school that values autonomous professional learning and the power of dialogue for personal and professional growth. It is interesting to read how encounters with a wide range of external partners and resources supports and sustains a homegrown approach to coaching and how BSB is exploring coaching for all members of their school community including students, staff, parents and beyond.

Chapter 12 endnotes

Final thoughts

We opened this chapter with the quote from Margaret Wheatley's inspirational 2009 book *Turning to Each Other: Simple Conversations to Restore Hope to the Future*. Writing this endnote 16 years later, her title still resonates. Wheatley states that 'If we want a different future, we have to take responsibility for what we are doing in the present' (p. 68). This is precisely what the CollectivED Award holders have done. They have used some of their time and effort in their multi-layered roles in educational settings to shift the gears on coaching, to acknowledge the tensions and appreciate the gains that emerge over time, and to situate it carefully within cultures that also focus on mentoring and wider professional learning. In doing so they have met the four award competencies of:

- encouraging and enabling collaborative conversations which create powerful professional learning
- building capacity in the work of educators and leaders to create contexts which support inclusive career-long and professional-wide learning
- working to break down barriers to professional development through positive engagement with the education sector and allied practitioners
- increasing the opportunities for educational change through enhanced professional agency and wellbeing.

Turning back to Wheatley's book title, we are aware that coaching in education is about shaping futures and that through the nature of coaching conversations change is possible and hope can be experienced. We also recognise that while coaching in education is a boundaried activity, it has permeable borders. We explore this further in chapter 18, using a model which conceptualises coaching in interacting contexts (see Figure 18.1). The encounters shared by CollectivED Award holders indicate the influences on the development of coaching in their settings and the ways that coaching has supported a sense of shared purpose and optimism. In the Venn diagrams of work and life, of learning and becoming, and of individual and community the experience of coaching can create a foundation for sustaining change.

Talking point

Share the four award competencies listed above with colleagues at a time when you have an opportunity for some thoughtful discussion. Which of these do you feel most strongly aligns with your current coaching intentions, practices and cultures in your setting? Do any of them provoke you to appreciate areas for focus or development? Listen carefully to each other's perspectives to ensure that initial assumptions are checked and challenged where necessary.

Ideas for action

This is an unusual suggestion for action. You may like to return to this chapter when you have read about the cycles of growth (CoG) model outlined in chapter 16. The reason for this is that the CollectivED Award design was implicitly influenced by the CoG model. In summary the key concepts are 'creativity, authenticity and solidarity' as attributes for professional learning and 'critique, articulate and expand' as resulting behaviours. If you do read this chapter again, keep these core ideas in mind and reflect upon how the encounters demonstrate these.

Chapter 13
Coaching as a way of developing purposeful conversational spaces

Facing the struggle and coming up with our own solutions is empowering and we usually know the best next steps to take. We can feel humiliated or disempowered if someone comes along and takes over, even if they solve the problem for us.

Kathryn Mannix (2021, p. 115)

Adopting a creative, critical and collaborative approach to the development of professional learning in education is a key principle of how CollectivED works. In this chapter we profile five examples of coaching which emerged through encounters facilitated directly by, or in partnership with, the CollectivED community. Like other encounters in this book these can be considered as an enhancement of the repertoire for coaching in education. They each offer scaffolds to help coaches, coaching participants and education leaders to sustain a coaching focus through intentional conversation and, as such, help to maintain the sense of purpose or roles of coaching in education. One of the common features of these approaches is that adopting the role of coach is not dependent on a formal training course or qualification. This is not to downplay the importance of professional learning and development in coaching quality or impact, but there is also a sense that being part of a community creating or using coaching approaches is an important opportunity for iterative professional learning.

We do not consider these approaches to be new 'types' of coaching – they all have what Knight would call 'dialogical' roots. In each case there are elements of enquiry and, as such, questions are used purposefully and considerately to support and empower the coachee to gain clarity, explore ideas and become aware of possibilities. They could also be considered relationally agentic forms of coaching, providing opportunities for goal-setting (where appropriate), with the coach enabling discussions about next steps, and acknowledging the potential of the coachee to make a positive difference in their educational setting with and for others.

The five encounters below all stem from specific projects based on partnerships with educators. The development of each coaching approach is described in the past tense, but where appropriate a present tense is used when practical advice for using the approach is given. It is anticipated that the approaches will continue to evolve over time as they are embedded in new programmes or contexts.

Encounter: dilemma-based coaching

Origins and development of dilemma-based coaching

Dilemma-based coaching (DBC) (CollectivED and Leeds Learning Alliance, 2024) was developed through an Erasmus+ project, called PROMISE, 'Promoting Inclusion in Society through Education: Professional Dilemmas in Practice'. The focus of PROMISE was the professional development of educators and the promotion of high-quality and innovative teaching, with a recognition that many of the challenges or professional dilemmas facing educators are embedded in issues related to inclusion (Beaton et al., 2021). DBC was first trialled online during the pandemic lockdowns by teachers, teacher educators and leaders from across a range of education phases and roles. It gave them the opportunity to engage in coaching-type conversations which were stimulated by sharing a specific dilemma related to inclusion that they were experiencing.

Following the emergence of DBC through the PROMISE project, two more sustained developmental opportunities emerged which helped us to engage a wider range of educators, over more sustained periods, to help them become familiar with DBC and to allow research and evaluation of the approach. CoachingLab involved an online network of educators in the UK, drawn from all phases, who met bimonthly in four 'gatherings'. During the CoachingLab gatherings participants were first introduced to DBC and then had multiple opportunities to use and discuss it together, with facilitated data-gathering related to their experience and perceptions of its value. The dilemmas brought to these gatherings were wide-ranging, extending the use of the approach beyond its origins in inclusion. DBC was also the basis of a year-long professional development and networking project hosted by Leeds Learning Alliance (LLA) and CollectivED. The network brought together teachers, teaching assistants and leaders from all types of school settings in half-termly in-person meetings. Their shared focus was acknowledgement of and desire to address the complexity and dilemmas of inclusion and they worked actively together to bring real situations to their DBC conversations, and to use these to surface areas of concern and uncertainty and to consider their capacities to respond well in their roles. Once again the participants in this network helped us to further enhance our understanding of DBC and gain a sense of it as a professional practice with potential for impact.

Scaffolding thinking using dilemma-based coaching

Learning from these three projects enhanced the guidance for engaging in DBC. First, the dilemma discussed in DBC should be introduced by the coachee, not assumed or imposed by the coach. Second, the quality of careful and considerate listening matters. This means questions should be used purposefully and sparingly to structure thinking and should also be introduced as appropriate, based on what is being discussed, rather than in an obligatory order. It is important that the coach allows the coachee to pause along the way rather than feel that they are being hurried along. Finally, as the DBC process is dialogical (rather than directive), questions are key tools to scaffold thinking.

The questions below are meant as a scaffold for the coach rather than a script. We do not promote a 'fidelity' concept, which would imply that positive outcomes of DBC were dependent on uniform uses of it as a direct intervention. However, it is completely appropriate to use the questions quite closely, especially when new to DBC. It is the case that more fluidity and flexibility develop through experience. It is also useful to think about whether the dilemma that is being discussed is 'emerging' or 'ongoing'. Most dilemmas are likely to be wrangled with over time and may be discussed across a sequence of coaching conversations because they remain live issues and are worthy of reflection on and as a source of learning. There are two sets of questions below and they may have more relevance at different stages of a coaching sequence.

If a dilemma is emerging or has not previously been discussed, the following questions were found to be helpful:

- What is the dilemma you are concerned with?
- Who does this involve?
- How does the situation make you feel?
- What seems to be influencing what is happening?
- Can you see any opportunities for change?
- How confident are you about your relevant knowledge and experience?
- How can I help you at this point?
- Who else might be worth discussing this with?

In ongoing conversations about a dilemma or when it has already started to be responded to, the focus may turn to the decisions and actions being taken and the professional learning that is emerging from working through dilemmas. At this stage the following questions were considered helpful:

- Did you try anything new in relation to this dilemma?
- What are you learning about others and yourself as you engage more with this dilemma?
- Do you see things differently at all and if so can you talk about that?
- What might be the legacy of this approach in your setting and practice?
- How might other educators gain insights from your experiences?

Experience and impacts of DBC

Through the opportunities to develop and apply DBC important clarifications emerged. Perhaps most important is the stance that recognising a dilemma does not imply fault. Dilemmas in education are persistent and multi-layered and, while they are experienced through the unique lives of individuals, their characteristics are rarely unique to the particular situation or person. Typical dilemmas related to:

- meaningful curriculum development and appropriate means of assessing learning
- tensions inherent in complex organisations and professional communication and management challenges
- relationships with parents
- complexities of meeting diverse learning needs
- diverse and conflicting expectations that society has of education provision
- working within systems of inequality to address bias, vulnerability and disadvantage.

Learning from professionals about how they have used DBC has helped to make sense of its form and function. The person taking the role of coach supports the coachee to think through a genuine dilemma that they are experiencing. In DBC coaches recognise the curiosities, anxieties, scepticism and ambitions that coachees experience in relation to dilemmas. Coaching conversations are therefore always unique. DBC creates opportunities for educators to embrace complexity rather than seek to reduce it, with an aspiration to learn from and work appropriately when dilemmas emerge. There is less focus on reacting to and resolving a discrete problem, and more focus on acknowledging and responding to an authentic dilemma.

Conceptualising DBC

Following the analysis of data emerging from the participants in CoachingLab key themes emerged, which included how DBC participants made connections with their values and ethics as educators, often triggered by recognising the emotions which were acknowledged during coaching. In addition a sense of ease with the capacity for shared responsibility was felt by some participants, accepting that dilemmas were often open-ended rather than easily solved. The experience of engaging in DBC also provided participants with alternative understandings of coaching and especially recognising the value of it as a counterweight to objective-led CPD, which they were more familiar with.

The CoachingLab work led to an enhanced conceptualisation of DBC and a visualisation of this is shown in Figure 13.1.

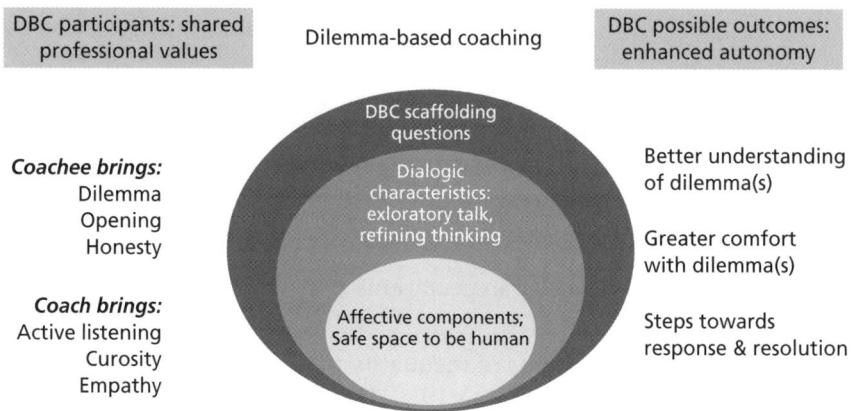

Figure 13.1 Dilemma-based coaching. © CollectivED, 2024

A DBC conversation dialogue

What follows is a coaching dialogue, transcribed and given here in full. It was a genuine DBC conversation held between Jasen and Rachel, relating to Jasen's teaching role. Reading it offers an opportunity to see how the questions proposed as a scaffold for DBC have been used responsively. It is also evident that as the conversation continued, a degree of dialogic co-construction is happening. Explanatory notes are added which demonstrate how the coach is actively listening and framing the conversation.

Coach   Jasen, you've said that you have a dilemma but I don't know what it is. So can you tell me what you're concerned about at the moment? *[This opening question is an invitation to the conversation and centres the focus on the dilemma.]*

Coachee   Yes. It relates really to the fact that I'm working in a range of schools in England. Because of Covid, early reading is a real issue. Catch-ups are needed, there's definitely some gaps, especially in the area of phonics – learning sounds to help with decoding. What I'm finding really tricky is that because there's this discussion and rhetoric of catch-up, I'm

Chapter 13 Coaching: developing purposeful conversational spaces

seeing many schools using online purchased resources for consistency. So it's allowing teachers and teaching assistants to all be on the same page and perhaps be able to teach this phonics without actually having to have a great depth of understanding. The issue for me is that I've got experience of over 20 years and a real passion for early reading. The idea of using a video, where in fact I'm pressing a button and someone else, a pre-recorded person is teaching the class, I find really tricky.

Coach So you're talking about this from the current position of teaching those classes. How old are the children that you're teaching? *[Here the coach is seeking clarity.]*

Coachee The children that I'm with at the moment are six- and seven-year-olds.

Coach So, six- and seven-year-olds learning reading, with post-pandemic concerns around some of the core skills around phonics. I'm assuming that it's not just you and your class that have been obliged to use these videos. Are you seeing this, it's not just because you're not a good enough teacher of reading, this is common practice, is it? *[The coach is summarising and checking context.]*

Coachee Yes. It's this catch-up agenda, closing the gap. It's because certain ways of teaching phonics require many, many adults to be involved. There are small groups. In many schools it's scheduled. So this teaching session, which is about 20 minutes, is scheduled at the same time every day, in different parts of the school. So it's literally like everybody is teaching at the same time and it has to be done within a certain amount of time. I think it's that whole idea of yes, you've got all of these people with different levels of skill but this session has to be done.

Coach I want to ask you how it makes you feel, but first of all let's clarify your position. So I guess I'm interested in how does it make you feel when you are the class teacher but also, how does it make you feel given that you're an experienced

	teacher and, if I'm hearing you right, with a specialism in teaching reading or a very keen interest in teaching reading? So we need to think about that in relation to who you are. So how does it make you feel that this is what you're given as a way of teaching now? *[The focus on emotional response is deliberately situated by the coach, who also shows the coachee that they have been listening and threading together the information.]*
Coachee	For me personally, as an experienced teacher with an expertise in this area, it does feel frustrating to be, well I'm not even going to say scripted because I'm not even the person talking. It's almost side-lined. So it feels, for me, I guess disempowering, taking away my professional autonomy. So a frustration really.
Coach	Clearly, you're entitled to that frustration. You're a professional. But we also have to acknowledge that we're there for the children and young people that we teach. You've acknowledged that there is a post-pandemic catch-up gap or anxiety. So there seems to be a response to that. How does it make you feel in terms of the pupils that you're working with? What do you notice? How are they being influenced by this, do you think? Is it good for them and just frustrating for you or are you worried about anything in relation to them? *[An extended set of questions, helping to centre the discussion around the learners and exploring the relationship between the teacher's response and the learners' needs.]*
Coachee	I mean weighing it up really, I suppose I feel that there's a benefit in that beyond the class that I may be teaching, there is a focus throughout the school and so at least there's this positive feeling that children are having regular input. But from my point of view, I know from experience that the resources that I have used or created or perhaps some of the language that I know from experience work, but for the sake of consistency, I am not really encouraged to let's say deviate from the programme.

Chapter 13 Coaching: developing purposeful conversational spaces

Coach
: I can understand this dilemma. I'm sure it's not unique to you and your setting. It's probably not unique to the teaching of reading. It might be the sort of thing that gets repeated over time but maybe with a different pedagogic or curriculum focus. It sounds like it might be quite an acute issue though. I am concerned that it might be that there are no opportunities for change. Can you see any opportunities for change? *[Coach offers reassurance that the expression of the dilemma is valid and begins to connect the specificity of it with wider school concerns. They are also starting to orientate the conversation towards the future.]*

Coachee
: Well, I would hope that as time progressed and that other teachers or teaching assistants became more confident in the process, I'm hoping that there would be some flexibility in the future for being able to use the resource but also to be able to bring your own flavours, your own teaching ways and methods, especially if you know they work, especially if over the years you've had success with those other ways.

Coach
: It sounds as if there's a glimmer of optimism and part of that is because you have some confidence that you, as an example of a teacher, have the relevant knowledge and expertise to help to flex this a little bit in the future. Is there anything that you are aiming to do, whether it is related to your own situation you find yourself in now as a teacher or in your role more widely in the school sector? If so, and I don't think there will be an answer to this that is easy, is there anything I can do to help you at this point as your coach? *[The coach is focusing on the coachee's potential role in the future, highlighting their agency.]*

Coachee
: I think what I realise and accept is an island of good practice actually isn't really sufficient within a school. A single teacher teaching in a certain way is not enough. So I accept the bigger picture, the need for many year groups to learn, not just the class that I may be teaching. But I think that what I would feel able to challenge moving forward is to perhaps ask why there might… No, not ask why there isn't

	the opportunity but ask for what areas of flexibility there might be once there's this fluency, once there's this perhaps basis of a common level of confidence? I'm not sure…
Coach	When you say you could ask, who were you going to ask? *[Coach notices a key future action and pushes for a little more detail.]*
Coachee	I mean it would be leaders within schools. For particular ways of teaching phonics, there are actually phonics leaders within schools and these people…
Coach	So like kind of key stakeholders who have got a level of responsibility but hopefully as well develop a level of expertise in relation to phonics and reading. It's that group perhaps, the people who might lever some change to some better understanding. I'm not an expert in this area. There's probably nothing I can do to help you at this point other than to encourage you to hold that space, to keep that in mind and to hold the space and to look for those opportunities. As well as those phonics leaders, is there anybody else that you might be discussing this with? There's just me but there's all those other people. Is there a first action in the next few weeks where you might be talking this through with somebody? *[Another extended response, with new questions starting to build towards co-construction of ideas.]*
Coachee	Yes.
Coach	Can I ask, have you talked to the children? I know you will talk to the children but have you talked to them about this? *[A provocation from the coach.]*
Coachee	It's interesting you ask that because I have wanted to ask the children about whether they feel that they are learning the best way for them or even are they enjoying. So that is a useful question that you've posed because that has been on my mind, that actually in the hurly-burly of being in the classroom, actually it is really important to…

Coach	I mean it's fraught with difficulties, isn't it? Asking the children because what are they comparing it with? They have their current experience. It's quite difficult for them to get the perspective. But I guess if you're concerned about children, you're concerned about how applicable and appropriate this is for all children. We're starting to get a sense from them. It might be a useful way to then lead into conversations with colleagues. We're going to have to stop now, Jasen, because I've got another class to teach and I think you're probably quite busy as well. So thank you. I appreciate this. Perhaps we'll come back and meet in maybe a few weeks' time. Let's keep this dilemma alive and maybe explore it again. But if you want to check in at any time, you're very welcome to. But I'm very keen to come back and think about how you might be responding to this and learning from it as an experienced professional, not as a naive professional but somebody who has more commitment to this. So thank you, thank you for sharing that with me. *[The coach is sharing their informed perspective and ensuring that while several next steps have been identified by Jasen these are connected to each other in a way that might aid further sense-making and a pathway to starting to respond to the dilemma. They also offer appreciation and closure of this conversation, with an assurance of future engagement.]*
Coachee	Thank you for listening and posing those questions, Rachel.

Experiencing hopefulness

A group of educators who had been using DBC to explore issues related to inclusion provided real insights into its value, including the experience of 'hopefulness'. Their perspectives are offered here. One participant noted that the DBC approach got quickly to the heart of 'it', with 'it' being the range of inclusion issues experienced in her education setting. She contrasted this with other models of coaching, which she described as valid but sometimes more laboured and less compatible with helping the coachee to gain clarity and insight in a timely fashion. In developing their coaching skills, and by taking the role of observers, the participants said that they had been conscious of enhancing their listening skills.

As teachers and managers, the participants felt that sometimes they were too quick to offer advice or even instruction, instead of creating enabling spaces for others to draw on their own understanding and skills in relation to dilemmas. They recognised that in developing a coaching repertoire they were breaking from these habits and instead opening up a quality space for reflection. They acknowledged how unique the coaching spaces created during the network meetings were compared to the daily rush of school life and the routine debriefings of incidents.

The network participants reflected on how the dilemma-based coaching approach was helping them to unpack the complexities and multiple dimensions of the situations they found themselves in and to explore options for change in inclusion practices. They valued the chance to engage in coaching conversations with members of the network who did not work in their schools and did not necessarily inhabit the same professional role. It was felt that colleagues in the network typically brought no assumptions or bias to the coaching conversations. For example, the working through of the dilemma led to one participant noticing that she had been correcting herself as she was talking and, as such, identified more clearly what the circumstances were, focusing more positively on the opportunities for change that had been present.

The fact that this quality space encouraged coachees to think positively in relation to inclusion dilemmas was a recurrent theme. Instead of seeing the dilemma as a stubborn problem the coaching conversation encouraged participants to understand it with more subtlety. They stated that they found themselves thinking in more depth and detail about the needs of individual pupils and students. They also said that this led them to recognise that while individual students are unique many of the associated inclusion dilemmas were shared rather than singular. The fact that the coach was neutral while always curious meant that although dilemmas may trigger an emotional response this was acknowledged, but tended not to overwhelm the conversation. Instead, the participants' values, beliefs and ethics seemed to be brought to the fore. The DBC approach was also deemed to be appropriate in helping to establish a balance between reflection and forward thinking. This forward thinking was described as 'planting seeds' which were already bearing fruit in creating new opportunities for inclusion.

Chapter 13 Coaching: developing purposeful conversational spaces

In our ever-more online professional world it is worth noting one last characteristic of the network which seemed powerful. The request from participants to retain the in-person regularly scheduled meetings, and the fact that they largely prioritised their attendance at these, demonstrated the value they saw in coming together as professionals. Being together and using DBC as a form of regular conversation were reported by the participants as helping them to feel reassured that their own professional experiences were shared and that the dilemmas they face are not because they themselves are in deficit. Holding the conversations in small groups scattered around the room with the opportunity to share the key issues that emerged created what was described as a lower-stakes scenario than the experiences that some of them had of line management, mentoring or coaching conversations conducted behind closed doors in schools and without the opportunity for shared reflection. They valued the expertise that each other brought as colleagues and coaches. They recognised that they were asking and being asked appropriate thought-provoking questions by people who could readily understand the terminology that was being used and the substantive nature of the contexts and communities in which each teacher worked.

Perhaps the most positive note, and one which was first highlighted by an individual in the thinking round but consolidated by others as they too reflected on the experience, was one of 'hopefulness'. While the sources of the coaching conversation were the authentic dilemmas that the educators brought into the space, the structure of the coaching conversation meant that the conversation was not woeful but instead became hopeful. The teachers, leaders and teaching assistants grappling with the dilemmas of inclusion found participating in the network and the adoption of a DBC approach both in the network and rippling out into their own settings to be a professional opportunity to create hope.

Reflections

It is hard to overstate how affirming creating hope is, particularly for professionals who have to grapple with many complexities, challenges and contexts which they cannot have full command over, which inevitably throw up dilemmas. It is also valuable that DBC was found to be usable in mixed and diverse groups, with relatively limited 'training', but instead with effective facilitation and a commitment to honour the time people had given to being part of the conversations. For some of the participants whose participation is reflected upon here, DBC was a first foray into coaching. This encounter is also an authentic example of a coaching approach that was rolled out with a degree of ease, and which continues to be practised in a number of informal and more organised situations.

Encounter: co-coaching for reimagining a positive direction for education

Origins and development of co-coaching

Following the PROMISE project, from which DBC emerged, and in response to the challenges of the pandemic a new Erasmus+ project was developed, called RAPIDE, Re-imagining a Positive Direction for Education. This time coaching was an approach we designed in from the start. The proposition was that in times of uncertainty and change educators can draw on their existing experiences, their often unexpected and rapidly adopted new ways of working and the challenges they and the learners face, to explore possible futures in education. We wanted to encourage positive, appreciative and exploratory conversations which were non-hierarchical and could be undertaken in person, online and both within and between specific education contexts. We called this approach 'co-coaching', which was a term easily translated across languages and inferred supportive and reciprocal opportunities.

In the RAPIDE project we found value in exploring education narratives emerging from the pandemic and then started to associate these with co-coaching. As an evidence base we interviewed teachers in the partner countries about their pandemic experiences and created 'narratives' from each contribution. As well as publishing these online we analysed them and started to note that their common features included:

- the realities
- the responses
- immediate and later reflections
- reimaginings.

The project named these the 4Rs. Most of the narratives opened with the changes that the pandemic created and, as such, they spoke to the realities of the situation. They also illustrated educators' reflections while the realities continued to unfold as they made sense of how learning was enabled through new platforms and practices. The 4Rs related to pedagogy, social and emotional aspects of remote and digital learning, altered forms of participation, new technologies and evolving professional and learner identities. As lockdowns ended, the future of education remained uncertain. The project narrative vignettes thus also offered insights into how educators were reimagining the future of teaching and learning. The 4Rs became themes which were explored across the project, including through the co-coaching dimension.

Scaffolding thinking using co-coaching

Tensions still exist between the pull of the pre-pandemic norms and the legacy of its consequences in education. The world has been changed by what was both challenging and possible during the pandemic. In many countries concerns about deteriorating school attendance and student and staff wellbeing are in the spotlight. Issues of behaviour and socialisation remain while the opportunities for enhanced digital support for learning have become more visible. Reimagining a positive direction for education is worthy of consideration and enabling individuals to consider their own roles, capacity, ambitions and desires to help create that future is a valid purpose for co-coaching conversations.

As co-coaching was developed and used within the RAPIDE project, we needed to be able to offer clear, concise guidance to participants using the approach. We were aware that the multilingual project meant that English was often a second or third language and that awareness of, or familiarity with, coaching in education varied significantly. Therefore our advice and question suggestions were deliberately accessible and easy to translate. It was not uncommon for co-coaching to be reciprocal (role-switching) within network meetings of professional development events.

Co-coaching is facilitated by a 'coach' who helps their coaching partner to explore experiences, opportunities and feelings related to their work in education. We encourage educators engaging in co-coaching to be curious, creative and supportive. Sharing narratives, stories and experiences is a good way to begin co-coaching. Some people like to write a short narrative to take into a coaching conversation. Other people liked to spend a little time reflecting on their experiences at the start of the conversation. Sharing narratives in co-coaching promotes voice, reflections and solidarity. The coach listens and begins to offer questions which support critical thinking, develop new perspectives and trigger decision making for actions. Figure 13.2 illustrates the types of questions which can be helpful and have resonance with the 4Rs of realities, responses, reflections and reimagining.

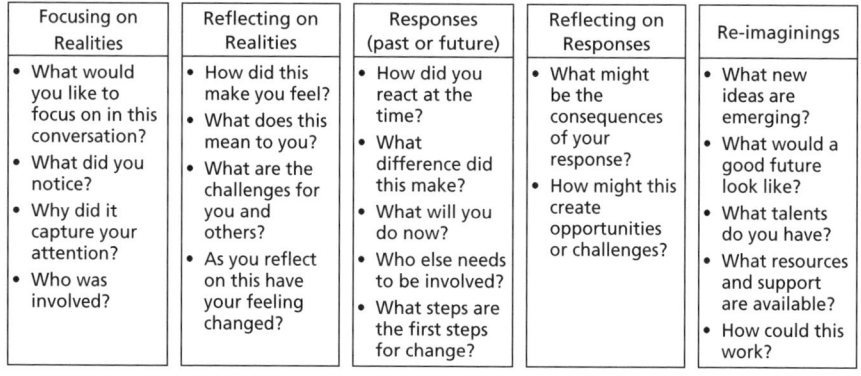

Focusing on Realities	Reflecting on Realities	Responses (past or future)	Reflecting on Responses	Re-imaginings
• What would you like to focus on in this conversation? • What did you notice? • Why did it capture your attention? • Who was involved?	• How did this make you feel? • What does this mean to you? • What are the challenges for you and others? • As you reflect on this have your feeling changed?	• How did you react at the time? • What difference did this make? • What will you do now? • Who else needs to be involved? • What steps are the first steps for change?	• What might be the consequences of your response? • How might this create opportunities or challenges?	• What new ideas are emerging? • What would a good future look like? • What talents do you have? • What resources and support are available? • How could this work?

Figure 13.2 Questions to scaffold co-coaching based on the 4Rs. Source: https://rapide-eu.net/engage

As a coach in co-coaching it is essential to avoid making judgements, offer unwanted solutions, break confidentiality or act as a therapist or counsellor. Applying these principles will help you build a co-coaching relationship which is based on trust and allows participants to be authentic, compassionate and open to learning.

Reflection

It has been interesting to take the co-coaching approach beyond the original Erasmus+ project remit and participants. Genuine interest has been shown in using it with pre-service and early career teachers to support them to make sense of their current experiences and to recognise their role as new professionals in shaping the future of education, whether it is at the scale of working with individual pupils or colleagues, contributing to discussions and decisions shaping future practice and understanding the significance of their own agency. The same has been suggested about using co-coaching at a time of transitions within careers, for example, when developing a new identity as a leader or within teams.

Encounter: attuned authentic coaching for teachers (AACT)

Origins and development of AACT

AACT (CollectivED, 2024) was co-created by a group of teachers, teacher educators and coaches as a response to the surge in teacher coaching (particularly from new 'providers' of instructional coaching). AACT is based on cycles of engagement and participation enabling co-enquiry between the coach and the teacher. It is an emergent model. As the initial work of the co-creation group ended, we invited colleagues working in and with schools to play with the approach, to deduce its potential and to adapt it to suit their contexts.

We based the development of AACT on the following key principles of teacher coaching:

> Teacher coaching is an overarching and personalised approach which, through sustained dialogue and enhanced support from a coach, provides the teacher with an opportunity to reflect, gain clarity, make decisions and to respond in the context of their own teaching and aligned with their professional purpose.

In developing the foundations for AACT we are advocating pedagogical knowledge and practice based on two foundations. The first is authentic instruction (Newmann and Wehlage, 1993) which still resonates 30 years on. Newmann and Wehlage researched and advocated for five key principles for learning which have meaning beyond the classroom:

1. learning activities which develop higher-order thinking
2. depth of knowledge (rather than a shallow, surface coverage of content)
3. connectedness to the world beyond the classroom
4. substantive conversation allowing students to talk meaningfully about their learning
5. social support for learning based on mutual respect and high expectations.

AACT also deliberately builds on attuned teaching (Gunning and Lofthouse, 2022), which has a foothold in trauma-informed and attachment-aware teaching. There are four key components which we

Coaching with purpose

call the ABCD of attuned teaching and which relate to wellbeing and inclusion in learning. In summary these are Adopt an anti-bias stance, Build relationships which make a difference, Create safe, enabling environments and Deepen understanding over time. Figure 13.3 expands these core ideas.

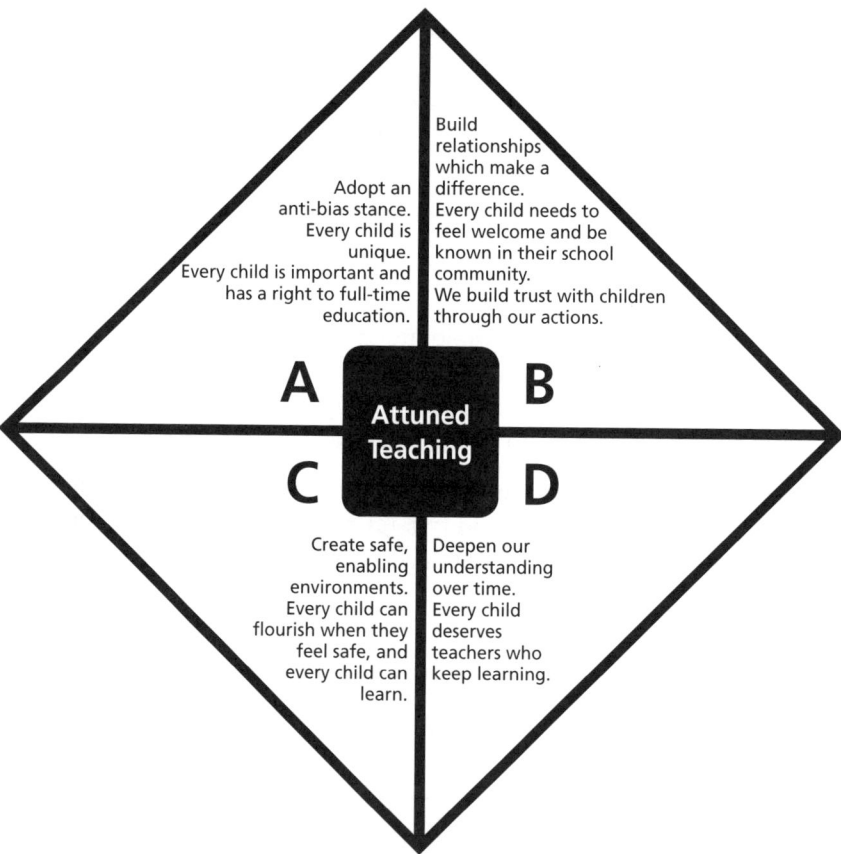

Figure 13.3 Attuned teaching. © CollectivED, 2024

It is the final piece of this jigsaw (D – deepen understanding over time) which motivates the AACT approach. We aim for this coaching approach to itself be pedagogic (based on learning) and have used the authentic and attuned principles to develop coaching guidance which

Chapter 13 Coaching: developing purposeful conversational spaces

respects teachers as unique individuals working in complex and diverse settings. We want coaching to support teachers to develop their own pedagogic practices grounded in meaningful learning and positive social relationships for their students. This is summarised in Figure 13.4.

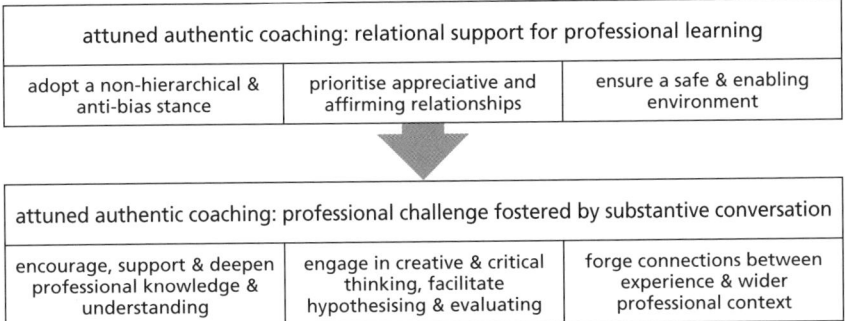

Figure 13.4 Professional and relational characteristics of AACT. Source: CollectivED (2024)

Scaffolding thinking using AACT

In practical terms this means that AACT starts with contracting and consent and agreed purpose to establish the relational support for professional learning. This component of contracting and consent corresponds with the proposition that while coaching may be offered as part of a wider school initiative, the choice to engage with it should rest with the teacher. It is also a reminder that the context might be whole-school, age-phase or subject-related, but the coaching focus should always be personalised and details of coaching conversations should remain confidential.

AACT is based on an underpinning cycle of co-enquiry shown in Figure 13.5.

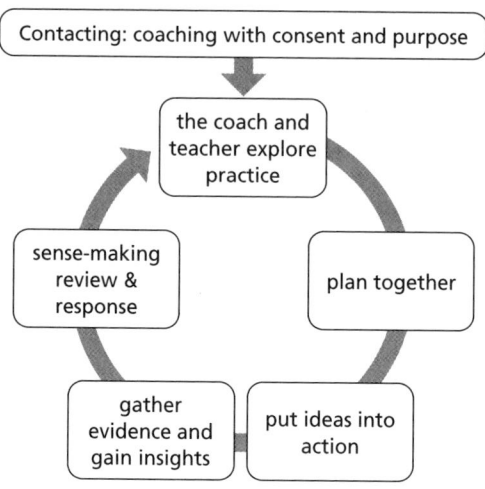

Figure 13.5 The co-enquiry cycle underpinning AACT. Source: CollectivED (2024)

It is suggested that three coaching cycles of coaching co-enquiry help deepen understanding and develop practice over time and can be undertaken at an appropriate and responsive (rather than predetermined) timescale. The co-enquiry coaching components will be adapted according to context, for example, there may be value in classroom observation, use of video, opportunity to engage with new training or reading as suits the purpose.

As an opportunity for co-enquiry the coach acts in a way to support the teacher to develop their knowledge and understanding through provoking reflection, seeking out information to guide decision-making, facilitating planned changes, exploring existing and new evidence, acknowledging both tensions and opportunities, engaging with their own values, feeling less discomfort with dilemmas and recognising the ways that they can respond within their professional roles and using their expertise. This is achieved by fostering substantive conversation which creates safe space for and enables sensemaking through higher-order thinking. Coaching conversations are characterised by analysis of information, questions and provocations which lead to creative and critical thinking, synthesising, hypothesising and evaluating. These lay the foundations of effective future decision-making. These outcomes are shared by both the coach and teacher.

Experiences and impact of AACT

AACT has started to be used in a range of contexts, and here four short accounts are offered as reflections on its contribution to the coaching repertoire, based on initial evidence emerging from practice. The first and last ones are from participants in the co-creation group, and the middle two are from practitioners using it following the emerging guidelines.

Account 1

As an experienced teacher and deputy headteacher in a primary school in England, I joined the AACT co-creation group because I am passionate about mentoring/coaching and have recently been looking into instructional coaching. Participating in designing the AACT model helped me connect with other professionals and listen to their ideas. It also helped me reflect on my role as a mentor/coach. I am drawn to AACT as it has a real focus on building relationships and personalising the support I can offer, with no 'one-size-fits-all' approach. As such it creates a safe space for teachers.

Account 2

I am the principal of an international school in Europe. I have wanted to develop coaching within the school since joining it recently and I used AACT to launch a pilot coaching programme. I chose it because of the useful guidance on how to coach as this was my first time as a coach, although I have been a mentor before. AACT provided a structure that was useful for both myself as a coach and the coachees as they knew what to expect. The structure meant that the coachees came up with a development plan in an area of their practice that they wanted to concentrate on. This meant that something tangible came from the process. In the pilot stage I had four coachees, all primary teachers, and with the exception of one, all have been teachers for several years. I shared the AACT information with them and they agreed to being part of the project. They all attended the first session with an idea of the area of practice they wanted to work on – so much of the focus on that session was listening to them talk through different ideas. The planning session was interesting as they all went off and planned their ideas with other members of staff. I think some of this was because they did not want to plan with the principal! I also think they were conscious of the fact that

I am a secondary specialist. So the second session was spent listening to them talking through their plan rather than planning with them. With the exception of one teacher whose enquiry related to a middle leadership role, I then observed part of their lesson and finally we met to review the observed lesson.

As a new coach I have had to learn to listen and not to interrupt with my great ideas! This has been the hardest part, which I am still working on. For my colleagues, I think it has been a tremendous success, one teacher has worked on her whole-school leadership skills by planning a whole-school sustainability day, another has improved how she deals with behaviour by developing a toolbox of strategies, one has applied for, and secured, a promotion to middle leadership and another colleague has introduced a maths carousel in her class which has provided challenge for students who need it and allowed her time to work with lower-ability students. The overall impact on students is improved outcomes in maths (she is extending the carousel idea to other subjects next year), a more robust middle leadership, greater awareness of sustainability across the school and improved behaviour management in early years. Above all, I think all of us have developed more confidence in ourselves as we have taken on new challenges.

AACT has brought the culture of coaching into the school. In a short space of just a few months using AACT has led to school improvements. Next year we plan to launch coaching as a professional learning community and will probably start with the AACT structure as I feel it is a good way to help coaches begin to build their coaching skills.

Account 3

I work in a small primary school in England and have a number of key leadership roles. I have been teaching for 11 years. A key feature of AACT that attracted me was that the values underpinning the approach strongly align with our school ethos.

We have completed one full cycle of AACT with a focus on improving writing in school. We left this very open though, and coachees could choose which area of writing they wanted to improve, e.g. writing in continuous provision, fine motor skills, writing in foundation subjects, grammar. As this was the first cycle, we dedicated a lot of staff meeting

Chapter 13 Coaching: developing purposeful conversational spaces

time to this. To begin with all teachers were trained on AACT as we thought it was important that teachers understood the reasons why we felt this coaching programme was beneficial to our school setting. We held staff meetings that focused on different points of the cycle, which gave teachers a clear focus. The overall schedule meant that coaches and coachees had time to research and implement any changes. Our staff were very engaged in AACT. They reported that they liked working with members of staff they would not normally interact with, e.g. across key stages. All staff members said they have gained something beneficial from taking part in the sessions. They also said that they liked having a coach as it made them accountable to enact change. For the first cycle, we were very structured in how we delivered it as I wanted to make sure that coaches and coachees understood each stage of the cycle. Now we've done the first cycle, we will start to provide more flexibility.

Despite it taking some time to set up and facilitate AACT I thoroughly recommend it! It supports creating a collaborative culture in school. Even early career teachers can be coaches as they do not need to be experts like a mentor. Everyone has something to gain from participating in a coaching programme like this.

Account 4

As a co-author of the original attuned teaching approach I am keen to see it being used widely to support pedagogy, education and teacher development and AACT is a way of bringing it into action. The attuned aspect enables me as a coach and mentor to intuitively respond to my coachee/mentee. It has become a way of being for me in work – listening, enabling thinking and reflection, identifying need, exploring and examining contexts and natures of people and children, studying their ways of being, and interweaving this with an attuned coaching mentoring response. Being introduced to authentic instruction has added another layer of integrity, quality assurance and equity to my approach. I have been using AACT across three areas of work. First, with a nursery school, focusing on developing and promoting a joy of outside learning through coaching and mentoring the whole staff team. The collaboration has triggered creative pedagogy in this area. Second, with an early years and foundation stage (EYFS) team, where I used AACT cycles with the EYFS leader and she in turn is using AACT cycles within her team to develop and deepen their pedagogy. Third, within a new professional development project 'SPACE to Flourish' – working with teacher peers and educator peers teaching them about attuned teaching and applying a loose AACT model to our development and journey with them across the year. So far I have appreciated the ability to use AACT with flexibility to personalise coaching cycles and create a responsive approach over time.

Reflection

The development of AACT through a CollectivED co-creation project forms part of the ongoing interest in how teachers can support each other to continue to engage in professional learning and to refine their practices. Being explicit about both pedagogic and relational principles and building on prior research and theory are important foundations for this work. It was undertaken outside of the commercial arena and this may mean it is not rapidly promoted or scaled up. However, it does mean that the invitation to explore the potential of AACT, make situationally appropriate adaptations and share with others is genuine. In the increasingly marketised and branded coaching world, where positive spin risks the over-promotion, rapid uptake and sometimes equally rapid abandonment of initiatives, we are satisfied that there is a purposeful place for approaches such as AACT to make a positive difference.

Encounter: Flourish programme

The details of this encounter are written by CollectivED graduate teaching assistant, Sheila Ball. In addition to supporting the inclusion of practices based on Kline's Thinking Environment™ (TE) (see chapter 2) into a postgraduate coaching and mentoring programme, Sheila has designed a new programme called 'Flourish'. We are not presuming a straightforward overlap between TE and coaching, but as its influence grows, the propositions underpinning it are worthy of consideration. Sheila opens this encounter by stating that Kline's TE is a philosophy of communication based on decades of practice and close observation. Sheila's PhD is exploring the role of the TE in educational settings. Flourish is an eight-month hybrid programme aimed at educators from early years to higher education, with or without positional leadership roles, interested in facilitating cultural change in their professional setting. Roles held by participants in the first cohort group include postgraduate student, learning support assistant, senior leader, lecturer, independent education consultant and coach. Sheila writes:

The purpose of the programme is to introduce participants to the ten components and building blocks which make up Kline's Thinking Environment. The hope is that participants can apply the principles and practices in their educational contexts with the aim of enabling children, young people and their colleagues to flourish without fear.

Ten components of Kline's Thinking Environment

Kline's Thinking Environment is a philosophy of communication based on the belief that human beings have an extraordinary capacity to think independently. In her 40 years of studying what enables people to think, Kline has concluded that the quality of everything we do in life depends on the quality of the thinking we do first (Kline, 1999). However, Kline has also observed that our capacity to think depends upon the behaviour of those who are with us while we are thinking (Kline, 1999). These two discoveries have led Kline to identify a set of behaviours to enable others to think independently in their personal and professional lives: Attention, Equality, Ease, Appreciation, Encouragement, Feelings, Information, Difference, Incisive Questions™ and Place. These behaviours are known as the ten components and can be used in one-to-one and group communicative contexts.

1. The foundational component **Attention** describes a particular mode of listening which connects people through a shared belief that what each other thinks matters (Kline, 1999). Whether one-to-one or in a group, a key ingredient of this mode of listening is the listener's promise not to interrupt the person who is thinking aloud or speaking. Knowing we won't be interrupted, Kline states, enables the development of exploratory and emergent thinking (2020). Such thinking, Kline has observed, comes in waves and pauses due to our capacity to think faster than we can produce the words to articulate our thinking. Knowing that the listener's generous attention will be maintained during these momentary silences and that our thinking is valued can deepen the process of thinking, enabling the scrutiny and resolution of personal or professional issues.

As opposed to listening to reply, **Attention** is about being in service to the person thinking aloud by activating three channels of focus: noticing the content of what is being thought aloud; noticing one's internal response to that and consciously encouraging the other to continue thinking aloud. Such encouragement is evident through non-verbal communication: warm gaze; eyes resting on the other's eyes; calm dynamic physical composure; not interrupting and being fascinated by the thinking that is about to emerge.

2. **Equality** is about treating each other as thinking equals, regardless of status, experience, identity, age or beliefs. This means that in a group gathering, through the creation of rounds, there is a balance of power. Everyone has the privilege to speak without being interrupted as well as the responsibility of respecting the time available so that as well as taking their turn to speak, others will have their opportunity to speak.

3. **Ease** is about creating psychological safety particularly in group situations where there may be internal or external pressure or competition to produce the best answers. When we know our thinking matters and that we will have our turn to think aloud without interruption (Attention and Equality), any tension or sense of urgency is dispelled and an easeful space can be created.

4. **Appreciation** is about noticing what is good and saying it. Referencing neuro-imaging research, Kline states that appreciative thinking and feeling positively impact blood flow to the brain, supporting our capacity to think effectively (Kline, 2009).

5. **Encouragement**, with the French '*cœur*' (heart) at its core and 'courage', is about emboldening others to venture wholeheartedly to the unexplored edge of their thinking. Encouragement makes explicit the nature of our listening and the quality of connection that is forged when we believe others can think independently. Through that connection, trust is built which enables others to be brave enough to share their tentative or radical thinking, which may lead to improvements, developments, innovations and better decision-making.

6. The component of **Feelings** is informed by the emerging field of neuroscience, which has revealed the intertwined nature of

emotional and cognitive processes and so the type of listening mentioned above welcomes others' feelings as well as thoughts.

7. **Information** is about ensuring that everyone present in a group situation, such as a meeting or workshop for example, has access to everything they need to know (documentation, agendas, reports, etc.) in good time to enable them to think well and fully participate, thus enhancing transparency and equitable sharing of power.

8. **Difference** is about committing to freedom from the untrue assumptions which drive prejudice. By listening without interruption to each person with whom we are communicating, offering that calibre of Attention, regardless of background, age, gender or faith, fascinated by where thinking may venture next, untrue assumptions that may be held consciously or otherwise about group identity can be challenged.

9. **Incisive Questions**™ are questions which enable high-quality independent thinking by removing limiting untrue assumptions (e.g. 'I'm no good at maths', 'I can't teach that class') lived as true which block thinking and can limit human potential.

10. The final component of **Place** is about creating an environment that shows people they are valued. This can be demonstrated through our physical composure when offering Attention as well as preparing the physical space in which the communication is to take place so that it is welcoming (e.g. light, positioning of furniture, refreshments, stationery, plants).

Influence of the Flourish programme on coaching

As I have been working with the participants in group and one-to-one sessions, I have been able to gain insights into the ways that the programme is impacting on coaching-type work in their settings, which suggests development of their self-awareness, listening practices, quality of reflection and capacity to create more inclusive and nourishing spaces in their professional settings for children, young people and adults.

Many participants have referred to becoming more aware of a perceived lack of time to think in their roles, an internal pressure to be productive and efficient and a lack of appreciation in day-to-day communication. Some have commented on their being aware of a judgemental presence driven by perceived pressures of hierarchy and time. There is a sense that the Flourish programme has helped them to slow down, notice how they listen to others and practise giving attention in a way that enhances reflection.

Some have shared how they are using some of Kline's strategies such as rounds and thinking pairs in lessons and in meetings and professional learning conversations with colleagues. They are hearing reflections from children and young people that they have 'never been listened to before' and that the use of thinking rounds at the beginning and end of a lesson helps them feel safe and that this practice makes them feel heard and valued. Another participant has noticed how the inclusion of rounds at the start and close of meetings which invite appreciation has made a significant difference to colleagues' behaviour.

The programme seems to be impacting on a range of professional learning practices. One participant who leads a regional teacher training programme has introduced the Thinking Pair question 'What are your thoughts and feelings?' as a tool to enable mentors to support early career teachers in developing their capacity to reflect. Rather than being dependent on the mentor's feedback and validation, the question encourages trainee teachers to think independently and this has implications for balance of power in the mentoring relationship. Other participants have highlighted for them the importance of creating spaces for educators to think rather than treating them as empty vessels to be entertained with inspirational stories and filled with examples of best practice, and of subtle changes to their organisation's coaching practice language, for example, replacing the term 'coach' with 'thinking partner'.

Finally, participants have commented on the power and value of hearing each other's thinking and how rare it is to think aloud in the presence of someone who is not giving approval or offering advice. For some, they have come to realise how vital thinking and providing the time and attention to thinking are for children, young people and adults. For others, Flourish has made them more aware of demands they have been placing on themselves and the importance of nourishing themselves to be better able to support others. The programme sessions appear to nurture a reflexive stance, with participants making connections between education theory and their practice. For some, Flourish is a tool for liberation from what they perceive to be the current imposition of restricted and reductive curricula and a homogeneous approach to initial teacher education consumed by compliance.

Reflection

Sheila's explanation and reflections in this encounter provide insights into the significance of creating and holding genuinely enabling spaces for others to think, without judgement and without interruption. For coaches there are opportunities to consider how such practices might complement or enhance their approach, paying particular regard to the feeling that many people in education settings have that such spaces are rare but impactful. The propositions behind Kline's TE, such as the conditions needed for independent thinking, may appear contradictory with some principles of coaching or social features of collaborative learning. There is value for coaches in exploring some of these tensions. For example, being able to engage in sustained independent thinking is a key goal and this is based on the presence of others who are facilitating conditions for this thinking actively, with intention and consideration. Counterintuitively, therefore, the independent thinking promoted is the product of a relational situation, just like coaching. The experience of independent thinking aligns with the concepts of ownership, voice and agency.

Encounter: holding the space for story exchange as collaborative curriculum innovation

Dr Lisa Stephenson is an academic, teacher educator and artist educator who built on her doctoral research to develop 'Story Exchange', a two-year creative curriculum project in Bradford, which is one of the most economically deprived and culturally diverse cities in England. The new curriculum and innovative pedagogies emerged through collaborative work between artists, primary teachers and the university team. Coaching was one of the components of the professional learning and development that underpinned the project. The project crossed boundaries between CollectivED and Storymakers Co., another research and practice centre at Leeds Beckett University. Drawing on a BERA blogpost by Stephenson et al. (Story Exchange, 2024) and a Chartered College of Teaching Impact article (Stephenson and Lofthouse, 2023), Lisa writes:

'Story Exchange' project

The 'Story Exchange' project set out to explore the impact of knowledge transfer between artists and teachers when embedding new imaginative curriculum approaches. It was a two-year funded project across seven primary schools in Bradford which focused on integrating drama and storytelling for cultural, socio-emotional literacy and communication across the curriculum. New approaches to pedagogy were co-created between teachers, artists, teacher educators and coaches through an emerging model of professional practice. Like other curriculum projects that I have led, the project used narrative enquiry, drama pedagogy and play to change classroom relationships placing collective imagination, literacies and affective learning at the heart of teaching and learning. The project drew from children's cultural linguistic strengths rather than a deficit model of oracy.

Coaching encounters

Central to the design and implementation of the project was that it created opportunities for 'holding spaces' for teachers and artists to co-plan, co-teach and co-reflect together – a co-enquiry-based approach to coaching. Teachers and artists collectively drew from a pedagogy of noticing significant moments within the learning. Regular coaching conversations occurred, facilitated by an additional member of the project team through which these significant moments were reflected on. In most cases the teacher and artist had each recorded their reflections on the lessons they had co-planned and co-taught, allowing the coach to gain insights into their experiences and sensemaking prior to the coaching conversation which they attended as partners. The aim of the coaching was to help create and sustain engaging, enabling and empowering conditions for the teachers, artists and their pupils within the curriculum project. Most of the coaching happened online and over the course of the project the participants had multiple opportunities to reflect on the coaching component itself. Further analysis of the coaching dialogue and how it relates to the developmental stages of the project is part of current research.

Impacts and legacy

Through sustained engagement of action research the teachers and artists produced a set of dispositions (attitudes, mindset, values) for social and emotional communication which activated and evidenced the impact of the project on pupil learning. The project methodology provided an iterative approach to gathering impact on learning. In professional development terms participants in the Storymakers project created new exploratory curriculum spaces, based on imaginative participatory story-based experiences which the teachers and artists first experienced, then experimented with and embedded over time.

Over 200 coaching conversations took place across the project and the analysis of these shows the changes in mindset for all stakeholders engaged in a community of practice. The coaching element supported boundary crossing as the teachers and artists worked in ways that were not always familiar to them, needing to negotiate and combine ideas and approaches. During coaching the teachers and artists reflected on a range of affective and embodied responses from uncertainty to wonder.

Alongside the immersive CPD experiences the coaching conversations supported the project purpose and helped participants gain confidence to approach curriculum learning differently. Practices were changed across time through professional noticing of 'significant moments' as a form of action research. 'Holding the space' through time allocation, coaching and collaborative CPD was highly significant during this process.

Reflection

This encounter is a good example of establishing a clear link between shared purpose and an appropriate coaching approach. Coaching was used to serve the teachers and artists, to help carve out a space beyond the co-planning and teaching during which they could reflect on experiences and outcomes as they encountered them, helping them to refine next steps as well as appreciate what was being achieved in the project. The coaching supported the project as a whole to become a relational space filled with hope for the young learners, their teachers and the artists.

Chapter 13 endnotes

Final thoughts

The five encounters in this chapter have different origins from the others in part 3. The coaching approaches emerged through specific and purposeful projects, all of which spanned a variety of educational contexts and involved developers and participants in a range of roles. They illustrate coaching as an emergent practice which has the potential to have core components and nuanced and adapted characteristics. Across all of the respective educational communities which have engaged with these coaching approaches are typical struggles, challenges, objectives and ambitions, but none of these are seen in isolation. Managed and supportive conversations, opportunities for enhanced thinking, respect for others and productive collaboration are key features in the capacity for coaching to contribute in understanding and agency required in the complexity of the work of educators.

The opening quote from Katherine Mannix, whose background is in palliative care and who is now an author, broadcaster and public educator, reminds us of the importance of feeling empowered rather than experiencing someone else stepping in and taking over. In each of the encounters in this chapter we see the significance of involvement and agency in addressing typical educational challenges or the desire for change, stimulated by scaffolded dialogue with a sense of shared purpose.

Talking point

In AACT we interweave coaching cycles with enquiry cycles. How does this sit with you and your colleagues? If you have experience of practitioner enquiry or action research, would coaching have complemented the process? What understandings can you bring from them to enhance coaching with purpose?

Ideas for action

Both DBC and co-coaching have been developed and used in networks where educators have engaged in scaffolded coaching conversations with shared intent and an opportunity for reflection on the experience.

Chapter 13 Coaching: developing purposeful conversational spaces

You may find a suitable opportunity to create this experience for colleagues. Be careful that this is not presented as a contextless CPD activity, but do feel free to 'play' with the approaches as we have done.

Chapter 14
Coaching as a way of enacting social justice, equity and decoloniality

Is it tenable to persist in the traditional coaching stance of moral neutrality – the Switzerland of the helping professions?

Hetty Einzig (2017, p. 43)

The CollectivED community is a global one, but without doubt it is dominated by educators working in a global minority, Western cultures. To some extent this mirrors the growth of international schools that are based on European and North American curriculum and assessment frameworks and employ large numbers of migrant teachers. As a community, we acknowledge the importance of work that explores coaching in context and considers how coaching approaches and frameworks are developed and adapted in different cultures. In this chapter we aim to extend our understanding beyond Western values and contribute to the growing discussion on interculturally sensitive coaching (van Nieuwerburgh, 2017), coaching for equity (Aguilar, 2020, 2024; Woulfin et al., 2023), coaching for social change (Chiu, 2022) and decolonising coaching (Roche, 2021).

In chapter 5 we focus on the concept of purpose. We extend this further here by considering how coaching with a higher or strong sense of purpose may influence behaviours and actions and can be highly relevant in addressing pressing social issues in our world today. Certain interconnected global issues such as climate change and social justice may seem almost unresolvable. But perhaps coaching with a sense of purpose might provide a more hopeful way of moving forward toward a more just and brighter future. An example of this relates to climate change engagement. Coaches may help individuals to not only acknowledge issues of climate change, but perhaps more importantly to create the space for positive conversations to explore how their values and purpose relate to steps forward in enhancing environmental sustainability. A recent review (Léger-Goodes et al., 2022) highlights the significance of eco-anxiety among teenage and young children globally, and a coaching stance may complement teaching about climate change, with the potential to support even young people to take action and make purposeful progress.

Coaching which acknowledges and addresses social and individual injustices embedded in racism and gender bias is also essential. Roche and Passmore (2021) highlight deficits in both coaching literature and norms of practice, which rarely acknowledge the power dynamics inherent in racialisation and systemic racism and other inequalities in the workplace or wider society. This poses ethical dilemmas about coaching, which may be usefully considered through the lens of decoloniality.

As Arshad (2021) writes:

> *Decolonising is not about deleting knowledge or histories that have been developed in the West or colonial nations; rather it is to situate the histories and knowledges that do not originate from the West in the context of imperialism, colonialism and power and to consider why these have been marginalised and decentred.*

It is interesting to reflect on how coaching in education, in terms of its purposes, processes, personnel, power structures, functions and outcomes, might support decolonising education or might reinforce the status quo. In our view it is essential to critique the emergence of globally ambitious education businesses and international schools that use coaching training and resources in their pursuit of the international market, yet fail to consider local context and needs.

We are inspired by the work of Charmaine Roche (2021), CollectivEd Advisory Group member, professional coach, doctoral researcher and former headteacher and her attention to decoloniality and coaching. She writes that:

> *Decoloniality is a critical theory and way of being that challenges the power structures of class, race, gender and heterosexual dominance that originate from European colonialism. It recognises that colonial patterns of power and knowledge creation continue to dominate in post-colonial times through Eurocentrism and globalisation. It brings the voices and narratives of the marginalised and excluded into mainstream discourse. (p. 12)*

As a coach her work both incorporates and extends beyond the education section. She is focused on how coaches can 'use their influence to co-create spaces that become emancipatory for those who feel marginalised and excluded' (p. 10). In companion work Roche is also focusing on coaching supervision, which may afford the critically reflective space needed to address the challenge of the 'universalised Eurocentric approach' and she advocates for 'drawing on the strengths and learning inherent in marginalised world views and epistemologies' (Roche, 2022, p. 46).

The encounters in this chapter include new reflections on recent experiences by Trista and Jasen which have supported their learning about decoloniality. There are also encounters which question and advocate for the role of coaching in challenging dominant power dynamics and discourses often embedded in school leadership and management decisions, including recruitment. In addition we include an encounter related to an international network of coaches whose focus is on the challenges of climate change. This chapter is an invitation for further discussion on coaching and social responsibility. The encounters presented are part of a growing body of work exploring allyship in coaching to promote social change (Chiu, 2022).

Encounter: empowerment and equity through executive and systemic coaching

Hannah Wilson is a qualified and accredited coach. She coaches individuals from her network, as an associate for different communities/networks and on different leadership programmes she has designed and curated. Hannah writes:

As a former school leader I undertook coaching training and when I was the founding headteacher of a school we adopted a coaching approach. I was also a volunteer coach through #WomenEd and for the Department for Education in England. Across my coaching roles my purpose is 'empowerment' and I undertake executive and systemic coaching to achieve this. The main coaching outcomes for individuals are confidence, clarity, values alignment, promotion and the capacity for negotiation. These support wellbeing and fulfilment.

My concerns about the use of coaching include schools not protecting the time of busy leaders to engage in coaching and insufficient funding to resource it. I also worry about in-house coaching being done to people to enhance performance, where line management and coaching are conflated, and when coaching is used as an intervention for diversity, equality and inclusion issues.

Reflections

Hannah's coaching purpose of 'empowerment' is well recognised and respected in the coaching community for using coaching as a means to promote social justice. Hannah shares our concerns on how coaching might not be supported well enough to be sustained and impactful. She also worries that coaching might be co-opted or weaponised in some contexts.

Encounter: coaching in Indigenous communities

This learning encounter is written by Trista and explores a transformational event that has had a significant impact on her experience with coaching in education. The moment occurred during a professional development session that she and a colleague were facilitating with Inuk coaches in the northern region of the province of Quebec. For Trista, this learning encounter led to a deeper exploration of the roots and guiding principles of coaching and to critical examination of the universality of key coaching skills and approaches. Being confronted with a blindspot when it comes to interculturally sensitive coaching offered an opportunity to engage more intentionally in the work of decolonising coaching as a researcher, practitioner and trainer. Below Trista briefly outlines her encounter in Kuujjuaq, Quebec, and the impact this experience has had on her work in coaching, teaching and professional learning.

In 2018 and again in 2019 I was invited by the Kativik School Board (KSB) along with my colleague Dr Lisa Howell to facilitate two two-day workshops on mentoring and coaching for Inuk educators in Kuujjuaq, Quebec. For context, Kuujjuaq is the largest village in the Nunavik region of the province of Quebec, Canada. Nunavik comprises the northern third of the province (almost equal to the size of France) and is the homeland of the Inuit of Quebec and part of the wider Inuit Nunangat. The educators participating in the professional development session were consultants who worked at the school board in Kuujjuaq and teachers from schools across the region's 14 communities. Teaching in Nunavik is done exclusively in Inuktitut, the mother tongue, from kindergarten to Grade 2. English and French are introduced to students as second languages in Grade 3, while Inuktitut continues to be taught as a subject. Like in many school boards in Quebec, teacher recruitment and retention are a challenge, especially in the region's most remote villages. Often, local community members are recruited as teachers without teaching qualifications and with little access to continuous professional development. The workshops were being offered to experienced educators who mentor and coach teachers in their remote villages. In order to attend the workshop many participants had to travel long distances and leave their families, school and communities for many days.

As facilitators, Lisa and I worked hard to make sure (to the best of our abilities) that the workshop would be culturally responsive, relevant and empowering for our participants. Our aim was to introduce what we understood as coaching and mentoring based on our own experience leading and working as mentor–coaches in the Western Quebec School Board (the 'South'). We also wanted to share current research, explore some of the key coaching skills, strategies and frameworks, and build a mentoring and coaching support network in the region.

The workshops were designed to provide a lot of time for participants to share their experiences and explore what mentoring and coaching meant in their own northern Indigenous context. From the feedback we received, it was clear that there were many elements during the four days we spent together that resonated for participants and they especially appreciated the time to connect with other coaches working in their region. Reflecting on the experience, I was also struck by how much of my own understanding of coaching was anchored in a Western and Global North perspective. Working with the Inuk educators I learned many critical lessons. I'll never forget one of the elders pulling me aside when Lisa and I were facilitating a discussion around what 'attentive listening' looks like, sounds like and feels like. He gently – but firmly – rejected the activity and reminded me that in his culture attentive listening was a way of being and how community members learned. 'Perhaps,' he smiled, 'you in the South might consider what you can learn from us.' Powerful! This encounter sparked me to consider how I might begin to decolonise coaching and find ways to disrupt and decentre some of the ways coaching is researched and practised. It has led me to explore what it means to coach 'across cultures' (van Nieuwerburgh, 2017) and whether coaching is a 'cross-cultural practice' (Abbott, 2010). I still have much to learn, unlearn and relearn and am grateful to the many teachers, mentors and coaches who are supporting this work.

'In Canada, we are also called upon to engage in the critical work of decolonization, dismantling the colonial infrastructures that maintain our K–12 and post-secondary education systems as we respond to the Truth and Reconciliation Commission of Canada's (2015) *Calls to Action*, which includes changes directly related to our schools and school systems' (Rodway, 2024). Since the learning encounter with Inuit educators in Kuujjuaq described above, I have been exploring different ways to decolonise coaching in my work. I have been conscious in diversifying the voices that are included in the assigned readings for my graduate course on 'Mentoring and coaching in professional contexts' that I teach at the University of Ottawa. I have also included a module focused specifically on 'coaching for equity' in the course, where we examine coaching in international and diverse contexts, what it means to centre equity in coaching and what we can learn from each other. Another way I try to put reconciliation into action is to share my learning encounter in Kuujjuaq as part of the land acknowledgement I offer in coaching workshops I facilitate. I have been fortunate to lead workshops and learn with and from Indigenous educators in Northern Saskatchewan, where I continue to learn more about Indigenous pedagogy and the ways in which it connects and informs coaching in Canada. Finally, through my research work on scaling collaborative teacher professional learning in Sierra Leone I am learning with and from local educators on how coaching and mentoring are understood in their context and ways to support them.

Reflections

This learning encounter occurred in an Inuit community, but it prompted Trista to reflect on how decolonising coaching is about actions we can all take in our everyday coaching work. It is essential to not compartmentalise decolonial thinking, but to use it as a new lens to help determine future decisions and actions in every context.

Encounter: coaching within the BAMEed Network

Lizana Oberholzer is a senior lecturer in education and uses, researches and writes about coaching in a number of contexts. This includes work related to National Professional Qualifications and the Early Career Framework, both of which are Department for Education (government) funded programmes in England. In this case study Lizana shares her work in developing coaching as part of the BAMEed Network (see www.bameednetwork.com/). This is a grassroots network aimed at ensuring our diverse communities are represented as a substantive part of the education workforce for teachers and leaders in education. They seek to address the inequities in the recruitment of Black, Asian and minority ethnic colleagues into the teaching profession and the lack of support to ensure progress in those careers. Lizana writes:

How we have developed coaching in BAMEed

I have been supporting BAMEed's coaching team for over eight years. I lead on coaching for BAMEed by developing and training the BAMEed coaching team, and I lead on their supervision which takes place once a month to support BAMEed coaches. The approach taken by the BAMEed team is to first understand the needs of the coachee as well as their context through 'narrative' coaching approaches; we move forward from there. We recognise that it is important to understand what is required, ensure that the coachee is fully heard and is in a calm, trusting space, to ensure that we are then able to move the learning conversation forward. We aim to make sure colleagues are clear how coaching can be of help to them and what coaching is. Once we are in a clear and safe space, we can then move forward with the learning relationship and the learning conversations.

We use a variety of thinking tools and creative approaches, such as drawings and semiotics, to help coachees to make sense of their world and to help them unpack their own thinking in a meaningful way (Oberholzer and Boyle, 2023). We also introduced the 'dilemma-based' coaching model (see chapter 13) to the BAMEed coaches, who use it when appropriate for the person they are supporting. We reflect regularly on the different models in the BAMEed supervision sessions and evaluated this model, and coaches found it to be highly effective in their coaching conversations, to help frame the key issues that colleagues might be experiencing within their contexts.

Addressing challenges and recognising impact

Because we know that time is often a barrier for colleagues in schools, we do our best to work flexibly with them as coaches. We sometimes experience tensions if our work is sponsored by larger organisations who would like to see impact and want reporting to happen. However, we contract carefully with both the sponsor as well as the coachee to be clear on the key roles and the importance of confidentiality as outlined by the European Mentoring and Coaching Council (EMCC), as well as the International Coaching Federation (ICF) in their ethical guidance. Coaches for BAMEed are fully trained on the contracting process as well to ensure that they are confident on how to move it forward.

In terms of BAMEed, we track the impact in relation to the outcomes of next steps and promotions for future leaders, or simply that the coachees continued to engage with education and are retained. Over the past few years, BAMEed supported 300 aspirational leaders to progress into leadership roles. We also supported colleagues to take on master's and doctoral studies, to enable them to further their professional learning journeys.

Reflections

BAMEed is a purpose-led network, utilising coaching to serve the best interests and aspirations of diverse communities. Representation is paramount in seeking to address inequities and importantly focus is given to nurturing future leaders of learning. Lizana highlights how BAMEed is negotiating some of the tensions around sponsorship, impact, reporting and the coaching principles of confidentiality and role of the coach. It is also interesting to read about how the network explores and evaluates different coaching models to find the ones that are most useful to their members.

Encounter: coaching for climate change and active hope

Rebecca Raybould, Brenda Marshall and Hazel Farrer host an online subgroup of Climate Coaching Alliance, called the 'Education Pod'. This is made up of parents, teachers, activists, leaders, coaches, volunteers and more who are interested in using a coaching approach with young people in the context of climate change. Rebecca, with support from other pod members, writes:

Why climate coaching?

Participants in the Climate Coaching Alliance (CCA) aim to 'participate in a positive shift in human awareness, to effect wider systemic changes in the world towards a truly regenerative future', to 'give life to the forest of life' and to 'influence the global professional coaching community to bring the deep and difficult questions of climate and ecological emergency into coaching conversations'. In the CCA Education pod our focus is on using a coaching approach with young people to empower them to take meaningful climate action. Our work has relevance because young people are concerned about the environment (e.g. Hickman et al., 2021; Children's Commissioner, 2021) and educators are keen to develop their teaching skills in this area (Teach the Future, 2021). As coaches we appreciate that we need to engage with the how (pedagogy) as well as the what (curriculum content) of our teaching (Hoath and Dave, 2022) and that the learning required to respond to the uncertainty and turbulence associated with the climate crisis call on educators 'to step beyond our traditional instructor role into more profound quality of mentorship' (Litfin, 2016, p. 117) and coaching.

It is in this context that we think coaching has the potential to be part of 'how' educators engage with the young people that they work with. The research about effective teaching approaches in climate change education is of course still an emerging field. But a key theme is the importance of engaging students in a way that enables them to take action within and beyond the school environment (Rousell and Cutter-Mackenzie-Knowles, 2020; Tannock, 2021). Coaching with its emphasis on active listening and empowering action may form part of our 'pedagogic toolkit'.

How our climate coaching is developing

As such, members of the Education Pod work and aim to work with young people, drawing on elements of a coaching approach. There is not one single approach to this work and we are also aware of the risk of causing psychological harm to young people when they surface their distress about climate change. Therefore, we highlight the need to build strong relationships, the importance of careful listening and questioning and the use of frameworks which promote active hope. We draw on Macy and Johnstone's (2022) work on the four stages of active hope: 'Gratitude, Honoring our Pain for the World, Seeing with New Eyes and Going Forth'.

While our work is still emerging, we have a strong sense of commitment and are actively learning together. Early indications suggest young people having a greater sense of agency and taking environmental action. We also acknowledge that this work with children and young people brings challenges, not least in:

- developing opportunities in the school curriculum
- adequately funding and resourcing student projects so young people are able to progress their ideas
- navigating the potential tension between wanting to support students to achieve successful climate action and wanting to support students in developing the resilience to work through setbacks and challenges.

Reflections

The united sense of purpose is extremely powerful in this account from the Climate Coaching Alliance. The Education Pod is aware of the potential risks to wellbeing of working with young people in relation to their anxieties about climate change and notes the importance of strong relationships and careful listening and questioning. With no one approach to guide this work, the pod members learn together and draw on their own research and experience in their emerging hopeful process. Chapter 3 introduced hope theory and the concept of 'active hope' aligns with Haesun Moon's (2022) reference to honouring the resourceful past and taking positive steps to move forward to a preferred future, which was discussed in chapter 2.

Encounter: wayfinding as a way of conceptualising coaching

This encounter is written by Jasen and develops the discussion of wayfinding as a way of conceptualising coaching. This theme has proved powerful to different members of the CollectivED community in support of their sensemaking. Jasen opens with the admission that 'In truth I hadn't heard of the concept of wayfinding prior to working in the Kingdom of Tonga, although the metaphor of learning journeys is often used in educational contexts.' Jasen draws on references to wayfinding in literature from the Global South as wayfinding typically aligns with navigating uncharted seas, exploring and discovering new territories, which has historical significance throughout Oceania. 'Wayfinding may be described as the process of embarking upon a purposeful, intentional, and self-regulated journey that takes an individual from an intended region in one landscape to another.' (Woods et al., 2020, p. 1). Jasen discusses the unique historical and cultural characteristics of wayfinding and reflects upon alignments that he feels coaching shares with this Polynesian navigation tradition.

Vā – the space between us

In Tongan culture the concept of *vā* is fundamentally important. *Vā* refers to the space that exists between things or people – a relational space – the space between us. Arguably, the historical Western, Global North perspective of space has focused more on the space that is beyond us, an expanse or void that lies ahead. In many traditional coaching models and frameworks the space beyond may be viewed as the goals and outcomes that we seek, aligning with the metaphor of visioning new horizons that offer possibilities and opportunities that we desire. As an advocate of 'solutions-focused' coaching (Jackson and McKergow, 2007), I believe in shining a light on the preferred future and focusing on affordances that we may orientate towards (see also chapters 2 and 3). In contexts of change, leaders are often heard saying 'We need to move forwards', implying a movement out of a problematic space. For me, wayfinding is more nuanced and far-reaching, as it aligns with the idea of 'moving forward with a collective sense of purpose', a concept that resonates with the idea of accompaniment that Trista discussed in chapter 8. The new horizon offers optimism for moving forward, but the *vā* between us importantly provides a sociospatial connection (Ka'ili, 2005, p. 89). Coaching encounters in the *vā* provide opportunities for nurturing and caring relationships that in turn may steer us purposefully forward. The Tongan concept of *tauhi vā* speaks beautifully to this as it relates to the power of relational connections.

Coaching stance and discriminating observation

Lewis (1972) describes wayfinding as discriminating observation which implies a knowledgeable, conscious effort to look closely at, or discern, a situation. A synonym for 'discriminate' that sits closely in meaning is 'discern'. Chris Munro (pers. comm.), uses the verb 'discern' when describing the concept of coaching stance, whereby a coach makes a reasoned decision on how facilitative or directive they need to be in supporting their coachee. I would suggest that coaches are truly agile and responsive when they listen to understand and refigure their stance accordingly. In the Tongan context of wayfinding, discriminating observation relates to much more than keenly viewing or monitoring: wayfinding is a truly responsive practice based on detecting environmental cues. This reminds me of the emphasis given to noticing small signs of positive change in 'solutions-focused' coaching. Personally, I see great value in framing wayfinding as an embodied coaching approach that utilises all the senses in the process of sensemaking. The following quote has wonderful resonance:

> *[...] wayfinding is an activity that confronts us with the marvellous fact of being in the world, requiring us to look up and take notice, to cognitively and emotionally interact with our surroundings.*
>
> O'Connor (2019, p. 20)

A different way of mapping

A fundamental distinction between Western and Polynesian seafaring practices relates to the concept of mapping and use of navigational tools. Early European sailors relied upon tools when navigating oceans. Such tools included charts and maps for plotting courses; a compass for determining direction; a sextant for calculating the angle between a celestial body and the horizon and an hourglass for measuring time intervals. In stark contrast, Polynesian navigators used a wayfinding methodology that was non-instrumental and beyond the thinking of a Western system of practical knowledge. Western navigators believed that without technology, the original colonisation of Oceania must have been accidental. The truth is that navigating by wayfinding was informed by a body of knowledge passed down through generations of Polynesian voyagers – it was certainly not accidental. Developing an expertise in wayfinding traditions required disciplined learning and skilful application which was far from haphazard.

It would be misleading to state that Polynesian wayfinders did not use maps. They learned and maintained vast mental maps of the islands' spatial relationships, but instead of fixed landmarks they used environmental cues such as sea swells, reef colours, wind directions, sun movements and, importantly, star courses and paths. Drawing a comparison between wayfinding and coaching principles and practice, it strikes me that wayfinding emphasises the importance of being truly present in the moment. A wayfinding coach would be highly attuned to the changing needs of the coachee, noticing small and subtle signs in behaviour and language; they would embody what it means to be truly responsive. They would show up for the person they are with and focus on a coachee's psychological safety. A coachee would feel well held and reassured by the wayfinding coach's positive intentions and way of being. A wayfinding coach would build a sense of trust and security by accompanying the coachee: navigating together would be key. Navigating a complex and uncertain path may be akin to travelling without a map. I, for one, would feel much safer voyaging in such circumstances accompanied by a highly attuned, responsive wayfinding coach.

Manifesting the movement

Perhaps the most cognitively challenging aspect of wayfinding relates to the idea that we can reach a destination *without* moving 'forward'. This seems a baffling contradiction, but I will try to make sense of this by exploring alignments with coaching approaches. Spiller (2016) describes Polynesian wayfinders as 'bringing the island to them through be-coming' (p. 31). It was the *waka* (canoe) which remained stationary and the world that moved closer. Clouds would arrive and draw nearer: in essence the environment would travel to you. Polynesian wayfinders valued stillness; being consciously present and in the moment, carefully making adjustments, drawing the destination closer. As a coach I thought long and hard about the idea of 'bringing the island to them'

(Spiller, 2016), wondering how this very different perspective speaks to my own coaching knowledge and experience. I feel a relatable coaching connection is the concept of visualisation in sports coaching. By mentally rehearsing the actions and outcomes they want to achieve, athletes strengthen their confidence and build self-efficacy. Visualising success in sporting contexts is not viewed as unusual as it sits comfortably alongside the idea of having a positive or growth mindset. Both 'bringing the island to them' and sports visualisation relate to the growing field of positive psychology (see chapter 3). In truth, Polynesian wayfinders and sports athletes reach their preferred futures through continuous practice and attention to detail, not chance occurrences!

The concept of manifestation involves the belief that one's thoughts and intentions can influence reality. Living in post-Covid times, with increased numbers of people affected by anxiety and related mental health issues, it seems plausible that manifesting a brighter future would be a comforting activity. The concept of manifesting feels like a natural fit with wayfinding. One reason is that both concepts appear to embody a sense of 'hope' for a positive discovery; hopeful thinking and manifesting seem to be synonymous. In terms of wayfinding-coaching, manifesting the preferred future is similar to the idea of 'bringing the change that people wish to see'. Perhaps for a wayfinding coach, an alternative expression for 'moving forward with purpose' might be 'making purposeful progress', an idea we discussed in chapter 5. 'Making progress' implies a sense of movement. However, we may view the positive movement as not necessarily forwards. Similar to the growth of a healthy plant, the movement may be upwards to the light and downwards to the nutrients. So I offer the technique of manifesting the movement (or progress) as a more relatable wayfinding idea to draw upon as a possible coaching approach.

Honouring the resourceful past

In chapters 2 and 5 we referenced Haesun Moon's (2020) dialogic orientation quadrant (DOQ), which I find immensely helpful in my coaching approach in Tonga. In Tonga I am referred to as *Palangi* by my Ministry of Education colleagues. In simple terms *Palangi* means 'not Tongan' and was originally used to describe white Europeans. Their use of the word is not expressed in a polarising or racially divisive way but refers to the fact that I do not have the lived historical and cultural experience of Tongan people. This is the undeniable reality; I have a huge amount to learn from my colleagues and need to respect the different ways of knowing and being in Tongan culture and society. For me personally, honouring the 'resourceful past' is the quadrant with vital significance and guides my way of being when working with Tongan colleagues. This aligns with the concept of appreciative inquiry (see chapter 3's description of positive psychology). Bungay Stanier advises us to 'tame the advice monster' which he states has the troubling persona of 'control-it'! (2020, p. 36). In my role, capacity building is a stated requirement from the Tongan Ministry of Education, but this does not mean that my Tongan colleagues need me to take control: we are wayfinding together and I adhere to the 'partnership principles' (Knight, 2022).

Appreciating what my colleagues have already achieved requires effort and energy to connect through the space between us (*vā*) and provide time (*tā*) to respectfully listen to understand. The Tongan historian Mahina (2008) has theorised the Tongan concept *tā-vā*, 'time-space', and describes an aspect of *tā-vā* as 'looking forward into the past' (p. 79). This aligns well with the idea of honouring the resourceful past as guidance in the present moment. Mahina (2008) argues that in early Polynesian thinking there was no future, only past and present. Again this is a challenging idea for me as a Palangi, but personally what makes sense is that a wayfinding-coach would take time to explore the solid success of past events to respect and amplify the great resourcefulness that human beings have accomplished.

Talanoa – a talking, connecting, thinking environment

Talanoa is often referred to as storytelling, especially in the context of Fijian *Talanoa*. However, it is worth noting that *talanoa* has different shades of meaning to different groups of Pacific people (Farrelly and Nabobo-Baba, 2014). For some, *talanoa* could be simply a casual chat, while in more formal contexts it could form the basis of a structured, ritualised methodology for resolving issues and conflicts. The unifying theme is 'connecting through dialogue', with the *vā* connecting space sharing equal importance. A key feature of *talanoa* is that the speaker is given the time they need to talk. There are parallels with 'listening without interruption' (Kline, 2020) and the 'ten components of a Thinking

Environment', introduced in chapter 2 and elaborated in chapter 13 (attention, appreciation, ease, encouragement, diversity, information, feelings, equality, place and incisive questions), which mirror the cultural practice of *talanoa*. It strikes me that Kline's component of 'place' aligns naturally and elegantly with the concept of *vā*.

Harris and Holman Jones (2019) state '*talanoa* embodies the power to connect and enact a movement of affect and action' (p. 564). Selecting the word 'affect' alongside 'action' speaks to a sense of physicality, embodiment and emotional presence. In Tongan culture, I view *talanoa* to be integrally connected to the concept of wayfinding. A wayfinding-coach will place value in the *vā* for relational, dialogic encounters. It strikes me that trusting relationships built through *talanoa* are likely to build confidence in the journey ahead. Wayfinding woven with *talanoa* would almost certainly foster a culture of collective efficacy and a united sense of purpose. Through *talanoa*, a wayfinding-coach listens to understand how to voyage confidently in partnership.

Culturally in Tonga, great importance is given to the concept of collectivism, supporting the need to appreciate all voices in the community space. The Polynesian concept of wayfinding illustrates that coaching is a collective endeavour. Navigating with a sense of purpose is fundamental.

Reflection

The emphasis in wayfinding of embarking on a purposeful journey has obvious resonance with the title and focus of this book. Jasen's reflections demonstrate that by engaging with and respecting the work of scholars and practitioners in the Global South, different perspectives can provide opportunities for reconsidering and enhancing coaching philosophy and practice.

Chapter 14 endnotes

Final thoughts

It is reasonable to expect coaching in education to both be scrutinised and enhanced when a social justice lens is applied. For example, decoloniality acknowledges historical injustices and empowers community voices through culturally respectful approaches by integrating Indigenous perspectives, creating inclusive spaces that honour unique identities and experiences, and fostering equitable personal growth and leadership development. It will be important not to isolate coaching from other features of education when doing so, but perhaps to allow it to create a vital critical perspective related to social justice on education ecosystems.

Talking point

Orientation typically refers to the process by which individuals acquire knowledge, skills, values, attitudes and behaviours that enable them to adapt and function effectively in a new environment. It would be useful to discuss the affordances and constraints that your current coaching practices offer for orientation towards social justice, equity and decoloniality.

Ideas for action

Engage with authors who are examining the equity, social justice and decolonisation of coaching and who challenge aspects of current research and practice. In what way can you bring these voices into your coaching practice and/or provision? Consider how you might respond to Lou Chiu's (2022) call: 'To fellow coaches, coaching educators, supervisors, professional bodies, and training providers, my question is, knowing what you know now, what will you do?'

Part 4
Coaching, context and change

What to look out for in part 4

In this section you will encounter:
- a discussion of the relationships between professional learning and coaching
- research-based considerations of how educational contexts influence coaching success and how coaching can help shape contexts
- consideration of educator wellbeing and the potential of coaching to support it
- explanation of three conceptual frameworks which can help determine the impacts and outcomes of coaching and the steps of change over time

- a discussion of educational change and the introduction of a new model through which the role of coaching can be explored
- insights from the CollectivED community on coaching as a powerful tool for positive and purposeful change in education

Writing this book has offered us a sustained opportunity for sensemaking (first introduced in chapter 4) and part 4 represents an extended synthesis of the sense that we have made in relation to coaching in education. In reality the writing has been a product of intense, ongoing peer interaction, familiarisation, defamiliarisation, enquiry, challenge and interpretation. As we entered into discussions we drew on the many encounters with coaching research and practice already shared in parts 1–3. We also revisited additional research that we undertook prior to writing this book and drew on new research evidence emerging from multiple focus groups with members of the wider coaching community who contributed case studies to part 3. Significant and recurring themes emerged in our discussions and they are the foundations for these chapters. These themes help us to ground our thinking about coaching in relation to purpose once again.

Coaching in education happens in settings, such as schools and colleges, alongside settings, often associated with leadership roles, at the intersection of settings, such as during career transitions into new posts, or in the relationships between school and wider communities. Educational policy and socio-economic and cultural characteristics of place, including changes over time, also influence how coaching is offered and what challenges or changes it seeks to support individuals to address. As such it is the context of educational coaching which gives meaning to its purpose. Thus, in chapter 15 we focus on coaching and context, drawing on research related to an understanding of contextual coaching, the relationship between coaching and other forms of collaborative professional learning models and the challenges of addressing concerns related to wellbeing. We introduce a new concept of terroir in relation to coaching, borrowed from the wine regions of the world. We return to this concept in chapter 17.

Understanding what coaching achieves for individuals and in terms of organisations is important in validating its use in education. As such the question of coaching efficacy is addressed in chapter 16. We propose that evaluating coaching is not straightforward, in part because of the complexities of context. We draw on three theoretical or conceptual frameworks to provide insights from research evidence about how efficacy might be understood. Once again this relates to purpose, including who sets the expectations for coaching. In chapter 17 we extend our thinking about the impact of coaching to situating it in the established ways of understanding change in education at individual and organisational levels. We conclude this chapter by introducing a new model of educational change, through which the concept of terroir is developed, and with the recognition of the dynamics of change and how coaching both influences and is influenced by them.

Chapter 18 is our final synthesis. Here we draw on the evidence emerging from CollectivED focus groups and share a new conceptualisation of 'Coaching in interacting contexts'. Key themes act as our sensemaking conclusions which both consolidate our understanding of coaching in education and create provocations for education practitioners and policy-makers.

We invite you to read this section through the sensemaking lens. We invited CollectivED focus groups to do this for chapters 15–17 and the endnotes on these chapters reflect their sensemaking. These are significant chapters, which are unlikely to be quick reads. As you read, consider how our conceptualisation aligns with the existing conditions and characteristics of your setting and practice. Consider what might be changing over time and whether this is by design or default. Think through the connections between coaching and the purposes that you have as a professional, and those that bring meaning to your work. We encourage you to share your reflections with others, those in similar roles to you, those whose work you influence and those whose understanding (and its limits) influences your work. Above all else read with curiosity and use what you learn to enhance your agency.

Chapter 15
Contextual coaching, collaboration and wellbeing

When it comes to the implementation of coaching, context (e.g. personal relationships, cultures and subcultures, and organizational mores) can produce functional complexities at a number of levels.

Trista Hollweck and Rachel Lofthouse (2021, p. 401)

Coaching in education forms part of ever-evolving professional, organisational and policy landscapes. Coaching has interactive properties; it is influenced by context and it also influences context. The coaching approaches that we have researched exist within education systems which are influenced by national policies that sometimes border on ideology. In many neoliberal political systems, for example, there is a policy assumption that competition ensures progress and often positions parents, children and young people as consumers of educational provision. The narrative is of school improvement, standards, league tables and quality assurance. It could also be argued that teachers and schools are primarily viewed as consumers who seek commodities as status symbols or the means to enhance outputs. In these systems data is currency, with exam results, rankings and inspection reports and 'user' reviews being used to represent the merit of individual learners and their teachers and of education settings as organisations. The role of coaching in such systems is not neutral.

In addition, and across many countries, concerns about poor mental health and wellbeing and attrition (both of young people and staff in schools, colleges and universities) are growing and coaching is being pursued as a possible remedial action which might trigger positive change. In our networks, on social media and in professional reporting teachers and school leaders often say that coaching helped them form connections with colleagues, that they like the chance to talk about their work and that it made them feel more trusted as professionals, leaving them feeling more positive about themselves and their work.

When considering education contexts it is impossible to ignore the local and global legacies of the Covid-19 pandemic, which had repercussions across society and all institutions including schools. There are significant concerns about the impacts of the pandemic and our responses to it on child and adolescent development, learning and attainment, the characteristics of professional communities, and health and wellbeing. In many countries absence from school is a growing concern, and teacher recruitment and retention patterns are worrying with the pandemic being cited as a consideration in both. In recent years there has been a rapid growth in coaching in education and, as such, the post-pandemic context is significant in understanding directions of travel when considering the relationships between coaching, collaboration and wellbeing.

Contextual coaching and coaching terroir

The term 'context' in this chapter refers to the personal relationships, cultures and subcultures, and organisational mores that make up a setting which can produce functional complexities at a number of levels. Contexts such as schools are made up of multiple interconnected and relational layers. For example, a teacher's classroom is nestled in a broader system that can include their school, community, district, government and society. Hence, introducing coaching into a setting cannot be understood without understanding the actions of the individuals in the setting. Reciprocally, the actions of individuals cannot be understood without understanding their setting. In the field of executive and organisational coaching, 'contextual coaching' (Gorrell and Hoover, 2009; Valentine, 2019) has been used as a way to recognise the significance of the relationship between context and coaching. We use the term 'contextual coaching' to signal that there is no one right way to 'do' coaching in education (Hollweck and Lofthouse, 2021). Rather, effective coaching must be attuned to the setting and contribute in a positive way to its context.

As a way to help us understand the role and influence of context and culture in coaching with purpose, we find the term 'terroir' a useful concept. Long considered an important factor in wine quality and style, 'terroir' is defined as an interactive 'cultivated ecosystem in which the vine interacts with factors from the natural environment, principally soil and climate' (Seguin, 1986). According to wine experts, the making of high-quality wines requires not only technical knowledge and experience but also the management of terroir, which is a matter of infinite complexity. 'Despite its complexity, the concept of terroir is a valuable one. The reductionist might find difficulty in appreciating its value for scientific analysis, but the fact that appellations have maintained their status over many years in French districts suggests the effects are real' (Jackson and Lombard, 1993). Considering there are excellent wines that come from a wide range of climates, topography and soil, it is impossible to define the best terroir. What is essential, however, is that the focus is on the interacting factors that influence the unique character of the grapes in their specific context. Like high-quality wine-making, coaching in education must take into consideration its terroir.

While there are effective coaching approaches available across a wide variety of settings, there is no one-size-fits-all solution. A coaching approach that works powerfully in one setting may not be as successful in another or, as Hargreaves and O'Connor (2018) write, 'Reform is like ripe fruit. It rarely travels well' (p. 131). This is not to say that we should not be focused on collective learning in education and exploring the many ways that coaching is working well in different contexts. In fact, this is at the heart of what CollectivED and this book are all about. Rather, what concerns us is the current conversation that there is a right way to 'do' coaching in education with little consideration of the role of context, culture or change theories.

Collaborative professional learning

We view deliberate collaboration as a critical element of coaching and also suggest that this goes beyond cooperation. Collaboration 'implies working cognitively on a challenge together, piecing together ideas or creating something through joint deliberation', whereas cooperation might be considered as 'task management processes' such as 'agreeing how to complete tasks, identifying who will complete tasks and fulfilling one's side of the bargain' (Lofthouse and Thomas, 2017, p. 49). As such, we propose that coaching is a form of collaborative professional learning (CPL), with the nature of the learning being related to the purpose to which coaching is put. It is likely that creating and sustaining strong and effective collaboration through coaching in education exists alongside other forms of CPL. Similarly where coaching is creating genuine opportunities for collaboration, rather than relying on the task management of cooperation, other forms of CPL are likely to become more meaningful. The opportunities for, and characteristics of, CPL form a significant part of the coaching terroir as part of the reciprocal and evolving relationship between coaching and context which underpins the concept of contextual coaching. As such, there is value in exploring CPL further, as illustrated with the following encounter.

Encounter: an ecosystemic analysis of collaborative professional learning narratives

Following their publication in CollectivED working papers, and with the authors' permission and later validation, Rachel undertook an analysis of nine cases of CPL using an ecosystemic approach (Lofthouse, 2019c). The sample included narratives from primary, secondary and further education settings in the UK. The authors identified them as coaching within a school improvement project (Ashley, 2018), lesson study (Lofthouse and King, 2017), use of the 'Thinking Environment' (Mycroft, 2019), narrative enquiry for leadership development (Bullough et al., 2019), use of discipline of noticing within a subject team (Brown, 2017), career development mentoring (Campbell, 2018), lesson chats (Ayliffe, 2019), alternative staff meetings (Jackson, 2017) and learning culture (Gilchrist, 2017).

The ecosystemic analysis allowed three broad and related components to be highlighted:

1. **inputs**: the people participating and facilitating the CPL, what theoretical frameworks or research were drawn on and how the CPL was designed
2. **engagement**: the nature of the dialogue in the CPL and the emotional experiences of engaging in the CPL. There were three dialogue subthemes (a, b and c) and three emotional experience subthemes (d, e and f):
   a. **content/focus of the discussion**: e.g. related to aspects of teaching and learning or drawing on research
   b. **collaborative nature of the dialogue**: e.g. developing conversation skills (such as listening, asking good questions, not interrupting), sharing experiences, building shared language, sense of ownerships, mutually beneficial
   c. **challenging aspect of the dialogue**: probing, developing critical thinking, making links, enabling others to problem-solve and making decisions, and this being sequenced over time
   d. **feeling willing to engage with the process**: not experiencing it as a threat and not being afraid to challenge each other, which leads to participants feeling less defensive, admitting when help is needed, and reframing perceived issues as positives and possibilities
   e. **building positive relationships**: feeling respected, experiencing kindness and support and gaining a heightened awareness of own and others' values
   f. **experiencing positive morale**: enthusiasm and willingness to participate in the collaborative practice
3. **outcomes**: the reported personal development and learning resulting from CPL, the changes to professional practice and cultural or collective changes occurring.

Threading throughout each ecosystem of CPL were constraints; some were systemic and not easily resolved. Others were, at least in part, addressed through the design of the collaborative practice and some became less problematic as the changes resulting from the collaborative practices evolved. When reviewing the original narratives, recurring tensions and affordances emerged.

The narratives of CPL act as an acknowledgement that schools and colleges and professionals working in them are often resistant to change. Some of the CPL approaches were developed to break down some of the norms of practice and existing hierarchies. Simple practical solutions were sought to do this in the 'alternative staff meetings' example where tendencies for staff to be preoccupied with other school-based tasks rather than fully attending the meetings were reduced by holding them off site (Jackson, 2017). More complex problems emerged when some past and existing practices had eroded trust, which needed to be regained to make progress. This was illustrated in the 'learning cultures' paper, 'When [teachers] have been exposed to those types of cultures, their ability to think and act like individual professional practitioners is taken away from them, as they get used to being told what to do, when to do it and what resources to use to deliver it! They lose the ability to think creatively, to take risks and to be professionally curious' (Gilchrist, 2017, p. 34).

Fortunately, the narratives demonstrated that trust can be established from a deficit or can be further enhanced through the experience of collaboration. Analysis of the CPL narratives suggested that a growth of trust during and resulting from collaborative practices was common. Of the examples analysed this was perhaps most explicitly designed into the practice in the 'thinking environment' (see chapters 2 and 13). 'Thinking environments can be sabotaged, but they can't be subverted: the sabotage is at least out in the open. Being upfront about this has been helpful for educators who are struggling with implementing radical, equalising new practices into organisations built on hierarchies of power' (Mycroft, 2019, p. 107)

There was, however, evidence that collaborative practices were difficult to establish and sustain. They took time to put into operation and they required sustained effort and appropriate resourcing. This meant that school and college leaders needed to make strategic and operational decisions to support them, by reallocating resources or redirecting time. In the 'lesson chats' example the headteacher stated that 'We have invested in these days because we know that "lesson chats" are a very effective way of putting CPD into practice' (Ayliffe, 2019, p. 89). The leadership team adopting 'lesson study' were grappling with the dilemma of how to resource it at a time of budgetary cuts and balancing the cost with its potential for capacity building for sustained impact: 'In a time of tightening budgets will an external role of "expert other" be affordable? If we prioritise it we need to consider how the time and effort afforded to it can be used to ensure that there is a sustainable future and builds on the growing expertise of teachers to support future Lesson Study, in our school or beyond' (Lofthouse and King, 2017, p. 18).

The narratives suggested that making these collaborative practices work required different leadership approaches to those often adopted in schools and colleges. This form of CPL could not be micromanaged but did need sustained support. This was an understandable challenge for school leaders, but it also presented a challenge to participants. To work effectively the collaborative practices required participants themselves to accept the associated challenge, and not only in terms of workload. They also needed to engage emotionally and cognitively and the demands of this were sometimes hard in already overcrowded professional lives. This was illustrated in the account of the 'discipline of noticing': 'Whilst all six teachers in the department considered The Discipline of Noticing to be a good idea, only three of us managed to systematically record accounts over a period of time. Setting oneself to notice and systematically record events requires commitment' (Brown, 2017, p. 13). However, the caveat was that the analysis demonstrated that when collaborative practices worked well, the participants took ownership and that led onto a way of addressing this tension. Workload remained an issue, but for many participants the effort of engaging in CPL was enjoyable, productive and created genuine learning opportunities.

The narratives also illustrated some of the wider potential of CPL when the tensions illustrated above can be responded to and, at least in part, resolved. They suggest that genuine opportunities for collaborative practices can make a difference to the working lives of teachers and leaders in schools and colleges. Teacher wellbeing and teacher retention are becoming problems which the system needs to address through policy decisions and changes to practice. These narratives were not collected with this in mind, but they do offer some insights into factors that might impact positively on teachers' capacities to sustain their work in the profession over time. Engaging in professional learning collaboratively offers them opportunities to meet some of the challenges of the job head-on, but in an environment where the challenges are shared and less anxiety is experienced. CPL can also play a part in developing new approaches suited to the needs of their pupils, students and colleagues. CPL can lead to teachers experiencing increased teacher collective efficacy (Donohoo, 2017). This may be in part the result of the chances for co-construction (Lofthouse et al., 2010a) as a consequence of the new dialogic processes which themselves rely on trust (Whitmore, 2017; Tschannen-Moran and Tschannen-Moran, 2010). In addition, some of the narratives indicated the existence of the first tenet of collaborative professionalism (Hargreaves and O'Connor, 2018), that of 'collective autonomy' through which educators are more independent of top-down administrators and school leaders but have less independence from each other. At a time when some schools are now being characterised as toxic for employees (Woodley and Morrison McGill, 2018), these narratives do offer hope that this is not inevitable (despite current pressures of accountability) and indeed demonstrate the value and impact of appropriately supported and intelligently designed workplace learning practices.

Contextual coaching as collaborative professionalism and contribution to school improvement

In general terms coaching and collaboration seem naturally linked, although as education settings can be very hierarchical it would be naive to suggest that in education all coaching is always positioned or experienced as collaborative. As we explored collaboration as a research theme in coaching, we became aware of the development of the concept of 'collaborative professionalism' (CP) (Campbell, 2016a; Hargreaves and O'Connor, 2018) as a way of understanding factors supporting school improvement. The conceptualisation of CP is based on ten tenets which relate to how teachers and leaders in a school community relate to each other and the students. The international evidence that Hargreaves and O'Connor draw on suggests the greater the presence of the tenets, the greater the chance of improvement in educational settings. The tenets are:

- collective autonomy
- collective efficacy

Chapter 15 Contextual coaching, collaboration and wellbeing

- collaborative enquiry
- collective responsibility
- collective initiative
- mutual dialogue
- joint work
- common meaning and purpose
- collaboration with students
- big picture thinking for all.

Explaining their conceptualisation of CP Hargreaves and O'Connor distinguish between professional collaboration and CP, stating that 'professional collaboration refers to how people collaborate within a profession', and noting that the 'collaboration may be strong or weak, effective or ineffective, and undertaken in one way or another' (Hargreaves and O'Connor, 2018, p. 4), which suggests that the essence of CP is enquiring together and acting upon the outcomes. One of their distinctions is that CP is deliberate and by design and that it is about 'creating stronger and better professional practice together' (p. 4). Being interested in coaching as a deliberate, intentional and designed collaborative practice we were curious about how coaching fits into the framing of CP and this led us to revisit examples of coaching which had explicitly set out to address the improvement agenda in their own contexts (Hollweck and Lofthouse, 2021). We used an abductive analysis approach to examine two case studies that are summarised in the encounters below. In both cases the coaching was developed in response to the policy challenges and the bespoke coaching approaches were adapted over time, with changes largely being the result of co-construction between coaches and/or coachees in the contexts of the schools.

Encounter: coaching within a government-funded school improvement model based on enhancing maths teaching

Teacher coaching was designed and introduced to support the development of maths teaching through enhancing metacognitive pedagogies. It was introduced in ten primary schools in the rural North of England, with significant numbers of children from military families. This group of children traditionally do not make as much progress as their peers as they go through school, often because they are more likely to move school but also because of the associated vulnerabilities of having a parent in the military. The coaching was part of a Strategic School Improvement Fund project (SSIF) funded by the government Department for Education (DfE) and which lasted just over two years. Funding was used to employ three additional members of staff (two full-time equivalent roles) who each worked regularly in three or four of the project schools as coaches. The first term of their employment gave them time to get to know the schools and to research both metacognition and coaching approaches. From the second term the coaching occurred weekly, with one lead teacher in each school, and included modelling of metacognitive teaching, joint planning, co-teaching and debriefing. Funded release time was given to the lead teachers to work with coaches and attend network meetings. The coaches had one week per half term to work together, share progress, develop adapted practice and informally coach each other through some of the inevitable complexities that arose.

Encounter: mentor-coaching to support teacher induction into new schools to improve retention and teaching quality

Mentor-coaching is an integrated feature of induction for teachers (new and experienced) joining schools in an English language school board in Quebec, Canada. As described in Trista's personal narrative in chapter 8, it was first introduced as a response to regional employment conditions which meant that up to one quarter of all teachers in the schools might be in this induction phase. The purpose of the coaching was to provide all teachers joining one of the board's schools (regardless of career stage) peer support and access to a self-sustaining professional learning process that focused on meeting the needs of children in their care. The coaches were experienced teachers in the district who continued to hold full-time teaching positions. The mentor-coach model included goal-setting, reciprocal classroom observations and debriefing, preparation of a reflective record, co-planning, and modelling of instructional strategies. The model supported mentor–coaches to move between the two stances of mentoring and coaching in response to the needs of their new colleagues. Mentor–coaches were supported by a small team working for the school board and took co-responsibility for their own practice through opportunities to engage with each other, both in and between schools in book clubs, coaches' breakfasts and networking meetings.

Understanding contextual coaching

Our analysis of the two cases of coaching in relation to the collaborative professionalism tenets revealed the significance of the contextualisation of the coaching. Both case studies of coaching were responses to the policy challenges and opportunities in their specific settings, which helped to provide clarity to the purpose of the coaching. The coaching approaches were adapted over time, with changes largely being the result of co-construction between coaches and/or coachees in the contexts of the schools. Our research findings can be outlined as follows:

- Effective contextual coaching leads to conditions underpinning school improvement.
- There are patterns of alignment with the ten tenets of collaborative professionalism.
- Contextual coaching is founded on mutual dialogue, joint work, collective responsibility and collaborative enquiry.
- In more mature coaching programmes, collective autonomy, initiative and efficacy emerge.
- There is also evidence that opportunities exist for contextual coaching to be further aligned with the remaining tenets.
- The study offers insight into how school improvement can be realised by the development of staff capacity for teacher leadership through contextual coaching.

This research indicated that the impact of coaching in education is enhanced by recognising the importance of context and the value of iterative design and co-construction of the coaching approach. We thus propose that contextual coaching relies on deliberate yet flexible designs and structures of support. The self-determining and iterative element of contextual coaching increased its sustainability and enabled collaborative professionalism to flourish across and beyond the active coaching cohorts. In our case studies the professionals involved began to take responsibility for shaping the coaching structure and design as a collective.

Contextual coaching is responsive to school culture and specific contexts. This suggests that coaching programmes cannot simply be inserted into schools and expected to work in isolation; they must be part of a broader programme design so that the intelligence gathered through coaching can feed back to the wider system and vice versa. In both cases the teachers and coaches had shared purpose and understood the pedagogic 'why' and 'how' underpinning the focus of contextual coaching, which led to greater buy-in, engagement and commitment. It was also critical that teachers had levels of autonomy and leaders ensured capacity for coaching. Although externally initiated, participants in both cases were given sufficient time, space, resources and agency to co-construct ongoing coaching delivery and design. Individual teachers also set their own coaching goals based on the areas of improvement and innovation that they had identified as important for their students.

To build and sustain coaching impact there needs to be long-term commitment and investment in the necessary resources. The research suggests that the principles of contextual coaching are generalisable, but models must be developed to be bespoke and aligned with each setting. It also indicates that collaborative professionalism might offer a useful framework to better design and implement contextual coaching programmes.

Coaching and educator wellbeing

As highlighted in the discussion about CPL, teacher wellbeing and teacher retention are becoming problems that need to be addressed through policy decisions and changes to practice. Students need passionate, competent and committed educators and we know students thrive when teachers thrive. Yet teachers and administrators are the professionals reporting the highest levels of negative emotion, job stress and burnout internationally (McCallum et al., n.d.; Sutcher et al., 2016). It is no wonder that there is a retention and recruitment issue across the globe (OECD, 2023). Interested in the role coaching played in educator wellbeing, Trista's doctoral research explored the influence of the mentor–coach role (as outlined in the contextual coaching encounter above and in chapter 8) on experienced teachers' professional learning, pedagogical practice and wellbeing. Whereas there is substantial research showing the positive impact of coaching on new teachers, much less is known about the impact being a coach has on the coach.

Encounter: a Canadian case study of mentor–coach wellbeing

This research used Seligman's (2011) PERMA wellbeing framework to highlight potential benefits, challenges and limitations of the mentor-coaching role (Hollweck, 2019b). Seligman (2011) defines wellbeing as a multidimensional construct that bridges the hedonic aspect of feeling good (positive emotion) with the eudaimonic aspects of living well: relationships, purpose, mastery, growth and autonomy (we discuss the theory of wellbeing in chapter 3). Five contributing wellbeing elements together form the acronym PERMA: positive emotion, engagement, (positive) relationships, meaning and accomplishment. Each element has three properties (Seligman, 2011, p. 16):

1. It contributes to wellbeing.
2. Many people pursue it for its own sake, not merely to get any of the other elements.
3. It is defined and measured independently of the other elements (exclusivity).

The combination of these five PERMA elements ultimately contributes to human flourishing (Goodman et al., 2018). Flourishing is defined by the World Health Organization (WHO, 2014) as a state in which every individual can realise their own potential, cope with the normal stresses of life, work productively and fruitfully and contribute to their own community. In this research study, wellbeing is considered a key component of human flourishing, but the terms are not synonymous.

From educational research, we have learned that teacher wellbeing is tied to the nature of their work (Nias, 1981). Teachers' work should buoy their sense of purpose (Pink, 2011), increase competence and mastery (Pink, 2011; Ryan and Deci, 2000), be anchored in *collaborative professionalism* based on solidarity and solidity (see discussion above), support a sense of *collective efficacy* (Donohoo, 2017, 2018) and lead to a sense of accomplishment (Pink, 2011). Teachers flourish when they are working as a collective doing meaningful work that is achievable and makes a difference in the lives of students.

For the mentor–coaches in Trista's study, being a mentor–coach contributed to their sense of wellbeing and aligned with the PERMA framework:

- **Positive emotion**: participants reported enjoyment and that the mentor–coach role was rewarding and linked to their personal and professional growth.
- **Engagement**: learning to be an effective mentor–coach took time, practice and collaborative professional learning activities. Participants appreciated the opportunity to learn skills and engage with their professional growth.
- (Positive) **Relationships**: participants reported positive and enduring relationships with their coaching partners, many noting they lasted long after the official mentor–coach role was finished.
- **Meaning**: although teachers had different reasons for becoming mentor–coaches, many shared that the role gave them an opportunity to give back to their school community and colleagues who may need their support.
- **Accomplishment**: participants reported feeling a sense of achievement when their coaching partner made improvements, felt effective and ultimately was successful at the end of the year.

Despite the majority of mentor–coaches reporting that the mentor–coach role contributed to their sense of wellbeing, the study also showed that coaching is not a panacea for wellbeing. In fact, some mentor–coaches reported that their increased emotional involvement and time commitment due to challenging relationships, disengaged partners and a negative perception of coaching in their school actually contributed to their sense of stress and illbeing.

Although the research and case studies captured in this book show many positive outcomes from coaching, including its potential to foster wellbeing for educators at different stages of their career, it is not a blanket solution. Caution should be taken when adopting any educational initiative, and coaching is no exception. The realities of constant change can be exhausting. Imposed reforms can be contradictory and are too often under-resourced. Educator stress and burnout can be triggered by such initiatives and coaching should not be an additional imposition if conditions are not conducive to it.

Chapter 15 endnotes

Final thoughts

When developing coaching across an organisation, investing in recruiting, training and resourcing coaches, it might be easy to fall into and then fall back on pre-designated coaching objectives and routines to sustain work over time. In the same way it might seem appropriate to ensure that the coaching provided to all colleagues (e.g. with regards to teaching) is uniform and consistent. Such decisions are often justified by an argument for equality. These routines might be established within the setting to meet the expectations of or be heavily influenced by a commercial provider. Managing coaching across complex settings will always be a balancing act, but ensuring flexibility and nuance and allowing for adaptation were seen as essential by the participants in our CollectivED focus group on coaching and context. This is illustrated by the following comments from a coaching leader from a large sixth form college who highlighted the need for coaching to enable staff:

> to feel safe to take risks and feel that coaching isn't being done to them [...] a place where people are openly sharing their creativity, that it is something that is welcomed and valued and encouraged. I think that ... kind of culture will encourage a really flourishing coaching programme because I feel that people will feel free to not go to be coached in order to be told how to do something and to be told how to adhere to a set of principles, but actually to get better and to find their [way of] improving something which is important to them within that culture. [...] It's really important that the context that the coaching programme is working within generates that ethos, if it's going to be in any way valuable, if it's going to be valued by the people that want to take part in it. [...] If it's going to work, it's got to be iterative, hasn't it? It's got to be able to change as time changes. We've all been through this hideous pandemic and seeing how that's affected people and changed the educational landscape. And I think it's really

important that the coaching context within your institution can reflect that and reflect that ability for us to stop and pause and go actually life looks different now.

These comments reflect the need to allow for individuality within coaching and also the significance of change over time, both within and beyond the control of the college. A key word used here is 'iterative', identifying the two-way dynamic relationship between coaching and context.

Talking points

In the opening quote of this chapter from Hollweck and Lofthouse (2021) the relationship between context (e.g. personal relationships, cultures and subcultures, and organisational mores) and the functional complexities of coaching is introduced. In addition, in the ecosystemic analysis of professional learning outlined in the first encounter in this chapter the following components of engagement were noted: the content/focus of the discussion, the collaborative nature of the dialogue, the challenging aspect of the dialogue, feeling willing to engage with the process, building positive relationships and experiencing positive morale. You might like to look back at the details given and then discuss them in relation to the ways that you and colleagues engage in professional development, including coaching. Are there any critical components that make a positive difference that are not identified here, but which you would also like to pay attention to?

Ideas for action

The final tenet of collaborative professionalism is 'big picture thinking for all'. This is often hard to achieve because of hierarchical decision-making structures that exist in education, in which some members of the community are more included than others. Knowing that this can be a challenge, reconsider the purposeful progress model introduced in chapter 5. You might like to undertake a review of coaching currently in place in your setting, considering both the coaching *with* and coaching *for* aspects to see how a sense of purpose supports the preferred future. Do current strategies and practices create more (or perhaps limit) the opportunities for 'big picture thinking for all'?

Chapter 16
Coaching efficacy: knowing what works

How can we do better? The answer is simple but the implementation is not. We would have to do three things: 1) do less telling; 2) learn to do more asking in the particular form of Humble Inquiry; and 3) do a better job of listening and acknowledging.

Edgar H. Shein (2013, p. 7)

Problematising the concept of efficacy

We believe in coaching, but not without question. It could be argued that its persistence in education systems and its apparent recent surge in use are evidence enough that it works. That alone suggests that it is adaptable over time and across contexts. However, it could also point to the potential for companies and consultants to make money from coaching and thus promote and sustain it. We might propose coaching as the answer to a deficit interpretation of education, a constant anxiety about gaps to be closed, challenges to be resolved. Encounters with coaching in this book do illustrate specific examples of how coaching has helped to address imbalances in educational experiences or outcomes. But they do not suggest that it is a quick or a sole fix in these situations. In this chapter we consider coaching efficacy based on its potential to create change. We don't assume that all change is necessary or good.

Probably the most cited coaching paper in education at the time of writing this book is Kraft et al. (2018), which is based on a meta-analysis of the causal evidence of the impact of teacher coaching on instruction (teaching) and achievement. They combined 60 research studies which gave a statistical analysis of effect and 'found pooled effect sizes of 0.49 standard deviations (SD) on instruction and 0.18 SD on achievement'. In some popular literature and instructional coaching programmes much is made of this data. However, what is rarely acknowledged is that the original research contexts were relatively limited to mostly North American literacy coaching in pre-kindergarten and elementary schools. Additionally, how coaching is defined and understood across the 60 studies included in the meta-analysis varies, a phenomenon in coaching research that we also highlight in chapter 2. For Kraft et al. (2018), teacher coaching programmes are defined 'broadly as an all in-service PD programs where coaches or peers observe teachers' instruction and provide feedback to help them improve' (p. 548). Although it fits under the broad teacher professional learning and development umbrella, coaching is distinct from most CPD since it is 'individualized, time-intensive, sustained over the course of a semester or year, context specific, and focused on discrete skills' (p. 548). There are inherent difficulties in extrapolation from education research in contrasting contexts with conflicting definitions and also from generalisations drawn from meta-analysis, which the paper's authors recognise, but this is sometimes lost in translation. What actually happens in feedback conversations and the type of coaching approach used matter when we are making judgements about coaching efficacy. For the purposes of this book we take an alternative, more localised, approach to understanding coaching efficacy, which we invite you to encounter alongside the wider literature.

It can be assumed that all forms of coaching in education share the broad purpose to support the learning and/or the wellbeing of educators and learners, with the coachee's focus being on changes in their own and others' learning and development. A legitimate question for policy-makers, leaders, researchers and practitioners is whether coaching actually does work. The CollectivED coaching case studies in part 3 offer specific examples of a range of types of coaching and their perceived value. They also demonstrate that coaching is not a quick-fix, one-size-fits-all approach or an activity that sits apart from other professional experiences. 'Coaching programmes cannot simply be inserted into schools and expected to work in isolation; they must be part of a broader programme design so that the intelligence gathered through coaching can feed back to the wider system and vice versa' (Hollweck and Lofthouse, 2021).

A number of key challenges in understanding coaching efficacy remain:

- Given the diversity of coaching practices we cannot expect to be able to answer the question about coaching efficacy in a few bullet points.
- Quantifying coaching activity, such as time spent, numbers coached and organisational reach, is not itself a measure of efficacy, particularly if ongoing participation is obligated rather than engaged with through informed, experienced and sustained consent.
- Claiming or even demonstrating that an approach is scalable does not equate to knowing that its impact is positive at scale when applied to lots of individual education settings.
- Knowing that a coaching model creates positive changes in one context does not guarantee that it can be transposed seamlessly and with the same impacts in a different context.

Thinking about coaching efficacy therefore is not as simple as knowing 'what works', but it is possible to make sense of 'what is working' in coaching at any given context and at a particular time.

In classic terms, as outlined in chapter 2, coaching typically creates opportunities for an individual to move through self-regulatory cycles, which include reflection, personal sensemaking and goal-setting. As such, judging the personal impact of coaching implies acknowledging that its value must be felt by the coachee (Grant, 2013). In education contexts it is necessary to reconcile the coachee's personal development with the impact of their work as a professional, and judging the wider efficacy of coaching needs to reflect these ripple effects on others. Therefore, to judge the impact and efficacy of coaching it is appropriate to start with Biesta's (2020) questions and to ask 'effective for what?' and 'effective for whom?' So, when we ask whether coaching 'works' in education we must remember the associated queries. These might be put simply as 5Ws and an H or 'who, what, why, where and when and then how' questions, such as:

- What are the knowledge, skills and attitudes that we need to foster in colleagues working in education to allow them to successfully participate in coaching?
- Who does coaching benefit?
- Why does coaching thrive in some organisations and flounder in others?
- Where is the limited resource that we have in education best deployed, and is coaching worth investing time and effort into when resources are tight?
- When might coaching be most valuable in the timelines of organisational change and individual development?
- How can we assess the impact of coaching when there are so many factors influencing success or struggle in education?

If coaching is about creating the conditions for change, a key question of its efficacy is whether coaching helps us to address a specific challenge and enhance a desirable quality or outcome of education. Plans for coaching will typically be framed by an objective: the positive impact we anticipate it can have. This might be related to teaching and learning, student experience or achievement, career development and role enhancement, teacher wellbeing and retention, community building or some other component of the education system. The stated objective will influence the selection and design of coaching programmes, which may be undertaken by individuals, developed within or across educational settings, be built into wider CPD provision or based on a published coaching model or commercial platform. Whatever the design there is a good chance that coaching will have impacts in addition to the stated objective, which itself may or may not be achieved, and these additional impacts may or may not be positive. It is also worth noting that while in many education settings objectives, targets and improvement plans are commonplace, we argue for a deeper consideration of purpose. As we pose coaching episodes as learning encounters, we need to consider what is being learned and what effect this learning is having, and whether the related learning is supporting individuals and organisations in their shared purpose.

When we consider the propositions and dilemmas above, it is clear that collecting data is only part of the process of exploring efficacy. Coaching in education is not easy to evaluate in simple terms. We need appropriate approaches, tools or lenses to analyse the information gathered which can help us to trace the ways that coaching influences change, enables learning and relates to purpose. This chapter offers three conceptual tools which also emphasise the significance of contexts of coaching. These are the use of:

1. a **theory of change** approach to support the development and localised evaluation of coaching (Laing and Todd, 2015)
2. **activity systems** (Engeström, 1987) as a means of illuminating the influences on the outcomes of coaching (Lofthouse et al., 2022; Lofthouse, 2022)
3. the **cycles of growth** model of professional learning as a sensemaking tool, allowing a consideration of affordances and changes in coaching (Lofthouse, 2021).

In this chapter theory of change and activity systems are first outlined and then illustrated through the unique case study of coaching first introduced in chapter 7: 'Interprofessional video-based coaching for communication rich pedagogies' (Lofthouse et al., 2018). This example is chosen as it is unusual and this unfamiliarity may help you remain curious about its efficacy as you encounter it. To illustrate the potential of the cycles of growth model in explaining how coaching supports professional learning we return to another encounter already introduced in chapters 6 and 14: 'Coaching within a government-funded school improvement project based on enhancing maths teaching'.

Starting with a theory of change for coaching

In education there is often a desire for change, a goal to which funding and time are allocated. Recognising the need for change is the first step, followed by starting to explore how that might be achieved. Without orientation towards a purpose there is a risk that any activity, such as coaching, gets established because it feels like the newest fad. There is also a risk that it acts as a distraction and gets in the way of the desired change by using up time and resources, and even colleagues' professional goodwill. One way to keep the purpose in mind and identify potential pathways to change through coaching is by creating a theory of change. Laing and Todd (2015, p. 3) describe theory of change as:

> *A theory-based approach to planning, implementing or evaluating change at an individual, organisational or community level. An assumption is made that an action is purposeful. A theory of change articulates explicitly how a project or initiative is intended to achieve outcomes through actions, while taking into account its context.*

While there are a range of approaches that can be used to create and make use of theory of change methods there are common features. One is that the intent for change is articulated and the context within which the desired change should occur is considered. Structure is added to the theory by developing propositions about what steps will be necessary and what shifts may occur over time. In education it is common to pay attention to steps and shifts that involve both staff and students, but not necessarily exclusively so. External partners, other experts, families and the wider community may also become interwoven into the theory of change. Typically a bespoke theory of change can be represented through visual means, allowing key people, activities, relationships and time frames to be mapped. These theory of change diagrams can be worked on by a range of stakeholders to ensure inclusion, value a range of perspectives and enable reality checks. The theory of change diagram will indicate potential causal relationships in an attempt to reveal the possible mechanisms for change. One of the major benefits of creating contextualised theory of change models is the opportunity to identify small steps and small gains which might otherwise be overlooked in the grand plan or overall evaluation. These can then both be designed for and also used as indicators that change is indeed underway. Rather than singular measures of success (or failure), theory of change approaches encourage the collection of a portfolio of data that might represent a more complex outcome.

Laing and Todd (2015) identify four possible approaches to developing a theory of change, which can be summarised as follows:

1. **deductive model**: developed from existing research literature and knowledge relevant to the contexts and desired change, which is then simplified into steps of change
2. **inductive model**: developed from observing phenomena in action rather than relying on what is already known or assumed about how it works
3. **mental model**: developed by drawing on the knowledge and experience of stakeholders, generated from their own ideas about how things work in context
4. **collaborative model**: developed through co-creation and collaboration, often between researchers who input evidence from existing research and practitioners, with the researcher able to act as a critical friend to offer support and challenge.

To illustrate the use of theory of change we return to the work undertaken by Jo Flanagan, Bibiana Wigley and Rachel Lofthouse, who collectively adopted a research-informed lens to support its development, implementation and evaluation stages in schools (Lofthouse et al., 2016), which was first introduced in chapter 7. Bibiana (Bib) and Jo were speech and language therapists who spent two years developing a video-based coaching approach that allowed them to work with teachers, early years practitioners and teaching assistants as coachees to support pupils with a range of speech, language and communication needs (SLCN) and pupils with English as an additional language (Lofthouse et al., 2016, 2018). The experiences that the coaches had of working directly with some of the children and with the families created the foundation from which they undertook situational and supportive work with school staff as coachees. In this developmental stage, across two schools, a theory of change approach was used to track the impacts of coaching over time. This is outlined in *Theory-based Methodology: Using theories of change for development, research and evaluation*, edited by Laing and Todd (2015).

A mental model of a theory of change was generated once each of the leadership teams in the two schools had decided to pursue the interprofessional coaching approach. This was facilitated through semi-structured interviews undertaken by Rachel. The first step was for

Rachel to interview the two headteachers about their own schools and objectives. The core questions used were:

- In terms of speech and language development what is the situation you face in your setting?
- What do you believe needs to change?
- How will these changes be made? What role will Bib and Jo (the speech and language therapists) play and what actions will you take (as headteacher)?
- What effect do you anticipate those actions will have?
- How will you know if change is happening?
- What will this be like for different members of your community (children, staff, parents, etc.)?

These interviews yielded significant evidence of the expectations of the headteachers, which were mapped as flow charts based on three core themes, each considered in relation to the staff and the children in the setting:

1. the starting situation: what is it like now and why, and what needs to change?
2. the steps to change and strands of action: what we are going to do about it?
3. the desired and intended outcomes.

The flowchart for one of the settings is shown in Figure 16.1.

Chapter 16 Coaching efficacy: knowing what works

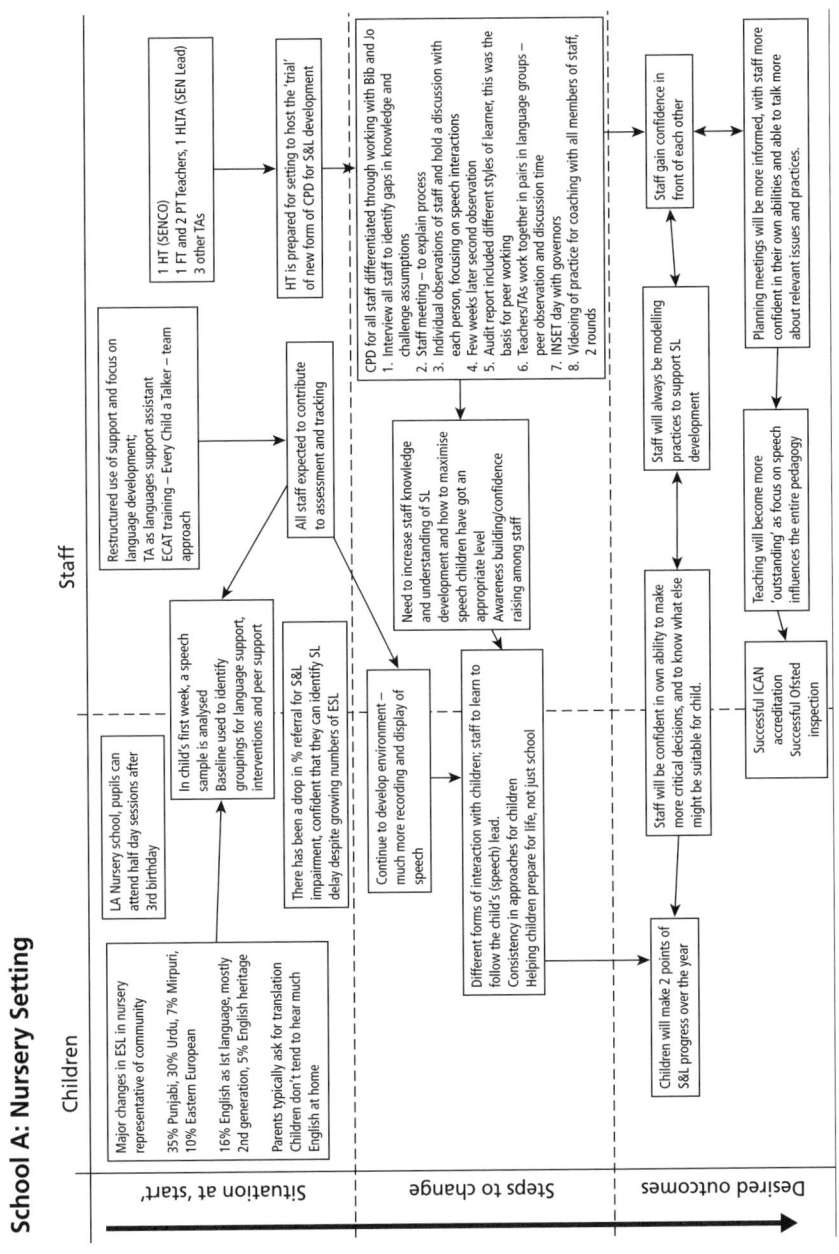

Figure 16.1 Example of initial theory of change flowchart. Source: Lofthouse, in Laing and Todd (2015)

Six months after the initial headteacher interviews, further interviews were conducted. In this round the teachers and teaching assistants who had been coached, as well as the headteachers, were interviewed. At the start of each interview participants were shown the theory of change flowchart for their setting, and their opinions were gathered as they reflected on the starting points, steps to change and outcomes, allowing the theorised leadership perspective and the actual experience of participating in the coaching to be reflected on and investigated. As Rachel reflected in the 2015 theory of change guide edited by Laing and Todd (p. 12):

> *The resulting interviews were expansive and informative. The interviewees frequently triggered new conversational threads as they reflected on what they could see represented on the flow diagram. They were able to determine what had come to fruition from the plan and what was more elusive. They added new arrows and notes to explain the experience from their perspective.*

In this case the theory of change was embedded in a research project, designed to help determine the efficacy of the coaching approach. The findings included the following:

- Interprofessional coaching helped to create conditions for bespoke workplace learning.
- Video-based coaching created a neutral, non-judgemental space in which teachers' own interactional practices with children were exposed and made open to co-construction, based on the relationship between pedagogic and communication knowledge and skills.
- Coaching formed a driver of focused professional development, providing participants with common understandings, a shared language and a willingness to share ideas and be more open to self-evaluation and critique.
- Coaching provided some of the 'glue' that supported access and learning from other CPD and the development of new leadership and support roles.

Reflecting on these outcomes in this case study of coaching shows how the theory of change approach was used to create focus, allowing the headteachers to be more deliberate in their coordination and leadership of the project. It also situates coaching within the context, to provide a sense of sequence rather than urgency and to create a base map from which further enquiry could be undertaken on the efficacy of the coaching approach. The sorts of insights supported by using the theory of change approach were invaluable as the model of interprofessional coaching was further refined and then offered in new settings.

Understanding how coaching functions as an activity system

Coaching can appear to take on a life of its own in any setting or programme, but it sits within a system in which it can be embedded or somewhat detached, but by which it is inevitably influenced. In addition, the object of coaching in educational systems may, or may not, be aligned with the actual outcomes of coaching. It is the situational understanding of the influences on and within coaching which an activity system can help us to understand. It is possible to use activity systems to review how education systems as a whole operate (e.g. to understand how an increasing use of performative measures to rank schools distorts the elements of the system and may create unwanted impacts). There is also potential to use activity systems at a case-by-case level. In coaching terms, for example, rather than assuming that rolling out the same coaching provision will have universal impacts across settings and educational systems, an activity systems approach acknowledges that each setting is unique, complex and dynamic.

Activity systems are rooted in cultural historical activity theory (CHAT), which is attributed to the Vygotskian sociocultural perspectives developed by Engeström (e.g. 1987, 2007). Rachel and her colleagues (2022, p. 154) used activity systems as a:

> *pragmatic tool, allowing an 'iterative process of theorising and verification' (Briggs, 2007, p. 590) [... demonstrating] the value of understanding the characteristics and impacts of distinct coaching provision to counter the over-generalisations of the role of coaching in education.*

Activity systems have a set of components, which are summarised in Table 16.1, with the components interacting with each other as indicated in Figure 16.2.

Table 16.1 Components of activity systems

Activity system component	Exploration of component in coaching activity systems
Object	The OBJECT of coaching is to facilitate self-reflection and effective decision-making in the context of the coachee's own personal and professional challenges. In education contexts this broad coaching object is further orientated towards the learning and wellbeing of educators (in any role) and their learners, with the coachee's focus being their own and others' learning and development. This will typically generate a more specific object, determined by the motivation driving coaching, for example, related to teaching or other professional skills or progression.
Subject	The coach is the SUBJECT of the system using a coaching approach to achieve with the intention of enabling the object to be achieved.
Tools	The coach deploys TOOLS such as language (e.g. coaching questions) frameworks or models (e.g. GROWTH coaching) and resources (e.g. content materials, digital technology and training) to support the coachee to make progress towards the object.
Mediating artefacts: Rules, community, division of labour	The RULES, COMMUNITY and DIVISION OF LABOUR are MEDIATING ARTEFACTS which influence the coachee's progress towards, and experience of achieving (or not), the object. They include the nature of coaching (a managed 1:1 conversation), the 'contracting' which frames the coaching, the relationship between coach and coachee and the communities that exist or are formed (e.g. cohorts of coachees, wider colleagues) and the ways that roles are adopted (e.g. respective contributions to coaching dialogue, the responsibilities assumed, power held or trust created).
Sensemaking and outcome	The OBJECT of the activity system is translated into OUTCOMES determined by the MEDIATING ARTEFACTS of the system and the SENSEMAKING process (e.g. self-awareness). The OUTCOMES of coaching may or may not be aligned with the object and will be experienced individually. Research into coaching effectiveness needs to consider both the object of (motivation for) coaching and also the lived experiences of participants and the education community within which they work. The outcomes will also be influenced by the extent to which other activity systems converge with or contradict the coaching in education activity systems in the policy and practice context.

Chapter 16 Coaching efficacy: knowing what works

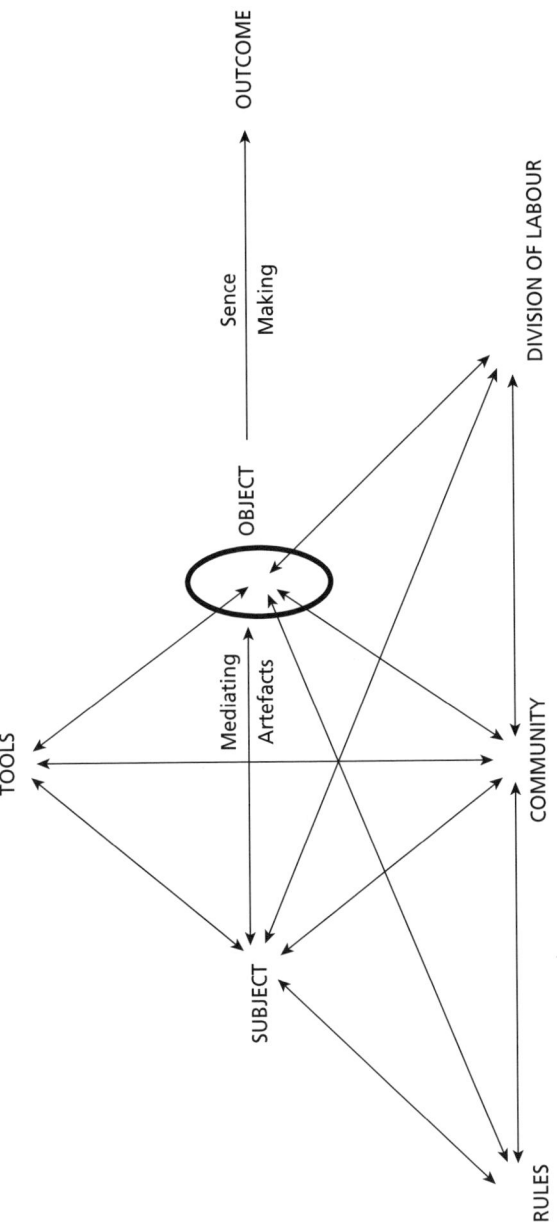

Figure 16.2 Interactions within a coaching activity system

Using the activity system as an analytical frame it is possible to explore the relationships between the original object of coaching and the actual outcomes. This gives an insight into the impacts of coaching and the extent to which it might be deemed a success. All of the components of the coaching activity system itself will influence or mediate the alignment or convergence between the object and outcomes, because they all contribute to the sensemaking that is happening both at individual and organisational levels (Lofthouse, 2022).

Returning to our interprofessional coaching case study to illustrate coaching as an activity system, we encounter what happened next. Following the development phase Bib and Jo were then able to offer coaching as a bespoke model to other schools as part of a year-long programme. At this stage of implementation, data was collected across a year from two primary schools led by a shared executive headteacher. In addition to data routinely collected in the schools, Rachel collected data using a series of focus groups, which allowed the experience of coaching and its impacts to be tracked. The findings were analysed using an approach based on activity systems (Lofthouse et al., 2022; Lofthouse, 2022). The core components of the resulting activity system are summarised as shown in Table 16.2. Following the table, examples of the sensemaking and outcomes are further outlined.

Table 16.2 Core components of the interprofessional coaching activity system

Activity system component	Exploration of component in the SLCN coaching activity system
Object	Coaching was introduced to support teachers to enhance communication-rich pedagogies in a context where over 95% of children were speaking and learning English as an additional language. Unlike some coaching models, the object of coaching included giving advice and guiding teachers to be more curious and insightful with respect to their pupils' SLCN.
Subject	The coaches were the speech and language therapists who had high levels of contextual knowledge related to the demographics and needs of the children in the city.

Activity system component	Exploration of component in the SLCN coaching activity system
Tools	The coaches used two key tools which helped to unlock the potential of coaching: 1. use of explanatory language underpinning the coaching which reflected the bringing together of the two professional domains 2. use of short video clips of the teachers' own recent lessons focusing on communication and interaction with children to enable shared scrutiny with teachers of the classroom pedagogic routines and opportunities.
Mediating artefacts: Rules, community, division of labour	Contextual mediating artefacts influenced the experience and outcomes of the coaching. The community involved in the coaching were school colleagues across a number of teaching roles, with the senior leadership teams of the two schools. A group of teachers had taken up the offer to be coached, using the specific coaching approach which had been developed and tested in the two previous settings (creating the rules). All staff were accessing associated training. Workload and participation can be recognised as a component of division of labour within an activity system, as can the decision by the senior leadership team to support rather than engage in coaching.

The outcomes of this specific case of coaching were dependent on the components of the activity system, the ways that these interacted and the sensemaking that went on. Some of the sensemaking occurred during the coaching cycles themselves, while other outcomes seemed to include resulting reflections on other aspects of professional life (such as planning and workload).

Unsurprisingly the coaching 'tools' made a difference, for example, the videos enhanced the teachers' capacities to focus on the SLCN of individual children and these insights led to more attuned pedagogic decision-making as described by teachers in focus groups: 'Things like group work, body language, using images with the words, using vocabulary that they could understand, giving short and simple instructions, repetition' and 'the positioning of children during an adult-directed session'. Becoming more confident about appropriate pedagogic decisions was itself attributed to a reduction in workload: 'It was everyday tweaks that made life a little easier […] It reduced my workload a little bit. Something as small as repositioning children within a group, to get them communicating with each other and join in, it did happen. So, the advice she gave, although very small, did have impact'. The discussion around workload gave additional insight into the perceived value of the coaching, as one teacher explained: 'Workload is one of those things that if you see the value of what you are doing it doesn't feel the same as if you don't.'

Some teachers volunteered to have their coaching meetings recorded for transcription and an analysis of the coaching sequences demonstrated a common pattern within coaching conversations. The coaching sessions typically had three distinguishable phases:

1. **orientation phase**: agreeing on the SLCN focus
2. **shared scrutiny phase**: coach and teacher reviewing classroom practice with respect to the SLCN focus, using video, recall and relevant documents as stimulus and drawing on existing professional knowledge (from the two professions), triggering some dissonance and realisation for the teacher
3. moving forward through the **co-construction phase**: coach prompting further reflection, problem-solving and suggestions for developing practice being co-constructed.

There was also evidence of some progression through the sequence of three coaching episodes. Changes occurred over time in the dynamic roles that the coach and teacher took in the conversations, the specificity of the SLCN focus under discussion and the teacher's familiarity with relevant vocabulary, concepts and tools to help her make more informed judgements, which helped the teacher move from being relatively tentative to more committed in pedagogic decision-making.

This worked example of a coaching activity system illustrates the complexity and specificity of what was occurring in these settings with their associated challenges and ambitions, with a particular model of coaching, at this point in the timeline of school development, sociocultural changes and education policy. Critically the activity system is a means by which to undertake analysis – making purposeful use of the data collected to create meaningful evidence and better understanding which can be used for future decision-making.

Cycles of growth enabled by coaching

If we consider coaching to be an opportunity for learning within the professional space, there is value in exploring examples of coaching practice through the lens of models of professional learning. Doing so may help us elevate our understanding of coaching as means to enhance ongoing teacher education or to create future capacity for individual and organisational change, rather than as a remedial act. Focusing on professional learning also helps to remind us that coaching is not the same as 'training' and that adults in professional contexts benefit from divergent outcomes and finding their own niche, as well as being able to meet the challenges of their context through developing a shared understanding and sense of purpose. Of course there are some conflicting perspectives on this, but here we draw on a model now known as the CoG model (see Figure 16.3), short for 'cycles of growth model', of professional learning (Lofthouse, 2021). This CoG model was developed through abductive analysis, which is a 'creative inferential process' (Tavory and Timmermans, 2014, p. 5) made possible by immersion in a range of research projects which led to Rachel's PhD.

Coaching with purpose

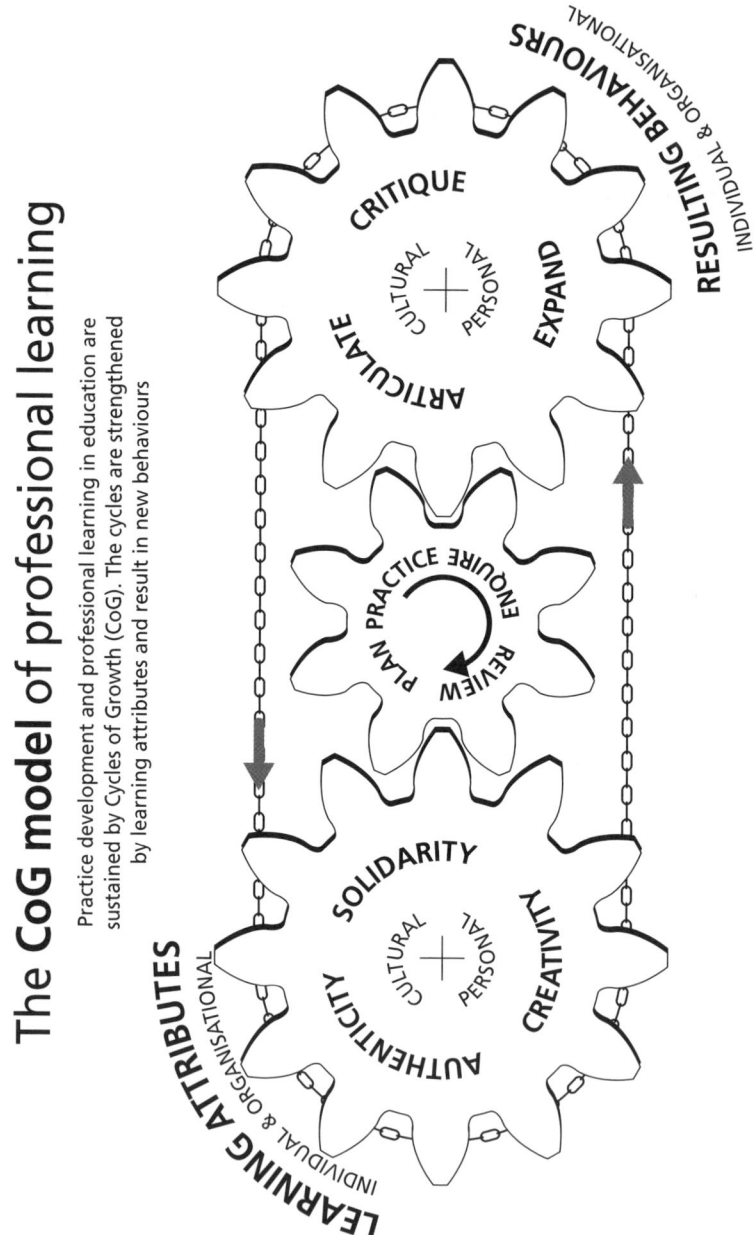

Figure 16.3 CoG model of professional learning. © Rachel Lofthouse, 2015

We can put coaching at the heart of the CoG model as it typically creates cycles of practice development taking place in, or influenced by, the professional context. Coaching cycles typically include processes of planning, doing, enquiring and reviewing. For example, a school leader may sign up to half-termly coaching sessions across a year, with opportunities for exploring challenges, setting goals and rehearsing ways to navigate decisions and actions with in-built check-ins within the coaching cycles. These sorts of professional learning activities take time, so it is important to ask whether coaching aids learning and development or just makes professionals increasingly busy. Having the right tools for the job can help to scaffold, frame and measure the learning experienced by the coachee. For example, if the coaching focus is teaching, useful tools might include video, observation frameworks and effective questions. If the focus is leadership, useful coaching tools might include the application of leadership theory or 360 evaluations. Tools have already been explored through discussion of activity systems above.

The CoG model indicates that three key attributes held by individuals and organisations can help to fuel professional learning. These are creativity, solidarity and authenticity. Creativity refers to being invited to problem-solve, being given opportunities to innovate and access to alternative practices and perspectives enabling practitioners to gain the capacity to develop original thinking and the confidence to go beyond routine practices. Developing a sense of solidarity requires teachers and school leaders to engage in collaboration and joint enterprises with others, including their own learners and the wider profession and to see beyond their personal experiences and immediate concerns. Authenticity in professional learning is enabled by practitioners understanding the tensions and priorities of the educational setting in which they work and taking account of the ethical dimensions of their practice.

The CoG model also defines valuable changes and behaviours resulting from professional learning. These changes work cumulatively to build individual and organisational capacity. As learners it is essential that professionals are able to articulate their dilemmas and ideas and to share their achievements from practice development, ideally through both internal and external networks, but often starting in the one-to-one conversations with peers, coaches or mentors. They also need to invite critique to ensure that their ideas and evidence are reviewed with an informed perspective, as well as to critique others' work with a generous spirit. As the cycles of practice development and professional learning go hand in hand, teachers' knowledge, professional repertoires and expertise expand and this allows their settings to become more effective in creating successful education for all.

The CoG model also demonstrates the potential of positive feedback loops between the changes and behaviours and the attributes. For example, as teachers experience the value of expanding their professional repertoire and share their work more frequently, they may help sustain the curiosity and creativity of colleagues to do the same, fostering a sense of professional togetherness. Teachers and leaders who become more critically aware as educators are likely to gain new insights which help them engage with the complexities of specific contexts and address the emergent challenges more authentically.

To illustrate the potential of the CoG model in explaining how coaching supports professional learning we return to the coaching case study first encountered in chapter 7 and referred to again in chapter 15: 'Coaching within a government-funded school improvement project based on enhancing maths teaching'. In this example the *cycles* of practice development included modelling, co-planning and observation as opportunities for the coaching conversations. The project was *authentically* designed with a focus on supporting the learning of children who were predominantly from military families and had lower levels of achievement compared with their peers. While attainment data is often complex, there was evidence over the project of improvements in the students' attitudes towards and achievement in maths. The coaches and lead teachers in each school built up working relationships over two years and developed a teacher network between the schools, building a sense of *solidarity* and shared purpose. While the project was focused on maths, the lead teachers engaged *creatively* with ideas and practices related to metacognition and developed them across the curriculum. The lead teachers gained a more nuanced and critical pedagogic understanding as well as the language and confidence to share their practices through observations, in network meetings and with colleagues in school and across the Teaching School Alliance, giving opportunities for *critique* and *articulation*. The evaluation evidence indicated that teachers had *expanded* their teaching repertoire and that their students had become more actively engaged and metacognitively aware. The teachers also *expanded* their capacity and motivation for subject leadership, for example, becoming specialist leaders in education or mathematics coordinators in the school and thus supporting the feedback loops of the CoG model.

Finally, in relation to the CoG model it is worth noting that it was used as the conceptual basis of the CollectivED Award, which is encountered in chapters 12 and 13. This further illustrates its capacity to be used to make sense of the efficacy of coaching, mentoring and professional learning over time.

Using the approaches to explore what and how coaching works in context

Kuusisaari (2013) proposed that coaching can be described as enabling 'developing talk', through which peers working in coaching relationships aim to develop something new through 'collaborative considerations, constructions and solution findings' (p. 56). This 'developing talk' should help to orientate activity, decision-making and problem-solving, often achieved through coaching with purpose.

Most coaching in schools is not the subject of a research project, but using tools such as theory of change, activity systems and models of professional learning (e.g. CoG) can help colleagues unpack what is happening beyond a 'head count' of activity or implausible and too often generalised claims of coaching impact. Theory of change approaches help to slow down thinking, ensuring that the context is taken into account as well as the steps that may need to be designed or noted as change happens. Like activity systems they can be a way to interrogate how the outcomes of coaching in education come about.

The activity system components shine a light on aspects of the coaching context and implementation that might be impacting positively or negatively on the desired purpose and indicate the types of information that may have value in evaluating coaching and explaining its efficacy. Activity systems also remind us to look beyond the original object and see what other outcomes are being generated. For example, the coaching designed to support primary teachers' maths teaching repertoire had the additional impact of building their confidence to apply for subject leadership roles (Lofthouse et al., 2022; Lofthouse, 2022). Activity systems are also useful when trying to unpick undesirable outcomes (Lofthouse and Leat, 2013) or to think through potential pitfalls.

The CoG model can also usefully be applied to coaching. Exploring the dimensions of creativity, solidarity, authenticity, articulation, critique and growth (expansion) generated by coaching is a good way to judge the extent to which coaching is creating rich opportunities for professional dialogue.

Using any of these tools to explore the efficacy of coaching in the spirit of 'humble inquiry' (Shein, 2013) can make a meaningful difference over time, helping you deepen and strengthen practice, and to check in against purpose rather than log metrics. In this spirit we believe that it is essential to approach evaluation or impact studies with genuine curiosity and as a further means to build relationships with others. This can only help rather than hinder the development of coaching and its value.

Chapter 16 endnotes

Final thoughts

Positive evaluations act as currency. They afford status to protagonists, provide affirmation of present effort and give legitimacy to future activity. Their perceived value, however, can result in a distortion of focus. Ensuring that coaching efficacy is understood holistically rather than just through what can be most readily measured takes both time and an open mind because it leads to greater depth of critique. Remembering that coaching in education is never a singular isolated activity is also essential. As a CollectivED colleague, experienced school leader and coach indicated 'This chapter marks an important moment for coaching in education – taking down the wrapping paper of coaching, and looking to see what is inside in how it is being applied, and understanding the impact it is actually having.'

During the CollectivED focus group on coaching and efficacy many interesting examples of practice were outlined, some of which have been shared through the encounters in part 3. It was also fascinating to listen to explanations of how coaching leaders and practitioners had changed their ways of understanding impact over time and how this related to purpose. This is well illustrated by this explanation from a senior MAT leader:

> *What really resonated for me was the transition from coaching 'with' and coaching 'for' [purpose] and that kind of journey of progress. What we found really interesting in our organisation. We started with the values and very much framing it with the coaching 'with', then we moved to what I would describe as a more rigorous approach using a trajectory model to kind of try to ascertain that progress and to track domains of knowledge and skill sets of teachers and all of those things for coaching for with those micro goals. And then we've moved back to coaching with purpose and I think that's probably where we're happiest and where we'll stay. As soon as we bring it back to the values, the work happens. We don't need to measure it on a trajectory. We've realised we felt that we did [need a trajectory] because I think there's an impetus in education to measure everything and assess everything. But as we've returned on the journey for coaching 'with' [purpose] we've held that space with more confidence and a greater sense of authenticity and our staff have understood that it's a values-driven model and we've seen big impact, we've seen bigger involvement [in coaching]. So that kind of makes me feel better as well that we feel comfortable about where we need [...] to hold the space for coaching with purpose.*

Understanding the efficacy of coaching in complex contexts such as education requires strategies that allow for both leaning in and leaning out. Knowing how the impact is perceived by individuals matters and knowing how the coaching is becoming more attuned and more sophisticated helps us to judge its evolution over time. Recognising the implications of coaching in a specific education setting, among different members of the community in that setting and for its contribution to a sustainable profession and to the self-confidence and self-efficacy of learners, takes more than a tick-box, traffic-light approach. Using the sorts of conceptual models offered in this chapter may enhance the holistic evaluation of coaching, as well as the quality of discussion and decision-making with regards to coaching in the wider education sector.

Talking points

In the opening quote for this chapter Shein advises us to 'do a better job of listening and acknowledging'. If you are to better understand coaching efficacy in your setting, who do you need to listen to, and what might you be overlooking or failing to acknowledge? What elements of the CoG model are evident in the experiences and outcomes of the coaching? Do colleagues recognise and prioritise these?

Ideas for action

Try using the theory of change approach when exploring opportunities for, and impacts of, coaching. Get colleagues involved to collaborate on this as leaders, coaches and coachees. This will help to join the dots and provide a base map to check in with and to amend over time.

Chapter 17
Coaching, change and the 5As

Coaching programmes cannot simply be inserted into schools and expected to work in isolation; they must be part of a broader programme design so that the intelligence gathered through coaching can feed back to the wider system and vice versa.
Trista Hollweck and Rachel Lofthouse (2021, p. 413)

Throughout this book we have been making the case that coaching in education is about creating conditions for purposeful and positive change. We consider educational change to be an extension of something familiar, a new set of skills, or in some cases a radical reorientation of practice. Change, in this sense, is a process and not a single event (Fullan, 2015). It is an evolution in attitudes, understanding and behaviours that most often happens over time. Whereas some people experience change as uplifting, revitalising and energising, others find unwelcome change can be profoundly disturbing and disorienting (James, 2009). When paired with coaching, we have found through our research and practice that the change process can be a more positive experience.

With coaching in education, change can take many forms and work across multiple levels: the individual, organisation (school) and system. For example, when a teacher is working with a coach, changes may occur in their pedagogical practice or professional understanding. Changes can also occur for individuals when they learn how to coach and become more experienced, competent and confident in their coaching. At the organisational or system level, changes can happen when coaching programmes are implemented in a school or district which can have an impact on professional routines and culture. Other school- and system-level changes might be when coaching is used to support the implementation of other educational initiatives, such as a new reform (see chapter 8) or increasing metacognition in maths instruction (see chapters 7 and 16). In some cases, the educational change process is happening (and needs to be managed) across multiple levels at the same time.

Recently there has been a shift in the discussion around coaching in education to include a focus on the role of context, culture and change (see Knight, 2021; Woulfin et al., 2023). While there remains a plethora of books and programmes that focus on the nuts and bolts or 'how-to' of coaching (what it is, the role of the coach, different coaching skills and approaches, etc.), there has been a growing recognition that context and culture can influence implementation, spread, sustainability and overall educator buy-in when it comes to coaching. We welcome this attention to *contextual coaching* (see chapter 14); it is essential to know who we are, where we have been and where we are going for purposeful and positive educational change.

In this chapter we unpack what we have learned over the past two decades in our practice and research work about educational change to better understand how and why coaching has an impact on some individuals, schools and systems more than others. We also explore the literature on organisational and systemic change to consider how and why some coaching programmes become deeply rooted and sustained in some contexts while others can flounder and fail. Researching and writing about change and improvement in educational settings (and beyond) has been in vogue for decades, and we thus draw on literature and theories from an extended period alongside more contemporary sources. Finally, we pull these ideas together and introduce the 5As model, a thinking tool we've developed to help individuals and organisations critically reflect on their educational change process across five dynamic phases.

Individual change

As discussed in part 1 of the book and evidenced in the CollectivED case studies, it takes time, experience and practice to become an effective coach. Although basic coaching skills, approaches and frameworks can be learned fairly easily, coaching expertise requires individuals to draw on experience and a more advanced repertoire of skills to respond to their coachee's needs (Hollweck, 2019b; Lofthouse, 2019b; van Nieuwerburgh and Love, 2019). So, how does an individual develop expertise in coaching? By now, there is general agreement that being an excellent educator is not the only ingredient in making an effective coach. As noted in chapter 3, Trista's doctoral research showed it took three years for experienced teachers who took on a mentor–coach role to be confident in their coaching skills, which they reported led to increased impact for their coachee (Hollweck, 2019a). Coaches need professional learning on different coaching skills and approaches, resources and opportunities to practise and get feedback on their coaching, and be part of a professional learning network that will support them to grow professionally and manage challenging situations (Hollweck, 2020). Understanding the developmental change process that happens when individuals learn something new is another useful tool. Not only does this understanding help those of us who are supporting coaches, but it is helpful for coaches who are working alongside teachers learning a new pedagogical practice or strategy. Below we describe four models that have informed our thinking and practice around individual change. Although 'no change model can capture all the intricacies of a particular instance of personal change' (van Nieuwerburgh and Love, 2019, p. 51), these models have each influenced the development of our 5As dynamic model of educational change.

Four stages of competence

The four stages of competence model or 'conscious competence' learning model is drawn from the fields of psychology and management. Often depicted as a ladder (see Figure 17.1), the model has been traced back to Martin M. Broadwell's (1969) 'levels of teaching' and describes the progress of individuals when they learn a new skill.

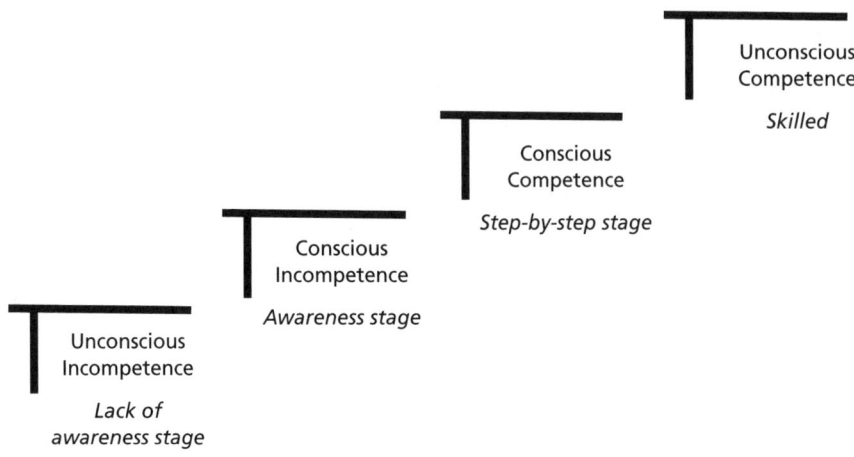

Figure 17.1 Ladder of competence

The initial stage describes the phase when individuals are unaware of how little they know (*unconscious incompetence*). Once they recognise their incompetence (*conscious incompetence*) they begin to consciously use, think about and practise the new skill (*conscious competence*). Finally, they move to the stage where they have mastered the skill and it becomes part of their unconscious repertoire or 'way of being' (*unconscious competence*).

When discussing this model in one of our writing sessions for this book, we noticed obvious connections to the self-actualisation (see chapter 3) stage in Maslow's (1943) 'hierarchy of needs' theory and Roger's (1995) 'way of being' (discussed in more detail in chapter 4). Another connection that we made was to the Johari window model (1955) by Joseph Luft and Harry Ingham (see Figure 17.2), which describes human interactions. Denoted as a feedback or disclosure model of personal awareness, the 'windows' divide what individuals reveal to others into four quadrants and relate to the consciousness component of the conscious competence model.

Figure 17.2 The Johari window

Concerns-based adoption model

Another useful model to help us understand the developmental change process that occurs when individuals learn to put new ideas and practices into use is the research-based concerns-based adoption model (CBAM) developed by Canadian researchers Gene E. Hall and Shirley M. Hord (Hall, 1974; Hall and Hord, 2020). Building on the teacher development work of Frances Fuller (1969) and grounded in change science, CBAM has been used as a research and implementation framework across a wide variety of educational settings (Haines, 2018; Hollingshead, 2009; Olson et al., 2020; Saunders, 2014). CBAM was found to be a useful thinking tool for participants in Trista's master's research, which explored educator experience with large-scale systemic change in the Canadian province of Quebec (see chapter 8).

CBAM has several guiding principles: change is always personal, takes time, relies on individual commitment to implement, is situated in a context that can either facilitate or hinder its desired outcome, and often takes a whole system effort (Hall and Hord, 2020). There are three components of CBAM: stages of concerns (SoC), levels of use (LoU) and innovation configuration (IC) map.

Stages of concerns

SoC is a developmental sequence that describes the seven stages of concerns individuals have as they carry out any innovation: unrelated, informational, personal, management, consequence, collaboration and refocusing (see Figure 17.3).

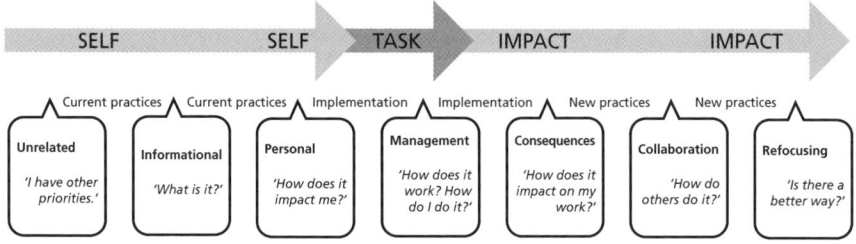

Figure 17.3 Stages of concerns

Supported by research, SoC is grounded in the notion that as both novice and experienced educators learn about, try and master new pedagogical methods and programmes, their feelings about the change evolve from a predominant focus on self (high personal concerns), to task (high management concerns), to impact (high consequence and collaboration concerns).

Levels of use

LoU identifies and categorises an individual's behaviours and actions during the change process as non-use, orientation, preparation, mechanical, routine, refinement, integration and renewal (see Figure 17.4).

Chapter 17 Coaching, change and the 5As

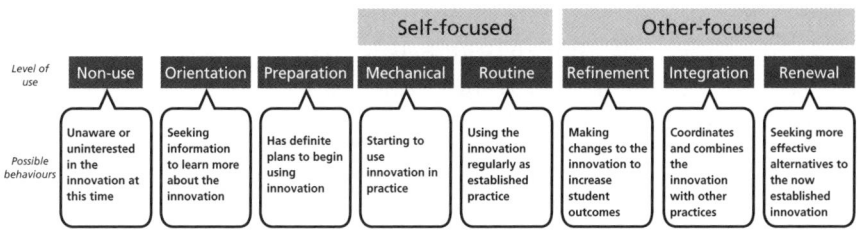

Figure 17.4 Levels of use

It takes time for educators to move from the more mechanical use of an innovation to being able to adapt, refine and integrate it with other instructional strategies. However, once educators develop higher levels of use and expertise with an innovation or change, research has shown that student learning also improves.

Innovation configuration (IC) map

The third and final component of CBAM is the bespoke IC map. Developed in partnership with those leading the change, the IC map is best described as an instrument that is used to define and quantify implementation of a new programme or practice. The IC map categorises the behaviours and expectations for individuals related to the implementation process of a specific innovation from ideal to less ideal. It also helps schools and systems to build on educators' prior knowledge, experiences and strengths, and to 'spread expertise among team members' and 'leverage complementary expertise efficiently to accomplish shared goals' (Learning Forward, 2022, p. 30).

Although the idea that individuals progress in a lockstep evolution through affective 'stages' can be misleading, CBAM is a useful framework to help us understand how educators respond to change. Not only can we use the tool to explore teachers' feelings and experience with new initiatives and innovations, but also it helps us to focus on meaningful ways to address their concerns. Of course, changes in individuals cannot be separated from the influence of other factors at play in the context and culture. As Anderson (2010) notes: 'CBAM theory posits that the nature and intensity of individual concerns about the implementation of new ideas and practices across and within each stage will be higher or lower, depending not only on the person's progress in mastering the change, but also on their organisational conditions (e.g., administrative and collegial support, fit with prior beliefs and practices) associated with the change, and the perceived impact or results of the change for those affected (teachers, students)' (pp. 66–67).

Stages of change (SoC) model

Another framework that can help us understand changes that are happening at the individual level is the stages of change model, also known as the transtheoretical model (TTM) (Prochaska et al., 1994). Developed by James Prochaska and Carlo DiClemente in the late 1970s, the model is based on their research that examined an individual's decision-making and motivation when it comes to quitting smoking. Widely used in health sciences, the model (DiClemente and Prochaska, 1998) describes six stages of change:

1. **precontemplation**: the individual is not considering change.
2. **contemplation**: the individual begins to think about making a change.
3. **preparation**: the individual has made a decision to act and is getting ready for change.
4. **action**: the individual works to implement the change.
5. **maintenance**: the individual works to maintain and consolidate the change.
6. **relapse** or **completion**: the individual reverts to earlier behaviour and/or previous stage of the change process or the change is sustained and incorporated into their way of being (adapted from Adams, p. 43).

In this model, it is understood that people do not change behaviours quickly or decisively. Rather, changes in behaviour occur continuously through a cyclical process with different people needing different strategies to make lasting and impactful change. Like CBAM's stages of concern model, the social context of an individual can influence their change process and there is no clear sense of how much time is needed for each stage or how long a person can remain in a stage.

The Dreyfus model

Dreyfus (2004) outlines five stages of skill acquisition for individuals learning a new innovation. These five stages are:

1. novice
2. advanced beginner
3. competent
4. proficient
5. expert.

In each of these stages Dreyfus outlines the role of context (context-free or situational), perspective (none, chosen or experienced), decision-making (analytic or intuitive) and commitment (detached or involved) and uses the examples of new drivers and chess players to explain how skill acquisition develops through experience. An adaptation of the Dreyfus model was used as a framework by Rachel and CollectivED fellow Lizana Oberholzer to help describe the difference between mentoring and coaching and how best to support educators at every stage of their career (Oberholzer and Boyle, 2023).

Although not an exhaustive list, we have found these four models useful to help us think about the changes that can happen for individuals during coaching or when individuals learn to coach. It is heartening to see the influence of change theory being addressed in recent coaching literature. Coaching expert Jim Knight (2021) has built on two of the models (CBAM and SoC) to describe five stages of implementation for individuals: non-use, awareness, mechanical, routine and proficient. It is our hope that these models and our own 5As dynamic model of educational change will be useful thinking tools to support critical reflection rather than be used as another checklist or blueprint for how change should unfold.

Organisational and systemic change

Educational change not only impacts individuals; it can also impact the people and places where they work. Change scientists have long been interested in organisational learning and ways to better understand, engage and lead change in settings such as schools and districts. In his management book *Fifth Discipline: The Art and Practice of the Learning Organization,* Peter Senge (2006) introduced the concept of 'systems thinking'. Systems thinking moves beyond the response of individuals to change and considers how organisations learn from research, experience and multiple sources outside their boundaries and fields, including other organisations. Senge argued that in order to successfully change the whole system, we need to be working on all different parts of the system. Thus, a systems thinking approach organises and integrates structure, organisation, resources and policy to support the desired change. Understanding the role an organisation's members and culture can play in shaping new ideas, initiatives and innovations helps explain why so often meaningful change is difficult to implement and sustain in complex contexts, like schools. In systems thinking, developing a strong 'learning culture' becomes an essential element in effective change management. However, this requires collaboration among staff, an openness to innovation and experimentation, and the space and capacity to reflect and adapt. The concept of systems thinking builds on the work of Donald Schön (1973, p. 28) who stated:

> We must become able not only to transform our institutions in response to changing situations and requirements; we must invent and develop institutions which are 'learning systems', that is to say, systems capable of bringing about their own continuing transformation.

It likely comes as no surprise that there has been a movement in the wider field of coaching to consider the systemic nature of organisations. Introduced briefly in chapter 2, 'systemic coaching' is gaining traction as a coaching approach that explores how individuals are part of an ecosystem and connected to the system in which they live and work (Hawkins and Turner, 2020; Whittington, 2020). Hannah Wilson provides a CollectivED case study on executive and systemic coaching in chapter 14. Rooted in systems thinking, Whittington describes this approach as coaching 'the individual client or team with the system in mind – exploring the part in the whole, and the whole in the part – so as to unlock the potential and performance of both' (quoted in Bayés, 2023). It is unlikely to be too long before we begin to see this new type of 'systemic coaching' brand in education. Despite our resistance to faddish coaching approaches, there is value in exploring the literature on organisational and systemic change, especially for those charged with implementing and leading coaching programmes in their schools and systems.

The study of what works and what doesn't in systemic educational change has a well-established scholarship base with its roots tracing back to the late 1960s and early 1970s (Louis, 2010). Over the past five decades, researchers have produced useful models and strategies to support schools and individuals living through (or managing) large- and small-scale change. Although these research studies vary, together they contribute to a powerful knowledge base that continues to evolve based on current areas of interest. For example, although earlier studies considered organisational and systemic change as a more technocratic and linear sequence described as research–dissemination–diffusion–utilisation (RDDU), in the 1980s and 1990s, researchers began to push back against the idea that there was a unidirectional flow from research to practice and argued for greater attention to be paid to the influence practitioners had on how an initiative was adopted into organisations, if it was adopted at all. Recent studies examine the dynamic complexity of educational change through a more critical lens with a focus on the human, organisational, political, cultural and contextual forces at play (Seashore Louis, 2010).

In the educational change discourse, four key ideas have become ingrained that have influenced our thinking and research. First, although initially referred to as innovation adoption, change is now understood as a process that takes time and its progress and outcomes are highly contingent on local context factors (Bentley, 2010). Second, the change process can be described in terms of three broad phases. Although these phases have different names, they have been referred to as the three Is or triple I model (Miles, 1987): initiation (adoption or mobilisation), implementation (initial use) and institutionalisation (incorporation, continuation or routinisation). While these phases are not static or prescribed, the implementation phase is the one that requires the most attention because it most often determines the likelihood of sustainability. In her master's research, Trista found these three phases a useful framework to explore large-scale change (see chapter 8). Third, the activities in these different phases are interactive, iterative and non-sequential in time. Finally, successful systemic change is not a process of direct replication but more a process of mutual adaptation. What this means is that changes should be in the spirit of the design and direction envisioned but must also respond to local circumstances.

Theoretical frameworks

There are several foundational theoretical frameworks that have been helpful in guiding our thinking around organisational learning, systemic change and the ways in which we can better strengthen, support and scale coaching in education. These frameworks draw on disciplines ranging from sociology, psychology, philosophy and business to curriculum and educational administration. In chapter 16, we introduced how Rachel and colleagues used cultural historical activity theory (CHAT) (Sannino and Engeström, 2018) to explore the impact of coaching and the ways in which the components of the coaching activity system influenced or mediated the alignment between the object of the coaching and its outcome. Systems theory also offers change scientists a useful framework to explore interacting processes within a system and the way they influence each other over time. In this theory, a system is conceptualised as more than the sum of its parts. Rather, it is defined by its structure, function and role, influenced by its context and expressed in its relations with other systems. Changing one component of a system may affect other components or even the whole system (Richardson, 2004). Like systems theory, complexity theory is also used in educational change because it is concerned with 'wholes, with larger systems or environments and the relationships among their constituent elements or agents' (Mason, 2008, p. 5). To better understand how systems develop and learn, researchers work 'within' the system level rather than at the individual level and examine the dynamics of connected factors. Key aspects of complexity theory include non-linearity, context, feedback, connectedness, unpredictability, chaos and order.

The diffusion of innovations (DoI) theory explores how, over time, an idea, product or technology gains momentum and spreads in a population or social system. Developed by communication theorist and sociologist Everett M. Rogers in 1962, DoI theory is used in many disciplines, such as marketing, social work, criminal justice, health sciences, business, agriculture, technology and education (Rogers and Cartano, 1962). Since individuals do not adopt innovations at the same rate, Rogers divided adopters into five categories based on the classical normal distribution curve: innovators (2.5%), early adopters (13.5%), early majority (34%), late majority (34%) and laggards (16%).

In DoI, innovators are described as those who are very willing to take risks and are often the first to develop new ideas. Early adopters are individuals who embrace change opportunities and enjoy leadership roles. They are likely to already be aware of the need to change so are more comfortable adopting new ideas. The early majority group don't necessarily lead the change but adopt new ideas before others. They like to see evidence that the innovation works before they are willing to adopt it. The late majority are sceptical of change and only adopt an innovation once it has been tried by the majority. The laggards are described as bound by tradition, conservative and the hardest group to bring on board. In DoI, there are five main factors at play that influence the adoption and, ultimately, the diffusion of an innovation. These five factors influence the five adopter categories to different extents.

1. **relative advantage**: the degree to which an innovation is seen as better than the idea, programme or product it replaces
2. **compatibility**: how consistent the innovation is with the values, experiences and needs of the potential adopters
3. **complexity**: how difficult the innovation is to understand and/or use
4. **triability**: the extent to which the innovation can be tested or experimented with before a commitment to adopt is made
5. **observability**: the extent to which the innovation provides tangible results.

Finally, in the field of educational change, there has been a move from the idea that change happens organically, one school at a time, to focusing more on large-scale systemic change that influences several schools at once (Datnow and Park, 2010). Co-construction theory is useful for exploring the dynamics involved in the implementation of large-scale educational change (Datnow et al., 2006; Datnow and Park, 2010). The co-construction perspective builds on the idea that contexts are embedded with multiple levels and the flow of influence is multidirectional and not top-down. For example, teachers can make decisions that not only affect the implementation of initiatives or policy but also may change the initiative or policy itself (Datnow and Park, 2010). So, any implementation strategy or effort to spread and scale an innovation must consider the ways in which people come to learn and adjust their own behaviour in social groups and organisations and the role of context as a dynamic shaping force (Bentley, 2010).

The 5As model: five dynamic phases of educational change

While writing this book, it became clear that we needed to consolidate what we had learned, experienced and researched on educational change into a thinking tool that would help us better understand the growth and development of individuals as coaches, coaching programmes in schools and systems, as well as other educational initiatives supported by coaching. The 5As model is the product of numerous reflective conversations and continues to be a 'work in progress'. Its usefulness as a thinking tool has been explored in several CollectivED gatherings. We are particularly grateful to colleagues Melanie Chambers, Emma Adams and Leslie Wallace from the British School of Brussels, who joined Rachel and Trista to present a symposium at the 2024 International Congress for School Effectiveness and Improvement (ICSEI). In this session the 5As model was used to think across and examine educational change at multiple levels: the individual coach, a school coaching programme, the CollectivED community and a national network. The model was also introduced in a workshop for school and district leaders in Prince Albert, Saskatchewan, which found it a valuable framework to examine large-scale system change focused on learning on the land and Indigenous ways of knowing, teaching and learning.

The 5As model shown in Figure 17.5 represents five dynamic phases of educational change. It can be used to critically reflect on coaching in education from three lenses – how we:

1. develop as coaches
2. implement coaching programmes in schools and systems and
3. create learning systems which sustain and create purposeful change in education through coaching.

As discussed earlier in this chapter, no individual responds to change in the same way and any individual change is influenced by – and can influence – their surrounding context and culture. Similarly, schools and school systems are complex entities with many interconnected parts and webs of relationships (Stoll, 2010; Wheatley, 2006). Any change – small or large – can have rippling effects on its context and culture. Concomitantly, the context can affect the impact and sustainability of any new change initiative, such as coaching. To represent this reciprocal influence, we include the term 'terroir' (see chapter 15) to represent the complete environment that surrounds the change and use the vine to show the mutually adaptive flow of influence that might occur during the change process.

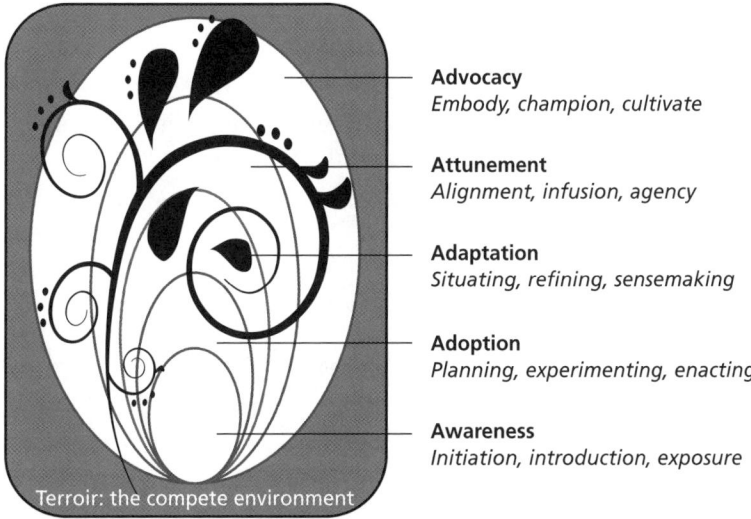

Advocacy
Embody, champion, cultivate

Attunement
Alignment, infusion, agency

Adaptation
Situating, refining, sensemaking

Adoption
Planning, experimenting, enacting

Awareness
Initiation, introduction, exposure

Terroir: the compete environment

Figure 17.5 The 5As dynamic model of educational change. © Lofthouse, Hollweck and Booton, 2025

Awareness

The first dynamic phase of the educational change process is awareness of a new idea, practice or innovation. This phase is less action-oriented and more focused on learning about the change. The three terms that describe this phase are:

- **initiation**: the action of beginning something

- **introduction**: an occasion when something is put into use for the first time
- **exposure**: a laying open or subjecting to the action or influence of something.

Adoption

Adoption describes the phase when there is a conscious decision to move from awareness to action. In this phase there is an acceptance to start something new. The three terms that describe this phase are:

- **planning**: the act of deciding how to do something
- **experimenting**: trying out new concepts or ways of doing things
- **enacting**: putting something into action.

Adaptation

This phase describes when there has been a commitment to the change and adjustments are made to improve ways of working within a context or setting. The three terms that describe this phase are:

- **situating**: fixing or building (something) in a certain place or position
- **refining**: improving an idea, method, system, etc. by making small changes
- **sensemaking**: the action or process of making sense of or giving meaning to something, especially new developments and experiences.

Attunement

In this phase the change is based on experience, on learning with and from others within and beyond the setting and on critical reflection of the innovation in relation to professional values, purpose and context. The three terms that describe this phase are:

- **alignment**: a state of agreement, cooperation or positionality based on a common cause or viewpoint
- **infusion**: the introduction of a new element or quality into something
- **agency**: the ability to take action or to choose what action to take.

Advocacy

The final phase is when the change becomes embedded as a way of being, seeing or relating. The innovation is fully integrated into the practice, context and culture and there is active support for it to grow. The three terms that describe this phase are:

- **embody**: to include or contain (something) as a constituent part
- **champion**: to support the cause of; defend
- **cultivate**: to promote the development or growth of.

Exploring educational change through the five dynamic phases of the 5As model

Although the 5As model depicts five dynamic phases of educational change, we see these phases as fluid, multidirectional and interrelated with no defined time schedule. As a sequence, we move from the bottom of the 5As model to the top, but it is possible to move forwards and backwards through the different phases. It is also not inevitable that the change process will progress through all five dynamic phases. As we've seen in the change literature and our own experiences, no matter how important and valuable the change might be, there is no guarantee that it will become embedded in an individual's practice or the larger system. The change process can stall and be abandoned at any phase without the right support, resources and attention. As we close this chapter, it is critical that we also ask ourselves some key questions around educational change, including coaching:

- How do we know if we are selecting and scaling the 'right' innovations in our classrooms, schools and school systems?
- What is our purpose for this change and what are our guiding principles?
- How do we know and measure our impact?
- Who benefits from the change?
- What challenges will we face?
- And, ultimately, is the change worth it?

Models such as the 5As model have value in part because they can create a shared language and allow for clarification. The 5As model helps us to consider change in relation to individuals, organisations and systems. The model is non-linear and, as such, describes the transgressions as much as the progressions of change. Schools and other educational settings are communities made up of people taking on diverse and often multiple roles, bringing with them varied forms of knowledge and skills, and influenced by unique personal and professional experiences. What one colleague may experience as a novel practice may be familiar and well tested by another. The fact that educational approaches can be suitably adapted to meet the challenges of a diverse curriculum, taught by a diverse workforce to meet the needs of a diverse student body, underlines the need to be cautious in response to driving forces of fidelity and uniformity. The same can be said of teacher learning and development. Change can still be supported and scaffolded, can take into account the fluidity of curriculum, community and policy and can help maintain a sense of direction towards desired purpose.

Coaching can support purposeful change, especially with consideration of the states described by the 5As. Coaching can help to support a growing *awareness* of others, their contexts, challenges and practices, and an awareness of other ways of working. Coaching can help support *adoption*, increasing access to ideas, offering guidance and being present to witness and enable trying new things out. Coaching can create conditions needed for *adaptation*, allowing the situating and refining of approaches in the specific contexts that practitioners find themselves in, and using dialogue about emerging experience and evidence to support sensemaking. Coaching can provoke greater *attunement*, encouraging ethical and conceptual alignment within and beyond the educational community, providing a safe space for challenge and consideration of dilemmas as well as opportunities. Coaching conversations themselves can enable *advocacy*, creating conversations in which values and beliefs are aired and critical thinking is rehearsed, in which credibility and expertise are honed, in which confidence is built to empower voice and collective agency through shared purpose.

Chapter 17 endnotes

Final thoughts

In this chapter we have considered educational change and introduced a new dynamic conceptualisation of educational change, made up of 5As: awareness, adoption, adaptation, attunement and advocacy. During the CollectivED focus group in which our discussion related to educational change a case was made about the value of coaching as a means of 'slowing down change'. This may seem counterintuitive in what are often highly performative cultures, with an inbuilt sense of urgency, but it was powerfully made by a very experienced coach and school leader who had worked in education across several continents. She said that:

> *Coaching slows down change in schools; that's what I notice. [...] I just see too much going through quickly in school sometimes and [...] coaching can really impact by just slowing that all down because people are thinking more about what they're going to do. [...] I noticed you can throw all the things you like at a group of people, but they're just going to stop taking it in and stop doing anything with it. So that relationship between coaching and change, it can have a very powerful effect, slowing everything down to enable people to really think about what they're doing and then making sure they're given time to think about things, and that's important as opposed to just responding, responding, responding and then at some point down the line going, 'Whoa, I just needed to step back.' So coaching and change for me within education can just mean a much more sustained impact for the better.*

In the opening quote of this chapter from a research paper by Trista and Rachel we propose that 'intelligence gathered through coaching can feed back to the wider system and vice versa'. This should not be mistaken as breaching confidentiality of coaching conversations but is an argument for the capacity that coaching has to contribute to the dynamic nature of change as proposed by the 5As.

Talking points

In a suitable discussion forum you might explore the 5As model of educational change further in your own context, either focusing on coaching itself or perhaps another desired change. Use the 5As as prompts to consider what you observe happening or what is noteworthy by its absence.

- awareness – initiation, induction, exposure
- adoption – planning, experimenting, enacting
- adaptation – situating, refining and sensemaking
- attunement – alignment, infusion, agency
- advocacy – embody, champion, cultivate.

Ideas for action

As a coach or coaching leader you may like to focus on advocacy as a key opportunity for influencing change. While advocacy is about having confidence and using voice, it is different from self-promotion or persuasion. Developing your advocacy of coaching should be for the genuine benefit of others in your education setting and beyond, rather than being a strategic move for your own benefit. It is about communicating from an informed stance allowing for criticality. It is about supporting others to gain experiences and insights that are valid to them. Being a witness to the realities of coaching in education, noticing the subtle and more significant changes that might result from coaching, celebrating small wins and being honest about tensions are all part of being an advocate. Advocacy for coaching is also part of a way of being built on forging positive relationships, finding shared purpose, being trusted, listening well, entering into thoughtful dialogue and creating learning encounters.

Chapter 18
Coaching connections: sensemaking through the CollectivED community

Dialogue involves respecting others and seeing them and their ideas as legitimate and responds to our universal, profound longing to be heard, to be validated and to feel connected to others.

Jim Knight (2016, p. 71)

Making sense of coaching in interacting contexts

Coaching is based on connections, most evidently between the coach and the coachee. The nature of these connections is defined by the purposes that coaching addresses, the relationships underpinning and forged by coaching, and the exploratory encounters and opportunities for learning and change that coaching can afford. We refer to these connections as creating the micro-context of coaching, created between the participating individuals and shaped by any coaching guidance that they are following. The characteristics and quality of this micro-context are often the focus of coaching literature, management of coaching and coaching training. However, to assume that coaching in education is simply determined by the ways that individuals work together as coach and coachee is naive.

Figure 18.1 provides a visual representation of contextual complexities related to coaching. It is resonant of Bronfenbrenner's (1979) ecological systems theory, which centres the child within nested systems influencing their development. In our conceptual framework the individual coach and coachee are centred in interacting contexts at a range of scales: the micro-context, meso-context, exo-context and macro-context, with change over time as the chrono-context. The relationship of contexts with each other is two-way, or reciprocal. For example, the micro-context of the coaching itself is influenced by the setting, professional roles and relationships that surround the coaching and over time the experiences and impacts of coaching have the potential to influence the contexts it exists in. The interrelated and interacting contexts are reminiscent of the concept of terroir (see chapter 15), which is featured in the 5As dynamic model of educational change (see chapter 17). Just as the context and culture of a school – or its terroir – influence the design, implementation and sustainability of a coaching programme, adopting a coaching approach or way of being (see chapter 4) can also influence its surrounding environment.

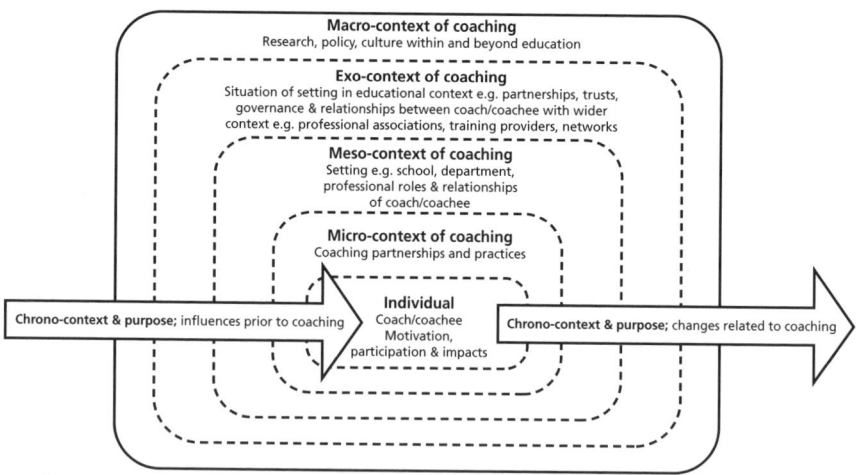

Figure 18.1 Coaching in interacting contexts. © Lofthouse, Hollweck and Booton, 2025.

The themes explored in this final chapter emerged from focus group discussions with 21 coaches, headteachers and senior leaders in primary and secondary schools, post-16 colleges and special schools in the state, independent and international school sectors who had contributed coaching case studies included in part 3 of the book. These discussions allowed a final sensemaking of coaching with purpose and its role in educational change and helped us to explore the active and significant relationships between the nested coaching contexts illustrated in Figure 18.1. The reflections were overwhelmingly positive and participants celebrated the value of coaching, acknowledged the time and energy needed to create successes and recognised the journeys that they and colleagues had been on as coaching had matured in their settings and professional roles. Key themes which emerged included the significance of leaders having confidence in authentic (rather than standardised) coaching, with a strong ethos of creating conversations which were relevant and had a sense of purpose. It was recognised that a priority for coaching is enabling individuals to be able to work together as thinking partners, where trust, openness and reflection are valued, and that the context is a significant factor in the cultures of coaching which emerge. There was also a sense that for coaching models to mature over time, thrive and build impact, advocacy, vision and a clear sense of purpose are essential.

It takes two: unique individuals and micro-contexts of coaching

It feels natural to start with the coaching partnership and ways of connecting and working that coaching participants adopt and develop. While this will inevitably be influenced by the affordances and constraints in the setting (e.g. time allocated to coaching), recognising that each coach and coachee will uniquely contribute to, and benefit from, the micro-context of coaching is essential. A primary school headteacher stated that coaching has value because 'people are more than willing to learn and grow and develop, but they're not quite sure how', and a director in a government-funded professional learning provider noted that, for both partners and course participants, coaching 'provides them with the opportunity of having a sense of agency and self-determination'.

From a leadership perspective decisions are made about who engages in coaching, in which roles and why. In the context of a MAT, a trust leader reflected on coaching induction and coaching trios provided to all staff and reported 'wellbeing benefits of coaching one another, and the connections with staff and bonds that form when you're speaking truly to other people'. A senior leader with responsibility for coaching talked about the teachers who form the instructional coaching team in her sixth form college as follows: 'The coaching team need to be authentic, they need to be enthusiastic. They need to be people who would benefit from it themselves.' She went on to say: 'It's about a process which allows people to have professional learning dialogues with a coach, it's a reciprocal process.' Also in the context of instructional coaching, but this time in an international school setting, a coaching and phase leader reinforced the significance of coaches 'turning up in a space with humility and respect and equality for people' and reflected on the shift that occurred when 'the coaching was coming to us, when we were flagged down in corridors [by colleagues asking], I just really want to have this conversation with you. Can you come in and help me with something?' She considered these interactions and the coaches responding with 'secret little happy dances' as 'something happening that was really lovely'.

When discussing coaching within a professional network, one focus group participant chose to emphasise 'the fact that coaching is all about the people and it's about the person in front of you and meeting their needs and everything else will fall in place and the impact will be evident. So we put the people first and you know, work with them.' Whatever else is shaping the micro-context, it is essential to remember that, as a former secondary headteacher and leadership consultant and coach clearly stated: 'Your purpose as a coach must be secondary to the purpose of those that are being coached.' The significance of the micro-context created within coaching partnerships was understood as part of its efficacy, as a coaching leader in a secondary school indicated. By providing multiple opportunities for colleagues to provide feedback on their experiences of coaching, he had received responses including 'My coach is so empathetic', 'It's focused on my wellbeing', 'I enjoy the freedom to focus on my own goals' and 'It's great to have someone listening to me enthusiastically, and it gives me a sense of purpose and confidence in what I do.'

There is a close relationship between the personal and professional motivations and attributes held by individuals who participate as coaches and coachees, the quality and characteristics of the micro-context of coaching that they co-create and the nature of the immediate and potential impacts that it has. This is pertinent whether coaching is a universal or reciprocal experience in a setting, whether it is resourced through the creation of a coaching team or independently engaged in beyond the employment setting by personal choice.

Flexible, situated and informed coaching

The micro-context of coaching is shaped by the approach taken, the tools used and the degree to which power or solidarity is expressed in the coaching relationship. While these characteristics may seem contained within coaching episodes, they are highly influenced by the individuals and their meso-context (itself influenced by the wider contexts), as well as being likely to evolve over time, which creates the chrono-context. A primary headteacher explained this well: 'It's iterative because we are all evolving. It's not just a one-size-fits-all and it's contextualised.'

These interacting contexts matter. A primary school co-head recognised that she needed

> to understand the landscape of the context and of the school. [...] Sitting in it, looking at it and listening to people from different points of view from different staff and families, from children, from teachers, from leadership team, from support staff. Understanding the landscape better allowed me then to get alongside individuals [...] a lot of time spent with all of the staff getting to know them. I found myself coaching, but sometimes mentoring, sometimes supervising and sort of morphing into all three depending on what the particular questions that were being asked or what my observations were, where that particular person wanted to go. It becomes a web of complexities.

As such she was immersing herself in the routines, relationships, roles, vulnerabilities and aspirations of individuals making up the meso-context of her school. As a leader adopting a coaching approach these insights shaped the micro-context of her work. For a professional network leader, understanding the challenges which are exerted by exo- and macro-contexts was seen as essential in enabling coaches working with educators of global majority backgrounds and heritages. This led to a focus on supporting coaches to understand 'narrative coaching and how that could be utilised to help [coachees] engage in a safe learning space to find ways forward'.

Coaching is thus inherently nuanced rather than formulaic. When leading coaching in a government-funded professional development provider working with partners, one focus group participant stated that she wanted 'thinking and listening coaches, rather than having coaches with an agenda' and that she had had to reassure colleagues using coaching who worried that 'I haven't got a form to fill in. I haven't got a set of questions to ask how, how do I go about this?' by 'articulating that they are thinking partners and that it is facilitative and dialogic coaching that they are using'. She indicated that she had aimed to create opportunities for 'coaching that's right for different contexts and really focuses on the principles of coaching being values-led rather than a set of steps'.

Arguing for nuance and flexibility in the micro-context of coaching does not imply that only limited coach development or training is required. A senior leader and qualified coach in an independent school reflected on this: 'I've been lucky enough to train quite a lot of teachers at the school in the basic skills of coaching […] although there's a model in the background of that, it's really about the kind of soft skills that go around that.' In the context of a large and diverse partnership of schools with embedded professional learning provision for colleagues at all career levels, a senior leader noted that 'in all of those spaces we've tried to create various models of coaching, depending on the individual context, and by that very nature by us introducing different coaching models'. In the focus groups there was much affirmation of a statement made regarding the need for leaders to have confidence in developing nuanced coaching, when a professional development sector leader stated that 'uniformity does not equal consistency'.

While the comments above reflected working with experienced professionals as coaches, another focus group participant had co-created a programme in which children in her primary school were trained as peer-coaches and she explained that 'Our school values are care, respect and empower, and we've really embraced coaching as the "empower" aspect.' In developing the coaching training for students she wanted them to see beyond a coaching formula: 'We obviously do talk about a lot of the things, trust, integrity and great questions. They are, as I said, very formulaic at the start and by the end of it the children are just doing the most amazing job, probably far better than some of our [staff] coaches.'

Developing awareness of and confidence in a coaching repertoire, of key skills and a range of approaches (see part 1), can result in the capacity to create micro-contexts of coaching which suit individuals at different life and career stages and who are necessarily being influenced by existing and changing characteristics in their settings and beyond. The meso- and exo-contexts can be positively influential in enabling positive experiences and impacts of coaching, including how it is led at school level and how the coaching draws on a breadth of knowledge and professional development opportunities. This was reinforced by a senior leader in a large secondary school setting who stated 'We've put a lot of [coaches] through the impact cycle, growth coaching or cognitive coaching. And what works is that we have good-quality coaches working with teachers. And, you know, if those coaches are coaching well, they're providing space for people to think, they make the person they're working with feel like they're the most important thing in the room. They are genuinely listened to. If you bring that way of being into your coaching, conversations like that build the culture.'

Learning through coaching: creating individual and organisational potential

Coaching is a collaborative learning practice leading to co-constructed outcomes. Coaching – as we define it in CollectivED (see part 1) – is not always well suited to meeting the challenges in some meso-contexts, for example, if staff turnover in a school is so rapid that simply ensuring basic routines and core competencies is the priority, mentoring and contextualised training are probably more appropriate in the immediate term. As a senior leader in a secondary school stated: 'Coaching is a kind of a tool. It's part of our armoury, but it's not the only tool that we use; sometimes it's not the best tool, sometimes you need to be directive.'

However, in many education settings there is the potential for a wonderful synergy between the ambitions that we have for students as learners and the need for the workforce to continually develop and learn. This was explored by a primary headteacher who stated that 'It wasn't a "done to" approach, it was "do together" and we decided on different topics, such as how can we enhance the teaching of vocabulary, metacognition, questioning, enquiry? And so on [...] I call it CPD by stealth, that they're all literally excited about what's next in the coaching session. They are training without me asking them to be trained and they're getting the answers from within and from valued members of the team.' Coaching may offer a route to enhancing professional decision-making, extending and enhancing teaching or leadership repertoires, and ensuring colleagues feel valued and able to make valid and unique contributions. A primary headteacher proposed that 'Sometimes you can't see the barriers to reaching your potential, so that's why it's so valuable having an external person or persons who are prepared to sit with you and be honest, have authentic conversations about some of the opportunities that are available and how you might access them and how you may access them in a more efficacious way than perhaps you have been.'

Coaching has the potential to generate and consolidate learning and can be transformative, for children, young people and adults alike. A coach who works with older secondary-age children helps them to capture their learning from engaging in coaching by asking them to respond to what she called a 'wonderful question' of 'I used to think that ... now I think ...', which helps them to recognise 'how they have moved on in their thinking'. A secondary school coaching leader working in the independent sector highlighted enhanced teacher agency:

> 'With regards to the staff it's the most exciting. I've been at this school for about 15 years. I think this is the most exciting period I've worked within the school because of the sense of agency that the staff here now have. And the number of things they're involved in that have stemmed from the coaching conversations that they've had with their coaches in school, that have then gone on to develop into something quite big and exciting.'

This illustrates the connections being forged through the micro-context of coaching between the individuals and their meso-contexts.

A further aspect of learning from coaching is what can be experienced and gained by the coach as they develop over time. This was exemplified by a coaching leader and experienced coach who said:

> 'When I went through coaching training, it actually changed my way of being. When I had to practise listening and coaching conversations, I became a better listener. You know, when I learn how to practise better questions, coach conversations, I actually ask better questions when I'm in social situations and with my friends and family. So I think training coaches and having coaches practise those coaching habits, some spread to their leadership qualities [...] and spread to families and friends. And I think that practising those habits changes the way people interact with each other and changes the way they communicate.'

As educators the macro-context and exo-contexts of educational policies and cultures can create overwhelmingly performative, convergent and linear thinking. In some contexts coaching has been co-opted to support the types of professional learning that might suit this context, but it can result in a distortion in the coaching micro-context away from a true coaching stance. When coaching is allowed to lead to divergent professional learning outcomes, based on supporting creative and critical thinking in a safe, enabling environment, it can be experienced as liberating, divergent and expansive.

Unseen, unbidden and unique coaching outcomes

One of the most fascinating things about coaching is the range of anticipated and sometimes unexpected changes that result for individuals and in the communities or organisations that they are part of. While coachees typically have a goal in mind (which may underpin, gain clarity during or emerge from coaching), the range of outcomes that are experienced often go beyond any specific goal. Stating that coaching outcomes can be unseen, unbidden and unique does not imply that coaching impacts should be assumed and that they do not need to be unaccounted for. A network leader whose coaching work relates to workforce representation and equality was clear that 'inclusivity and social mobility is an important part of the work that we do, so for us tracking is important'. Being aware of the unintended outcomes is also valuable. This was noted by an instructional coach leader who started to code the changes in teaching that he observed his colleagues making or sharing, in part to be able to report impact to the senior leadership team. He stated that 'I started to codify using Jim Knight's BIG 4. Has it been a change in instruction or content or community building [classroom management] or assessment? I also added leadership and wellbeing as well because I found those other two that came out quite a lot.' This acknowledgment that coaching allows for personal and professional learning and is often differentiated and divergent was also indicated by another coaching leader in a secondary school: 'What's transformative for one person is different for another, and that could be on all sorts of scales.'

Remembering that coaching can have reciprocal benefits rather than simply unidirectional ones is critical, particularly when making resource-based decisions. As an experienced coach, senior leader and teacher described: 'I feel I'm such a better teacher now because of what I know through coaching. It's improved me as a communicator and consequently as an educator, I think I'm able to get more from the kids, which is a wonderful thing and therefore we're able to learn more together and that's a wonderful thing too. I also feel as a colleague I'm able to support people better than I ever have done before.' In a similar vein an accredited coach and former special school headteacher indicated how the coaching role complemented the leadership role, for example, when she was working with parents: 'And what coaching probably did in that scenario is enable me to be a better listener and, where appropriate, ask the questions that helped, kind of like move them from a place of frustration and "I feel stuck and I can't do anything" to something else.'

When individuals in a setting have positive experiences of coaching and value the outcomes, they become more open to new coaching opportunities and thus have the potential to become more agentic. In an international school the coaching leader welcomed the fact that 'coaching began to show up in unexpected places. We did a lot of work around anti-bias, anti-racist work in early years, thinking about being with the children and how we were going to consider families and difference. And I can remember halfway through one of these conversations somebody said, oh, we could coach that, that could be a moment where we could work with other teachers and it just kind of started to take off. So coaching started to show up in more curriculum work and in different areas.'

In education we are often urged to scale up and roll out initiatives such as coaching, as if observed or measurable impacts in one context or at one scale will be replicated with mass activity. This can also create tensions when considering who makes decisions about what coaching is 'for', particularly in schools with inherent hierarchy and finite resources. A senior leader working across a MAT explained 'We've started to actively move away from this educationalist desire to measure every single thing and we have given ourselves permission as leaders of our different organisations to not obsess with the micromanagement of the coaching, and therefore the micro outcomes, which is what we perceive to be the individual one-to-one, because we do believe in the absolute integrity of confidentiality within those coaching conversations.' This is a vivid example of how macro-contexts, which normalise the emphasis on performativity, can be buffered by the exo-context of the MAT partnership of schools, allowing more authentic coaching engagement in the meso- and micro-contexts.

Changing culture to cultures of change

In education settings the details and formality of schedules and deadlines, role descriptions and deployment, targets and evaluation, budgetary constraints and line management mechanisms are functions that are thought to underpin efficiency and improvement planning. It is valuable to remember that coaching may not be best served by the same foundations. Tightly managing coaching through timetables of activity and objectives, externally defined expectations and hierarchical roles is likely to thwart its potential. True coaching goes beyond the level of surface learning and may aid the application of set routines or performance, and in education this can really impact teachers and the culture of teaching. This was reflected on by a freelance coach and teacher educator who specialises in early years and education for care-experienced children. She talked about coaching as 'learning and deepening learning and diving deep into learning [...] the coaching conversations that I have are around sharing knowledge and sharing research and sharing learning to help other teachers and educators in their deepening pedagogy because practice improves when pedagogy is deepened'. In her work – which includes using Kline's thinking environment to facilitate group coaching (see chapter 2) – 'sharing' within coaching is reciprocal and co-constructive.

Simple changes matter over time, as indicated by a primary headteacher: 'Every member of staff has a teaching and learning partner with whom they do some observations and coaching so that we can reflect, genuinely in a non-threatening, non-judgemental way, reflect on our aim and practice and how we can improve.' Another primary headteacher used the parable of the hummingbird to describe this. She said 'The hummingbird lives in a forest. The forest is on fire. All the animals are fleeing from the fire and the hummingbird goes back and forth with a droplet of water from a local lake, and the animals laugh and say, "What are you doing? That's not going to do anything to it." And the hummingbird says "I'm doing what I can" and I think we all need to be a bit more hummingbird because collectively all the small changes can create a big wave of change.'

As coaching evolves and matures, it can evoke outcomes with significant educational and organisational impacts. A senior leader with coaching responsibility described how 'the biggest change and one of the reasons I love coaching so much is just its ability to change the culture of a school. That's the way people talk to each other because [...] they listen a bit better, you know, they seek first to understand and then be understood. And these small changes in a large group of people over time really do shift the vibe of a school and an organisation.' This reinforces the importance of the micro-context creating the culture coaching through which relatedness develops.

Coaching can lead to decision-making and actions in education settings (made up of the meso- and exo-contexts) which are enhanced because they are routinely considered with caution and curiosity, underpinned by care and compassion and a shared purpose. This was well summed up by a MAT senior leader:

Coaching with purpose [...] as soon as we bring it back to the values, the work happens. We don't need to measure it on a trajectory. We've realised we felt that we did because I think there's an impetus in education to measure everything and assess everything but as we've returned on the journey for coaching, we've held that space and gained more confidence and a greater sense of authenticity and our staff have understood that it's a values-driven model and we've seen big impact, we've seen bigger involvement. [...] It's not a kind of finite journey, it's that kind of evolution and it should feel very natural and very holistic. I think that's something that we've felt very proud to have discovered ourselves almost and I know probably many people have been on that journey before. But I feel like we've done that and that's been a really important part of our journey for coaching.

Meaningfully connecting what happens in education settings to the opportunities and challenges in the wider world through coaching also helps to create cultures of change (see chapter 17). A coach, coaching supervisor and network leader expressed this in the context of climate change proposing that we 'move our attention to thinking how might a coaching approach be useful in helping to really listen to young people and also helping young people to develop a sense of agency, that there were a whole range of actions possible within that sphere'. She talked about the importance of a coaching 'way of being' with a focus on 'listening to other people' as the foundation of 'coaching as part of social movements' with the potential to connect the micro-context and purpose of coaching with the macro-context of current and potential policies and cultures with local, national and global significance.

Interestingly in a separate focus group her co-leader in the international network, who lives and works in New Zealand, highlighted the Māori concept of *mana* as 'kind of like someone's unique special value as a person. So it's like, it's like a treasure. It's like a gift. It's something that you value and so for me, that's really important in a coaching conversation to really uphold that special uniqueness about an individual'.

Cultures of change develop when individuals, groups and communities develop a sense of purpose and agency, when they feel connected, confident and valued. Coaching can be a space in which individuals are gifted the opportunity to experience optimism, support and hope. It can also be a space of resistance, where tensions and anxieties are shared for oneself and others, and where change begins to feel possible.

Finding and sustaining purpose: coaching values and goals

The values held by educators and developed in the communities that they create give shape to the sense of purpose. Finding and sustaining purpose is a driving force towards establishing optimistic and contextualised goals which orientate decisions and actions. For a former headteacher, now coach and teacher developer, this was fundamental: 'In my education journey as a teacher and advisor specialising in early years and early childhood, I think seeing the significance of children's uniqueness and very young children coming with so much and how they are so vulnerable and influenced by adults either doing right or wrong or good or bad to them is something I'm really fired up about. Having a sense of purpose about children's rights and entitlement to safety and belonging and relationships with trusted adults [...] so that their early life experience is the best it can be, because that's what they need and deserve.'

A former school leader, coach and sector professional development leader reflected on her core focus as an educator 'that was directly impacting on social communities, working with communities and through those communities impacting on children, children's potential and their ability to achieve and be successful in the world, not always through academic levels, but to go out into the world with confidence and be successful'. Coaching in education (like education itself) is inherently a future-focused endeavour, where milestones can help generate success and where the present and potential become connected. A sector professional development leader expressed this in relation to the participants on leadership programmes, stating that coaching helped to 'provide them with the opportunity of having that sense of agency and that self-determination which goes against many, many school [and sector] cultures that I've been involved in. [Coaching] helps to spark that excitement about their learning.'

Chapter 18 Coaching connections

Purpose-orientated connections between coaching and wellbeing were frequently made in the discussions. This in part is a function of the macro-context, with legitimate societal concerns about wellbeing being aired more often, and also perhaps a function of what becomes familiar in the meso-context, including the difficulty of retaining staff in some settings, leaders and teachers experiencing depression and burnout, and students presenting with higher levels of anxiety. Increasing agency among students and staff is fundamentally future-focused and the micro-context of coaching can create a dynamic potential across the boundaries between individuals and their multiple contexts. This was illustrated by a contribution focused on coaching young people within the context of climate change:

One of the other big things about coaching is it's about developing agency in the person that you're coaching, and when young people feel that they have agency, they feel they can do something. They feel they can act, and they can make a difference. It might just be in their family, it might be in this school and their community, but they feel they can do something. That gives young people a real boost to their wellbeing. So yeah, it's really quite awesome to see how that can have positive impacts on young people's mental health.

Coaching is values-based: the way coaches and coachees engage with each other in the micro-context relates to the attributes that they perceive about themselves as individuals, that they see in their coaching partner and that they recognise in the relationship, dialogue and focus of coaching. For some people this extends to what they refer to as a coaching 'way of being', in addition to any designated coaching activity. The senior leader, coach and coaching network leader quoted in the previous paragraph expressed the values that he brought to coaching both young people and professionals: 'You've got to have those values and that way of being [...] in terms of my values, a real influential concept came when I read Carl Rogers [...] about the unconditional positive regard for somebody. So holding someone in the highest regard and with the greatest respect.' Another coaching leader identified the 'moral purpose' and 'strengths-based approach' that she drew upon when coaching. Purposefully working towards environments and activities in which educators find their potential and feel good in their roles is fundamental. A coaching leader within a network emphasised 'that co-constructive relationship in [coaching] spaces and that huge element of trust really helps to enable people to find their place and to flourish and to thrive' and suggested that in coaching 'we find a space, I think, where our values align' and reminded us that 'the one thing that underpins all of it is kindness and that ability to empathise and put yourself in the shoes of others to unlock their potential.'

Working with children and young people using coaching provided a former middle leader and now specialist coach with an opportunity to work in a way that was consistent with her values: 'I'm very passionate about social justice and I feel that undiagnosed neurodivergent young people have really had a bad deal. And I want to expose that and to help [these young] people to see that they're not broken. They don't need to be fixed, but we do need to be attuned to them and to make accommodations for them. So I want them to be critical thinkers as well, and not just to take things lying down and to question it and see, you know, does this fit?' Another coach who often worked with young people, particularly around their engagement with climate change issues, stressed how coaching allowed her to maintain her 'stubborn optimism and part of what I feel I want to do for young people generally, and for my son, is to create that active hope.' On establishing peer coaching among students a senior leader reflected that 'my purpose as an educator is ownership for children and people who are being coached to understand that education is not something that is done to you. You actually own that.'

Coaching way of being: agency and transformation

Educators can bring an almost unique perspective to coaching – their core role is one with a focus on learners' growth and development, engagement with knowledge, skills and dispositions, and coaching in education is an extension of this. There are, however, some teaching and leadership habits that sometimes act against a coaching way of being. In the same way, there are some dispositions and beliefs that can become limiting factors for learners, and recognising and addressing these through coaching, both with young people or professionals, is valuable. A coach and former school headteacher expressed this as 'I think that's always been something, that's been supporting human flourishing [...] it's not just about the flourishing of the individual, but it's the flourishing of the collective' and with reference to her focus in terms of climate change she continued: 'flourishing of all of the other aspects of nature that are around us because we are part of nature'. A primary headteacher who is both a coach and coachee stated that 'I'm just committed to other people, to enabling them to transform their lives and committed to myself being coached and enabling that as well.'

In this regard creating and sustaining agency becomes a key purpose of coaching. A leader and qualified coach with expertise in special education offered her perspective: 'My purpose as an educator is about seeing people grow and being confident in themselves and believing in themselves. [...] with my coaching hat, working with many neurodivergent adults [...] often limiting beliefs are unpicked and they often relate back to experiences in school, so, I've no doubt that's influenced how I see it, because I think it's important that individual individuals, young people [...], understand themselves. They understand what makes them the best version of themself and they understand what's difficult and navigating that, just as I want that for anybody in my team. And I think the other big thing about coaching is the levelling out. So often in schools, we're all about what's on the organisational chart and [coaching] really turned that on its head a lot. [...] The agency thing has been so important and it continues to be really important because actually if you're wanting to get that common purpose, you've got to have people who are able to bring their best versions of themselves to their workplace to make that difference.' A CollectivED Award coach considered why many of the award holders had engaged in the process: 'Their purpose is to create cultural change, maybe around wellbeing, to move away from didactic ways of working, to really give teachers agency, to think about "How can we improve through our professional development?"'

For many school and sector leaders a key concern is developing organisational cultures which are values-based, and in our focus groups key themes emerged of inclusion, children's rights and the quality of relationships within school, with parents and with the wider community. One primary headteacher emphasised the importance of 'creating a context in which we can develop as good human beings doing good human doings, so the "being" isn't enough, we have to "do". And bell hooks talked about "love is an act" and that inclusion piece is really, really important to us in all of its senses.' She went on to say: 'We hold those values in a really safe way and through all of the conversations, and through all of the interactions that we have, whether that be with the children or the parents or the staff.'

In relation to connecting values with actions a senior leader in a primary school offered fundamental questions: 'Something else I've been sort of grappling with is: how can we align our common work? And to a vision? So teachers work hard in their spaces and bringing teachers together around the table is a really important honouring of time. But how can we make sure that that coaching experience for that team is aligned to the collective vision and the collective work as well?' A primary headteacher reflected on her journey: 'There was a complicated web of indicators of whether or not we were moving in the right direction. There was purpose there, there was the structure, there was a framework and over time there was definitely change.'

A leader in a secondary school stated that 'our ethos in the school is all about respect. Over time [through coaching] we've built a culture which is much more collaborative and communication overall is better and that's a wonderful thing to be able to say.' A MAT leader noted that 'our relationships are fundamental to our decision-making and our actions and they are the driving force behind the work we try to do and the things we try to achieve'. A primary headteacher reflected that 'for me, it's people's skills, making sure that everybody understands that everybody is different and to respect that and to value that […] if somebody feels a part of that team that they're valued and supported and appreciated and professionals who are given the time to think, then I think that that's just the magic that we're all looking for.'

A final quote suggests what is possible when coaching with purpose. It comes from the MAT leader quoted above: 'The reason that we're so dedicated and so intent on getting a culture of coaching right in our schools is because we believe it's one of the essential transformative competencies. We feel it is reflective of us as a humanist organisation [with a] vision around interconnectedness and the cross-pollination of ideas and co-creation of ideas. And so all of our coaching is really about how we connect with other people, how we are better in collaboration and

[...] this commitment and this dedication to working with colleagues, with students, with other people to really kind of make progress towards this vision of interconnectedness and being able to hold the individual at the forefront of everything that we do. And so that's really how it connects to our purpose, our moral purpose and our motivation as an organisation.'

Chapter 18 endnotes

Final thoughts

When we reflect on coaching, purpose and change, it is clear that coaching is not just an interactional micro-context bringing individuals together. It is also highly influenced by the meso-, macro- and exo-contexts it exists in. This influence is two-way, with coaching intentionally or by outcome enabling individuals to shape the contexts that they are part of. The chrono-context is critical here: acknowledging the difference that happens over time and therefore recognising the value in letting coaching cultures mature rather than simply be rolled out as standardised approaches. This is at the heart of the 5As model introduced in chapter 17, including the concept of coaching terroir.

Given these interrelationships, a clear case exists for coaching with purpose. Learning encounters through coaching have the power to create change. It therefore makes sense to allow coaching to be a practice which helps educators to find, reconnect with and sustain their individual and collective purposes, and through the coaching dialogue to enable them to connect their goals and their values by active reflection, enhanced decision-making and an extended and agentic professional and personal repertoire.

Talking point

The reflections and conclusions offered in this chapter originate from focus groups in which we used thinking rounds to allow each participant time to contribute without interruption. This allowed for sustained individual responses, drawing on experience, reflecting attitudes and values and recognising tensions as well as successes. The thinking rounds also encouraged attention and listening (both of which are important coaching skills). Why not try to create some small thinking round discussions with colleagues? Perhaps share a section of this chapter with them as a stimulus.

Ideas for action

You might like to use the coaching in interacting contexts model as a way to explore the ways in which aspects of your setting and its situation, relevant policies and educational influences, and individual attributes and attitudes may be impacting on coaching. Once you have started to draw some conclusions, test these out with others, to consider what assumptions you might be making and what you might have overlooked. Then don't just file it away. Take your analysis to a future planning meeting where your thinking might make a difference to decision-making.

Epilogue
A call to action and advocacy

> *Psychologists find that in cultures where people pursue happiness individually, they may actually become lonelier. But in cultures where they pursue happiness socially – through connecting, caring and contributing – people appear to be more likely to gain well-being.*
>
> Adam Grant (2021)

We draw this book to a close with consideration of the ambitions we had in authoring it, our conclusions about the current position of coaching in education and a call for action. As co-authors we believe that 'life-worthy' learning implies 'a life of learning *with* a sense of purpose' and consider coaching to be able to play a significant part. Although coaching in education is not solely related to wellbeing, and indeed that might not be its primary purpose, we are persuaded by the conclusion summarised by Grant in the opening quote. There is psychological value in connecting, caring and contributing, and coaching certainly creates opportunities for all three.

As we wrote this book four clear ambitions emerged:

1. We wanted to draw heavily on our own experiences and those of colleagues, peers and allies who have immersed themselves in coaching in education. This allowed us to reflect the realities of the work of school leaders and coaches in creating opportunities for purposeful practice and values-based change. We respect the hard work that has gone into developing coaching infrastructure, resources and capacity, and into gaining insights, qualifications and expertise over time and we wanted to acknowledge that.

2. We wanted to illustrate a breadth of coaching in education and how it is used to make a positive difference to members of school communities. In doing so we wanted to emphasise the significance of visioning and sustaining educational purpose, and how this can be supported by integrating coaching approaches into the lives of teachers, leaders and students.

3. We wanted to ensure that this book was unique and significantly research-informed. We have done this by gathering and analysing a substantial number of brand-new case studies of coaching as empirical data, by conducting research and enquiry as scholars and in line with ethical approval granted by a university ethics panel, and by maintaining an objective stance to sensemaking. We have also engaged with existing literature, including peer-reviewed research and key professional and academic texts in the field of coaching in education. This new data and revisiting of evidence have allowed unique analysis and synthesis to emerge.

4. We wanted to provide value to readers who come to this book from multiple roles in education and with varied intentions in relation to their own study and professional development and practice. We know that coaching cannot be successfully adopted through top tips and that it is not a quick fix. As such we have framed the book around encounters with coaching to provide concrete examples of sustained practice from a wide range of settings. We have added endnotes including questions for discussion and ideas for action alongside reflections. Finally we have used the emergence of key themes from the book as a way of providing new and existing conceptual sensemaking models which we anticipate readers can reflect on and refer to in the light of their own contexts.

It is our engagement from within the CollectivED community that has enabled us to meet these ambitions.

There are lots of good news accounts in this book which support our view of 'purposeful' coaching conversations as 'energising' and 'valuable' discussion. At the present time we see coaching as a way of working in support of educators and education which is still in its infancy. Despite the significant commercial interests in the field and the additional resource that is being allocated to it in some settings, there are areas of resistance and concern in how coaching is designed, being deployed and scaled up. Coaching risks becoming another cog in the machine that keeps professionals busy and is used to reproduce systems, and to recycle ideas rather than challenge and support educators to imagine and create educational futures they might truly aspire to and be party to the creation of. Just as coaching ought to spotlight and support the potential of those who engage in it, our book has deliberately shone a light on support coaching as a fertile, contextual and dynamic practice which still has so much untapped potential to make a positive difference.

We continue to advocate for coaching in education because we know that at its best it can:

- create supportive relationships between colleagues
- provide educators with opportunities and space to be valued, seen and heard
- personalise professional learning and development
- become a vehicle through which educators can explore research and make connections with practice
- scaffold reflection and enquiry
- enable experimentation and evaluation
- support professionals to make autonomous, situated decisions
- ensure educators find their niche and utilise their talents
- foster a sense of agency by enabling voice, choice and ownership
- support educators to accompany one another through individual and systemic change
- enhance wellbeing and feelings of hopefulness in education communities.

Our research and sensemaking have allowed us to develop our thinking about coaching in new ways. We fundamentally believe that coaching can take a number of forms and fulfil a number of functions and that this requires it to be malleable and adaptive as a practice. We make a clear distinction between coaching and training, acknowledging the value of each in professional contexts, but emphasising coaching as a way that individuals within a community can learn with and from each other and engage critically and reflectively with ideas and influences that emerge or are introduced to the setting.

We recognise coaching as a co-constructive and considerate space, usually undertaken as a one-to-one activity in which the participants should always be assured of care and confidentiality as essential qualities. In this respect we would propose coaching as a form of 'connective labour' (Pugh, 2024), being relational at heart, with coaches relying on emotional understanding and having the capacity to create a sense of belonging and social intimacy. Such qualities have the potential to address many of the concerns faced in contemporary education systems across both their workforces and student bodies.

We recommend that professional development for coaches is prioritised, opportunities for working in networks are ongoing, that consideration is given to ensuring informed consent and contracting (agreeing terms) for participants and that the value of supervision for coaches is appreciated. We encourage education leaders to ensure that coaching is not undertaken or perceived as remedial action, but that it is developed as a nuanced, sophisticated and optimistic form of professional and personal learning.

Coaching can be celebrated as a means to create conditions worthy of our purpose as educators. It offers hope for supportive change and growth for individuals. Individuals shape coaching and coaching can shape individuals. More than that though, coaching can become a way of being together and of wayfinding, and thus it can shape our education communities. Coaching can be an integral element in fostering positive and productive change in schools and organisations, but context – or the coaching terroir – must always be considered and integrated in any coaching initiative.

We hope that this book forms part of a call for action. There is more that can be researched to ensure that coaching in education fulfils its potential as an integrated, sustained and sustainable practice. There are more approaches to developing coaching further than any individual or organisation can promote. There are many ways to begin, to develop and to strengthen expertise in coaching, and those who are fortunate enough to experience them form an invaluable part of the education workforce.

We know we have been fortunate to be part of the CollectivED community and we hope that all readers of this book have opportunities to find a sense of shared purpose and a network in which they can grow and contribute. We close this book with a few quotes from participants in our community, about what their engagement has meant to them.

Learning and growth comes from:

the uniqueness of talent, knowledge and skill that each person brings [...] under the shared values and beliefs that allow each person's strengths to have purpose and impact within the group.

It has been essential to:

continue to challenge our thinking and develop our practice beyond the influence of our own communities. We need to look beyond the horizon and, as such, new ideas are formed and developed.

This is possible because:

loose connections are made, sometimes the tiny flicker of connection, then somehow you find yourself working more closely with that person, contributing to their project, getting that vital piece of guidance, sharing an energy.

Engagement creates opportunities for change:

Being part of this network has given me huge confidence. And that confidence has enabled me to initiate research into the puzzles that presented to me whilst I was working.

We value human connection, empowerment and growth:

And maybe that's just a human thing – that we want to actually contribute, something that is useful along the line [...] it is about improvement or creating positive change.

This book has only been possible because of the advocates for coaching who have contributed to it directly and who have informed our thinking and our work over decades. We hope that this book helps a new generation of advocates for coaching with, and for, purpose in education.

References

Abbott, G. (2010) 'Cross-cultural coaching: A paradoxical perspective', in Cox, E., Bachkirova, T. and Clutterbuck, D. (eds.) *The Complete Handbook of Coaching*. SAGE Publications Ltd, pp. 324–340.

Abrams, J. (2009) *Having Hard Conversations*. Corwin Press.

Adams, M. (2016) *Coaching Psychology in Schools: Enhancing Performance, Development and Wellbeing*. Routledge.

Aguilar, E. (2013) *The Art of Coaching: Effective Strategies for School Transformation*. John Wiley & Sons.

Aguilar, E. (2020) *Coaching for Equity: Conversations that Change Practice*. John Wiley & Sons.

Aguilar, E. (2024) *Arise: The Art of Transformational Coaching*. Jossey-Bass.

Allen, K. E. (2019) *Leading from the Roots: Nature-Inspired Leadership Lessons for Today's World*. Morgan James.

Anderson, S. E. (2009) 'Moving change: Evolutionary perspectives on educational change', in Hargreaves, A., Lieberman, A., Fullan, M. and Hopkins, D. (eds.) *Second International Handbook of Educational Change*. Springer, pp. 65–84.

Arshad, R. (2021) 'Decolonising the curriculum – how do I get started?', *The Times Higher Education*, 14 September 2021. Available at: www.timeshighereducation.com/campus/decolonising-curriculum-how-do-i-get-started (Accessed: 1 September 2024).

Ashley, K. and North Star TSA (2018) 'Working together: Coaching as the compass in the journey of implementation', *CollectivED Working Papers*, 5, pp. 12–16. Available at: www.leedsbeckett.ac.uk/-/media/files/research/collectived/collectived-sept-2018-issue-5-final.pdf (Accessed: 25 July 2024).

Ayliffe, P. (2019) '"Lesson Chats" @ Mayfield', *CollectivED Working Papers*, 8, pp. 86–89. Available at: www.leedsbeckett.ac.uk/-/media/files/research/collectived/collectived-issue-8-may-2019-final2.pdf (Accessed: 25 July 2024).

Bambrick-Santoyo, P. (2016) *Get Better Faster: A 90-day Plan for Coaching New Teachers*. John Wiley & Sons.

Bandura, A. (1977) 'Self-efficacy: Toward a unifying theory of behavioral change', *Psychological Review*, 84(2), pp. 191–215.

Bar-On, R. (2010) 'Emotional intelligence: an integral part of positive psychology', *South African Journal of Psychology*, 40(1), pp. 54–62.

Baumfield, V., Hall, E., Higgins, S. and Wall, K. (2009) 'Catalytic tools: understanding the interaction of enquiry and feedback in teachers' learning', *European Journal of Teacher Education*, 32(4), pp. 423–435.

Bayés, M. (2023) 'Systemic coaching: Attending to whole, part, and greater whole', *Human Systems Dynamics Institute*. Available at: www.hsdinstitute.org/resources/systemic-coaching.html#:~:text=Systemic%20coaching%20extends%20this%20framework,the%20entire%20system%20in%20mind (Accessed: 9 September 2024).

Beaton, M. C., Thomson, S., Cornelius, S., Lofthouse, R., Kools, Q. and Huber, S. (2021) 'Conceptualising teacher education for inclusion: Lessons for the professional learning of educators from transnational and cross-sector perspectives', *Sustainability 2021*, 13, pp. 21–67.

Beere, J. and Broughton, T. (2013) *The Perfect Teacher Coach*. Independent Thinking Press.

Beijaard, D. (2019) 'Teacher learning as identity learning: models, practices and topics', *Teachers and Teaching,* 25(1), pp. 1–6.

Bentley, T. (2009) 'Innovation and diffusion as a theory of change', in Hargreaves, A., Lieberman, A., Fullan, M. and Hopkins, D. (eds.) *Second International Handbook of Educational Change.* Springer, pp. 29–46.

Biesta, P. G. (2020) *Educational Research: An Unorthodox Introduction.* Bloomsbury.

Boniwell, I., Kauffman, C. and Silberman, J. (2010) 'The Positive Psychology Approach to Coaching', in Cox, E., Birakova, T. and Clutterbuck, D. (eds.) *The Complete Handbook of Coaching.* SAGE Publications, pp. 157–169.

Booton, J., Hollweck, T. and Munro, C. (2023) 'Mentors Who Coach – Coaches Who Mentor: Accompaniment and Stance as Unifying and Liberating Concepts', *CollectivED Working Papers,* 17, pp. 5–14. Available at: www.leedsbeckett.ac.uk/-/media/files/research/collectived/collectived-issue-17-gci-conference-2023.pdf (Accessed: 25 July 2024).

Boyatzis, R. (2002) 'Unleashing the power of self-directed learning', in Sims, R. (ed.) *Changing the Way We Manage Change.* Quorum Books.

Boyatzis, R., Smith, M. and Van Oosten, E. (2019) *Helping People Change: Coaching with Compassion for Lifelong Learning and Growth.* Harvard Business Review Press.

Boyes-Watson, C. (2008) *Peacemaking Circles and Urban Youth: Bringing Justice Home.* Living Justice Press.

Briggs, A. R. J. (2007) 'The use of modelling for theory building in qualitative analysis', *British Educational Research Journal,* 33(4), pp. 589–603.

Broadwell, M. M. (1969) 'Teaching for learning (XVI)', *The Gospel Guardian,* 20(41), pp. 1–3.

Brock, V. (2014) *Sourcebook of Coaching History.* Library of Congress.

Bronfenbrenner, U. (1979) *The Ecology of Human Development: Experiments by Nature and Design*. Harvard University Press.

Brown, B. (2021) *Atlas of the Heart: Mapping Meaningful Connection and the Language of Human Experience*. Random House.

Brown, D. (2017) 'Researching our practice using The Discipline of Noticing', *CollectivED Working Papers*, 1, pp. 12–15. Available at: www.leedsbeckett.ac.uk/-/media/files/research/collectived/collectived-dec-2017-issue.pdf (Accessed: 25 July 2024).

Brown, P. and Brown, V. (2012) *Neuropsychology For Coaches: Understanding The Basics*. Open University Press.

Browne, L., Luckham, E., Prebble, G. and Zacharia, C. (2012) 'Coaching students in a secondary school: a case study', in van Nieuwerburgh, C. (ed.) *Coaching in Education. Getting Better Results for Students, Educators and Parents*. Karnac, pp. 191–198.

Buck, A. (2020) *The BASIC Coaching Method Workbook*. Cadogan Press.

Buckingham, M. and Coffman, C. (2005) *First, Break All the Rules: What the World's Greatest Managers Do Differently*. Pocket Books.

Buckingham, M. and Goodall, A. (2019) *The Feedback Fallacy*. Harvard Business Review. Available at: www.physicianleaders.org/articles/the-feedback-fallacy (Accessed: 29 July 2024).

Bullough, M., Crawford, L. and Hughan, C. (2019) 'Three questions for school leaders' *CollectivED Working Papers*, 7, pp. 91–93. Available at: www.leedsbeckett.ac.uk/-/media/files/research/collectived/collectived-issue-7-mar-2019.pdf (Accessed: 25 July 2024).

Bungay Stanier, M. (2016) *The Coaching Habit: Say Less, Ask More and Change the Way You Lead Forever*. Box of Crayons Press.

Bungay Stanier, M. (2020) *The Advice Trap: Be Humble, Stay Curious & Change the Way You Lead Forever*. Page Two.

Bungay Stanier, M. (2022) *How to Begin*. Page Two.

Campbell, C. (2016a) 'Collaborative professionalism: of, by and for Catholic school leaders', *Principal Connections*, 20(1), pp. 6–7.

Campbell, J. (2016b) 'Framework for Practitioners 2: The GROWTH model', in van Nieuwerburgh, C. (ed.) *Coaching in Professional Contexts*. SAGE Publishing, pp. 235–240.

Campbell, J. and van Nieuwerburgh, C. (2018) *The Leader's Guide to Coaching in Schools: Creating Conditions for Effective Learning*. Corwin Press.

Campbell, P., Hollweck, T. and Netolicky, D. M. (2023) 'Grappling with pracademia in education: Forms, functions, and futures' in Dickinson, J. and Griffiths, T. L. (eds.) *Professional Development for Practitioners in Academia: Pracademia*. Springer International Publishing, pp. 65–83.

Campbell, S. (2018) 'Being mentored through CTeach', *CollectivED Working Papers*, 4, pp. 44–46. Available at: www.leedsbeckett.ac.uk/-/media/files/research/collectived/collectived-june-2018-issue-4.pdf (Accessed: 25 July 2024).

Chestnutt, H., Hollweck, T., Baradaran, N. and Jiménez, M. (2024) 'Mapping distributed leadership using social network analysis: accompaniment in Québec', *School Leadership & Management*, 44(1), pp. 8–29.

Children's Commissioner (2021) *'The big ask, the big answer'*. Available at: www.childrenscommissioner.gov.uk/the-big-answer/ (Accessed: 27 July 2024).

Chiu, L. (2022) 'Conceptualising allyship for coaching to promote social change', *International Journal of Evidence Based Coaching and Mentoring*, (S16), pp. 40–54.

CollectivED, 2024 *AACT guide*. Available at: www.leedsbeckett.ac.uk/research/collectived/guide-to-coaching/ (Accessed: 29 November 2024).

CollectivED and Leeds Learning Alliance, *2024 DBC guide*. Available at: www.leedsbeckett.ac.uk/research/collectived/guide-to-coaching/ (Accessed: 29 November 2024).

Cooperrider, D. L. and Whitney, D. (2005) *Appreciative Inquiry: A Positive Revolution in Change*. Berrett-Koehler Publishers.

Cormier, D. (2008) 'Rhizomatic education: Community as curriculum', *Dave's Educational Blog*, 30 June 2008. Available at: https://davecormier.com/edblog/2008/06/ (Accessed: 30 July 2024).

Costa, A. L. and Garmston, R. J. (1994) *Cognitive Coaching: A Foundation for Renaissance Schools*. Christopher Gordon Publishers.

Costa, A. L. and Garmston, R. J. (2016) *Cognitive Coaching: Developing Self-Directed Leaders and Learners*. 3rd edn. Rowman & Littlefield.

Cox, E., Bachkirova, T. and Clutterbuck, D. (2010) *The Complete Handbook of Coaching*. 2nd edn. SAGE Publishing.

CUREE (2005) 'National Framework for Mentoring and Coaching'. Available at: www.curee.co.uk/resources/publications/national-framework-mentoring-and-coaching (Accessed: 24 July 2024).

Damon, W. (2008) *The Path to Purpose: How Young People Find Their Calling in Life*. Free Press.

Datnow, A., Lasky, S., Stringfield, S. and Teddlie, C. (2006) *Integrating Educational Systems for Successful Reform in Diverse Contexts*. Cambridge University Press.

Datnow, A. and Park, V. (2009) 'Large-scale reform in the era of accountability: The system role in supporting data-driven decision making', in Hargreaves, A., Lieberman, A., Fullan, M. and Hopkins, D. (eds.) *Second International Handbook of Educational Change*. Springer, pp. 209–220.

De Haan, E. (2008) *Relational Coaching: Journeys Towards Mastering One-to-One Learning*. John Wiley & Sons.

Department for Education (2019) 'ITT Core Content Framework'. Available at: www.gov.uk/government/publications/initial-teacher-training-itt-core-content-framework (Accessed: 27 July 2024).

Department for Education (2021) *National Professional Qualifications Frameworks*. Available at: www.gov.uk/government/publications/national-professional-qualifications-frameworks-from-september-2021 (Accessed: 27 July 2024).

De Shazer, S., Dolan, Y., Korman, H., Trepper, T., McCollum, E. and Berg, I. K. (2021) *More than Miracles: The State of the Art of Solution-Focused Brief Therapy*. Routledge.

DiClemente, C. C. and Prochaska, J. O. (1998) 'Toward a comprehensive, transtheoretical model of change: Stages of change and addictive behaviors', in Miller, W. R. and Heather, N. (eds.) *Treating Addictive Behaviors*. 2nd edn. Plenum Press, pp. 3–24.

Donohoo, J. (2017) *Collective Efficacy: How Educators' Beliefs Impact Student Learning*. Corwin Press.

Donohoo, J. (2018) 'Collective teacher efficacy research: Productive patterns of behavior and other positive consequences', *Journal of Educational Change*, 19(3), pp. 323–345.

Dowley, M. and Lovell, O. (2024) *Classroom Management Handbook: A Practical Blueprint for Engagement and Behaviour in Your Classroom and Beyond*. John Catt.

Downey, M. (2003) *Effective coaching: Lessons from the Coach's Coach*. Texere.

Drago-Severson, E. (2004) *Helping Teachers Learn: Principal Leadership for Adult Growth and Development*. Corwin Press.

Drago-Severson, E. and Blum-DeStefano, J. (2016) *Tell Me So I Can Hear You: A Developmental Approach to Feedback for Educators*. Harvard Education Press.

Dreyfus, S. (2004) 'The five-stage model of adult skill acquisition', *Bulletin of Science Technology and Society*, 24(3), pp. 177–181.

Dweck, C. S. (2006) *Mindset: The New Psychology of Success*. Random House.

Einzig, H. (2017) *The Future of Coaching: Vision, Leadership and Responsibility in a Transforming World*. Taylor & Francis.

Elek, C., Page, J. and Eadie, P. (2024) 'Identifying the theoretical foundations of coaching as a form of ongoing professional development in early childhood education: a meta-narrative review', *Professional Development in Education*, pp. 1–21.

Elliott, K., Hollingsworth, H., Thornton, A., Gillies, L. and Henderson, K. (2022) 'School leadership that cultivates collective efficacy: Emerging insights 2022', *Australian Council for Educational Research*. Available at: https://research.acer.edu.au/educational_leadership/10/ (Accessed: 16 September 2024).

Ellis, C. (2012) *Quilt Love: Simple Quilts to Stitch and Treasure*. Taunton Press.

Engeström, Y. (1987) *Learning by Expanding: An Activity-Theoretical Approach to Developmental Research*. Orienta-Konsultit.

Engeström, Y. (2007) 'Putting activity theory to work: the change laboratory as an application of double stimulation', in Daniels, B., Cole, M. and Wertsch, J. V. (eds.) *The Cambridge Companion to Vygotsky*. Cambridge University Press. pp. 363–382.

Eraut, M. (2007) 'Learning from other people in the workplace', *Oxford Review of Education*, 33(4), pp. 403–422.

Evans, K. and Vaandering, D. (2016) *The Little Book of Restorative Justice in Education: Fostering Responsibility, Healing and Hope in Schools*. Good Books.

Evered, R. D. and Selman, J. C. (1989) 'Coaching and the art of management', *Organizational Dynamics*, 18(2), pp. 16–32.

Fa'avae, D. (2021) 'Critical autoethnographic encounters in the moana: Wayfinding the intersections of to'utangata Tonga and indigenous masculinities', in Iosefo, F., Holman Jones, S. and Harris, A. (eds) *Wayfinding and Critical Autoethnography*. 1st edn. Routledge, pp. 69–79.

Farmer, P. (2011) 'Accompaniment as policy', *Science of Implementation Initiative*, 25 May 2011. Available at: https://siidata.org/paul-farmer-accompaniment-as-policy/ (Accessed: 2 September 2024).

Farrelly, T. and Nabobo-Baba, U. (2014) 'Talanoa as empathic research', *Asia Pacific Viewpoint*, 55(3), pp. 319–330.

Frankl, V. E. (2006) *Man's Search for Meaning*. Beacon Press.

Fullan, M. (2015) *The New Meaning of Educational Change*. Teachers College Press.

Fuller, F. (1969) 'Concerns of teachers: A developmental conceptualization', *American Educational Research Journal*, 6(2), pp. 207–226.

Gallacher, G. (2022) *Coaching Women: Changing the System Not the Person*. Open University Press.

Gallucci, C., Van Lare, M. D., Yoon, I. H. and Boatright, B. (2010) 'Instructional coaching: Building theory about the role and organizational support for professional learning', *American Educational Research Journal*, 47(4), pp. 919–963.

Gallwey, W. T. (2024) *The Inner Game of Tennis: The Classic Guide to Peak Performance*. Random House.

Gilbert, A. and Whittleworth, K. (2009) *The OSCAR Coaching Model*. Worth Publishing.

Gilchrist, G. (2017) 'Developing a learning culture in schools', *CollectivED Working Papers*, 1, pp. 33–37. Available at: www.leedsbeckett.ac.uk/-/

media/files/research/collectived/collectived-dec-2017-issue.pdf (Accessed: 25 July 2024).

Goleman, D. (1998) *Working with Emotional Intelligence*. Bantam Books.

Goodman, F. R., Disabato, D. J., Kashdan, T. B. and Kauffman, S. B. (2018) 'Measuring well-being: a comparison of subjective well-being and PERMA', *The Journal of Positive Psychology*, 13(4), pp. 321–332.

Goodrich, J. (2024) *Responsive Coaching: Evidence-informed instructional coaching that works for every teacher in your school*. John Catt.

Gorrell, P. and Hoover, J. (2009) *The Coaching Connection: A Manager's Guide to Developing Individual Potential in the Context of the Organization*. American Management Association.

Grant, A. (2021) 'There's a Specific Kind of Joy We've Been Missing', *The New York Times*. Available at: https://www.nytimes.com/2021/07/10/opinion/sunday/covid-group-emotions-happiness.html (Accessed: 1 September 2024).

Grant, A. M. (2006) 'An integrative goal-focused approach to executive coaching', in Stober, D. and Grant, A. M. (eds.) *Evidence Based Coaching Handbook*. Wiley, pp. 153–192.

Grant, A. M. (2013) 'The efficacy of coaching', in Passmore, J., Peterson, D. B. and Friere, T. (eds.) *The Wiley-Blackwell Handbook of the Psychology of Coaching and Mentoring*. Wiley-Blackwell, pp. 15–39.

Grant, A. M. (2014) 'Foreword', in *Sourcebook of Coaching History*. 2nd edn. Library of Congress.

Grant, A. M. and Cavanagh, M. J. (2004) 'Toward a profession of coaching: Sixty-five years of progress and challenges for the future', *International Journal of Evidence Based Coaching and Mentoring*. 2(1), pp. 1–16.

Grant, A. M. and O'Connor, S. (2019) 'A brief primer for those new to coaching research and evidence-based practice', *The Coaching Psychologist*, 15(1), pp. 3–10.

Gruenert, S. and Whitaker, T. (2015) *School Culture Rewired: How to Define, Assess, and Transform It*. ASCD.

Gunning, C. and Lofthouse, R. (2022) 'A Manifesto for attuned teaching', in McGovern, W., Gillespie, A. and Woodhouse, H. (eds.) *Understanding Safeguarding for Children and their Educational Experiences: A Guide for Students, ECTs and School Support Staff*. Emerald Publishing.

Haines, K. J. (2018) 'Professional development for new classroom spaces: Extending the Concerns-based adoption model', *Journal of Perspectives in Applied Academic Practice*, 6(2), pp. 58–66.

Hall, G. E. (1974) *The Concerns-Based Adoption Model: A Developmental Conceptualization of the Adoption Process Within Educational Institutions*. University of Texas.

Hall, G. E. and Hord, S. M. (2020) *Implementing Change: Patterns, Principles, and Potholes*. 5th edn. Pearson.

Halvorson, H. G. (2012) *9 Things Successful People Do Differently*. Harvard Business Review Press.

Hammond, S. A. (2013) *The Thin Book of Appreciative Inquiry*. Thin Book Publishing Co.

Hargreaves, A., Lieberman, A., Fullan, M. and Hopkins, D. W. (eds.) (2014) *International Handbook of Educational Change: Part Two*, Volume 5. Springer.

Hargreaves, A. and O'Connor, M. (2018) *Collaborative Professionalism: When Teaching Together Means Learning For All*. Corwin Press.

Harris, A. and Holman Jones, S. (2019) 'Activist affect', *Qualitative Inquiry*, 25(6), pp. 563–565.

Hattie, J. A. C and Fierier, K. (2018) *Ten Mindframes for Visible Learning: Teaching for Success*. Routledge.

Hawkins, P. and Turner, E. (2020) *Systemic Coaching: Delivering Value Beyond the Individual*. 1st edn. Routledge.

Hickman, C., Marks, E., Pihkala, P., Clayton, S., Lewandowski, R. E., Mayall, E. E., Wray, B., Mellor, C. and van Susteren, L. (2021) 'Climate anxiety in children and young people and their beliefs about government responses to climate change: a global survey', *The Lancet Planetary Health*, 5(12), pp. 863–873.

Hoath, L. and Dave, H. (2022) 'Climate Change Education: Creating the Foundations for Effective Implementation'. Available at: www.capealliance.org.uk/reports-articles (Accessed: 26 July 2024).

Hobson, A. J. and Malderez, A. (2013) 'Judgementoring and other threats to realizing the potential of school-based mentoring in teacher education', *International Journal of Mentoring and Coaching in Education*, 2(2), pp. 89–108.

Hollingshead, B. (2009) 'The concerns-based adoption model: A framework for examining implementation of a character education program', *NASSP Bulletin*, 93(3), pp. 166–183.

Hollweck, T. (2017) 'Threading the needle: Examining the teacher induction program (TIP) in the Western Québec School Board', in Kutsyuruba, B. and Walker, K. (eds.) *The Bliss and Blisters of Early Career Teaching: A Pan-Canadian Perspective*. Word and Deed Publishing Inc., pp. 205–226.

Hollweck, T. (2019a) *A Patchwork Quilt: A Qualitative Case Study Examining Mentoring, Coaching, and Teacher Induction in the Western Québec School Board* [Doctoral dissertation], Université d'Ottawa/University of Ottawa. Available at https://ruor.uottawa.ca/items/049a00a1-26c6-4a70-828c-8355a9b71944 (Accessed: 9 September 2024).

Hollweck, T. (2019b) '"I love this stuff!": a Canadian case study of mentor–coach well-being', *International Journal of Mentoring and Coaching in Education*, 8(4), pp. 325–344.

Hollweck, T. (2020) 'Growing the top: Examining a mentor–coach professional learning network', in Schnellert, L. (ed.) *Professional Learning Networks: Facilitating Transformation in Diverse Contexts with Equity-Seeking Communities*. Emerald Publishing Limited, pp. 141–170.

Hollweck, T. and Baradaran, N. (2022) 'Accompaniment project overview', a report prepared for the *Leadership Committee for English Education in Québec* (LCEEQ). Available at: https://lceeq-files.s3-ca-central-1.amazonaws.com/documents/accompaniment/Phase_I_Needs_Assessment_Final_Report_and_LCEEQ_Accompaniment_Overview_2021%E2%80%932022.pdf (Accessed: 1 September 2024).

Hollweck, T. and Lofthouse, R. M. (2021) 'Contextual coaching: Levering and leading school improvement through collaborative professionalism', *International Journal of Mentoring and Coaching in Education*, pp. 399–417.

Hollweck, T., Netolicky, D. M. and Campbell, P. (2021) 'Defining and exploring pracademia: Identity, community, and engagement', *Journal of Professional Capital and Community*, 7(1), pp. 6–25.

Hollweck, T., Netolicky, D. M. and Campbell, P. (2022) 'Pracademia: exploring the possibilities, power and politics of boundary-spanners straddling the worlds of practice and scholarship', *Journal of Professional Capital and Community*, 7(1), pp. 1–5.

Hollweck, T., Reimer, K. and Bouchard, K. (2019) 'A missing piece: Embedding restorative justice and relational pedagogy into the teacher education classroom', *The New Educator*, 15(3), pp. 246–267.

Hook, P., McPhail, I. and Vass, A. (2006) *Coaching and Reflecting Pocketbook*. Teachers' Pocketbooks.

hooks, b. (1994) *Teaching to Transgress: Education as the Practice of Freedom*. Routledge.

International Coaching Federation (ICF) (website). Available at: https://coachingfederation.org/about (Accessed: 9 September 2024).

Jackson, P. and McKergow, M. (2007) *The Solutions Focus: Making Coaching and Change SIMPLE*. 2nd edn. Nicholas Brealey International.

Jackson, R. (2017) 'Breathing Space; enabling professional learning through alternative staff meetings', *CollectivED Working Papers*, 1, pp. 22–25. Available at: www.leedsbeckett.ac.uk/-/media/files/research/collectived/collectived-dec-2017-issue.pdf (Accessed: 25 July 2024).

Jackson, D. and Lombard, P. (1993) 'Environmental and management practices affecting grape composition and wine quality – A review', *American Journal of Enology and Viticulture*, 44, pp. 409–430.

James, C. (2009) 'The psychodynamics of educational change', in Hargreaves, A., Lieberman, A., Fullan, M. and Hopkins, D. (eds.) *Second International Handbook of Educational Change*. Springer, pp. 47–64.

Ka'ili, T. O. (2005) 'Tauhi vā: Nurturing Tongan sociospatial ties in Maui and beyond', *The Contemporary Pacific*, 17(1), pp. 83–114.

Kemmis, S., Wilkinson, J., Edwards-Groves, C., Hardy, I., Grootenboer, P. and Bristol, L. (2014) *Living Well Now and in the Future: Why Sustainability Matters*. Sense Publishers.

Kennedy, H., Landor, M. and Todd, L. (eds.) (2015) *Video Enhanced Reflective Practice: Professional Development through Attuned Interactions*. Jessica Kingsley.

Kline, N. (1999) *Time to Think: Listening to Ignite the Human Mind*. Hachette UK.

Kline, N. (2009) *More Time to Think*. Fisher King.

Kline, N. (2020) *The Promise that Changes Everything: I Won't Interrupt You*. Penguin Life.

Knight, J. (2007) *Instructional Coaching: A Partnership Approach to Improving Instruction*. Corwin.

Knight, J. (2016) *Better Conversations: Coaching Ourselves and Each Other to Be More Credible, Caring and Connected*. Corwin.

Knight, J. (2018) *The Impact Cycle*. Corwin.

Knight, J. (2021) 'Moving from talk to action in professional learning', *Educational Leadership*, 78(5), pp. 16–21.

Knight, J. (2022) *The Definitive Guide to Instructional Coaching: Seven Factors for Success*. ASCD.

Knight, J., Hoffman, A., Harris, M. and Thomas, S. (2020) *The Instructional Coaching Playbook*. One Fine Bird Press.

Knight, S. (2009) *NLP at Work (Neuro Linguistic Programming): The Essence of Excellence*. 3rd edn. Nicholas Brealey Publishing.

Knowles, M. S. (1984) 'Introduction: The Art and Science of Helping Adults Learn', in Knowles, M. S. (ed.) *Andragogy in Action: Applying Modern Principles of Adult Learning*. Jossey-Bass, pp. 1–21.

Kosiorek, C. and Thompson, J. (2017) *A Quick Guide to Video Coaching: The Best Practice to Improve the Art and Craft of Teaching Through Guided Reflection* (self-published, Amazon).

Kraft, M. A. and Blazar, D. (2018) 'Taking Teacher Coaching to Scale: Can personalized training become standard practice?', *Education Next*, 18(4), pp. 68–74.

Kraft, M. A., Blazar, D. and Hogan, D. (2018) 'The effect of teacher coaching on instruction and achievement: A meta-analysis of the causal evidence', *Review of Educational Research*, 88(4), pp. 547–588.

Kuusisaari, H. (2013) 'Teachers' collaborative learning – development of teaching in group discussions', *Teachers and Teaching: Theory and Practice*, 19(1), pp. 50–62.

Lafortune, L. and Deaudelin, C. (2001) *Accompagnement socioconstructiviste: Pour s'approprier une réforme en éducation*. Presses de l'Université du Québec.

Lafortune, L., Lepage, C., Persechino, F., Bélanger, K. and Aitken, A. (2009) *Professional Accompaniment Model for Change*. Presses de l'Université du Québec.

Laing, K. and Todd, L. (eds.) (2015) 'Theory-based methodology: Using theories of change in educational development, research and evaluation', Research Centre for Learning and Teaching, Newcastle University. Available at: https://www.ncl.ac.uk/mediav8/centre-for-learning-and-teaching/files/theory-based-methodology.pdf (Accessed: 25 July 2024).

Learning Forward (2022) *Standards for Professional Learning*. Learning Forward.

Leat, D., Lofthouse, R. and Taverner, S. (2006) 'The road taken: professional pathways in innovative curriculum development', *Teachers and Teaching*, 12(6), pp. 657–674.

Lee, R. (2013) 'The role of contracting in coaching: balancing individual client and organizational issues', in Passmore, J., Peterson, D. B. and Friere, T. (eds.) *The Wiley-Blackwell Handbook of The Psychology of Coaching and Mentoring*. Wiley-Blackwell, pp. 40–57.

Léger-Goodes, T., Malboeuf-Hurtubise, C., Mastine, T., Généreux, M., Paradis, P.-O. and Camden, C. (2022) 'Eco-anxiety in children: a scoping review of the mental health impacts of the awareness of climate change', *Frontiers in Psychology*, 13, pp. 1–21.

Leider, R. J. (2015) *The Power of Purpose: Find Meaning, Live Longer, Better*. 3rd edn. Berrett-Koehler Publishers.

Lemov, D. (2021) *Teach Like a Champion 3.0: 63 Techniques that Put Students on the Path to College*. Jossey Bass.

Lewis, D. (1972) *We, the Navigators: The Ancient Art of Landfinding in the Pacific*. University of Hawaii Press.

Litfin, K. T. (2016) 'Person/planet politics: Contemplative pedagogies for a new Earth', in Nicholson, S. and Jinnah, S. (eds.) *New Earth Politics: Essays from the Anthropocene*. MIT Press.

Lofthouse, C. and King, C. (2017) 'From teachers being accountable to taking collective responsibility: using Lesson Study for cultural change', *CollectivED Working Papers*, 1, pp. 16–18. Available at: https://www.leedsbeckett.ac.uk/-/media/files/research/collectived/collectived-dec-2017-issue.pdf (Accessed: 25 July 2024).

Lofthouse, R. (2018) 'Long live metacognition, lessons learned from a life in the field', *CollectivED Working Papers*, 4, pp. 70–76. Available at: www.leedsbeckett.ac.uk/-/media/files/research/collectived/collectived-june-2018-issue-4.pdf (Accessed: 24 July 2024).

Lofthouse, R. (2019a) 'In conversation with Rachel Lofthouse', *Practice: Contemporary Issues in Practitioner Education*, 1(1), pp. 4–8.

Lofthouse, R. (2019b) 'Coaching in education: a professional development process in formation', *Professional Development in Education*, 45(1), pp. 33–45.

Lofthouse, R. (2019c) 'Narratives of collaboration in practice; discourses, dimensions and diversity in collaborative professional development', *CollectivED Working Papers*, 8, pp. 116–125. Available at: www.leedsbeckett.ac.uk/-/media/files/research/collectived/collected-issue-8-may-2019-final2.pdf (Accessed: 25 July 2024).

Lofthouse, R. (2021) 'Creating the engine room for professional learning: Explaining a research-based model', *Impact*, 13. Available at: https://my.chartered.college/impact_article/creating-the-engine-room-for-professional-learning-explaining-a-research-based-model/ (Accessed: 25 July 2024).

Lofthouse, R. (2022) 'How can we judge the impact of coaching in schools?' *Schools Week*, 29 June 2022. Available at: https://schoolsweek.co.uk/how-can-we-judge-the-impact-of-coaching-in-schools/ (Accessed: 25 July 2024).

Lofthouse, R. (2024) 'Coaching: Creating a golden thread through a lived professional curriculum', in *BERA (2024) Curriculum in a Changing World: 50 think pieces on education, policy, practice, innovation and inclusion*, pp. 108–111.

Lofthouse, R., Flanagan, J. and Wigley, B. (2016) 'A new model of collaborative action research; theorising from inter-professional practice development', *Educational Action Research*, 24(4), pp. 519–534.

Lofthouse, R., Flanagan, J. and Wigley, B. (2018) 'Talking it through: Using specialist coaching to enhance teachers' knowledge from speech and language sciences', *Impact Journal*, 2. Available at: https://my.chartered.college/impact_article/talking-it-through-using-specialist-coaching-to-enhance-teachers-knowledge-from-speech-and-language-sciences/ (Accessed: 25 July 2024).

Lofthouse, R., Greenway, C., Davies, P., Davies, D. and Lundholm, C. (2020) 'Pre-service Teachers' conceptions of their own learning: does context make a difference?' *Research Papers in Education*, 36(6), pp. 682–703.

Lofthouse, R. and Hall, E. (2014) 'Developing practices in teachers' professional dialogue in England: using coaching dimensions as an epistemic tool', *Professional Development in Education*, 40(5), pp. 758–778.

Lofthouse R. and Leat D. (2006) 'Coaching for geography teachers', *Teaching Geography*, 31(3), pp. 130–132.

Lofthouse, R. and Leat, D. (2013) 'An activity theory perspective on peer coaching', *International Journal of Mentoring and Coaching in Education*, 2(1), pp. 8–20.

Lofthouse, R., Leat, D. and Towler, C. (2010a) 'Coaching for teaching and learning: a practical guide for schools', CfBT Education Trust. Available at www.ncl.ac.uk/mediav8/centre-for-learning-and-teaching/files/coaching-for-teaching.pdf? (Accessed: 24 February 2025).

Lofthouse, R., Leat, D., Towler, C., Hall, E. and Cummings, C. (2010b) 'Improving coaching: evolution not revolution', CfBT Education Trust. Available at https://dera.ioe.ac.uk/id/eprint/2085/7/improving-coaching_Redacted.pdf (Accessed: 24 February 2025).

Lofthouse, R. M., Rose, A. and Whiteside, R. (2022) 'Understanding coaching efficacy in education through activity systems: privileging the nuances of provision', *International Journal of Mentoring and Coaching in Education*, 11(2), pp. 153–169.

Lofthouse, R. and Thomas, U. (2014) 'Mentoring student teachers; a vulnerable workplace learning practice', *International Journal of Mentoring and Coaching in Education*, 3(3), pp. 201–218.

Lofthouse, R. and Thomas, U. (2017) 'Concerning collaboration: teachers' perspectives on working in partnerships to develop teaching practices', *Professional Development in Education*, 43(1), pp. 36–56.

Lofthouse, R. and van Nieuwerburgh, C. (2019) 'Making most of the spectrum of mentoring and coaching in education', *CollectivED Working Papers*, 9, pp. 67–70. Available at: www.leedsbeckett.ac.uk/-/media/files/research/collectived/collectived-issue-9-oct-2019-final.pdf (Accessed: 6 March 2025).

Lofthouse, R. and Whiteside, R. (2020) 'Sustaining A Vital Profession: Evaluation of A Headteacher Coaching Programme', Project Report, Leeds Beckett University. Available at: www.leedsbeckett.ac.uk/-/media/files/schools/school-of-education/sustaining-a-vital-profession--final-report.pdf? (Accessed: 24 July 2024).

Lofthouse, R. and Wright, D. (2012) 'Teacher education lesson observation as boundary crossing', *International Journal of Mentoring and Coaching in Education*, 1(2), pp. 89–103.

Louis, K. S. (2009) 'Better schools through better knowledge? New understanding, new uncertainty', in Hargreaves, A., Lieberman, A., Fullan, M. and Hopkins, D. (eds.) *Second International Handbook of Educational Change*. Springer, pp. 3–27.

Luft, J. and Ingham, H. (1955) 'The Johari window, a graphic model of interpersonal awareness', *Proceedings of the western training laboratory in group development*. UCLA.

Macy, J. and Johnstone, C. (2022) *Active Hope (Revised): How to Face the Mess We're in with Unexpected Resilience and Creative Power*. New World Library.

Mahina, O. (2008) 'From vale (ignorance) to 'ilo (knowledge) to poto (skill), the Tongan theory of ako (education): Theorising old problems anew', *AlterNative: An International Journal of Indigenous Peoples*, 4(1), pp. 67–96.

Mannix, K. (2021) *Listen: How to Find the Words for Tender Conversations*. William Collins.

Maslow, A. (1943) 'A theory of human motivation', *Psychological Review*, 50(4), pp. 370–396.

Mason, M. (2008) 'Complexity theory and the philosophy of education', *Educational Philosophy and Theory*, 40(1), pp. 4–18.

Maxwell, J. A. (2005) *Qualitative Research Design: An Interactive Approach*. 2nd edn. SAGE Publishing.

Mayer, J. D., Caruso D. R. and Salovey, P. (1999) 'Emotional intelligence meets traditional standards for an intelligence', *Intelligence*, 27(4), pp. 267–298.

McCallum, F., Price, D., Graham, A. and Morrison, A. (n.d.) 'Teacher well-being: a review of the literature', a report prepared for the AISNSW Education Research Council. Available at: https://apo.org.au/node/201816 (Accessed: 1 September 2024).

Mezirow, J. (2003) 'Transformative learning as discourse', *Journal of Transformative Education*, 1(1), pp. 58–63.

Miles, M. (1987) 'Practical Guidelines for School Administrators: How to Get There', paper presented at American Educational Research Association annual meeting, March 1987. Washington, DC.

Miller, W. R. and Rollnick, S. (2002) *Motivational Interviewing: Preparing People for Change*. 2nd edn. Guilford Press.

Miller, W. R. and Rollnick, S. (2013) *Motivational Interviewing: Helping People Change*. 3rd edn. Guilford Press.

Ministère de l'Éducation (2020) Education Act, Québec. Available at: www.legisquebec.gouv.qc.ca/en/document/cs/I-13.3 (Accessed: 2 December 2024).

Moon, H. (2022) *Coaching A to Z: The Extraordinary Use of Ordinary Words*. Page Two.

Moon, H. (2024) 'The boundary is not a barrier', *Canadian Centre for Brief Coaching*, 7 December. Available at: www.briefcoaching.ca/blog/the-boundary-is-not-a-barrier (Accessed: 9 September 2024).

Munro, C. and Campbell, J. (2022) 'Coaching as a way of leading', *Australian Educational Leader*, 44(4), pp. 28–32.

Mycroft, L. (2019) 'Teaching the Thinking Environment – A personal reflection', *CollectivED Working Papers*, 8, pp. 105–108. Available at: www.leedsbeckett.ac.uk/-/media/files/research/collectived/collectived-issue-8-may-2019-final2.pdf (Accessed: 25 July 2024).

Nesbit, R., Moulton, S., Robinson, S., Smith, C., DeHart-Davis, L., Feeney, M. K., Gazley, B. and Hou, Y. (2011) 'Wrestling with intellectual diversity in public administration: avoiding disconnectedness and fragmentation while seeking rigor, depth, and relevance', *Journal of Public Administration Research and Theory*, 21(1), pp. i13–i28. doi: https://doi.org/10.1093/jopart/muq062

Newmann, F. M. and Wehlage, G. G. (1993) 'Five Standards of Authentic Instruction', *ASCD*. Available at www.ascd.org/el/articles/five-standards-of-authentic-instruction (Accessed: 24 February 2025).

Nias, J. (1981) 'Teacher satisfaction and dissatisfaction: Herzberg's 'two-factor' hypothesis revisited', *British Journal of Sociology of Education*, 2(3), pp. 235–246.

Oberholzer, L. and Boyle, D. (2023) *Mentoring and Coaching in Education: A Guide to Coaching and Mentoring Teachers at Every Stage of Their Careers*. Bloomsbury Publishing.

O'Brien, T. (2015) *Inner Story: Understand your mind. Change your world.* Ideational.

O'Connor, M. R. (2019) *Wayfinding: The Science and Mystery of How Humans Navigate the World.* St Martin's Press.

OECD (2023) 'Teacher employment', *Review Education Policies.* Available at: https://gpseducation.oecd.org/revieweducationpolicies/#!node=41733&filter=all (Accessed: 1 September 2024).

O'Leary, M. (2022) 'Rethinking teachers' professional learning through unseen observation', *Professional Development in Education*, 50(6), pp. 1–14.

Olson, K., Lannan, K., Cumming, J., MacGillivary, H. and Richards, K. (2020) 'The Concerns-Based Adoption Model and strategic plan evaluation: Multiple methodologies to understand complex change', *Educational Research: Theory and Practice*, 31(3), pp. 49–58.

Passmore, J. and Brown, A. (2009) 'Coaching non-adult students for enhanced examination performance: a longitudinal study', *Coaching: An International Journal of Theory, Practice and Research*, 2(1), pp. 54–56.

Pellman, R. and Pellman, K. (1984) *The World of Amish Quilts.* SAGE Publishing.

Perkins, D. (2014) *Future Wise: Educating our Children for a Changing World.* Jossey-Bass.

Peterson, D. and Hicks, M. (1996) *Leader as Coach: Strategies for Coaching and Developing Others.* Personal Decisions International.

Pink, D. (2011) *Drive: The Surprising Truth About What Motivates Us.* Riverhead Books.

Price, D. (2013) *Open: How We'll Work, Live and Learn in the Future.* Crux Publishing.

Prochaska, J. O., Norcross, J. C. and DiClemente, C. C. (1994) *Changing for Good*. Avon Books.

Pugh, A. (2024) *The Last Human Job: The Work of Connecting in a Disconnected World*. Princeton University Press.

Reimer, K. E. (2018) *Adult Intentions, Student Perceptions: How Restorative Justice is Used in Schools to Control and to Engage*. IAP.

Richardson, K. A. (2004) 'Systems theory and complexity: Part 2', *Emergence: Complexity and Organization*, 6(4), pp. 77–82.

Roche, C. (2021) 'Decolonising Coaching', *Coaching Perspectives*, 21, pp. 10–12. Available at: https://cdn.ymaws.com/www.associationforcoaching.com/resource/resmgr/Roche_-_Decolonising_coachin.pdf (Accessed: 1 September 2024).

Roche, C. (2022) 'Decolonising reflective practice and supervision', *Philosophy of Coaching: An International Journal*, 7(1), pp. 30–49.

Roche, C. and Passmore, J. (2021) *Racial Justice, Equity and Belonging in Coaching*. Henley Business School.

Rodway, J. (2024) 'Introduction to the symposium: Decolonizing professional learning', *International Education News*, 7 April 2024. Available at: https://internationalednews.com/2024/04/12/decolonizing-professional-learning-lead-the-change-interviews-part-7/ (Accessed: 2 December 2024).

Rogers, C. R. (1961) *On Becoming a Person: A Therapist's View of Psychotherapy*. Constable and Robinson.

Rogers, C. R. (1995) *A Way of Being*. Houghton Mifflin Harcourt.

Rogers, E. M. and Cartano, D. G. (1962) 'Methods of measuring opinion leadership', *Public Opinion Quarterly*, 26(3), pp. 435–441.

Rousell, D. and Cutter-Mackenzie-Knowles, A. (2020) 'A systematic review of climate change education: giving children and young people a "voice" and a "hand" in redressing climate change', *Children's Geographies*, 18(2) pp. 191–208.

Ryan, R. M. and Deci, E. L. (2000) 'Intrinsic and extrinsic motivations: Classic definitions and new directions', *Contemporary Educational Psychology*, 25(1), pp. 54–67.

Sachs, J. (2003) *The Activist Teaching Profession*. Open University Press.

Sannino, A. and Engeström, Y. (2018) 'Cultural-historical activity theory: Founding insights and new challenges', *Cultural-Historical Psychology*, 14(3), pp. 43–56.

Saunders, R. (2014) 'Effectiveness of research-based teacher professional development: A mixed method study of a four-year systemic change initiative', *Australian Journal of Teacher Education* (Online), 39(4), pp. 166–184.

Schein, E. H. (2009) *Helping: How to Offer, Give, and Receive Help*. Berett-Koehler Publishers.

Schön, D. A. (1973) *Beyond the Stable State: Public and Private Learning in a Changing Society*. Penguin.

Scott, K. (2017) *Radical Candor: How to Get What You Want by Saying What You Mean*. Macmillan

Seashore Louis, K. (2010) 'Better schools through better knowledge? New understanding, new uncertainty', in Hargreaves, A., Lieberman, A., Fullan, M. and Hopkins, D. (eds.) *Second International Handbook on Educational Change*. Springer, pp. 3–28.

Seguin, G. (1986) '"Terroirs" and pedology of wine growing', *Experientia*, 42, pp. 861–873.

Seligman, M. (2011) *Flourish: A Visionary New Understanding of Happiness and Well-being*. Simon and Schuster.

Senge, P. M. (2006) *The Fifth Discipline: The Art and Practice of the Learning Organization*. Broadway Business.

Sharratt, L. and Fullan, M. (2012) *Putting Faces on the Data: What Great Leaders Do!* 1st edn. Corwin.

Shein, E. H. (2013) *Humble Inquiry: The Gentle Art of Asking Instead of Telling.* Berrett-Koehler Publishers.

Sherrington, T. (2019) *Rosenshine's Principles in Action.* John Catt.

Sieler, A. (2010) 'Ontological coaching', in Cox, E., Bachkirova, T. and Clutterbuck, D. (eds.) *The Complete Handbook of Coaching*, SAGE Publishing. pp. 104–119.

Snyder, C. R. (2002) 'Hope theory: Rainbows in the mind', *Psychological Inquiry: An International Journal for the Advancement of Psychological Theory*, 13(4), pp. 249–275.

Snyder, C. R. and Lopez, S. J. (2007) *Positive Psychology: The Scientific and Practical Explorations of Human Strengths.* SAGE Publishing.

Spiller, C. (2016) 'Calling the Island to You: Becoming a wayfinder leader', *Academia.edu*. Available at: www.academia.edu/31231487/Calling_the_Island_to_You_Becoming_a_Wayfinder_Leader (Accessed: 8 August 2024).

Stephenson, L. and Lofthouse, R. (2023) 'A pedagogy of professional noticing and co-inquiry: Embedding drama for oracy across the primary curriculum', *Impact*, 18, pp. 36–39.

Stober, D. R. and Parry, C. (2005) 'Current challenges and future directions in coaching research', in Cavanagh, M., Grant, A. M. and Kemp, T. (eds.) *Evidence-Based Coaching, Vol. 1. Theory, Research and Practice from the Behavioural Sciences.* Australian Academic Press, pp. 13–19.

Stoll, L. (2009) 'Connecting learning communities: Capacity building for systemic change', in Hargreaves, A., Lieberman, A., Fullan, M. and Hopkins, D. (eds.) *Second International Handbook of Educational Change.* Springer, pp. 469–484.

Sutcher, L., Darling-Hammond, L. and Carver-Thomas, D. (2016) 'A coming crisis in teaching? Teacher supply, demand, and shortages in the US', *Learning Policy Institute*, 16 September 2016. Available at: https://learningpolicyinstitute.org/product/coming-crisis-teaching (Accessed: 1 September 2024).

Tannock, S. (2021) *Educating for Radical Social Transformation in the Climate Crisis*. Palgrave Macmillan.

Tavory, I. and Timmermans, S. (2014) *Abductive Analysis: Theorizing Qualitative Research*. The University of Chicago Press.

Thomas, W. and Smith, A. (2009) *Coaching Solutions: Practical Ways to Improve Performance in Education*. Network Continuum Education.

Tschannen-Moran, B. and Tschannen-Moran, M. (2010), *Evocative Coaching: Transforming Schools One Conversation at a Time*. Jossey-Bass.

Tschannen-Moran, B. and Tschannen-Moran, M. (2018) *Evoking Greatness: Coaching to Bring Out the Best in Educational Leaders*. Corwin.

Valentine, M. (2019) 'Contextual coaching: leveraging context for alignment in the system', *Philosophy of Coaching: An International Journal*, 4(1), pp. 93–106.

van Nieuwerburgh, C. (2014) *An Introduction to Coaching Skills: A Practical Guide*. SAGE Publishing.

van Nieuwerburgh, C. (2017) 'Interculturally-sensitive coaching', in Drake, D., Spence, G. and Bachkirova, T. (eds.) *The SAGE Handbook of Coaching*. SAGE Publishing, pp. 439–452.

van Nieuwerburgh, C. and Love, D. (2019) *Advanced Coaching Practice: Inspiring Change in Others*. SAGE Publishing.

van Nieuwerburgh, C. and Tong, T. (2013) 'Exploring the benefits of being a student coach in educational settings: a mixed method study',

Coaching: An International Journey of Theory, Research and Practice, 6(1), pp. 5–24.

Vass, A. (2016) *Coaching Schools Pocketbook.* Teachers' Pocketbooks.

Walker, D. (2010) 'Being a pracademic – combining reflective practice with scholarship', keynote address for the AIPM Conference, Darwin, Australia, 10–13 October. Available at: https://leishman.conference-services.net/resources/266/2110/pdf/AIPM2010_0092.pdf.

Weiss, R., Edgerton, N. and Palmer, S. (2017) 'The SPACE coaching model: an integrative tool for coach therapists', *Coaching Today*, October 2017, pp. 12–17.

Wheatley, M. J. (2006) *Leadership and the New Science.* 3rd edn. Berrett-Koehler Publishers.

Wheatley, M. J. (2009) *Turning to Each Other: Simple Conversations to Restore Hope to the Future.* 2nd edn. Berrett-Koehler Publishers.

Whitmore, J. (2009) *Coaching for Performance: The Principles and Practice of Coaching and Leadership.* 4th edn. Nicholas Brealey Publishing.

Whitmore, J. (2017) *Coaching for Performance.* 5th edn. Nicholas Brealey Publishing.

Whittington, J. (2020) *Systemic Coaching and Constellations: The Principles, Practices and Application for Individuals, Teams and Groups.* Kogan Page Publishers.

WHO (2014) 'Definition of mental health', World Health Organization. Available at: www.who.int/features/factfiles/mental_health/en/ (Accessed: 1 September 2024).

Wilkinson, M. T. and D'Angelo, K. A. (2019) 'Community-based accompaniment and social work—A complementary approach to social action', *Journal of Community Practice*, 27(2), pp. 151–167.

Wilson, C. (2011) 'Solution-focused coaching and the GROW model', in Wildflower, L. and Brennan, D. (eds.), *The Handbook of Knowledge-Based Coaching*. Wiley and Sons, pp. 279–285.

Wilson, V. (2014) 'Examining teacher education through cultural-historical activity theory', *Tean Journal*, 6(1) pp. 20–29.

Winch, A. (2022) 'Are we instructional coaches or simply coaches now? The changing role of instructional coaches during unpredictable times', *CollectivEd Working Papers*, 14, pp. 4–7. Available at: www.leedsbeckett.ac.uk/-/media/files/research/collectived/collectived-issue-14.pdf (Accessed: 24 February 2025).

Woodley, H. and Morrison McGill, R. (2018) *Toxic Schools*. John Catt Educational.

Woods, C. T., Rudd, J., Robertson, S. and Davids, K. (2020) 'Wayfinding: How Ecological Perspectives of Navigating Dynamic Environments Can Enrich Our Understanding of the Learner and the Learning Process in Sport', *Sports Med - Open*, 6, 51. doi: https://doi.org/10.1186/s40798-020-00280-9

Woolman, C. (2018) *Edubabble: A Glossary of Teacher Talk*. FriesenPress.

Woulfin, S. L., Stevenson, I. and Lord, K. (2023) *Making Coaching Matter: Leading Continuous Improvement in Schools*. Teachers College Press.

Additional resources

These resources and weblinks have been found to be of value by members of the CollectivED community and are referred to in the encounters in part 3.

CollectivED blogs and resources

CollectivED coaching videos, guides, blogposts and working papers can be accessed at www.leedsbeckett.ac.uk/research/collectived/ in addition to the following resources and blogposts referred to in the encounters:

CollectivED Award, CollectivED website. Available at: www.leedsbeckett.ac.uk/-/media/files/schools/school-of-education/des01022---collectived-award-flyer.pdf (Accessed: 29 July 2024).

CollectivED, *2024 AACT guide*. Available at: www.leedsbeckett.ac.uk/research/collectived/guide-to-coaching/ (Accessed: 29 November 2024).

CollectivED and Leeds Learning Alliance, *2024 DBC guide*. Available at: www.leedsbeckett.ac.uk/research/collectived/guide-to-coaching/ (Accessed: 29 November 2024).

Dilemma-based coaching blogpost 1, Carnegie Education. Available at: www.leedsbeckett.ac.uk/blogs/carnegie-education/2021/04/exploring-and-learning-from-educational-complexity/ (Accessed: 29 July 2024).

Dilemma-based coaching blogpost 2, Carnegie Education. Available at: www.leedsbeckett.ac.uk/blogs/carnegie-education/2023/03/coaching---from-dilemmas-to-hope/ (Accessed: 29 July 2024).

Attuned Teaching, Carnegie Education. Available at: www.leedsbeckett. ac.uk/blogs/carnegie-education/2022/12/attuned-teaching-a-framework-built-on-relationships-for-learning/ (Accessed 27 July 2024).

ACCT, Carnegie Education. Available at: www.leedsbeckett.ac.uk/blogs/carnegie-education/2024/03/time-to-acct/ (Accessed: 27 July 2024).

Erasmus+ websites and resources

PROMISE project. Available at: https://promise-eu.net/ (Accessed: 27 July 2024).

Guide to Co-Coaching from the RAPIDE project. Available at: https://rapide-eu.net/engage (Accessed: 27 July 2024).

Networks, organisations, consultants and associations

BAMEed network website. Available at: www.bameednetwork.com/ (Accessed: 27 July 2024).

Climate Coaching Alliance website. Available at: www.climatecoachingalliance.org (Accessed: 27 July 2024).

Crowther Centre for Applied Educational Research, Crowther Centre website. Available at: www.crowthercentre.org.au/ (Accessed: 29 July 2024).

European Mentoring and Coaching Council, EMCC website. Available at: www.emccglobal.org/ (Accessed: 27 July 2024).

Growth Coaching International website. Available at: www.growthcoaching.com.au/ (Accessed: 27 July 2024).

Instructional Coaching Group website. Available at: www.instructionalcoaching.com/ (Accessed: 27 July 2024).

International Coaching Federation, ICF website. Available at: https://coachingfederation.org/ (Accessed: 27 July 2024).

Joanne Miles Consulting website. Available at: https://joannemilesconsulting.wordpress.com/about/ (Accessed: 30 July 2024).

Kaizen. Available at: https://kaizen.com/what-is-kaizen/ (Accessed: 29 July 2024).

LLSE. Available at: www.llse.org.uk/ (Accessed: 30 July 2024).

Olevi Coaching website. Available at: www.olevi.com/coaching/ (Accessed: 29 July 2024).

Walkthrus website. Available at: https://walkthrus.co.uk/ (Accessed: 26 July 2024).

WomenED website. Available at: https://womened.com/ (Accessed: 27 July 2024).

Online resources, podcasts, articles and blogposts

Centre for Creative Leadership's SBI (Situation–Behaviour–Impact) model. Available at: www.ccl.org/articles/leading-effectively-articles/closing-the-gap-between-intent-vs-impact-sbii/ (Accessed: 26 July 2024).

Graydin Coaching blog. Available at: www.graydin.com/blog/grow-vs-start-with-heart-coaching-models-in-education (Accessed: 29 July 2024).

GROW model, Coaching Culture at Work website. Available at: www.coachingcultureatwork.com/the-grow-model/ (Accessed: 27 July 2024).

Growth Coaching Framework. Available at: www.growthcoaching.com.au/documents/10/Coaching_using_the_GROWTH_model.pdf (Accessed: 26 July 2024).

Harvard's 'Best Foot Forward' Research. Available at: https://visiblybetter.cepr.harvard.edu/best-foot-forward-project (Accessed: 26 July 2024).

Hattie 'collective efficacy'. Available at: https://visible-learning.org/2018/03/collective-teacher-efficacy-hattie/ (Accessed: 26 July 2024).

ISMART. Available at: www.growthcoaching.com.au/resource/performance-development-goal-setting/ (Accessed: 26 July 2024).

Leadership Matters' 360 Tool. Available at: www.leadershipmatters.org.uk/diagnostic-tools/lm-360 (Accessed: 26 July 2024).

Nora Bateson 'warm data' and 'data storytelling'. Available at: https://batesoninstitute.org/ (Accessed: 26 July 2024).

Outward Mindset, Arbinger Institute website. Available at: https://arbinger.com/blog/what-is-an-outward-mindset/ (Accessed: 30 July 2024).

Positive Intelligence. Available at: www.positiveintelligence.com/ (Accessed: 26 July 2024).

Seven Eyed Model, Living Therapy website. Available at: www.livingtherapy.co.uk/seven-eyed-model (Accessed: 27 July 2024).

SPACE Coaching Model, Rowan Consultancy website. Available at: www.rowan-consultancy.co.uk/Documents/RowanResources/TheSPACECoachingModel%20_CoachingTodayOct%202017.pdf (Accessed: 27 July 2024).

Spiral of inquiry, Educational Leaders website. Available at: www.educationalleaders.govt.nz/Pedagogy-and-assessment/Evidence-based-leadership/The-spiral-of-inquiry (Accessed: 29 July 2024).

Story Exchange, BERA blog post. Available at: www.bera.ac.uk/blog/boundary-crossings-with-artists-teachers-and-children-integrating-creative-pedagogies-for-young-peoples-wellbeing (Accessed: 27 July 2024]

STRIDE. Available at: https://media.bloomsbury.com/rep/files/Coaching_Questions.pdf (Accessed: 27 July 2024).

Tannock, S. (2022) 'What kind of climate change education do we actually need?', UCL podcast. Available at: www.ucl.ac.uk/ioe/news/2022/nov/

what-kind-climate-change-education-do-we-actually-need-rftrw-s18e02 (Accessed: 27 July 2024).

Teach the Future (2021) 'Teaching the Future – Research with UK Teachers on the current state and future of climate education', Teach the Future website. Available at: www.teachthefuture.uk/research (Accessed: 27 July 2024).

Wheatley, M. and Frieze, D. (2010) 'Hero to Host: Leadership in an Age of Complexity'. Available at: www.margaretwheatley.com/articles/Leadership-in-Age-of-Complexity.pdf (Accessed: 27 July 2024).